Quality Literacy Instruction for Students With Autism Spectrum Disorders

Quality Literacy Instruction for Students With Autism Spectrum Disorders

**Edited by Christina Carnahan, Ed.D.,
and Pamela Williamson, Ph.D.**

Foreword by Kathleen Quill, Ed.D.

AAPC Textbooks
A Division of AAPC
P.O. Box 23173
Shawnee Mission, Kansas 66283-0173
www.asperger.net

© 2010 Autism Asperger Publishing Co.
P.O. Box 23173
Shawnee Mission, Kansas 66283-0173
www.asperger.net

Publisher's Cataloging-in-Publication

Quality literacy instruction for students with autism spectrum disorders / edited by Christina Carnahan, and Pamela Williamson ; foreword by Kathleen Quill. -- 1st ed. -- Shawnee Mission, Kan. : AAPC Textbooks, c2010.

p. ; cm.
ISBN: 978-1-934575-66-6

Has companion volume, "Quality literacy instruction for students with autism spectrum disorders: instructor manual" by the same editors.
Includes bibliographical references and index.

1. Autism spectrum disorders--Patients--Education--Study and teaching. 2. Autistic children--Education--Study and teaching. 3. Literacy--Study and teaching. 4. Teachers of children with disabilities--Study and teaching. I. Carnahan, Christina. II.Williamson, Pamela, 1960-

LC4717.85 .Q35   2010 2010921398
371.94--dc22   1003

This book is designed in Tarzana and Helvetica Neue.

Cover illustration: ©istockphoto: Monkey Business Images

Printed in the United States of America.

Dedication

We dedicate this book to the children and families
whom we have had the honor of serving.

In addition, we dedicate the book to our husbands, Shane and Joe,
our children, Ellie, Jack, Caitlin, and Jennifer, and our parents,
whose love and support make our work possible.

Acknowledgments

We would like to extend a special thank-you to the individuals and families living with autism who continue to teach us about the importance of quality literacy instruction for ALL individuals on the spectrum.

This book would not be possible without the hard work and support of many individuals. We extend our sincerest gratitude to Ruth Aspy and Brenda Smith Myles of the Ziggurat Group and to the entire AAPC staff, especially Kirsten McBride. Thank you for your efforts in reviewing chapters and editing content. We truly value and appreciate your support.

We would also like to thank the chapter authors without whom this book would not be possible. Finally, to our husbands, children, and other family members, thank you for your unconditional love and support.

Table of Contents

About the Editors

Christina Carnahan, Ed.D., is an assistant professor of special education at the University of Cincinnati, where she coordinates the special education master's degree program. She received her doctorate from the University of Cincinnati. Dr. Carnahan began working in recreational settings with individuals with significant disabilities as a teen. After completing her undergraduate degree in special education, she taught in K-12 settings where she served individuals across the autism spectrum. Currently, she works with preservice and practicing teachers, preparing them to meet the diverse needs of individuals with autism and other complex disabilities. She also conducts research in special education, focusing on literacy, evidence-based practice, and teacher effectiveness. In addition to her teaching and research, she is involved with local and state organizations working to improve educational services for individuals with ASD. She speaks and publishes locally and nationally, including on such topics as literacy and educational programming for individuals with ASD.

Pamela Williamson, Ph.D., is an assistant professor of special education at the University of Cincinnati. She received both her doctorate of philosophy and her master's degree from the University of Florida. Her work in K-12 settings was in inclusive classrooms where she served a diverse group of students, including individuals with autism. Currently, she works with preservice teachers, preparing them to deliver high-quality literacy instruction to all students with special needs. In addition, she works with inservice teachers to prepare them to assume roles as formal and informal teacher leaders. Her research interests include reading and autism, attention deficit-hyperactivity disorder, teacher leadership, and inclusion. Her work is published in *Exceptional Children, Qualitative Heath Research, Social Science and Medicine, Journal of Child and Family Studies, Learning Disabilities Research and Practice, Field Methods, Beyond Behavior,* and *Childhood Education.*

Contributors

Christina Carnahan, Ed.D., University of Cincinnati

Pamela Williamson, Ph.D., University of Cincinnati

Kara Hume, Ph.D., University of North Carolina, Chapel Hill

JoAnne Schudt Caldwell, Ph.D., Cardinal Stritch University

Sandra M. Grether, Ph.D., Cincinnati Children's Hospital Medical Center, and
  Communication Sciences and Disorders, University of Cincinnati

Christina Yeager Pelatti, M.A., Cincinnati Children's Hospital Medical Center

Elizabeth B. Keefe, Ph.D., University of New Mexico

Susan R. Copeland, Ph.D., University of New Mexico

Heather DiLuzio, M.A., Albuquerque Public Schools

Lesley Mandel Morrow, Ph.D., Rutgers, The State University of New Jersey

Allison Breit-Smith, Ph.D., University of Cincinnati

Laura Justice, Ph.D., The Ohio State University

Hope Smith Davis, Ed.D., Indiana University South Bend

Jenni Jacobs, M.Ed., Linden Grove School, Ohio

Susan Watts-Taffe, Ph.D., University of Cincinnati

David A. Koppenhaver, Ph.D., Appalachian State University

Jennifer C. Wolfe, M.S., Linden Grove School, Ohio

Betty Y. Ashbaker, Ph.D., Brigham Young University

Kate Snyder, M.Ed., Middletown City Schools, Ohio

Foreword

Ask any college student why he or she wants to be a teacher, and the answer is likely to be, "I love to watch children learn." Ask any veteran educator about his or her biggest challenge, and the reply will likely be, "I struggle to meet the needs of diverse learners." This textbook, *Quality Literacy Instruction for Students With Autism Spectrum Disorders*, is an extremely important resource for the educators of both today and tomorrow. It will strengthen the skills of a veteran teacher and better prepare the teachers of tomorrow.

Today, we have a wide variety of resources on autism spectrum disorders (ASD) to guide our understanding and support our teaching efforts. There is a large body of literature that addresses the core aspects of the disorder: differences in the development of social understanding, communication competencies, and cognitive and emotional flexibility. We know to ask "why" when faced with a student's challenging behavior, and there are books to guide us. We know to ask "why" when faced with a student's problematic social relationships or breakdowns in communication, and there are resources to help. And now, we are finally getting answers to every educator's question, "why does this student struggle to read, and how can I teach him to comprehend what he is reading?" This question is on the forefront of teachers' minds, given the status of education reform today.

The federal mandate of the No Child Left Behind Act of 2001 clearly states that we need to improve teaching and learning outcomes for all students, including students with disabilities. Standards-based education reform establishes measurable goals for all students in language arts, math, and other core subject areas. As a result, educators are being asked to differentiate instruction so that every student's learning can be seen and measured. These academic standards must be aligned with the assessment, individualized education program (IEP), curriculum, and achievement measures of every special education student. At the same time, standards-based instruction must provide opportunities for students with disabilities to learn critical skills needed for maximum lifelong independence. In the case of students with ASD, this means addressing their need for social skills, communication skills, problem-solving skills, and emotional resilience. Acquisition of these core skills is supposed to be embedded within the academic curriculum.

An understanding of how students with ASD learn is necessary to accomplish this mandate. The editors and chapter authors of *Quality Literacy Instruction for Students With Autism Spectrum Disorders* have laid the foundation for educators to do this. They have woven a tapestry to connect comprehensive information about balanced literacy instruction with a thorough description of how to teach literacy to students with ASD. Step-by-step, the reader is given a conceptual framework to understand the complexity of literacy, an explanation of where and why students with ASD need literacy support, and how to address their individual instructional needs.

A balanced approach to literacy includes instruction in phonemic awareness, fluency, vocabulary, reading comprehension, and writing. Each aspect of literacy is linked to the unique cognitive, social, and communication issues inherent in ASD. In each chapter, careful attention is given to filling the gap between research and practice through the use of organized tables that summarize key concepts, case studies that illustrate key teaching constructs, and recommended hands-on activities for the university student or veteran teacher to apply the information. It is clear that the authors have both a wealth of knowledge about literacy instruction and a solid understanding of ASD.

I compliment Christina Carnahan and Pamela Williamson for taking on this project and producing a manuscript that will benefit every current and future teacher of literacy. My thanks go to all the chapter authors for the positive impact that they will make on the lives of students with ASD who deserve to learn to read with meaning, and can learn so much about life through reading.

Whether you are a university student or a veteran reading teacher, you are about to embark on a "journey of knowledge" that will impact your teaching skills for the rest of your career. Read it once, read it twice, and then refer to it again and again. The quality of your literacy instruction will improve for all your students, with and without ASD.

Kathleen A. Quill, Ed.D.

Overview of Textbook Features

The *Quality Literacy Instruction for Students With Autism Spectrum Disorders* textbook contains the following features to help strengthen your understanding of material discussed in each chapter, as well as share this knowledge with parents and colleagues and apply it to your everyday work with children and adolescents with ASD:

- **Chapter learner objectives** – Refer to the list of learner objectives at the beginning of each chapter for a preview of the chapter's content, as well as to learn what information you are expected to understand and be able to explain after reading the chapter.

- **Vocabulary** – Note the terms included in highlighted text within each chapter for at-a-glance reminders of key vocabulary. The definitions of these terms are included in the glossary in Appendix B.

- **Chapter highlights** – Review the points listed at the end of each chapter to recall the main points discussed within the chapter.

- **Chapter review questions** – Answer the questions at the end of each chapter to check your understanding of and ability to explain the information discussed within the chapter. The review questions may also be used as a study guide when preparing for tests and/or exams.

- **Chapter review answers** – Refer to Appendix A to confirm your answers to the review questions that accompany each chapter.

- **Glossary** – Refer to Appendix B for an alphabetical listing of all vocabulary terms included in highlighted text within the textbook.

Part One

Conceptualizing Literacy Instruction for Students With ASD

Chapter 1
A Conceptual Framework for Literacy Instruction: Meeting the Needs of All Students on the Autism Spectrum

Christina Carnahan, Ed.D., University of Cincinnati

Pamela Williamson, Ph.D., University of Cincinnati

Learner Objectives:

After reading this chapter, the learner will be able to:

- Describe the culture of autism
- Discuss the components of literacy
- Describe cognitive processing differences exhibited by individuals with ASD that may influence literacy instruction
- List the components of this textbook

L iteracy skills, including reading, writing, speaking, and listening, are critical components of success during and after the school years for all students. Not only do literacy skills allow students greater access to academic curriculum, such skills are important for participating in the community, engaging in social relationships, and living independently as adults. Most important, literacy skills provide the foundation for improving one's quality of life, regardless of ability or functioning level.

The purpose of this textbook is to provide a detailed discussion of literacy instruction for students with autism spectrum disorders (ASD). Because assumptions, rather than proper assessment and screening, are frequently made about their cognitive and communication functioning, many individuals with ASD are excluded from literacy experiences (Kluth & Darmody-Lathom, 2003; Mirenda, 2003). Behavioral differences are often viewed as anomalies that make individuals with ASD incapable of learning. Such views can lead to complacency, poor instruction, and acceptance of poor outcomes. This text emphasizes that all individuals, including all individuals with ASD, have the ability to participate in meaningful literacy experiences that enrich their lives.

Mesibov, Shea, and Schopler suggested the existence of a "culture of autism" (2005, p. 19). Recognizing the spectrum of differences in individuals with ASD, the notion of a specific autism culture suggests "predictable patterns of thinking and behavior" that guide our understanding and interactions (p. 19). We adhere to this view, seeing the way individuals with ASD perceive and interact with their world as being different from that of individuals without ASD. It is important here to note our very deliberate word choice: We discuss differences and patterns of thinking – not deficits. That is, we choose to view the way people with ASD think about and perceive their world as differences (rather than deficits or problems) that require differentiated instruction and support. These beliefs, combined with an understanding of the unique strengths and interests of each individual, guide our practice. It is with this same understanding that we hope you approach this text and your work with individuals with ASD.

Key Concept

Based on the notion of a "culture of autism" (Mesibov et al., 2005), the way individuals with ASD think and behave should not be seen as deficits. Rather, literacy experiences should build on each individual's strengths and interests.

The way individuals with ASD perceive and think about their worlds (Attwood, 2008; Mesibov et al., 2005) influences how they interact with and comprehend communication and printed materials, two components of literacy. Thus, traditional literacy instruction without regard for the characteristics of autism and of the individual is ineffective.

Research on reading instruction for students with ASD is emerging. Similarly, research on the brain and processing styles of individuals with ASD continues to grow. The foundation for this book is the intersection between our knowledge about ASD, our knowledge about quality literacy instruction, and the emerging research on literacy instruction for students with ASD (see Figure 1.1). As you will note, most of the chapter authors comment upon the paucity of research on literacy and autism. At times, they make suggestions that are grounded in the literature bases of quality literacy instruction and the characteristics of autism, moving away from the intersection that includes research. This decision was made in response to the fact that students on the spectrum and their teachers cannot wait for the research to catch up to their needs.

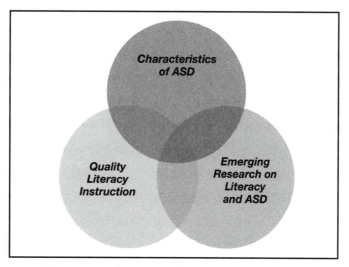

Figure 1.1. ASD and quality literacy instruction.

What Is Literacy?

There is no universally accepted definition of literacy, but definitions in the literature frequently are based on theoretical models of literacy instruction. For example, models of instruction that emphasize bottom-up processing rely upon notions of the importance of understandings of letter-sound correspondences that gradually move toward recognizing whole words and associating those words with meaning. Top-down models, on the other hand, emphasize meaning first and then gradually work toward learning patterns frequently used in the English language. Still other definitions blend these two models and are more interactive or transactional in nature. Further complicating definitional issues for students on the spectrum are distinctions between so-called academic literacy versus functional literacy, as well as what Alberto, Fredrick, Hughes, McIntosh, and Cihak (2007) referred to as visual literacy, or understanding information communicated through images.

Each of these definitions brings with it a certain set of values, benefits, and drawbacks in relation to meeting the needs of individuals with ASD. Rather than subscribing to one strict definition, we believe in what Mirenda (2003) described as "balanced literacy theories, (or) the use of a wide range of technologies, and the belief that students with autism and other developmental disabilities can, indeed, participate meaningfully in literacy learning experiences," no matter their age or level of need (p. 274). Throughout this text, we refer to literacy as the skills that allow an individual to have increased, meaningful engagement with his or her environment (e.g., home and school communities) and those in it. Important literacy skills go beyond reading and writing. Literacy also includes (a) the development of functional communication systems, which may be speech based or use augmented systems; (b) listening comprehension; (c) understanding the pragmatic aspects of communication; (d) reading, which can include comprehending sight words and other visual symbols in addition to written words; (e) critical thinking; and (f) engaging in literacy experiences for pleasure (Alberto et al., 2007; Browder, Trela, & Jimenez, 2007; Mirenda, 2003).

Regardless of the precise definition of literacy, we have learned from our work with students and teachers that all students on the spectrum benefit from quality literacy instruction that is informed by deep understandings of the individual student and thorough assessment. The ends must inform the beginning and the middle. In other words, we must answer such questions as What are the long-term goals for each student? and What literacy experiences will the student need to meet these goals? To help students on the spectrum to reach their literate potentials, teachers must provide thoughtful instruction that may include instruction from disparate theoretical models based upon student needs.

Literacy and Autism

Although there is great heterogeneity among the literacy experiences and skills of individuals with ASD, some generalities do exist. Communication, cognition, and literacy are closely connected, with experiences or skills in one area affecting the others (Chiang & Lin, 2007; Kluth & Chandler-Olcott, 2008; Mirenda, 2003; Nation, Clarke, Wright, & Williams, 2006). Communication and cognition will be addressed in further detail later in the text, but a brief discussion at this point is warranted, as they are core concepts for understanding literacy and ASD. The following list summarizes these concepts.

1. **Constructing meaning and learning from any environment requires attention to many different aspects of that environment** (Reed & Gibson, 2005).
   a. To truly understand the nature of what another person says, we must attend to multiple stimuli, including tone of speech, facial expressions, and body language. Similarly, when learning a new concept or following a new set of directions, we attend to verbal directions while looking at or manipulating a variety of materials.

2. **Many individuals with ASD demonstrate overselective attention** (Reed & Gibson, 2005), or attention to a limited number of environmental cues at one time. They are unable to attend to multiple stimuli or environmental cues (Quill, 2000).
   a. These individuals may attend to specific parts or aspects of a situation without regard for the context within which the situation occurs (Happé & Frith, 2006; Quill, 2000). Over the past several decades, research and personal accounts have indicated that overselectivity and visual perception influence how individuals with ASD process environmental stimuli (Caron, Mottron, Berthiaume, & Dawson, 2006; Edgin & Pennington, 2005; Grandin, 2006; Happé & Frith).
   b. Individuals with ASD are less likely to engage in the top-down processing necessary for making connections and understanding the big picture of events (Frith, 2008).
   c. The significant focus on details makes it difficult to integrate information for meaningful purposes and comprehension. Regardless of whether individuals with ASD have a strength and/or preference for processing specific details, or lack the ability to process information in context (Dakin & Frith, 2005; Porter & Colheart, 2006), stimulus overselectivity inhibits their ability to attend to and process important aspects of the educational environment (Frith, 2003; Happé & Frith, 2006; Koegel, Koegel, & Carter, 1999; Reed & Gibson, 2005). Attention, without regard for context, inhibits the ability to integrate new information with previous experiences, translate knowledge into meaningful learning, and understand global concepts (Happé & Frith; Koegel et al.; Quill, 2000). This is especially critical, as task demands increase in the higher grades or situations become more complex (Reed & Gibson).

3. **Approximately 33-50% of children with ASD do not use functional speech as their primary form of communication** (Noens & van Berckelaer-Onnes, 2005).
   a. While the rest of the ASD population develops speech, both groups demonstrate impairments related to the pragmatic aspects of language (Mundy & Markus,

1997; Rapin & Dunn, 2003). Research suggests that these differences correlate with the cognitive processing style described earlier (Hale & Tager-Flusberg, 2005; Mundy, 2003; Quill, 2000).

4. **People with ASD attend to specific words or phrases** with limited attention to the situation or context that influences meaning (Noens & van Berckelaer-Onnes, 2005).

   a. Their verbal skills often overshadow their language comprehension abilities; they may have a large vocabulary but fail to understand simple comments or directions (Lord & Rhea, 1997).

   b. They may have strong word-decoding skills, but struggle with reading comprehension (Attwood, 1998). Another challenge is the propensity among individuals on the autism spectrum toward literal/factual thinking (Noens & van Berckelaer-Onnes, 2005), which makes understanding idioms, sarcasm, and other pragmatic aspects of communication difficult.

5. **Together, cognition and communication influence literacy.**

   a. Many students with ASD demonstrate strength in word decoding, with greater challenges in comprehension (Newman et al., 2007). Hyperlexia, or the ability to decode text written significantly above one's comprehension level, has been noted in many individuals with ASD.

   b. Individuals with ASD tend to be concrete, literal thinkers. Concrete thinkers have difficulty generalizing information or skills learned in one setting to other settings or situations. Similarly, they are often able to demonstrate skills in static situations, but unable to perform them in complex or real-world situations (Volkmar, Lord, Bailey, Schultz, & Klin, 2004). Figure 1.2 demonstrates the connection between the characteristics seen in many individuals with ASD and literacy skills.

   c. Accessing and integrating relevant background knowledge at the global text level can be challenging, but individuals with ASD appear to have the ability to access background knowledge (Saldaña & Frith, 2007). Thus, although students with ASD may be able to comprehend short passages of text, creating meaning from longer passages such as those faced in academic settings is generally difficult for them.

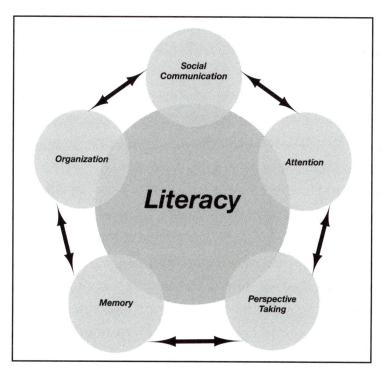

Figure 1.2. Linking the characteristics of ASD and literacy.

Based on the interface between the characteristics of ASD, quality literacy instruction, and the emerging research, we have identified several big ideas to guide literacy instruction for students with ASD.

1. All students, regardless of their perceived functioning level, should have access to quality literacy instruction.

2. A student-centered approach is crucial for building the literacy experiences of students with ASD. Instruction must incorporate the characteristics of the individual child (i.e., strengths, needs, and interests), the characteristics of ASD, and the components of effective literacy instruction, or more specifically, the components of effective literacy instruction for students with ASD.

3. Literacy experiences must be authentic and functional. Authentic literacy activities are meaningful to each person's daily life – what is authentic for one is not necessarily authentic for another. Most important, literacy experiences must be functional, designed so that skills and concepts learned are applicable to the needs of the child and allow him to experience increased participation in all aspects of life – at home, at school, and in the community.

4. Literacy experiences must take into account what we know about the cognitive processing style of individuals with ASD. Many report that visual supports, including objects, pictures, written directions, and even well-organized physical space, increase their understanding and comprehension (Grandin, 2006). Therefore, literacy experiences that highlight salient information are crucial. Further, specific strategies, such as use of visual supports, which capitalize on a student's strengths, help communicate information without overwhelming the learner.

5. Literacy instruction must incorporate or build on the special interests of each student. Many children with ASD demonstrate intense interests in a variety of topics. Although specific topics or areas of interest may change with age or experience, they offer an excellent tool for beginning literacy instruction. Using a special interest or topic is helpful for several reasons. First, highly motivating topics increase active engagement in the learning process. Second, for students who feel intimidated by or are fearful of literacy learning materials, the special interest topic may increase motivation and decrease anxiety. Third, using topics of interest provides a foundation from which literacy experience can broaden the student's horizons.

Overview of the Text

This textbook is divided in three parts. The first part, Conceptualizing Literacy Instruction for Students With ASD, details our conceptual framework for literacy instruction. Chapters 2 and 3 build on this framework through discussions of the relationship between cognition and literacy for students with ASD and general guidelines for working with students in educational settings. Part Two, Designing Effective Literacy Environments for Students With ASD, focuses on understanding the characteristics of effective readers, linking communication and literacy, understanding the reading process, and designing print rich environments. Finally, Part Three, Building Literacy Skills for Students With ASD, addresses the various components of literacy. These include emergent literacy, word recognition, fluency, vocabulary, comprehension, and written communication.

Each chapter contains the following components to help organize your thinking and guide you through the book:

1. Learner objectives
2. Vocabulary
3. Case examples
4. Chapter highlights

5. Review questions
6. Focused comments on assessment, technology, and diversity

Finally, to help readers visualize how instruction occurs, chapters contain rich descriptions of functioning classrooms. Because we believe that *everybody* should receive quality literacy instruction, we have decided not to have a separate chapter on designing literacy experiences for students with the most intense needs. Instead, each chapter addresses the needs of learners across the spectrum. As the editors of this text, we hope that each chapter supports your understanding of and ability to design high-quality literacy experiences for individuals with ASD.

Chapter Highlights

- Literacy skills provide the foundation for improving quality of life, regardless of ability or functioning level.

- Many individuals with ASD are excluded from literacy experiences because of assumptions made about their cognitive and communicative abilities.

- The "culture of autism" (Mesibov, Shea, & Schopler, 2005) frames the way in which individuals with ASD perceive and interact with their world as different, but not as a deficit.

- Traditional literacy instruction without regard for the characteristics of ASD and the individual is ineffective.

- Research on effective literacy instruction for individuals with ASD is still emerging.

- For the purposes of this text, literacy is defined as the skills that allow an individual to have increased, meaningful engagement with his or her environment and those in it. Literacy includes:
  - ✔ Reading
  - ✔ Writing
  - ✔ Developing functional communication systems
  - ✔ Listening comprehension
  - ✔ Understanding pragmatics
  - ✔ Reading (including sight words and other visual symbols in addition to written words)
  - ✔ Critical thinking
  - ✔ Engaging in literacy experiences for pleasure

- Quality literacy instruction should be informed by knowledge of the individual student and assessment.

- Two areas specifically influence the literacy experiences of individuals with ASD: communication and cognitive processing style.

- Communication requires simultaneous attention to multiple stimuli. Individuals with ASD demonstrate stimulus overselectivity, or attention to a limited number of environmental cues at one time.

- Research suggests that the cognitive processing style of individuals with ASD reflects a tendency to hyperfocus on details, leading to challenges with comprehension of more global concepts.

- Approximately 33-50% of individuals with ASD do not use functional speech as their primary form of communication. Nearly all individuals with ASD, including those who do develop functional speech, struggle with pragmatic language.

- Many individuals with ASD demonstrate strength in word decoding but are challenged by comprehension.

- The interface between the characteristics of ASD, quality literacy instruction, and emerging research leads to the development of central components in literacy instruction for individuals with ASD. These components include:
  - ✔ All students, regardless of perceived level of functioning, should have access to quality literacy instruction.
  - ✔ A student-centered approach is crucial for building the literacy experiences of individuals with ASD.
  - ✔ Literacy experiences must be authentic and functional.
  - ✔ Literacy experiences must be responsive to the cognitive processing style of individuals with ASD.
  - ✔ Quality literacy instruction incorporates or builds on the special interests of each student.

Chapter Review Questions

1. What is literacy?

2. Discuss the link between the culture of autism and literacy skills.

3. Discuss the big ideas for designing literacy instruction for individuals with ASD.

References

Alberto, P., Fredrick, L., Hughes, M., McIntosh, L., & Cihak, D. (2007). Components of visual literacy: Teaching logos. *Focus on Autism and Other Developmental Disabilities, 22*(4), 234-243.

Attwood, T. (2008). An overview of autism spectrum disorders. In K. Dunn Buron & P. Wolfberg (Eds.), *Learners on the autism spectrum: Preparing highly qualified educators* (pp. 19-43). Shawnee Mission, KS: Autism Asperger Publishing Company.

Browder, D., Trela, K., & Jimenez, B. (2007). Training teachers to follow a task analysis to engage middle school students with moderate and severe developmental disabilities in grade appropriate literature. *Focus on Autism and Other Developmental Disabilities, 22*(4), 206-219.

Caron, M. J., Mottron, L., Berthiaume, C., & Dawson, M. (2006). Cognitive mechanisms, specificity and neural underpinnings of visuo-spatial peaks in autism. *Brain, 129*, 1789-1802.

Chiang, H. M., & Lin, Y. H. (2007). Reading comprehension instruction for students with autism spectrum disorders. *Focus on Autism and Other Developmental Disabilities, 22*(4), 259-267.

Dakin, S., & Frith, U. (2005). Vagaries of visual perception in autism. *Neuron, 48*, 497-507.

Edgin, J., & Pennington, B. (2005). Spatial cognition in autism spectrum disorders: Superior, impaired or just intact? *Journal of Autism and Developmental Disorders, 35*(6), 729-745.

Frith, U. (2003). *Autism: Explaining the enigma* (2nd ed.). Oxford, UK: Blackwell.

Frith, U. (2008). *How cognitive theories can help us explain autism.* Retrieved August 22, 2008, from http://www.ucdmc.ucdavis.edu/mindinstitute/events/dls_recorded_events.html

Grandin, T. (2006). *Thinking in pictures and other reports from my life with autism.* New York: Vintage Books.

Hale, C., & Tager-Flusberg, H. (2005). Social communication in children with autism: The relationship between theory of mind and discourse development. *Autism, 9*(2), 157-178.

Happé, F., & Frith, U. (2006). The weak coherence account: Detail-focused cognitive style in autism spectrum disorders. *Journal of Autism and Developmental Disorders, 36*(1), 5-25.

Kluth, P., & Chandler-Olcott. (2008). *A land we can share: Teaching literacy to students with autism.* Baltimore: Paul H. Brookes Publishing Company.

Kluth, P., & Darmody-Lathom, J. (2003). Beyond sight words: Literacy instruction for students with autism. *Reading Teacher, 56*(6), 532-535.

Koegel, R., Koegel, L., & Carter, C. (1999). Pivotal teaching interactions for children with autism. *School Psychology Review, 8*(4), 576-594.

Lord, C., & Rhea, P. (1997). Language and communication in autism. In D. V. Cohen (Ed.), *Handbook of autism and pervasive developmental disorders* (2nd ed., pp. 195-225). New York: John Wiley & Sons.

Mirenda, P. (2003). "He's not really a reader ...": Perspectives on supporting literacy development in individuals with autism. *Topics in Language Disorders, 23*(4), 271-282.

Mesibov, G., Shea, V., & Schopler, E. (2005). *The TEACCH approach to autism spectrum disorders.* New York: Kluwer Academic/Plenum Publishers.

Mundy, P. (2003). Annotation: The neural basis of social impairments in autism: The role of the dorsal medial-frontal cortex and anterior cingulated system. *Journal of Child Psychology and Psychiatry, 44*(6), 793-809.

Mundy, P., & Markus, J. (1997). On the nature of communication and language impairment in autism. *Mental Retardation and Developmental Disabilities, 3*, 343-349.

Nation, K., Clarke, P., Wright, B., & Williams, C. (2006). Patterns of reading ability in children with autism spectrum disorders. *Journal of Autism and Developmental Disorders, 36*, 911-919.

Newman, T., Macomber, D., Naples, A., Babitz, B., Volkmar, F., & Grigorenko, E. (2007). Hyperlexia in children with autism spectrum disorders. *Journal of Autism Developmental Disorders, 37*(4), 760-774.

Noens, I., & van Berckelaer-Onnes, I. (2005). Captured by details: Sense-making, language and communication in autism. *Journal of Communication Disorders, 38,* 123-141.

Porter, M., & Colheart, M. (2006). Global and local processing in Williams syndrome, autism, and Down syndrome: Perception, attention, and construction. *Developmental Neuropsychology, 30*(3), 771-789.

Quill, K. A. (2000). *Do-watch-listen-say: Social and communication intervention for children with autism*. Baltimore: Paul H. Brookes Publishing Company.

Rapin, I., & Dunn, M. (2003). Update on the language disorders of individuals with autistic spectrum. *Brain & Development, 25,* 166-172.

Reed, P., & Gibson, E. (2005). The effect of concurrent task load on stimulus over-selectivity. *Journal of Autism and Developmental Disorders, 35*(5), 601-614.

Saldaña, D., & Frith, U. (2007). Do readers with autism make bridging inferences from real world knowledge? *Journal of Experimental Child Psychology, 96,* 310-319.

Volkmar, F. R., Lord, C., Bailey, A., Schultz, R. T., & Klin, A. (2004). Autism and pervasive developmental disorders. *Journal of Child Psychology and Psychiatry, 45*(1), 1-36

Chapter 2
Autism, Cognition, and Reading Comprehension

Christina Carnahan, Ed.D., University of Cincinnati

Pamela Williamson, Ph.D., University of Cincinnati

Learner Objectives:

After reading this chapter, the learner will be able to:

- List the factors that influence how individuals construct meaning from text

- Discuss the influence of theory of mind, executive function, and central coherence on the cognitive processing style of students with ASD

- Discuss the influence of cognitive characteristics common in ASD on reading comprehension

■ ■ ■

Charlie is an eighth grader with high-functioning autism. He loves school, especially reading. He spends all of his free time immersed in books. However, Charlie also has several challenges at school. First, it is almost impossible for him to work independently. When the teacher gives directions, Charles usually waits until she provides several prompts, including very explicit directions, before he initiates the task. Further, though Charlie is able to repeat the directions, he does not independently recognize and self-correct off-task behavior. He is easily distracted and requires reminders about the materials necessary to complete his assignments. He is frequently found wandering the room or meandering in the hallways on his way to the restroom.

■ ■ ■

Literacy skills are crucial for promoting academic engagement, communication, critical thinking, independence, and lifelong learning (Erickson, 2003; Hanser & Erickson, 2007). Most important, literacy skills provide the foundation for improving quality of life, regardless of one's ability or functioning level. Students with autism spectrum disorders (ASD) often demonstrate social communication and cognitive processing differences that may influence how they engage in literacy activities (Carnahan, Hume, Clarke, & Borders, 2009). As a result, they are frequently excluded from literacy instruction (Mirenda, 2003). Further, the instruction they do receive is limited to basic skills such as decoding sight words and letter-sound correspondence. Although these skills are important, active engagement in meaningful literacy experiences is crucial.

From a cognitive-constructivist perspective, the construction of meaning from a text includes contributions from the reader (e.g., student characteristics, background knowledge), the text (e.g., length, genre, text difficulty), and the context (e.g., teaching strategies) (Jennings, Caldwell, & Lerner, 2006). As a result, skilled comprehenders (a) access relevant background knowledge, (b) make inferences, and (c) monitor reading comprehension (Graves, Juel, & Graves, 2007). These readers also demonstrate fluency, understand both the structure and vocabulary of the text, and integrate relevant information from their own world to make meaning (Koppenhaver, this text, Chapter 12; Koppenhaver & Erickson, 2009; Mirenda, 2003).

Together, these abilities support an individual in creating a situation model (Kintsch, 2004), or a "mental model or representation of textual information and its interpretation" (Gunning, 2010, p. 309). Situation models call on a reader's schema, or knowledge related to a topic. Understanding the cognitive characteristics in individuals with ASD, especially those clearly linked to comprehension such as accessing background knowledge and difficulty making inferences, is crucial to helping students develop comprehension skills.

Research suggests that although individuals with ASD demonstrate strengths in decoding and word calling, reading comprehension skills are generally lacking (Chiang & Lin, 2007; Myles et al., 2002; Nation, Clarke, Wright, & Williams, 2006). Thus, although they may be fluent readers, individuals with ASD often need support for comprehension. This chapter presents what is currently known about the cognition of students with ASD and the influence the specific cognitive processing style may have on reading comprehension.

Cognition and Reading Comprehension in Individuals With Autism Spectrum Disorder

According to the National Research Council (NRC), "educational interventions cannot assume a typical sequence of learning; they must be individualized, with attention paid to the contribution of each of the component factors to the goals most relevant for an individual child" (2001, p. 83). This notion is especially important in this textbook and our discussion of cognition. We are only beginning to understand reading comprehension and literacy skill development in the context of the unique cognitive styles of ASD. As we apply what we know about effective literacy instruction, we must do so based on what we understand about ASD, cognition, and each individual student.

ASD is defined by behavioral characteristics, including differences in socialization, communication, and restricted interests and behaviors (American Psychiatric Association [APA], 2000). These behavioral manifestations are expressions of neurological differences or cognitive processing styles that we are only beginning to understand. Over the past two decades, three models or constructs have provided great insight into the nature of ASD: theory of mind, executive function, and central coherence. Although each addresses unique features or characteristics, taken together, they help explain the cognitive processing style often seen in individuals with ASD and are crucial to conceptualizing reading for individuals with ASD. When applying these concepts to individual learners, it is important to begin with thorough assessments that paint a clear picture of the specific factors that influence learning for each child.

This chapter focuses on the cognitive processing style often seen in individuals with ASD. However, no two individuals are exactly alike. Understanding cognition in the context of an individual's life is crucial for building comprehension and other literacy skills. Assessment is the foundation for such understanding. The Ziggurat Model (Aspy & Grossman, 2008) is designed to assist in building this understanding. The foundation of this model is the Underlying Characteristics Checklist (UCC), an informal assessment tool that provides information about how ASD manifests in an individual's life. As such, the UCC is designed to identify characteristics of ASD across eight domains: Social, Restricted Patterns, Communication, Sensory Differences, Cognitive Differences, Motor Differences, Emotional Vulnerability, and Known Medical or Biological Factors. There are currently two versions of the UCC (high functioning and classic). Table 2.1 provides a discussion of assessment-related considerations that may guide you in understanding the role of the cognitive profiles and the needs of each individual.

Table 2.1
Assessment and Diversity

The following considerations, summarized from Wilder, Dyches, Obiakor, and Algozzine (2003), may be beneficial when working with individuals from diverse backgrounds:

1. Assessment teams should include a bilingual speaker, whenever possible.
2. Assessments must account for the norms of the individual's native culture.
3. Whenever possible, two assessments, one using the language from the dominant culture and one from the native culture, should be conducted.

Communication norms differ across cultures, and assessments must account for these differences. However, it is not enough to simply recognize behavioral manifestations (e.g., avoiding eye contact) of cultural differences. Understanding the values reflected in these behaviors is also important. Values shape experiences, world knowledge, and vocabulary, to name a few. In turn, these factors influence reading comprehension.

Additionally, using instructional materials that reflect the experiences of the learner is crucial for building interest and motivation, as well as supporting connections between learners' lives and learning material. For individuals with ASD, such materials are especially important. Learning materials that are not authentic compound challenges in perspective taking, active engagement, and understanding the gist of a story – all core challenges for individuals with ASD. On the other hand, beginning with personally relevant materials tends to increase the connection to the story, thereby increasing engagement and attention. Identifying personally relevant materials requires communication and planning. Do not make assumptions about culture or values (Rogers-Adkinson, Ochoa, & Delgado, 2003). Rather, ask questions of the family or others who know the individual well that provide insights related to individual interests and, when necessary, invite an interpreter who understands both the individual's language and culture.

Theory of Mind

In a seminal article, Baron-Cohen, Leslie, and Frith (1985) first discussed the notion of theory of mind (ToM) in the context of ASD. ToM refers to two important abilities, (a) the capacity to recognize the thoughts, beliefs, and intentions of others and understand that these mental states are different from our own; and (b) using this understanding to predict the behavior of others.

More recently, Baron-Cohen and colleagues (2005) discussed two other terms, *empathizing* and *systematizing*, in the context of ToM. Empathizing implies an extension of the terms *recognize* and *predict* mentioned above. Thus, it encompasses not only the ability to recognize the thoughts and feelings of others, but also the fact that a person has an "emotional reaction that is appropriate to the other person's mental state ... [an] affective reaction such as sympathy" (Baron-Cohen et al., p. 629). Whereas empathizing involves understanding others, systematizing addresses our understanding of systems. That is, we strive to understand the components of systems, how the components of a system function together, and how systems work. According to Baron-Cohen (2009), where many students with ASD struggle to empathize, they excel at understanding systems.

Theory of mind, ASD, and reading comprehension. Predicting behavior based on an understanding of others' mental states is challenging for individuals with ASD, and these challenges are central to their social-communication differences (Mason, Williams, Kana, Minshew, & Just, 2008; Mitchell & O'Keefe, 2008). They particularly manifest in areas such as language comprehension (e.g., tendency toward literal interpretations) and pragmatic language use. Cognitive style cannot be separated from the social-communication patterns found in autism (NRC, 2001). That is, factors discussed in relation to social-communication also influence cognition and vice versa.

Frith (2008) suggested that the prototypical example of a child with ToM difficulties, including empathizing and systematizing, is one who seems to live in his or her own world with little regard for the thoughts of others. In other words, these individuals have difficulty recognizing and understanding the perspectives of others.

Within a literacy context, perspective taking is important to "make sense of the actions of characters in a story" while reading or listening (Colle, Baron-Cohen, Wheelwright, & van der Lely, 2008, p. 28; Mason et al., 2008). Understanding how and why a character behaves in a certain way is crucial for accurate comprehension. That is, understanding that different characters have different perspectives and shifting between those perspectives is how we come to understand a text. Failure to recognize each character's perspective makes it difficult to make inferences or reconcile actions and behavior while reading (Happé, 1994).

In addition to difficulty putting oneself in someone else's shoes and recognizing that someone else's knowledge, interests, or feelings differ from one's own, ToM challenges are characterized by several observable behaviors that often manifest in social and academic situations. These include difficulty interpreting another person's figurative language (e.g., not recognizing that someone may say one thing but mean something else), continually discussing intense interests in certain topics or activities, and challenges engaging in shared experiences. For example, when told by a teacher, supervisor, or parent to "get moving" on a seated activity such as a puzzle, a student with ASD may actually stand up and move around the room. Additionally, when reading, individuals with ASD often interpret words, phrases, or sentences verbatim without regard for euphemisms or implied meanings. This literal thinking combined with difficulty understanding others' perspectives negatively influences their ability to make both causal and predictive inferences (Hundert & van Delft, 2009; Myles et al., 2002), which is a crucial component of building a situation model consistent with the text.

Consider the example of Charlie at the beginning of this chapter. Charlie loves anything that moves in the air, and he has the uncanny ability to link any lesson or conversation back to the topic of helicopters, jets, and skydiving. Most people do not share Charlie's awe of these topics, and, as a result, his conversations, writing, and comprehension are one sided. Although listeners usually indulge him at first, after a few minutes they become bored or even aggravated.

When engaged in conversation, we continually assess and monitor our partner's affect and spoken language to make predictions about what is coming next. Unfortunately, Charlie does not recognize others' facial expressions, body posture, or tone of voice. Similarly, his intense interests color his comprehension in conversations or when reading. As a result, Charlie often misses specific comments and other obvious clues that suggest that the listener is bored. For example, although his conversation partner stops nodding or providing other affirming comments and begins to look away, Charlie is often surprised when peers or adults walk away in the middle of one of his sentences. Indeed, he frequently continues talking until the person is no longer in the room.

Big Ideas in ToM

ToM influences:
- The ability to recognize and empathize with the thoughts and perspectives of others, and
- The ability to use these to predict or explain behavior.

ToM, ASD, and literacy: Individuals with ASD may:
- Have difficulty understanding the motivation or emotions of characters in a text.
- Have difficulty making predictions and inferences.

What does the research say? As mentioned, Baron-Cohen and colleagues (1985) first discussed the notion of impaired ToM in ASD. In what has become a classic example, the authors used two dolls (Sally and Anne) to assess ToM.

At the start of the experiment, the two dolls are in the same area. Sally places a marble in a basket and leaves the scene. While she is gone, the other doll, Anne, hides the marble in a box. Sally then returns to the scene. The researchers ask the participants where Sally will look for the marble. The correct answer is that Sally will look in the basket. However, 80% of the children with ASD failed the experiment, reporting that Sally would look in the box.

Since the original study, a significant body of research has employed higher-order tasks to address ToM, with mixed results (Hutchins, Prelock, & Chace, 2008; Joseph & Tager-Flusberg, 2004; Kaland, Callesen, Moller-Nielsen, Mortensen, & Smith, 2008; Melot & Angeard, 2003; Peterson, Slaughter, & Paynter, 2007; Ruffman, Garnham, & Ridout, 2001; Salter, Seigal, Claxton, Lawrence, & Skuse, 2008). While some participants with ASD demonstrate significant impairments, others accurately complete even higher-order ToM tasks.

It is not yet clear exactly how ToM develops or the specific role it plays in ASD (Oberman & Ramachandran, 2007). Even when individuals with ASD accurately complete ToM tasks, they do not use the same cognitive systems as those without ASD (Mason et al., 2008; Tager-Flusberg, 2007). That is, rather than using social networks, they often rely on linguistic patterns and general problem-solving skills.

At this time, language skills and intelligence appear to be the best predictors of performance on false-belief tests such as the Sally and Anne test (Kaland et al., 2008;

Tager-Flusberg, 2007). Moreover, and perhaps most important to our discussion, the ability of an individual with ASD to complete a static ToM task does not imply an ability to perform similarly in complex, real-life situations (Salter et al., 2008). Thus, inferring mental states and predicting behavior in very complex social situations or when reading complex narratives will likely be challenging for these learners.

Executive Function

Generally speaking, executive function (EF) refers to the set of skills or abilities that are important for "maintaining a mentally specified goal and for implementing that goal in the face of distracting alternatives" (Fisher & Happé, 2005, p. 757; see also, Pennington & Ozonoff, 1996). EF processes are crucial for planning and carrying out goal-directed behavior while tuning out unnecessary distractions or information. In other words, EF allows us to direct, monitor, and regulate our attention, thoughts, and behavior in many different situations (Carlson, 2005; Kenworthy, Yerys, Anthony, & Wallace, 2008). Planning and initiation, working memory, inhibition, cognitive flexibility, and fluency are examples of processes often discussed in the context of EF (Pennington & Ozonoff; Rajendran & Mitchell, 2007; Yerys, Hepburn, Pennington, & Rogers, 2007).

EF, ASD, and reading comprehension. Executive function accounts for differences in ASD, including repetitive behaviors and restricted patterns and interests (Geurts, Verte, Oosterlaan, Roeyers, & Sergeant, 2004; Kenworthy et al., 2008; Pennington & Ozonoff, 1996). These EF characteristics manifest as difficulty organizing information from the environment, transitioning from one activity to another, completing activities with several steps, and self-monitoring to correct errors (Dettmer, Simpson, Myles, & Ganz, 2000; Pelios, Macduff, & Axelrod, 2003; Swanson, 2005). For example, when faced with a seemingly simple task, persons with ASD usually have difficulty determining where to begin, what materials are needed, and the sequence of the steps. Unfortunately, it often falsely appears that the person does not know specific content or is refusing to work.

Some individuals with ASD have difficulty inhibiting responses or managing impulses (Attwood, 2008; Bishop & Norbury, 2005; Geurts et al., 2004; Hill, 2004). These children appear to act "without thinking of the context, consequences, and previous experience" (Attwood, p. 32). That is, students with ASD seem not to integrate new experiences with previous knowledge and use the integrated information to inform their behavior.

Again, think of Charlie. Recently, he sat working on a writing assignment. The classroom teacher, Mrs. Copper, realized that her small-group lesson had run over the allotted time. Therefore, she decided to skip the daily brainteaser activity to get the class back on schedule. She informed the class about the schedule change, suggesting that students make some final notes about their writing pieces in the five minutes left before lunch.

Charlie knew the class rules about raising his hand, he knew where to find his individual schedule, and he also understood about the necessity of change. However, since this was the first schedule change in fourth grade, he hadn't yet learned the routine for managing the change. He was unsure of when, or if, the brainteaser activity would occur. He interrupted Mrs. Copper four times in three minutes about the schedule change. And when she was giving the class some last-minute instructions about recess, he interrupted her again ... loudly. Although Charlie felt anxious, he wasn't able to appropriately communicate his anxiety to his teacher.

In addition to social-behavioral implications, EF challenges also have academic implications. Frith (2008) noted that individuals with EF differences have trouble generating and manipulating ideas. That is, they find it difficult to integrate new information, situations, or rules with existing concepts and knowledge, especially in times of stress. This is particularly true when the new information is not congruent with existing knowledge. In such a case, existing knowledge seems to inhibit the integration process.

There is limited research on the ability of individuals with ASD to access and integrate prior knowledge or experience in the context of reading (Saldaña & Frith, 2007; Wahlberg & Magliano, 2004). However, though limited, the data suggest that while individuals with ASD are able to access background knowledge, applying relevant knowledge across texts may be challenging. In the case of reading comprehension, integrating text with *relevant* previous experience is crucial. As Gunning (2010) suggested, "To make sense of the selection, you have to rely heavily on the knowledge you bring to the text" (p. 308). This knowledge, combined with the inferences one makes while reading, supports a reader's situation model. If students with ASD struggle both with making inferences and accessing relevant background knowledge, developing situation models that align with the information from the text may be difficult.

For Charlie, his love of things that fly in the air is a double-edged sword. At times, he is able to recall details about different types of planes, helicopters, and insects and use the information to inform his understanding. However, if he reads a book or hears a lecture presenting new content, Charlie frequently tunes out or interrupts the speaker. When asked to answer questions about the content, he often responds with default answers based on his prior knowledge rather than the new information. For example, Charlie's current focus is military helicopters, especially those used during World War II. Recently, Charlie's teacher presented him with a short news article about Pave Hawk helicopters used to provide humanitarian aid or conduct search-and-rescue missions. After reading the article, Charlie's teacher asked him to talk about two different ways that Pave Hawk helicopters can be used. Rather than answering with information from the story, Charlie quickly began talking about the different ways the military used helicopters during WW II.

Reading is a complex process; it is more than the sum of all of its parts. True comprehension requires attention to some details with little regard for others. However, comprehension is not simply attention to detail. As we read, we monitor our comprehension and self-correct as necessary (Graves et al., 2007). Monitoring comprehension involves asking, "Did I understand what I read?" Put another way, when monitoring, we ask, "Is my understanding in line with what actually happened in the text?" Monitoring and self-correcting comprehension is crucial for accurate understanding. When we misunderstand a word, sentence, or paragraph, our comprehension diminishes. Once we realize we do not understand, we use a variety of strategies (e.g., reread the text) to correct our understanding. Executive function differences related to attention and memory, as well as organizing and planning, may make both monitoring and self-correcting comprehension challenging for individuals with ASD.

Big Ideas in EF

EF influences:
- The ability to organize/plan, implement, and self-monitor cognition and behavior.
- The ability to integrate new knowledge with previous experiences.

EF, ASD, and literacy: Individuals with ASD may:
- Access background knowledge but struggle to determine background knowledge that is relevant.
- Have limited ability to integrate what they read with previous experiences.
- Need support to self-monitor while reading.

What does the research say? There appears to be a direct link between EF and ToM in students with ASD (Hill, 2004; Pellicano, 2007; Pennington & Ozonoff, 1996; Rajendran & Mitchell, 2007). Although it is not completely clear whether one predicates the other, support is emerging to suggest that EF is foundational to ToM (Pellicano). Two thorough reviews (Pellicano; Rajendran & Mitchell) discuss the ToM-EF relationship and should be consulted for detailed information.

Similar to the issues surrounding ToM, the nature and role of EF in ASD are not clear. Not all individuals with ASD demonstrate EF challenges, and even among those who do, there is no one universal deficit. While most studies support some level of executive dysfunction in ASD, data across studies are often contradictory. Kenworthy et al. (2008) suggested there is a "struggle to capture executive control with traditional measures of the construct for a number of reasons" (p. 325). These struggles include the developmental course of EF, the complex nature/definition of EF, variance across the spectrum, comorbidity of other disorders, and methodological research issues (Verte, Geurts, Roeyers, Oosterlann, & Sergeant, 2006).

Of particular interest are the methodological issues that may influence research outcomes, specifically the artificial data-collection strategies often employed. That is, lab settings do not reflect the complex nature of everyday life. Performing a task in a static situation is drastically different from performing the same task in complex social settings.

Also of interest are emerging data suggesting that the way in which EF tasks are delivered (e.g., face to face with a researcher or via computer) influences the ability of individuals with ASD to perform (Ozonoff et al., 2004). That is, a computer-generated task may filter out the social and motivational factors that influence performance of EF tasks delivered by a real person. For a full review of these issues, see Hill (2004) and Kenworthy and colleagues (2008).

Many questions remain regarding the exact role EF or EF profiles play across the autism spectrum. However, practically speaking, in authentic settings EF challenges influence the daily lives of individuals with ASD, including planning, monitoring, and adapting thoughts and behaviors. These challenges have implications for the behaviors students engage in and the cognitive strategies they employ as they approach literacy experiences.

Central Coherence

Frith and colleagues noted that typically developing individuals focus on meaning or the big picture of events at the expense of small details (Frith, 2003; Happé & Frith,

2006). Our primary goal when presented with an event, concept, or task is to understand the central tenets and create meaning from the smaller pieces. The importance of this global focus cannot be underestimated. The inclination toward global processing allows us to attend to important information from our environment and integrate it for meaningful purposes, which is crucial for later recall and use (Quill, 2000).

Weak central coherence, ASD, and reading comprehension. Unlike ToM and EF, weak central coherence (WCC) is concerned not only with deficits, but also with the strengths and abilities found in ASD (Frith, 2003, 2008; Happé & Frith, 2006). Frith postulated that individuals with ASD demonstrate a propensity toward detail-focus processing, but debate continues on whether they have a weakness in global processing or simply a preference or strength related to detail-focused processing (see below). Regardless, research suggests a propensity toward detail-oriented processing, which influences how individuals with ASD function in everyday life (Happé, 2005; Happé & Booth, 2008).

Manifestations of the WCC processing style are obvious in many scenarios that require attention to the big picture in the daily lives of individuals with ASD (e.g., completing daily living routines) (Happé, 2005). Happé described several implications that are especially important to a discussion of literacy, in particular reading: differences in memory, categorization, and comprehension. The overarching theme of these differences is meaning making (Attwood, 2008; Frith, 2003).

Students with ASD demonstrate attention to and memory for specific details and rote facts over conceptual or "big picture" ideas. The implications of such a detailed focus are enormous when making meaning from text. When reading, many minor details are parsed out as we come to understand the essence of a story or passage. However, until the big idea forms, it is often necessary to hold smaller details in our working memory. Some research suggests that as the complexity (amount or nature) of a reading passage amplifies, students with ASD have increasing difficulty integrating the information for meaningful purposes (O'Connor & Klein, 2004).

Think again of Charlie. As he reads a passage about a little girl who falls and needs stitches, he focuses on the red coat the girl is wearing rather than the injury. Charlie is also prone to remembering specific details about individual characters, such as the day of the week they were born or the color of glasses they wore years before. He seems to store these details in his memory without connecting the relationship between the main characters in the story.

Relationship to memory and categorization. Categorization facilitates our understanding of patterns, and helps us make connections and come to know something at a deep or automatic level. Students with ASD may not attend to the semantic relationships between words, concepts, or experiences and, thus, not use these relationships to categorize and store information in memory. Their focus is on the individual word, concept, or experience rather than the link between a set. As a result, storage occurs in isolation, without connections to similar words, concepts, or experiences.

Finally, WCC influences comprehension. Students with ASD demonstrate a propensity toward local-oriented processing, or an eye for details. At the same time, they process and integrate (make meaning about) global information in close-ended contexts. This has been demonstrated through sentence comprehension (Saldan & Frith, 2007). That is, when individuals with ASD are directed to attend to sentences as opposed to individual words, their ability to make meaning (as opposed to simply decode or word call) grows (O'Connor & Klein, 2004).

However, sentence comprehension is drastically different from comprehending paragraphs, chapters, or books. The ability to integrate words to create meaning at the sentence level does not imply the same ability exists when faced with lengthy and complex tasks. Gunning (2010) suggested that, "as they read, adept readers ask themselves 'why' questions about processes … The cause, which is often answered in the next sentences, is then connected to the effect. Causal connections are made in rapid-fire fashion. These causal connections are the glue that hold the information together" (p. 309). An intense focus on specific details, as is often seen in individuals with ASD, may limit the ability to make connections beyond sentences and paragraphs. As the complexity of text increases either conceptually or in length, the ability of students with ASD to integrate information for meaningful purposes will likely change.

Big Ideas in CC

CC influences:
- An individual's attention to details.
- An individual's drive for meaning.
-

CC, ASD, and literacy: Individuals with ASD may:
- Focus on small details with little regard for the overarching theme or main idea.
- Have difficulty connecting information at the paragraph and text levels.

What does the research say? As with EF and ToM, the research on WCC is not conclusive (Happé & Booth, 2008). While data suggest a strong proclivity toward local processing (Morgan, Maybery, & Durkin, 2003), individuals with ASD can process global information for single objects. The challenge seems to lie in making connections or creating meaning between the individual objects. Moreover, as stated, individuals with ASD are capable of processing larger pieces of information when given specific directions or when presented with close-ended task (Happé, 2005; Lopez & Leekam, 2003). Similar to EF, the types of activities used in many research studies do not replicate or take into account real-world demands. The ability to complete a close-ended WCC activity does not necessarily translate to the ability to use CC in daily activities.

Happé and Booth (2008) suggested an alternative to the either-or way of understanding CC, proposing that a "reduced tendency to integrate information and increased tendency to featural processing" (p. 60) may explain the WCC characteristics in individuals with ASD. Stated simply, strength in one area does not necessarily imply deficit in another. Additional research is needed to parse out these tendencies and to investigate the role of WCC across the autism spectrum (Happé & Frith, 2006).

Language and Comprehension

In addition to the three constructs just discussed – ToM, EF, and CC – a few comments about language use in students with ASD are warranted. Language comprehension plays a critical role in reading comprehension. Specific factors related to syntax and semantics may influence comprehension (Carnahan & Borders, in press). *Syntax*, or the structure of language, develops in young children as they begin to create two-word phrases. *Semantics* is about meaning. Children demonstrate an understanding of semantics when they begin to change words to denote different relationships (e.g., plurals, verb tense, prefix, and suffix).

Children with ASD generally demonstrate strengths in understanding the rules of language. However, differences exist that may influence how they construct meaning from text (Tager-Flusberg, Paul, & Lord, 2005). First, they often acquire certain vocabulary forms before others. For example, many children demonstrate a greater capacity for learning nouns (e.g., *boat*) over verbs (e.g., *boating*). Second, they appear to have difficulty using bound morphemes (e.g., *play* versus *played*, *work* versus *worked*) to mark past tense. Finally, many have difficulty with pronouns. For example, they reverse pronouns, using *You* instead of *I*, as in "You want a cookie?"

These language skills are closely linked to the cognitive processing characteristics previously discussed. Literacy instruction, which also incorporates language and communication skills, focused on basic, discrete skills alone is not enough; students with ASD need integrated, contextualized instruction that is based on an understanding of their unique learning characteristics and individual interests.

Table 2.2 provides a discussion of technology considerations that may be helpful in building quality instruction to address both comprehension instruction specifically, and literacy instruction globally.

Table 2.2
Technology

An abundance of technology is available (software, hardware, etc.) that can support meaningful engagement in literacy experiences and build reading comprehension. Many of these tools are undervalued and underutilized. Rather than providing an exhaustive list of technology, we offer suggestions for utilizing technology on a consistent basis. In addition, the online resources section at the end of this table contains links to several valuable tools.

The cognitive processing characteristics combined with the communication differences of individuals with ASD can make developing quality literacy experiences for students a daunting task. However, these experiences are not just about academics, but also about quality of life. Thus, understanding the unique learning needs of each student and designing creative, engaging literacy experiences is crucial, no matter how severe the student's challenges seem.

In a recent article, Mirenda (2008) commented that, when traditional methods are slow or ineffective, it is crucial to ask, "Is there another way we can make this happen …?" (p. 2). Rather than presuming the student cannot learn or develop a new skill, we push on, finding alternate routes or options. Though Mirenda's article is specifically about AAC (augmentative and alternative communication), it provides important insights about using technology to support reading comprehension and literacy for students with ASD.

The following points summarize Mirenda's suggestions:

1. Ignore an individual's previous history or apparent lack of readiness skills. Although previous history may provide important information, just because something did not work in the distant past does not mean it will not work now.
2. Begin with interventions and technologies that build on interests and strengths.
3. Consider any underlying motor challenges (e.g., motor planning challenges) that may influence an individual's ability to use the technology.
4. Presume that individuals with ASD have the same potential to become literate as anyone else. Provide many, many opportunities to use the technology and engage in quality literacy experiences.

Finally, start with something simple or something complex, something high tech or something low tech, but get started. Again, building comprehension and other literacy skills for students with ASD may seem overwhelming, but accessing and implementing the appropriate technology can make literacy achievable.

> **Online Resources**
>
> The first two web sites are links to specific instructional tools that may be useful for students who demonstrate some of the comprehension challenges discussed in this text. The third web site offers an abundance of theoretical and practical resources for building quality literacy experiences for students with disabilities.
> - Thinking Reader – http://www.scholastic.ca/education/tom-snyder/la-thinking_reader.html
> - Kidspiration – http://www.inspiration.com/Kidspiration
> - The Center for Literacy and Disability Studies – http://www.med.unc.edu/ahs/clds/

This chapter discussed the influence that ASD may have on reading comprehension. The reader, the text, and the learning context all contribute to comprehension (Jennings et al., 2006). Factors related to each area, such as integrating relevant background knowledge, making inferences, and attending to some details while ignoring others, influence the situation model an individual develops (Gunning, 2010). However, cognitive processing characteristics may influence the way that individuals with ASD approach text and, thus, their comprehension. Specifically, the profile includes a propensity toward literal and concrete thinking, limited ability to recognize and understand the perspective of others, difficulty making inferences, and differences with organization and attention (Happé & Frith, 2006; Quill, 2000; Reed & Gibson, 2005).

Perhaps most important, the ASD profile includes a propensity toward bottom-up processing suggested by Frith (2008). Hyperfocus on minute details rather than the big picture poses challenges for comprehending and storing information in context and for gaining meaningful purpose, especially as text complexity increases. Thus, many individuals with ASD become so consumed by a detail that they miss the greater meaning of the text. These cognitive characteristics do not only apply to individuals with ASD who use verbal communication. Individuals who do not use verbal communication may have similar cognitive processes. These cognitive processes should be considered when designing literacy instruction for all individuals with ASD, regardless of communication.

Taken together, ToM, EF, and WCC provide a beginning glimpse at the cognitive processing style of students with ASD. However, it is important to acknowledge the limited research on how the cognitive characteristics influence the reading comprehension of individuals with ASD. Although there is still much to learn, these theories provide the foundation for thinking about how individuals with ASD may approach literacy activities, especially reading comprehension.

Chapter Highlights

- Literacy skills provide the foundation for improving quality of life, regardless of ability or functioning level.

- Many students with ASD demonstrate social communication and cognitive processing difficulties that influence how they engage in literacy activities. As a result, they are often excluded from literacy instruction.

- Skilled comprehenders do the following:
    - ✔ Access relevant background knowledge
    - ✔ Make inferences
    - ✔ Monitor reading comprehension
    - ✔ Demonstrate fluency
    - ✔ Understand structure and vocabulary of text
    - ✔ Integrate relevant information from their own world to make meaning

- Individuals with ASD may be able to fluently decode a text as a result of strengths in word calling and decoding but often struggle with comprehension skills.

- Implementation of effective literacy instruction must occur based on knowledge of ASD, cognition, and the individual student.

- Characteristics of ASD include differences in socialization, communication, and restricted interests and behaviors. These characteristics are expressions of neurological differences or cognitive processing styles.

- Three models or constructs provide insight into the nature of ASD: theory of mind, executive function, and central coherence.

Theory of Mind

- Theory of mind, first introduced by Baron-Cohen, Leslie, and Frith in 1985, refers to two important abilities:
    - ✔ The capacity to recognize the thoughts, beliefs, and intentions of others and understand that these mental states are different from our own
    - ✔ Using this understanding to predict the behavior of others

- Two other terms, *empathizing* and *systematizing*, have recently been introduced in the context of theory of mind.
  - ✔ Empathizing includes the ability to recognize the thoughts and feelings of others, as well as demonstrate an affective reaction to another person's mental state.
  - ✔ Systematizing addresses understanding of systems.

- Differences in social communication manifest in areas such as language comprehension and pragmatic language and are founded in difficulties predicting behavior based on an understanding of others' mental states.

- Challenges with perspective taking impact reading or listening comprehension in a literacy context. For example, understanding how and why a character behaves in a certain way is crucial for accurate comprehension.

- Literal interpretation of language, intense interests in certain topics, and challenges in engaging in shared experiences are all characteristics linked to theory of mind that can impact literacy development.

Executive Function

- Executive function processes are critical for planning and carrying out goal-directed behavior while tuning out unnecessary distractions or information. Some of these processes include planning and initiation, working memory, inhibition, cognitive flexibility, and fluency.

- Executive function accounts for differences in ASD, including repetitive behaviors and restricted patterns and interests. Some individuals with ASD have difficulty inhibiting responses or managing impulses.

- Research suggests that while individuals with ASD are able to access background knowledge, applying relevant knowledge across texts may be challenging.

- Monitoring and self-correcting is critical for accurate understanding; differences related to attention, memory, organizing, and planning may make monitoring and self-correction challenging for individuals with ASD.

- Though the research on the relationship between executive functioning and ASD is not yet conclusive, it is likely that challenges in planning, monitoring, and adapting thoughts and behaviors impact how individuals with ASD approach literacy experiences.

Central Coherence
- While typically developing individuals tend to focus on meaning or the big picture of events, individuals with ASD tend to focus on specific details rather than the big picture.

- Weak central coherence impacts literacy development related to making meaning from text, where selecting important details to create a larger picture becomes critical to comprehension.

- The ability to identify relationships between words, concepts, and/or experiences is also impacted by weak central coherence and leads to missed connections.

- As complexity of text increases, the ability of individuals with ASD to integrate information for meaningful purposes may be challenged.

Language Comprehension
- Individuals with ASD often demonstrate strengths in understanding the rules of language.

- Differences exist in how individuals with ASD construct meaning from text. These differences include
  - ✔ Acquiring certain vocabulary forms before others (i.e., nouns before verbs)
  - ✔ Difficulty using bound morphemes to mark past tense (e.g., *play* versus *played*)
  - ✔ Challenges with pronouns (e.g., using *you* instead of *I*)

Chapter Review Questions

1. What factors influence reading comprehension?

2. Define ToM, EF, and CC.

3. How might differences related to ToM, EF, and CC influence reading comprehension in individuals with ASD?

4. Provide at least three detailed examples that demonstrate the influence of these differences on reading comprehension.

References

American Psychiatric Association. (2000). *Diagnostic and statistical manual for mental disorders* (4th ed., text revision). Washington, DC: Author.

Aspy, R., & Grossman, B. (2008). *Designing comprehensive interventions for individuals with high-functioning autism and Asperger Syndrome: The Ziggurat model*. Shawnee Mission, KS: Autism Asperger Publishing Company.

Attwood, T. (2008). An overview of autism spectrum disorders. In K. D. Buron & P. Wolfberg (Eds.), *Learners on the autism spectrum: Preparing highly qualified educators* (pp. 18-43). Shawnee Mission, KS: Autism Asperger Publishing Company.

Baron-Cohen, S., Leslie, A., & Frith, U. (1985). Does the autistic child have a "theory of mind"? *Cognition, 21*, 37-46.

Baron-Cohen, S., Wheelwright, S., Lawson, J., Griffin, R., Ashwin, C., Billington, J., & Chakrabarti, B. (2005). Empathizing and systemizing in autism spectrum disorders. In F. Volkmar, R. Paul, A. Klin, & D. Cohen (Eds.), *Handbook of autism and pervasive developmental disorders* (3rd ed., pp. 628-639). Hoboken, NJ: John Wiley & Sons.

Bishop, D., & Norbury, C. F. (2005). Executive functions in children with communication impairments in relation to autistic symptomatology: 2: Response inhibition. *Autism, 9*(1), 29-43.

Carnahan, C., & Borders, C. (in press). Language and communication in autism. In A. Boutot & B. S. Myles (Eds.), *Autism education and practice.* Boston: Pearson.

Carnahan, C., Hume, K., Clarke, L., & Borders, C. (2009). Using structured work systems to promote independence and engagement for students with autism spectrum disorders. *Teaching Exceptional Children, 41*(4), 6-15.

Carlson, S. (2005). Developmentally sensitive measures of executive function in preschool children. *Developmental Neuropsychology, 28*(2), 595-616.

Chiang, H. M., & Lin, Y. H. (2007). Reading comprehension instruction for students with autism spectrum disorders. *Focus on Autism and Other Developmental Disabilities, 22*(4), 259-267.

Colle, L., Baron-Cohen, S., Wheelwright, S., & van der Lely, H. (2008). Narrative discourse in adults with high-functioning autism or asperger syndrome. *Journal of Autism and Developmental Disorders, 38*, 28-40.

Dettmer, S., Simpson, R., Myles, B. S., & Ganz, J. (2000). The use of visual supports to facilitate transitions of students with autism. *Focus on Autism and Other Developmental Disabilities, 15*, 163-169.

Erickson, K. (2003). Reading comprehension in AAC. *The ASHA Leader, 8*(12), 6-9.

Fisher, N., & Happé, F. (2005). A training study of theory of mind and executive function in children with autistic spectrum disorders. *Journal of Autism and Developmental Disorders, 35*(6), 757-771.

Frith, U. (2003). *Autism: Explaining the enigma* (2nd ed.). Oxford, UK: Blackwell.

Frith, U. (2008). *How cognitive theories can help us explain autism*. Presentation to the U.C. Davis Mind Institute. Retrieved June 29, 2009, from http://www.ucdmc.ucdavis.edu/mindinstitute/events/dls_recorded_events.html

Geurts, H., Verte, S., Oosterlaan, J., Roeyers, H., & Sergeant, J. (2004). How specific are executive function deficits in attention deficit hyperactivity disorder and autism. *Journal of Child Psychology and Psychiatry, 45*(4), 836-854.

Graves, M. F., Juel, C., & Graves, B. B. (2007). *Teaching reading in the 21st century* (4th ed.). Boston: Pearson.

Gunning, T. (2010). *Creating literacy instruction for all students*. New York: Allyn & Bacon.

Hanser, G., & Erickson, K. (2007). Integrated word identification and communication instruction for students with complex communication needs: Preliminary results. *Focus on Autism and Other Developmental Disabilities, 22*(4), 268-278.

Happé, F. (1994). An advanced test of theory of mind: Understanding of story characters' thoughts and feelings by able autistic, mentally handicapped, and normal children and adults. *Journal of Autism and Developmental Disorders, 24*(2), 129-154.

Happé, F. (2005). The weak central coherence account of autism. In F. Volkmar, R. Paul, A. Klin, & D. Cohen (Eds.), *Handbook of autism and pervasive developmental disorders* (3rd ed., pp. 640-649). Hoboken, NJ: John Wiley & Sons.

Happé, F., & Booth, R. (2008). The power of the positive: Revisiting weak coherence in autism spectrum disorders. *The Quarterly Journal of Experimental Psychology, 61*(1), 50-63.

Happé, F., & Frith, U. (2006). The weak coherence account: Detail-focused cognitive style in autism spectrum disorders. *Journal of Autism and Developmental Disorders, 36*(1), 5-25.

Hill, E. (2004). Executive dysfunction in autism. *TRENDS in Cognitive Sciences, 8*(1), 26-32.

Hundert, J., & van Delft, S. (2009). Teaching children with autism spectrum disorders to answer inferential "why" questions. *Focus on Autism and Other Developmental Disabilities, 24*(2), 67-76.

Hutchins, T., Prelock, P., & Chace, W. (2008). Test-retest reliability of a theory of mind task battery for children with autism spectrum disorders. *Focus on Autism and Other Developmental Disabilities, 23*(4), 195-206.

Jennings, J. H., Caldwell, J., & Lerner, J. W. (2006). *Reading problems: Assessment and teaching strategies* (5th ed.). Boston: Pearson Education, Inc.

Joseph, R., & Tager-Flusberg, H. (2004). The relationship between theory of mind and executive functions to symptom type and severity in children with autism. *Development and Psychology, 16*, 137-155.

Kaland, N., Callesen, K., Moller-Nielsen, A., Mortensen, E., & Smith, L. (2008). Performance of children and adolescents with asperger syndrome or high-functioning autism on advanced theory of mind tasks. *Journal of Autism and Developmental Disorders, 38*, 1112-1123.

Kenworthy, L., Yerys, B., Anthony, L., & Wallace, G. (2008). Understanding executive control in autism spectrum disorders in the lab and in the real world. *Neuropsychology Review, 18*, 320-338.

Kintsch, W. (2004). The construction-integration model of text comprehension and its implications for instruction. In R. Ruddell & N. Unrau (Eds.), *Theoretical models and processes of reading* (5th ed., pp. 1270-1328). Newark, DE: International Reading Association.

Koppenhaver, D., & Erickson, K. (2009). Literacy in individuals with autism spectrum disorders who use AAC. In P. Mierenda & T. Iacono (Eds.), *Autism spectrum disorders and AAC* (pp. 385-412). Baltimore: Paul H. Brookes Publishing Company.

Lopez, B., & Leekam, S. (2003). Do children with autism fail to process information in context? *Journal of Child Psychology and Psychiatry, 44*(2), 285-300.

Mason, R., Williams, D., Kana, R., Minshew, N., & Just, M. (2008). Theory of mind disruption and recruitment of the right hemisphere during narrative comprehension in autism. *Neurophyschologia, 46*, 269-280.

Melot, A., & Angeard, N. (2003). Theory of mind: Is training contagious? *Developmental Science, 6*(2), 178-184.

Mirenda, P. (2003). "He's not really a reader ...": Perspectives on supporting literacy development in individuals with autism. *Topics in Language Disorders, 23*(4), 271-282.

Mirenda, P. (2008). A back door approach to autism and AAC. *Augmentative and Alternative Communication, 24*, 219-233.

Mitchell, P., & O'Keefe, K. (2008). Brief report: Do individuals with autism spectrum disorder think they know their own minds? *Journal of Autism and Developmental Disorders, 38*, 1591-1597.

Morgan, B., Maybery, M., & Durkin, K. (2003). Weak central coherence, poor joint attention, and low verbal ability: Independent deficits in early autism. *Developmental Psychology, 39*(4), 646-656.

Myles, B. S., Hilgenfeld, T. D., Barnhill, G. P., Griswold, D. E., Hagiwara, T., & Simpson, R. L. (2002). Analysis of reading skills in individuals with Asperger Syndrome. *Focus on Autism and Other Developmental Disabilities, 17*(1), 44-47.

Nation, K., Clarke, P., Wright, B., & Williams, C. (2006). Patterns of reading ability in children with autism spectrum disorder. *Journal of Autism and Developmental Disorders, 36*, 911-919.

National Research Council. (2001). *Educating children with autism.* Washington, DC: National Academy Press.

Oberman, L., & Ramachandran, V. (2007). The simulating social mind: The role of the mirror neuron system and simulation in the social and communicative deficits of autism spectrum disorder. *Psychological Bulletin, 133*(2), 310-327.

O'Connor, I. M., & Klein, P. D. (2004). Exploration of strategies for facilitating the reading comprehension of high-functioning students with autism spectrum disorders. *Journal of Autism and Developmental Disorders, 14*, 115-127.

Ozonoff, S., Cook, I., Coon, H., Dawson, G., Joseph, R., Klin, A., et al. (2004). Performance on Cambridge Neuropsychological Test automated battery subtests sensitive to frontal lobe function in people with autistic disorder: Evidence from the collaborative programs of excellence in autism network. *Journal of Autism and Developmental Disorders, 34*(2), 139-150.

Pelios, L., Macduff, G., & Axelrod, S. (2003). The effects of a treatment package in establishing independent academic work skills in children with autism. *Education and Treatment of Children, 26*, 1-21.

Pellicano, E. (2007). Links between theory of mind and executive function in young children with autism: Clues to developmental primacy. *Developmental Psychology, 43*(4), 974-990.

Pennington, B., & Ozonoff, S. (1996). Executive function and developmental psychopathology. *Journal of Child Psychology and Psychiatry, 37*(7), 51-87.

Peterson, C., Slaughter, V., & Paynter, J. (2007). Social maturity and theory of mind in typically developing children and those on the autism spectrum. *Journal of Child Psychology and Psychiatry, 48*(12), 1243-1250.

Quill, K. A. (2000). *Do-watch-listen-say: Social and communication intervention for children with autism.* Baltimore: Paul H. Brookes Publishing Company.

Rajendran, G., & Mitchell, P. (2007). Cognitive theories of autism. *Developmental Theories of Autism, 27*, 224-260.

Reed, P., & Gibson, E. (2005). The effects of concurrent task load on stimulus over-selectivity. *Focus on Autism and Developmental Disorders, 35*(5), 601-614.

Rogers-Adkinson, D. L., Ochoa, D. L., & Delgado, B. (2003). Developing cross-cultural competence: Serving families of children with significant developmental needs. *Focus on Autism and Other Developmental Disabilities, 18*(1), 4-8. Ruffman, T., Garnham, W., & Ridout, P. (2001). Social understanding in autism: Eye gaze as a measure of core insights. *Journal of Child Psychology and Psychiatry, 42*(8), 1083-1094.

Saldaña, D., & Frith, U. (2007). Do readers with autism make bridging inferences from world knowledge? *Journal of Experimental Child Psychology, 96*, 310-319.

Salter, G., Seigal, A., Claxton, M., Lawrence, K., & Skuse, D. (2008). Can autistic children read the mind of an animated triangle? *Autism, 12*(4), 349-371.

Swanson, T. (2005). Provide structure for children with learning and behavioral problems. *Intervention in School and Clinic, 40,* 182-187.

Tager-Flusberg, H. (2007). Evaluating the theory of mind hypothesis of autism. *Current Directions in Psychological Science, 16*(6), 311-315.

Tager-Flusberg, H., Paul, R., & Lord, C. (2005). Language and communication in autism. In F. Volkmar, R. Paul, A. Klin, & D. Cohen (Eds.), *Handbook of autism and pervasive developmental disorders* (3rd ed., pp. 335-364). Hoboken, NJ: John Wiley & Sons.

Verte, S., Geurts, H., Roeyers, H., Oosterlaan, J., & Sergeant, J. (2006). Executive functioning in children with an autism spectrum disorder: Can we differentiate within the spectrum? *Journal of Autism and Developmental Disorders, 36*(3), 351-372.

Wahlberg, T., & Magliano, J. (2004). The ability of high function individuals with autism to comprehend written discourse. *Discourse Processes, 38*(1), 119-144.

Wilder, L., Dyches, T., Obiakor, F., & Algozzine, B. (2003) Multicultural perspectives on teaching students with autism. *Focus on Autism and Other Developmental Disabilities, 19*(2), 105-113.

Yerys, B., Hepburn, S., Pennington, B., & Rogers, S. (2007). Executive function in preschoolers with autism: Evidence consistent with a secondary deficit. *Journal of Autism and Developmental Disorders, 37*, 1068-1079.

Chapter 3

Effective Instructional Strategies for Students With Autism Spectrum Disorders: Keys to Enhancing Literacy Instruction

Kara Hume, Ph.D., University of North Carolina, Chapel Hill

Learner Objectives

After reading this chapter, the learner should be able to:

- Describe why specialized instructional strategies may be necessary to engage students with ASD in literacy instruction

- Identify six broad categories of instructional strategies that benefit students with ASD during literacy instruction

- Provide examples of specific instructional strategies under each broad category that can be used with students with ASD

- Illustrate how several instructional strategies may be implemented during literacy activities with students with ASD

■ ■ ■

Ms. Walker, principal of Mountain Shadows Elementary School, was concerned. For the third year in a row, the students with disabilities in her building had not progressed as expected on yearly reading assessments. Her building housed a specialized program for students with ASD serving 46 students, ages 3-10. Students were served in both general and special education classrooms, and few were meeting expectations in literacy skill development.

Ms. Walker understood that students on the spectrum had a wide variety of strengths and needs and that currently used assessments may not best capture a student's true skills. However, she felt certain that more could be done to ensure improved literacy skills for her students with ASD. Though the school had recently invested in a comprehensive reading program, Ms. Walker was worried that it wasn't meeting the needs of these students. What else could be done?

■ ■ ■

The goal of educators is to increase students' engagement and active participation in classroom activities, with specific materials, and during interactions with peers and staff across the school day. Research has indicated that engaged behavior is the single best predictor of academic gains for students with disabilities (Bulgren & Carta, 1993). Similarly, the amount of time a student with autism spectrum disorders (ASD) is actively engaged in or attending to activities and interactions has been cited as one of the best predictors of outcomes for these students (Iovannone, Dunlap, Huber, & Kincaid, 2003). However, characteristics related to a student's ASD often make active engagement in the school setting difficult. Such characteristics can impede student progress and performance during literacy instruction despite the use of new and well-researched curricular materials.

Students with ASD have differences in executive functions (see Chapter 2) that impact planning and organizing (Hill, 2004). Such differences may make it difficult to organize the materials necessary to complete an activity and/or to follow a sequence of steps to meet a desired result. Both planning and organizing require the skill of dual focus – the ability to consider the immediate situation, such as a given literacy assignment, as well as the desired outcome, such as an idea about what the finished project may look like. This ability may be impaired in students with ASD.

Many individuals with ASD also demonstrate differences in inhibitory control – the ability to ignore competing information while processing a given task (Hill, 2004). These students likely have difficulty in prioritizing the importance of details in the environment and may be highly distracted by internal thoughts. In addition, the information processing style of students with ASD appears to be impacted (Hill). This processing style, also termed weak central coherence, impairs a student's ability to process information within context. As a result, events may be experienced and remembered as a series of unrelated occurrences without clear connections or themes. For example, when retelling a story, students with strong central coherence might describe the general ideas or themes, whereas students with ASD, who typical have weak central coherence, may recall only specific details. Weak central coherence may also impact the ability to understand abstract concepts such as figurative language like metaphors, similes, irony, and parables (Happé, 1993).

In addition to executive function and information processing differences, the learning of students with ASD may be impacted by several other characteristics. They may have difficulty learning through traditional instructional strategies such as verbal instruction, modeling, and social reinforcement. For example, studies have indicated that students with ASD are likely to attend only to select parts of a verbal message since processing several stimuli (e.g., the verbal instruction, the gestures of the teacher, the classroom environment) can be difficult (Burke & Cerniglia, 1990). In addition, deficits in imitation and attending to others may make it difficult for students to observe and replicate staff/peer behavior (Thurm, Lord, Li-Ching, & Newschaffer, 2007). Finally, the effectiveness of social praise (e.g., "I'm proud of you!") with students with ASD is questionable (Mesibov, Shea, & Schopler, 2005). These students may respond more favorably to other forms of reinforcement more specific to their special interest areas or preferred routines (Attwood, 2003). Examples include earning time to draw pinball machines, read about Thomas the Tank Engine, or talk about vampire movies.

Although students with ASD may face a number of difficulties while participating in literacy activities, the research has clearly identified strengths that can be enhanced through well-implemented instructional strategies. These strengths include (a) visual-spatial processing (Garretson, Fein, & Waterhouse, 1990); (b) a keen awareness of visual and/or cognitive detail; (c) strong rote memory; and (d) an attachment to routine, which can be easily cultivated to teach meaningful skill sequences (Mesibov et al., 2005). To achieve active engagement of students with ASD, instruction must be deliberately designed with these strengths, as well as some of the likely difficulties, in mind. Careful planning of how information will be presented, how students will respond, and how the environment will be modified is required to help ensure that engagement will occur.

The instructional strategies discussed in this chapter were chosen for several reasons. First, an evidence base supports their use with students on the autism spectrum.

The National Professional Development Center on Autism Spectrum Disorders (PDA, 2009) has identified 22 instructional strategies that meet criteria to be deemed evidence-based practices. Strategies discussed in this chapter that meet the stringent requirements of the PDA will be noted. Other strategies have a strong evidence base with other populations of students, and the literature is emerging on their application with students with ASD. Emerging strategies will also be noted. Second, these strategies are easily applicable in a classroom setting with one or more students with ASD. Third, the strategies are designed around the unique strengths and needs of individuals with ASD. And last, they are practices that, although intended primarily for students with ASD, can benefit a broad range of students, including those with attention, organization, and processing issues. The instructional strategies fall under six broad categories:

1. Organized Classroom Environment
2. Visual Supports
3. Structured Instruction
4. Curricular Modifications
5. Embedded Supports
6. Maintenance and Generalization Planning

Organized Classroom Environment

The environment for students with ASD should be carefully arranged so that a student's attention is available to focus on the most meaningful information – the literacy instruction. The teaching environment should communicate expectations, and only the most salient and relevant information should be highlighted.

The literature has identified two steps that assist in clarifying expectations and reducing competing information: (a) segmenting the space and (b) minimizing auditory and visual distractions (Heflin & Alberto, 2001; Mesibov et al., 2005). These strategies, named Stimulus Control/Environmental Modification by the PDA, meet the requirements as evidence-based practices.

Segmenting Space

It is helpful if the environment is arranged so there are clear boundaries, either physical or visual, that differentiate areas in the classroom. These separated spaces provide contextual information for students about what is to happen in each area. The organized spaces help students to understand the environment and function more effectively and independently. They can reduce anxiety as students gain clarity about expectations (Mesibov et al., 2005). When students are directly taught the behaviors for each space within the classroom, the area becomes a cue for appropriate behavior (Heflin & Alberto, 2001).

Bookshelves, file cabinets, desks, tables, dividers, and other classroom furniture can help designate specific classroom areas. In addition, visual boundaries such as rugs, tablecloths, masking tape, and/or labels posted on the wall assist in dividing space in the classroom. Visual boundaries can be particularity effective in spaces that are used for more than one activity, such as a small-group table that is used for both reading and math groups. A colored cue placed on the table may signal what activity will be occurring each time a student arrives to the location (e.g., a red sign represents math, and a blue sign represents reading).

Spaces in a classroom for young students may include centers with play materials, large- and small-group areas, and a space for eating snacks or completing art projects. These spaces would be created by using classroom materials such as bookshelves, Lego table, small partitions, curtains, and student cubbies. Boundaries may also help communicate to younger students, or those who are impulsive or motor-driven, where each area begins and ends, and where they are supposed to be/stay in the classroom during specific activities.

For older students, the spaces may include a student desk that is part of a co-operative group, an additional quiet work space, a computer center, and a small library area. These areas may be labeled with signs, a small rug, or colored cues that indicate what is to happen in each location (e.g., independent work, group work, silent reading time). Within each segmented space, only the relevant materials should be available for students, further clarifying how each space will be used.

■ ■ ■

Using Segmented Space to Support Students During Literacy Instruction

Mr. Garcia, a teacher at Mountain Shadows, decided he needed to do something differently during his language arts activities. He taught second-grade students; three of them had an autism diagnosis, and he was concerned about their progress. Mr. Garcia realized he spent a great deal of time reminding students of the expectations, "Be quiet – it's silent reading," "You're supposed to be reading to you partners now – it's buddy reading," or "Pull your chairs together for your book club group – everybody should be participating!"

Currently all of these activities happened at the students' individual desks, and Mr. Garcia recognized the environment might not be clearly indicating what the expectations were. He decided that students would stay at their desks for silent reading to emphasize that they were to work alone. For buddy reading, Mr. Garcia pulled out carpet squares and placed them in pairs around the room. He labeled each square with the names of the partners that should be sitting together. For book club, he assigned groups to labeled areas in the room (e.g., the small-group table, the carpeted area).

Once Mr. Garcia had taught the students how to move to these spaces and what the expectations were once they arrived, he found that he was spending less time clarifying the activities to students and was able to spend more time engaged with students around literacy activities. The environment and the segmented spaces now provided much of the information to the students.

■ ■ ■

Minimizing Auditory and Visual Distractions

The second key concept in organizing the classroom involves minimizing auditory and visual distractions. This helps students to focus on the concepts that are being taught instead of details that may not be relevant. Often when students with ASD are presented with too many stimuli (visual or auditory), their processing slows down or, if overloaded, their processing stops completely. This is a natural response. Consider the bulletin board used for announcements in the teacher's lounge, church lobby, or at the grocery store. When information is presently in an orderly fashion and the space is not cluttered, readers are much more likely to process and digest the information. When papers are stacked on top of one another and the space is disorderly, readers are likely to pass by the bulletin board without processing any of the information posted.

Minimizing distractions involves considering how much information is posted on classroom walls and determining if it is relevant to the class activity. Teachers may consider either reducing the amount of stimuli or placing the information out of the field of vision of the most distractible students (see Figures 3.1-3.3). Putting all extraneous materials and supplies in cabinets, boxes, drawers, or folders is beneficial. Covering open shelves with solid-colored fabric can be helpful as well.

Being aware of sources of noise like that coming from the hallway, playground, cafeteria, bathroom, and intercom is also important when organizing classroom spaces. Similarly, visual distractions like windows, doorways, reflective surfaces, fans, computer screens, ceiling decorations, and classroom traffic should be assessed. Often these potential distractions can be easily covered with butcher paper, fabric, a rolling divider, or cardboard, or the item and/or student can be moved to a better location.

Focusing on removing possible distractions is important across the age range and functioning level for students on the spectrum. It is important not to assume that as students get older, or if students are higher functioning, they no longer need or profit from being educated in a highly organized environment.

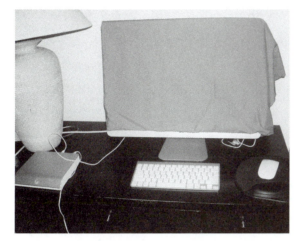

Figure 3.1. A sheet covers the computer screen when not in use to reduce competing visual distractions.

Figure 3.2. To reduce distraction, fabric covers the bottom shelf of materials that are not needed.

Figure 3.3. Extra teacher and student materials are stored in tubs and clearly labeled to reduce visual distractions.

Visual Supports

Using visual supports to communicate information to students with ASD is beneficial for several reasons. Supplementing verbal instructions with visuals provides information that is stable over time and is accessible to students even after the verbal instructions have been given. As such, visual information can serve as a continual reference, reminding students of instructions or expectations. In addition, anxiety and difficulty around transitions can be reduced if students are able to "see" the upcoming activities and events (Kluth, 2003). Numerous visual supports can be used when instructing students on the autism spectrum. Several that can easily be applied to literacy instruction will be discussed in this chapter. These strategies are all evidence based per the PDA.

Internet Resources

Creating visual supports is much easier than it used to be and often doesn't even require the use of a digital camera. A number of web sites provide high-quality photos or icons of almost any picture that is needed – from covers of books, to pictures for alphabetizing, and even photos of popular authors and illustrators. Google Images (www.google.com) has thousand of photos; just type in the name of the picture you need. Free clipart is available on a number of sites, including http://school.discoveryeducation.com/clipart/. Photos from http://pics.tech4learning.com/ can also be very useful.

Visual Schedules

A visual schedule (see Figures 3.4-3.6) communicates the sequence of upcoming activities or events through the use of objects, photographs, icons, words, or a combination of tangible supports. A visual schedule tells a student where he/she should be and when he/she should be there. Visual schedules are designed to match the individual needs of a student and may vary in length and form.

Typically two kinds of schedules should be in use – an overall classroom schedule and individual schedules for students who benefit from additional concrete information. General classroom schedules are important for outlining activities the whole class will be participating in, such as art or lunch, and should vary only minimally from week to week depending on special events or school activities. They should be posted in a visible location in a format, using words, photos, or icons, that can be understood by the students.

Individual schedules are designed separately for each student. This type of schedule may present the sequence of activities that will occur throughout the school day or only portions of the school day displayed at a time. They should be manipulated by the student throughout the day and should move with the student as he/she transitions from location to location. Additional resources related to making and using individual schedules may be found in the resource section.

Using Visual Supports With English Language Learners (ELL)

The use of visual supports also benefits students who are learning English as a second language (ESL or ELL). Washburn (2008), describing effective strategies when working with ELL students, stated, "Say everything at least three of several ways: speech; written words, drawings, diagrams on the board, or photos; actual objects; or action. Do not rely solely on the students' listening comprehension. Use manipulatives to illustrate what you mean …" (p. 249). This is similar to what is recommended for students with ASD – using pictures, icons, objects, or the written word to increase understanding.

■ ■ ■

Using Visual Schedules to Support Students During Literacy Instruction

In Mrs. Harper's resource classroom at Mountain Shadows, students with varying disabilities, including four on the autism spectrum, came in and out of the room throughout the day. Some students stayed for much of the morning, whereas others came only for one period. The activities changed often, depending on the student groups and their needs. Throughout much of the day, Mrs. Harper responded to questions like, "What are we doing today?," "Where am I supposed to be?," and "What are we doing next?" These questions, coupled with the off-task behavior her students demonstrated as she tried to get them organized, were reducing the time for literacy instruction.

Mrs. Harper decided that implementing individual visual schedules for several of her students would be a beneficial instructional strategy. Because her students had varying comprehension levels, she made several formats based on her students' needs. Two students were given schedules that showed photographs of the different locations they were to visit while in the resource class. One student had a written schedule, and another used icons. The schedules showed the students where to go and in what sequence activities would occur.

Now when students entered the classroom, Mrs. Harper only needed to direct them to their schedules and then begin instruction. The schedules guided the students to the correct locations, such as the listening center, the independent work area, the small-group table, or the handwriting station. When the first activity was finished, students went back to their visual schedules to get information about what activity would be next.

Figure 3.4. A visual schedule using photographs to indicate sequence of the activities during literacy instruction (listening center, reading group, independent work).

Figure 3.5. A visual schedule using icons to indicate the sequence of activities during literacy instruction (listening center, reading group).

1. Listening Center
2. Reading Group
3. Work Alone
4. Back to Room

Figure 3.6. A visual schedule using words to indicate the sequence of activities during literacy instruction.

Work Systems

The next layer of visual information can be provided through the use of a work system (see Figure 3.7-3.8). While a visual schedule instructs a student *where to go*, a work system answers questions about *what to do* once a student has arrived at the scheduled location. Work systems attempt to provide students with a meaningful and organized strategy for approaching several tasks or activities (Mesibov et al., 2005). They visually answer four questions for students when they arrive at an assigned location, such as the math table or the cafeteria, or when they are expected to complete an assigned activity or routine, such as participating in a group project or turning in homework. The four questions answered by the use of effective work systems are:

1. *What* task or activity is the student supposed to engage in?
2. *How much work* (or how many tasks) is required during the specific work period OR *how long* will the activity last?
3. How will the student know that *progress* is being made and that the activity is *finished*?
4. *What happens next*, after the work or activity is finished? (Mesibov et al.)

Information in a work system is presented visually at a level students can understand, and can range from a written list for individuals with strong reading and comprehension skills to pictures or objects for more concrete learners. This visual information assists students in understanding that they are making progress in activities and helps emphasize a sense of competence and closure when an activity is complete (Mesibov et al., 2005). Additional resources about developing and implementing work systems may be found in the resource section.

Use of PowerPoint® to Create Schedules and Work Systems

Schedules and work systems can also be created using PowerPoint®. Several studies have found this method of presentation to be effective. Rehfeldt, Kinney, Root, and Stromer (2004) included step-by-step instructions for embedding sound, animation, and graphics into PowerPoint® schedules and work systems. Below is an example of a combined schedule and work system. The first slide instructs the students where to go (listening center); the following slides instruct the students what to do once they have arrived at the assigned location.

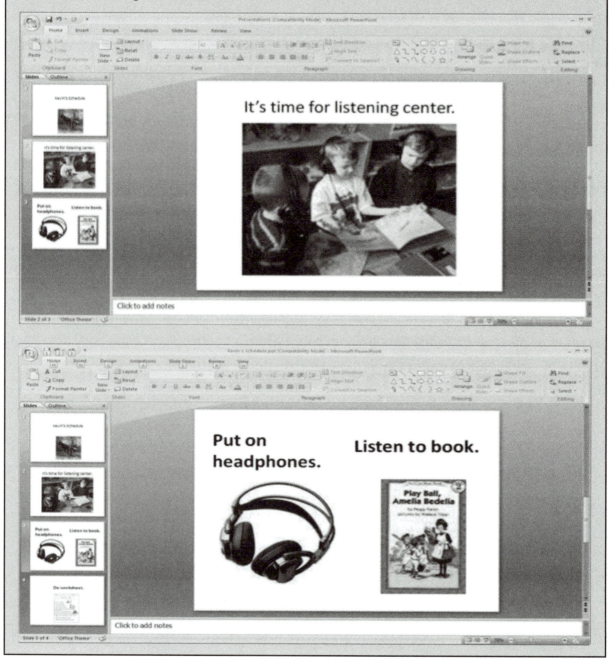

■ ■ ■

Using Work Systems to Support Students During Literacy Instruction

Mrs. Harper was pleased with the increased time on task she observed after implementing individual visual schedules. Students were able to get to their assigned locations quickly and independently. Once they arrived at the assigned location, however, students continued to have questions about what was expected. "What do we do first, Mrs. Harper?," "What's next?," or "Are we done yet?"

Mrs. Harper wanted to visually answer those questions for her students, so she decided to implement work systems at each activity. When students arrived at the small-group table, Mrs. Harper presented a work system to be used by the group. Icons and words identified each activity they would be doing, such as guided reading, answering questions, word wall, and dictionary activities, such as using guide words. As each activity was finished, it was removed from the work system and placed in a "finished" box. She also implemented work systems at each literacy center that instructed students on what to do when they arrived.

Mrs. Harper found that once students were clear about the expectations and knew when they would be finished and what would be coming next, they were calmer and more engaged in classroom activities.

■ ■ ■

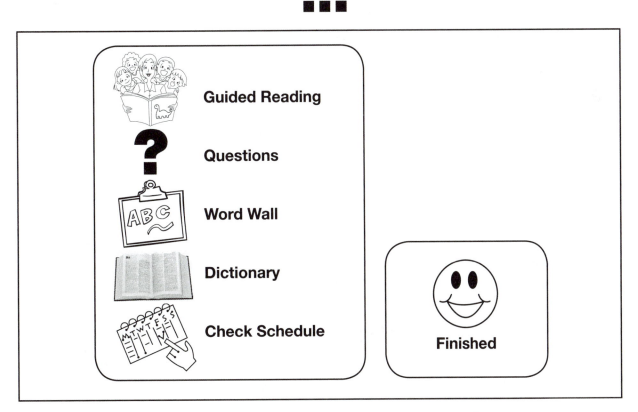

Figure 3.7. A written/icon work system that answer questions about what will occur during reading group.

Figure 3.8. Photo work system that answers questions about what will occur at the listening center (listen to assigned book, do assigned work sheet, check schedule when finished).

Visual Instructions and Organization

An additional question can be answered for students through the use of visual supports – *How do I do the activity?* When designing activities for students with ASD, it is important to consider how instructions will be provided. In most cases, it is essential to supplement verbal directives with visual information. Visual information allows students to function more independently, as they can be taught to look to the materials for information rather than relying solely on a staff member to guide them through the task. Supplementing instructions with visuals also helps to teach students that materials can be used for multiple purposes. For example, students can learn through visual instructions that the reading flash cards can be used for a cloze activity, as well as for alphabetizing and for placing in order to form sentences.

Visual instructions can be provided in a variety of ways depending on the students' needs and functioning level. For the most concrete learners, the materials themselves provide the instruction information. For students who understand pictures/words, those abstract systems can provide instructions.

Next, it is important to decide what types of organization will need to be incorporated into the activity to enable the student to be more successful and independent. It is helpful here to consider stabilizing materials, containing task materials in/on a tray, limiting the number of parts or pieces, reducing the number of problems or directions on a page, and setting up some of the task for the student ahead of time (see Figure 3.9-3.11).

Figure 3.9. An early literacy activity – recognizing letters from non-letters. The materials provide the instructions for the student, and the activity is organized with a tray.

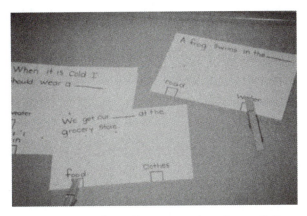

Figure 3.10. A reading comprehension activity. Written words provide the instructions, and the activity has limited parts and pieces to assist with organization.

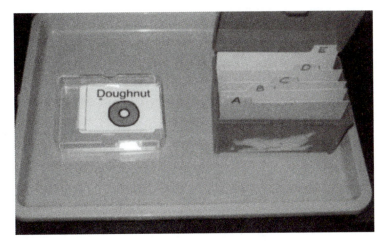

Figure 3.11. An alphabetizing activity. The materials provide the instruction, and the file box is organized and stabilized on a tray so students can manipulate the activity with ease.

Structured Instruction

It is important to first establish a supportive classroom environment for students with ASD (Heflin & Alberto, 2001). Next, and equally important, is instructing students in a structured and systematic way. When teaching new skills, such as those related to literacy, several strategies within the applied behavior analysis (ABA) framework are effective (Alberto & Troutman, 2006). Applied behavior analysis refers to the use of behavioral techniques to teach new skills or modify behavior. Numerous instructional strategies fall under the ABA umbrella. These include discrete trial training, pivotal response training, punishment, and self-management. In addition, a number of important classroom practices stem from ABA, including frequent data collection and analysis and functional behavior assessment (see assessment box). Several instructional strategies that employ the behavioral principles of ABA will be described in this chapter. Each meets the PDA's criteria for being evidence based, and each can be used in daily literacy instruction to increase student engagement and performance.

Functional Behavior Assessment

If a student is consistently engaging in challenging or interfering behavior during literacy instruction, a functional behavior assessment (FBA) may provide information that can guide your selection of instructional strategies. FBAs include observational data that analyze (a) the antecedents and consequences related to the target behavior across contexts; (b) interviews with staff and families; and (c) manipulation of antecedents and consequences to observe behavior change. The goal is to determine why the target behavior is occurring (its function) and how it can be replaced through effective instructional and/or behavioral strategies. Additional information about FBA and the training required to conduct one may be found at this interactive web site that provides video examples: http://jabba.edb.utexas.edu/mainstep/ms/index1.cfm

---

Task Analysis

Breaking complex behavior into its component parts is called task analysis (Alberto & Troutman, 2006). It is the foundation of many instructional strategies for students with ASD. Skills, such as identifying the title of a book, can be broken into many steps and taught in a number of phases.

It is important to first identify what skills the student currently has, such as orienting the book properly and identifying the title page. Next, all components of the task should be listed in the order in which they are to be performed. For the skill of identifying the title of a book, for example, these may include recognizing the features of a title such as capitalization, placement on a page, and position relative to other text. Once each component step has been taught and the skill has been mastered, it can be incorporated into a more complex task, such as finding a specific title at the library, identifying the author of specific titles, or grouping books by designated genres based on titles.

Conducting task analyses requires practice but is valuable when teaching students with ASD. Systematically identifying skills that students can already demonstrate and the steps needed for skills mastery will greatly reduce student failure and, in turn, increase engagement (Alberto & Troutman, 2006).

To sharpen your task analysis skills, select a simple task like brushing teeth and list its component parts in sequence. Then read the steps out loud to a partner while he/she does what you instruct. It will quickly be evident what steps you missed (e.g., if the partner is trying to put toothpaste on the brush with the cap still on), and your skills will improve over time. Additional information may be found in the resources section.

Prompting

Once the steps necessary to complete an activity have been identified, teachers may begin instructing students. Typically in an ABA framework, staff members provide a prompt or cue, also known as a stimulus, such as "Who is the author of this book?" The student should respond, and a consequence should follow. To encourage the correct response, teachers often need to provide prompts.

A great deal of research has been conducted on the use of prompting with students with ASD, including studies on effective prompts, the appropriate timing of prompts, and how to fade prompts. One evidence-based prompting strategy that can be effective during literacy instruction is least-to-most prompts (Neitzel & Wolrey, 2008). Teachers arrange prompts from the least to most intrusive, beginning with the lowest level of prompting and proceeding to prompts that offer more assistance if students are not successful. After selecting the target skill (e.g., identifying the author), teachers decide what type of prompt in the prompting hierarchy to give. Least-to-most prompts may follow this hierarchy:

- Gestural
- Verbal (full, partial)
- Visual
- Model (full, partial)
- Physical (full, partial) (Neitzel & Wolrey)

If students respond correctly after receiving a cue or instruction, they may be reinforced. If students do not respond or respond incorrectly, teachers can provide prompts based on the hierarchy, ensuring eventual success for the student.

Positive Reinforcement

Reinforcement is used to increase the use of a target skill or behavior. Positive reinforcement is the contingent presentation of a reinforcer immediately following a student's use of the target skill (Neitzel, 2008). The relationship between the student's use of the target skill and receiving reinforcement increases the likelihood of the student demonstrating the target skill again.

To effectively use positive reinforcement, teachers must first establish a target skill and performance criteria. For example: *Kate will respond to the cue "Where is the title?" with only gestural prompts for 3 consecutive days*. Next, teachers need to identify meaningful positive reinforcers for individual students. These may be primary reinforcers such as snacks or secondary reinforcers such as social praise or preferred activities. When selecting reinforcers, use a reinforcer checklist and consider the age and interests of the students as well as the targeted skill. (More information about reinforcer checklists may be found in the resource section.)

Once the target skill, performance criteria, and reinforcers have been identified, teachers may begin implementing positive reinforcement during instruction. For example, when the teacher provides the cue "Kate, where is the title?" and Kate responds correctly with only gestural prompts as assistance, a meaningful reinforcer is immediately provided (e.g., a token that may later be exchanged for time on the computer). After the stated performance criterion has been met, a new criterion that is more challenging, such as Kate responding correctly with no prompts, is established, and reinforcement is provided when the new skill is demonstrated.

Chaining

The steps in a task analysis form a behavioral chain that can be taught. When the sequence of behaviors occurs correctly, students are reinforced. Initially students are reinforced after completing each step of the task. As steps are mastered, students are reinforced only when successfully completing two steps of the sequence, then when three steps are completed correctly, and so on. This strategy of reinforcing responses that occur in a sequence to form more complex behavior is called chaining. Chaining can be used across curriculum areas and is particularly effective when teaching students with ASD (Hall, 2008).

■ ■ ■

Using Structured Instructional Strategies to Support Students During Literacy Instruction

Ms. Hinson, a special education teacher at Mountain Shadows who works with students with moderate disabilities, was trying to encourage her students with ASD to access their reading programs on the computer.

When the students arrived at the computer, they were often unengaged, off task, and unaware of where to begin. Ms. Hinson realized that perhaps her students didn't know how to find the appropriate programs on the computer desktop, so she decided this needed to be a piece of her literacy instruction.

She first developed a task analysis related to finding, opening, and beginning the reading computer program:

1. Press the computer power button.
2. Press the monitor power button.
3. Place hand on the mouse.
4. Move the cursor with the mouse until it points to the Kidspiration® icon.
5. Double-click the Kidspiration® icon.
6. Move the cursor with the mouse to the Sign In box.
7. Left-click in the box.
8. Type in your name (use visual cue if needed).
9. Place hand back on mouse.
10. Move cursor to the box labeled "Beginning Letters."
11. Single-click the box.
12. Begin activity.

Then she began teaching the steps to her students using a least-to-most prompting hierarchy. Ms. Hinson started by using gestures to direct her students' attention to the correct location on the computer or screen. If students didn't respond to the gestural prompt, she added a verbal instruction, "Press the power button." If students still were not able to respond, Ms. Hinson either pushed the button for them and modeled the skill or physically helped the students to push the button.

Initially, she reinforced students after completing step one ("Good work, Keisha!" or providing a primary reinforcer). When that was mastered, she reinforced the students after completing steps one and two ("Way to go – the computer is on!"). Slowly, as stu-

dents mastered additional steps of the behavioral chain, Ms. Hinson reinforced less frequently, until the students were able to demonstrate the skill independently. Using task analysis, prompting, reinforcement, and chaining, Ms. Hinson was able to successfully instruct her students on how to access their literacy practice on the computer.

She realized that more complex skills could also be taught using task analysis. She passed on the strategies to her colleague, Ms. Pena, an itinerant special educator who supported students with ASD in fifth grade at Mountain Shadows. Ms. Pena developed a more complex task analysis that assisted students in gathering relevant information from Internet searches to use in book reports and research papers.

When writing book reports, the students she supported went to the computer lab with several index cards that helped guide their searches. Each index card had a question written on it, and student was to find the answer through the Internet search. The questions were generated and written by staff/students depending on students' ability levels.

1. Select Internet search engine.
2. Type in search topic of interest.
3. Read the question on first index card (e.g., "How did Judy Blume come up with the title *SuperFudge*?").
4. Read/scan the content on the web site to determine if the answer to the question can be found on that page.
5. If the answer can be found on the web site, write the answer on the front of the index card.
6. Turn the index card over. Write the name of the web site (e.g., www.judyblume. com/books/fudge/superfudge) on the back of the index card.
7. If the answer cannot be found on the web site, use the mouse to click on the green "Back" arrow.
8. Move the cursor with the mouse down to the web site of choice.
9. Single-click the web site of choice.
10. Read/scan the content on the web site to determine if the answer to the question can be found on that page.
11. If the answer can be found on the web site, write the answer on the front of the index card.
12. Turn the index card over. Write the name of the web site on the back of the index card.
13. Read the question on your second index card.

14. Read/scan the content on the web site to determine if the answer to the question can be found on that page.

15. If the answer can be found on the web site, write the answer on the front of the index card.

16. Turn the index card over. Write the name of the web site on the back of the index card.

The task analysis continued until students had located answers to each of their questions. Although this task analysis and skill area required assistance for several of her students, Ms. Pena was very pleased that the structured instruction had led to better book reports and a higher percentage of time engaged in literacy instruction.

■ ■ ■

Embedded Supports

Numerous instructional strategies will likely benefit students with ASD. Following are several more that have strong support in the literature and can easily be embedded in literacy instruction.

Choice

Allowing students with ASD opportunities to make choices throughout the day has proven an effective instructional strategy in several studies. Though not yet considered an evidence-based practice by the PDA, choice making is a well-established intervention across disability areas (Dyer, Dunlap, & Winterling, 1990; Umbreit & Blair, 1996). For example, providing choices has been shown to increase task engagement, correct responding, and homework completion, as well as to decrease disruptive behavior (Moes, 1998).

Choices can be implemented in many ways. Improvements in engagement have been observed when students are able to choose the order in which activities are to occur (Watanabe & Sturmey, 2003). For example, when assigned to the listening center, students could choose which of the assigned books they would listen to first. During reading group, students could choose if they would complete the word wall or the dictionary activity first. The choices are controlled by the staff members, but the order of completion is chosen by the student.

Decreases in challenging behavior have been noted when students are able to choose materials within an assigned activity (see Figure 3.12). At the handwriting station, students could choose if they will complete their assignment on paper or on a dry-erase board. During a journal writing activity, students could choose what they would like to write with, and from a field of topics, they could decide what they would like to write about. In addition, students could choose from a field of preferred reinforcers after demonstrating the target behavior to the established criterion. Rather than the teacher selecting the reinforcer, the student could use a "reinforcer menu" upon completion (see Figure 3.13).

Figure 3.12. Choices for students at the handwriting station.

Figure 3.13. A reinforcer menu – students can choose their positive reinforcement after completing given tasks.

Priming

Priming is a procedure that allows individuals to preview an activity or event before it occurs so that it becomes more predictable. For example, using priming prior to receiving a classroom assignment, students are exposed to the activity that will occur the following day. This preparation can take place at home, in the classroom, or in some other setting. Priming has been successful in teaching students academic and social skills, as well as in decreasing off-task and other problem behavior (Schreibman, Whalen, & Stahmer, 2000). An increase in academic responding has also been noted across studies (Koegel, Koegel, Frea, & Hopkins, 2003).

Successful implementation of priming requires a team approach. Teams may include student caregivers as "primers," or primers may be school staff members, such as special education teachers or paraprofessionals. Teachers pass on the next day's assignment to the primer, who then introduces the material to the student. Primers are not responsible for teaching the materials – the goal is to familiarize the student with the material prior to it being taught the next day. Simply orienting the student to the material and providing a brief introduction is sufficient to achieve the purpose of priming: making thinks more predictable.

■ ■ ■

Using Priming to Support Students During Literacy Instruction

Mr. Lindsey was the student teacher in the kindergarten class at Mountain Shadows. In one of his methods classes, they were talking about priming, and he decided he had several students who could benefit from this strategy. For example, he had two students with ASD who had great difficulty attending during circle time. They often disrupted other students, especially when he was reading a story to the group.

Mr. Lindsey decided to introduce the book to the students with ASD the day before he read it to the large group. Near the end of the day, he pulled the two students aside at a small table and read the book to them. He pointed out the pictures and asked a few questions, but he did not spend as much time with the book as he typically did during circle. Instead, he used this time to allow the students to become familiar with the story and the pictures and tried to keep the priming session fun and motivating. He began to notice that during circle time, the two students demonstrated less problem behavior, and after several weeks they began answering a question or two during the story.

■ ■ ■

Video Modeling

Another strategy that can assist in preparing students with ASD for literacy assignments and activities is video modeling. This evidence-based practice (per the PDA) uses video clips to teach students a specific behavior. Once a target behavior has been identified, such as presenting original student writing to the class, staff recruits a student or adult model to demonstrate the target behavior on video. Staff may provide the model with a script that can break the target behavior into clear steps. These may include where to stand in the front of the room, what voice volume to use, how to show the class illustrations, and how to scan the audience while presenting. These steps are videotaped and may require editing or voiceovers to ensure that they are modeled smoothly with no errors.

Once the tape is complete, it is viewed by the student with ASD. After viewing the video several times with support and guidance from staff, the student may be asked to demonstrate the skill in class. Research indicates that skills taught through video modeling have a high rate of acquisition and are likely to be maintained and generalized (Bellini & Akullian, 2007).

Video Modeling Tips

Video modeling does not require much technological savvy or complicated equipment. In fact, very basic and inexpensive camcorders are now available that plug right into the computer after capturing the video and allow for easy editing and viewing (www.theflip. com). Make sure that your recording space is well lit and free of obvious distracters. Use a tripod to ensure a steady shot, and be sure that only the appropriate target behavior is captured on film. When editing, review the clip to ensure the length is suitable (3-5 minutes is recommended) and that the pacing is normal. After some practice, most teachers find that creating a tape for video modeling is an efficient and effective instructional strategy (Banda, Matuszny, & Turkan, 2007).

Curricular Modifications

This chapter has addressed modifying instructional strategies, *how students are taught*, to increase the success of individuals with ASD. Along with instruction is an equally important variable – the curriculum, the *content that is taught*. Several curricular variables can impact the engagement of students with ASD and, if modified appropriately, make instruction more meaningful and successful (Kern, Delaney, Clarke, Dunlap, & Childs, 2001). In the following, we will look at the use of high-interest, functional materials and the importance of using a wide variety of materials.

Using High-Interest, Functional Materials

The processing style of students with ASD tends to make seeing the "big picture" difficult. Class activities and the connections between them may not be apparent to these students and, thus, the lessons may not be as meaningful (Mesibov et al., 2005). One curricular variable that can be modified to increase meaning is the materials that are used during instruction. Using materials that are related to a student's interest area or that will impact functional outcomes is likely to increase student engagement and decrease problem behavior (see Figures 3.14-3.15) (Dunlap, Foster-Johnson, Clarke, Kern, & Childs, 1995). The change in materials does not mean that the instructional objectives should change (although that may be required for some students); instead only the context and student response would be modified.

Dunlap et al. (1995) described a curricular modification made for Jill, a 13-year-old with multiple disabilities and interfering behavior. Jill had great difficulty completing handwriting worksheets related to letter formation and spacing. However, she was very interested in taking photos in the classroom and school and sharing them with staff and peers. Staff modified her curricular materials, and her new handwriting assignment was to write captions for her photos that would be placed in a photo album. She was still to work on the same instructional objectives, letter formation and spacing, but the materials were adjusted to include her interest area and a functional outcome. Along with improved engagement, Jill's affect greatly improved with the modified materials.

Kern et al. (2001) presented another example of the benefits of modifying curricular materials. An elementary school student was struggling to complete writing tasks. He was to copy sentences from a handwriting worksheet into a journal. The standard worksheets included sentences about the solar system or dinosaurs. The student consistently demonstrated off-task behavior during this activity. When the staff modified the materials to include sentences from the manual of his favorite video game system, Sega Genesis, great improvements were seen in the student's engagement and task completion.

An additional benefit of using high-interest and functional curricular materials is that it can reduce student reliance on staff members to provide reinforcement. Earlier in this chapter reinforcement was discussed as an event that occurred after a target behavior was displayed. This requires that an adult is present to provide the reinforcement during and/or after activities.

An additional reinforcement strategy is using embedded reinforcement, where the student engages in a positive and preferred activity while demonstrating the target behavior. For example, instead of earning time to read about Thomas the Tank Engine *after* completing a given activity, the student is reading about Thomas *during* the activity. This can reduce the need for frequent adult reinforcement, which can lead to a reduction in prompt dependency and passivity that is often found in students with ASD (Goodson, Sigafoos, O'Reilly, Cannella, & Lancioni, 2007). Including high-interest materials in every activity is not feasible for most teachers. However, if reinforcing materials are regularly interspersed in the daily activities, students' engagement is likely to increase (Koegel & Koegel, 1986).

SpongeBob has a friend named Patrick.
Patrick is pink.
SpongeBob and Patrick like to go swimming together.
SpongeBob and Patrick feel happy when they go swimming.

What color is Patrick? _____

What do Patrick and SpongeBob like to do together? _____
How do SpongeBob and Patrick feel when they are swimming? _____

Figure 3.14. A reading comprehension activity using a student's interest in SpongeBob.

Figure 3.15. A reading activity using a student's interest in Superman.

Using High-Interest and Functional Materials to Support Students During Literacy Instruction

Mrs. Tsang taught students with ASD in grades 3-5 at Mountain Shadows. Several of her students who were not yet reading were working on early literacy goals like recognizing sight words and matching words to pictures. Mrs. Tsang selected her sight words from the Dolch word list, but found that her students weren't making progress as she had hoped and were often off task during literacy instruction.

She decided to choose words that were of greater interest and were more meaningful to her students. She assessed the interests of her students and chose words they were likely to encounter in their environment, such as McDonald's, Nintendo, Honda, Disney, *and* Cheerios. *She began by teaching the students to match the words to the correct logos, which they greatly enjoyed. Then she was able to teach them to recognize the words without the logos. Eventually, as students' interest in print grew and their attention was sustained, she was able to intersperse other basic sight words and environmental print. Her objectives remained the same, but the change in materials positively impacted her students' success.*

Using a Wide Variety of Materials

A wide variety of curricular materials should be used with students with ASD for several reasons (Kluth, 2003). First, using a broad range of resources increases the likelihood of skill generalization. Students may become rigid in their use of a material if a range of options is not presented. For example, if students are learning to match upper- and lowercase letters and only letter magnets are used, the skill may not generalize to matching letters on a worksheet, on a felt board, or in a computer game. Using multiple exemplars for each skill is essential if generalization is to occur. This will be discussed further in the following section.

Next, traditional teaching materials such as worksheets and overhead presentations may not hold a student's attention due to processing differences. A range of materials can also make the difference between students simply being present and students participating and being engaged (Kluth, 2003). When a variety of materials are used, students have a chance to be successful and learn in a way that suits them. Students with ASD have reported that hands-on opportunities to learn most beneficial (Grandin, 1995).

Last, students with ASD often present a co-occurrence of fine-motor difficulties (Ming, Brimacombe, & Wagner, 2007), and a wide range of materials can assist in alleviating many fine-motor difficulties.

Several studies have indicated that varying materials can decrease challenging behavior and increase time on task (Dunlap et al., 1995; Kern et al., 2001). For example, Kern et al. found that when a student was asked to complete tasks requiring fine-motor skills, he engaged in challenging behaviors. When a laptop computer or tape recorder was provided, self-injury decreased, and all assignments were completed. Similarly, Dunlap et al. found that when a student was required to assemble ballpoint pens, problem behavior occurred. When the materials were changed, and the student assembled sandwiches instead, on-task behavior increased. Kluth (2003) provides some examples (see Figure 3.16).

IN ADDITION TO TRYING:	TRY USING:	
Books	Adapted books (laminating pages, rewriting text to make it easier or more relevant), magazines, comic books, advertisements, audio books, movies *An adapted book – several picture choices are provided for students. Students choose the correct picture and match it to the page.*	
Worksheets	Adapted worksheets (highlight information), laminated sheets and EXPO marker or grease pencil, small chalkboard or wipe board, overhead projector *An adapted math worksheet – worksheet is laminated so students can use dry-erase markers, and manipulatives are included.*	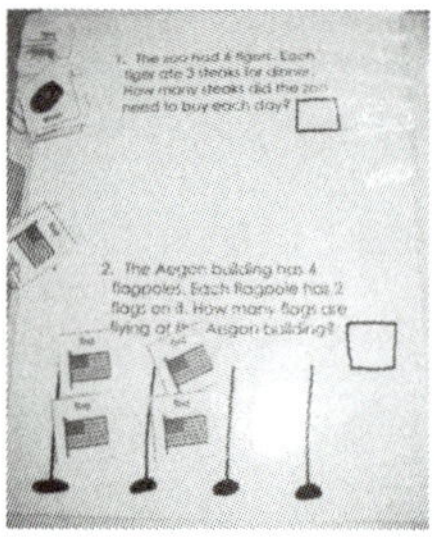
Pencils	Computer, typewriter, rubber stamps, magnetic letters or words, markers *An activity to practice ordering letters. Students can put tiles in the correct order rather than writing letters.*	

Figure 3.16. Examples of varying materials. From *You're Going to Love This Kid* (p. 191), by P. Kluth. 2003, Baltimore: Brookes. Reproduced with permission.

Maintenance and Generalization Planning

Implementing the instructional strategies and curricular modifications described in this chapter will likely increase students' engagement during literacy instruction. However, a challenge arises for students with ASD as they leave the setting in which instruction took place and attempt to apply the skills in a new setting, with new materials, or with new people. Students with ASD have difficulty generalizing new skills to new contexts (Hall, 2009). Challenges in generalization may be present for several reasons, including poor flexibility, difficulty relating new stimuli to past experiences, and lack of responsiveness to cues (Fein, Tinder, & Waterhouse, 1979).

Instructional strategies must include support for these generalization difficulties. Students should have multiple opportunities to practice their literacy skills in a number of environments using a variety of materials and with a number of peers and adults. Following are several instructional strategies that support the generalization of skills.

Sufficient Exemplars

Stokes and Baer (1977) described strategies designed to increase generalization of skills in students with disabilities. One of those strategies, "train sufficient exemplars," essentially encourages staff to provide many examples when teaching a skill or concept. Because of the rote-memory strengths of students with ASD, it is often difficult to discern whether a student has memorized an activity or assignment or if he truly understands the content.

For example, when presented with a series of 10 flash cards to be put in alphabetical order, Andrew, a 7-year-old with an ASD, put them in perfect order each time. The teacher thought Andrew had the skill of alphabetizing mastered until she presented Andrew with a new group of 10 words. He did not know where to start. Once the teacher showed him the order of the words, he memorized it and could then order the words correctly on his own, but he did not understand the concept of alphabetical order. Using several trials like this identified this critical piece of information.

Using multiple examples also ensures that students become familiar with materials that they will encounter outside of the classroom in generalization settings. If students are able to alphabetize flash cards as well as names in a phone book, CDs on a CD rack, and authors on a library shelf, it is more likely that the skill of alphabetizing will generalize when students are faced with these tasks and materials outside of the instructional setting. Conversely, if students have limited exposure to reading materials (e.g., most literacy instruction comes from a basal reader with little application), the literacy skills are less likely to transfer across setting and material (e.g., reading the bus schedule at the bus stop, reading the movie reviews in the newspaper to make a movie selection).

In addition, it is essential that the way in which students respond to cues is diverse. For example, asking students to place magnetic letters in order during every spelling lesson provides a limited number of ways students can respond during instruction. Limited responses minimize generalization opportunities and may limit student understanding of concepts. Additional responses could include students filling in missing letters in words, spelling words out loud with peers, using a variety of materials such as letter blocks or paper and pencil, or typing words on the computer.

Program for Independence

Independent functioning can also be difficult for students on the autism spectrum. After learning and demonstrating a skill with teaching staff, students may continue to rely on the presence of an adult or some form of reinforcement to remain engaged or to complete activities (Stahmer & Schreibman, 1992). The removal of close supervision, adult prompting, or contingencies may lead to a backslide, such as reoccurrence of off-task behaviors or a decline in engagement and productivity across settings (Dunlap & Johnson, 1985). As a result, instruction must include strategies to enhance independent performance. Such strategies may include a planful effort to reduce teacher prompting as quickly as possible (e.g., utilizing the "least" prompts whenever possible) or reducing the amount of reinforcement provided and instead embedding reinforcement in the curricular materials. Teaching students how to independently manipulate schedules and work systems is another helpful approach. In addition, teachers can implement self-management strategies during literacy instruction. These strategies teach students how to monitor and record their behavior on a target skill and then reinforce themselves when agreed-upon performance criteria are met (Alberto & Troutman, 2006).

■ ■ ■

Using Independence Programming to Support Students During Literacy Instruction

Ms. Henke was worried about how her student with ASD, David, would do next year when he went from his fifth-grade class at Mountain Shadows to middle school. As long as Ms. Henke was right on top of David, he could complete most literacy activities, even editing his essays. But if she was helping another student, David was typically off task and unengaged while students went through the editing process.

She decided to implement some self-management strategies. She selected a target goal for David that included editing his essays for punctuation, capitalization, spacing, and correct headings. She developed a checklist for him that asked questions such as "Have I put a period at the end of sentences?" and "Have I capitalized the first word of each sentence?" She added a spot for him to check off each question as he completed the editing. She then taught him how to use the self-recording tool, and together they agreed if David completed the editing independently and accurately.

Ms. Henke was pleasantly surprised to see how well the self-management strategies worked in supporting David's independence during literacy activities, and she was much more hopeful about his upcoming transition to middle school.

Conclusion

Students with ASD have often been left out of literacy instruction due to the misguided belief that they couldn't or wouldn't learn to read (Lanter & Watson, 2008). Recently, however, the field has recognized that these students can benefit tremendously from literacy instruction. These benefits are more likely to occur if educators are thoughtful about how alterations in the environment, instruction, and curriculum may improve the literacy skills of their students with ASD.

Ms. Walker felt hopeful. Her staff was now better equipped with both an understanding of how autism may impact a student's engagement in literacy activities and a repertoire of techniques to increase student participation and understanding. She felt certain that her staff would see steady progress in literacy skill development and that her students with ASD would be more involved in literacy instruction. Although she knew some of the changes in classroom environments, instructional strategies, and curriculum materials may take some time to implement, she was certain that her staff would see that the modifications and adaptations resulted in improvements in both literacy skills and classroom behavior.

Chapter Highlights

- Research indicates that engaged behavior is the single best predictor of academic gains for students with disabilities.

- Individuals with ASD demonstrate differences in executive functioning (planning and organizing) and inhibitory control (the ability to ignore competing information while processing a given task) that make engagement in the classroom challenging.

- Individuals with ASD may also have difficulty learning through traditional instructional strategies, such as verbal instruction, modeling, and social reinforcement.

- Well-implemented instructional strategies can build upon identified strengths of individuals with ASD. These strengths include:
  - ✔ Visual-spatial processing
  - ✔ Keen awareness of visual and/or cognitive detail
  - ✔ Rote memory
  - ✔ Attachment to routine

- Six categories of instructional strategies with a strong evidence base are:
  - ✔ Organized classroom environment
  - ✔ Visual supports
  - ✔ Structured instruction
  - ✔ Curricular modifications
  - ✔ Embedded supports
  - ✔ Maintenance and generalization planning

- Two steps to assist in clarifying expectations and reducing competing information are (a) segment the space and (b) minimize auditory and visual distractions.

- Segmented space involves clear boundaries, either physical or visual, to differentiate specific areas in the classroom. Classroom areas might include small group, computer center, or library.

- Only relevant materials should be available in each segmented space.

- Minimizing auditory and visual distractions helps individuals with ASD focus on concepts being taught rather than details that may not be relevant.

- Visual supports support individuals with ASD by:
  - ✔ Providing information that is accessible and stable over time
  - ✔ Reducing anxiety and difficulty around transitions since students are able to "see" upcoming events and activities

- One type of visual support is a visual schedule. Visual schedules communicate the sequence of upcoming activities or events through the use of objects, photographs, icons, words, or a combination of tangible supports.

- Typically, two kinds of schedules should be in use – an overall classroom schedule and individual schedules for students who benefit from additional concrete information.

- While a visual schedule instructs a student where to go, a work system answers questions about what is to be done once a student has arrived at the scheduled location.

- Work systems visually answer four questions:
  - ✔ What task or activity is the student supposed to engage in?
  - ✔ How much work (or how many tasks) is required during the specific work period, OR how long will the activity last?
  - ✔ How will the student know that progress is being made and that the activity is finished?
  - ✔ What happens next, after the work or activity is finished?

- When designing activities for individuals with ASD, it is often important to supplement verbal directives with visual information.

- Incorporating levels of visual organization in an activity helps a student to be more independent. Levels could include containing materials in/on a tray, limiting the number of parts or pieces, reducing the number of problems on a page, or setting up some of the task for the student ahead of time.

- It is important to instruct students in a structured and systematic way. Several strategies in the applied behavior analysis (ABA) framework are effective. Some of these strategies include task analysis, prompting, reinforcement, and chaining.

- Task analysis is an instructional strategy that employs the principles of ABA. It involves breaking complex behavior into its component parts. Skills can be broken into many steps and taught in a number of phases.

- In an ABA framework, a prompt or cue (a stimulus) is provided to the student; the student responds, and a consequence follows.

- Least-to-most prompts is a prompting strategy that can be used in effective literacy instruction. Least-to-most prompts may follow this hierarchy:
  ✔ Gestural
  ✔ Verbal (full, partial)
  ✔ Visual
  ✔ Model (full, partial)
  ✔ Physical (full, partial)

- Reinforcement is used to increase the use of a target skill or behavior. It is the contingent presentation of a reinforcer immediately following a student's use of the skill.

- To effectively use positive reinforcement, teachers must first establish a target skill and performance criteria.

- The steps in a task analysis form a behavioral chain that can be taught. The process of reinforcing responses that occur in a sequence to form complex behavior is called chaining.

- Other instructional strategies that can be embedded to support individuals with ASD include:
  - ✔ Choice
  - ✔ Priming (a procedure allowing individuals to preview an activity or event)
  - ✔ Video modeling (using video clips to teach a specific behavior)

- In additional to instructional strategies, which address how students are taught, curriculum (the content that is taught) can impact the engagement of individuals with ASD.

- Curricular modifications include using high-interest, functional materials and a wide variety of materials.

- Individuals with ASD have difficulty generalizing new skills to new contexts. Generalization can be supported with sufficient exemplars (providing many examples) and programming for independence (e.g., plan to reduce teacher prompting).

Chapter Review Questions

1. Why are specialized instructional strategies beneficial when teaching literacy skills to students with ASD?

2. How might an educator organize his/her environment to better support literacy instruction?

3. How can the use of visual schedules reduce student anxiety during literacy instruction?

4. What are several components of structured instruction that can assist students with ASD?

5. What additional materials can an educator use during literacy instruction if students do not respond to basal readers? Why might these materials be effective in increasing engagement?

6. How might educators encourage independent performance of literacy skills?

7. How can technology assist in teaching literacy to students with ASD?

References

Alberto, P., & Troutman, A. (2006). *Applied behavior analysis for teachers.* Upper Saddle River, NJ: Pearson Education.

Attwood, T. (2003). *Why does Chris do that? Some suggestions regarding the cause and management of the unusual behavior of children and adults with autism and Asperger Syndrome.* Shawnee Mission, KS: Autism Asperger Publishing Company.

Bellini, S., & Akullian, J. (2007). A meta-analysis of video modeling and video self-modeling interventions for children and adolescents with autism spectrum disorders. *Exceptional Children, 73,* 264-287.

Bulgren, J., & Carta, J. (1993). Examining the instructional contexts of students with learning disabilities. *Exceptional Children, 59,* 182-191.

Burke, J., & Cerniglia, L. (1990). Stimulus complexity and autistic children's responsivity: Assessing and training a pivotal behavior. *Journal of Autism and Developmental Disorders, 20,* 233-253.

Dunlap, G., Foster-Johnson, L., Clarke, S., Kern, L., & Childs, K. (1995). Modifying activities to produce functional outcomes: Effects on the problem behaviors of students with disabilities. *Journal of the Association for Persons with Severe Handicaps, 20,* 248-258.

Dunlap, G., & Johnson, J. (1985). Increasing the independent responding of autistic children with unpredictable supervision. *Journal of Applied Behavior Analysis, 18,* 227-236.

Dyer, K., Dunlap, G., & Winterling, V. (1990). Effects of choice making on the serious problem behaviors of students with severe handicaps. *Journal of Applied Behavior Analysis, 23,* 515-524.

Fein, D., Tinder, P., & Waterhouse, L. (1979). Stimulus generalization in autistic and normal children. *Journal of Child Psychology and Psychiatry, 20,* 325-335.

Garretson, H., Fein, D., & Waterhouse, L. (1990). Sustained attention in children with autism. *Journal of Autism and Developmental Disorders, 20,* 101-114.

Goodson, J., Sigafoos, J., O'Reilly, M., Cannella, H., & Lancioni, G. (2007). Evaluation of a video-based error correction procedure for teaching a domestic skill to individuals with developmental disabilities. *Research in Developmental Disabilities, 28,* 458-467.

Grandin, T. (1995). How people with autism think. In E. Schopler & G. Mesibov (Eds.), *Learning and cognition in autism* (pp. 137-156). New York: Plenum Press.

Hall, L. (2008). *Autism spectrum disorders: From theory to practice.* Upper Saddle River, NJ: Pearson Publishing.

Happé, F.G.E. (1993). Communicative competence and theory of mind in autism: A test of relevance theory. *Cognition, 48,* 101-119.

Heflin, J., & Alberto, P. (2001). Establishing a behavioral context for learning for students with ASD. *Focus on* Autism *and Other Developmental Disabilities, 16,* 93-102.

Hill, E. (2004). Executive dysfunction in autism. *TRENDS in Cognitive Sciences, 8,* 26-32.

Iovannone, R., Dunlap, G., Huber, H., & Kincaid, D. (2003). Effective educational practices for students with autism spectrum disorders. *Focus on Autism and Other Developmental Disabilities, 18,* 150-166.

Kern, L., Delaney, B., Clarke, S., Dunlap, G., & Childs, K. (2001). Improving the classroom behavior of students with emotional and behavioral disorders using individualized curricular modifications. *Journal of Emotional and Behavioral Disorders, 9,* 239-247.

Kluth, P. (2003). *You're going to love this kid.* Baltimore: Brookes Publishing.

Koegel, L., & Koegel, R. (1986). The effects of interspersed maintenance tasks on academic performance in a severe childhood stroke victim. *Journal of Applied Behavior Analysis, 19,* 425-430.

Koegel, L., Koegel, R., Frea, W., & Hopkins, I. (2003). Priming as a method of coordinating educational services for students with autism. *Language, Speech, and Hearing Services in Schools, 34*, 228-235.

Lanter, E., & Watson, L. (2008). Promoting literacy in students with ASD: The basics for the SLP. *Language, Speech, and Hearing Services in Schools, 39*, 33-43.

Mesibov, G., Shea, V., & Schopler, E. (2005). *The TEACCH approach to autism spectrum disorders.* New York: Plenum Press.

Ming, X., Brimacombe, M., & Wagner, G. (2007). Prevalence of motor impairment in autism spectrum disorders. *Brain & Development, 29*, 565-570.

Moes, D. (1998). Integrating choice-making opportunities within teacher-assigned academic tasks to facilitate the performance of children with autism. *Journal of the Association for Persons with Severe Handicaps, 23,* 319-328.

National Professional Development Center on Autism Spectrum Disorders. (PDA, 2009). FPG Child Development Institute, UNC-Chapel Hill, http://www.fpg.unc.edu/~autismPDC/

Neitzel, J. (2008). *Positive reinforcement: Steps for implementation.* Chapel Hill: The University of North Carolina at Chapel Hill, National Professional Development Center on Autism Spectrum Disorders, Frank Porter Graham Child Development Institute.

Neitzel, J., & Wolery, M. (2008). *Least-to-most prompting: Steps for implementation.* Chapel Hill: The University of North Carolina at Chapel Hill, National Professional Development Center on Autism Spectrum Disorders, Frank Porter Graham Child Development Institute.

Rehfeldt, R., Kinney, E., Root, S., & Stromer, R. (2004). Creating activity schedules using Microsoft® PowerPoint®. *Journal of Applied Behavior Analysis, 37*, 115-128.

Schreibman, L., Whalen, C., & Stahmer, A. (2000). The use of video priming to reduce disruptive transition behavior in children with autism. *Journal of Positive Behavior Interventions, 2,* 3-11.

Stahmer, A., & Schreibman, L. (1992). Teaching children with autism appropriate play in unsupervised environments using a self-management package. *Journal of Applied Behavior Analysis, 25*, 447-459.

Stokes, T., & Baer, D. (1977). An implicit technology of generalization. *Journal of Applied Behavior Analysis, 10*, 349-367.

Thurm, A., Lord, C., Li-Ching, L., & Newschaffer, C. (2007). Predictors of language acquisition in preschool children with autism spectrum disorders. *Journal of Autism and Developmental Disorders, 37*, 1271-1734.

Umbreit, J., & Blair, K. (1996). The effects of preference, choice, and attention on problem behavior at school. *Education & Training in Mental Retardation & Developmental Disabilities, 31,* 151-161.\

Washburn, G. (2008). Alone, confused, and frustrated: Developing empathy and strategies for working with English Language Learners. *The Clearing House, 81*, 247-250.

Watanabe, M., & Sturmey, P. (2003). The effect of choice-making opportunities during activity schedules on task engagement of adults with autism. *Journal of Autism and Developmental Disorders, 33*, 535-538.

Additional Resources

Evidence-Based Practices: More information about the criteria for evidence-based practices, as well as the full list of practices, may be found at http://www.fpg.unc.edu/~autismPDC/about/

Reinforcer Checklist: A thorough checklist may be found at http://www.lessons4all.org/downloads/reinforcement_checklist.pdf

Task Analysis: Additional examples of task analysis sequences may be found at http://www.behavioradvisor.com/TaskAnalysis.html

Visual Schedules: An online module by Dr. Shelia Smith detailing how to create and use visual schedules is available through the Autism Internet Modules (AIM): http://www.autisminternetmodules.org

Work Systems: An online module by Dr. Christi Carnahan detailing how to create and use work systems is available through the Autism Internet Modules (AIM): http://www.autisminternetmodules.org

PART TWO

Designing Effective Literacy Environments for Students With ASD

Chapter 4
What Is Reading and What Do Good Readers Do?

JoAnne Schudt Caldwell, Ph.D., Cardinal Stritch University

Learner Objectives

After reading this chapter, the learner should be able to:

- List different theories that attempt to explain the reading process

- Describe the behaviors of good readers

- Clarify key predictors of reading achievement

- Explain the five components of the reading process as described by the National Reading Panel

- Describe formal and informal measures of assessment for each of the five components

- Compare and contrast advantages and disadvantages of assessment measures

- Discuss instructional implications for each of the five components

- Explain factors that impact reading comprehension

You would expect a chapter entitled "What Is Reading and What Do Good Readers Do?" to begin with a definition of reading. However, given the complexity of the reading process, this is not easy to do. Some define reading as the ability to say the words. However, of what use is saying words that do not result in comprehension? Very briefly, reading represents "a combination of print processing skill and comprehension" (Morris, 2008, p. 5).

Many have attempted to describe the reading process in greater detail. Bottom-up models depict reading as a "one-way street" that begins with letter perception, moves to word pronunciation, and ends in comprehension of individual words, sentences, and text (Gough, 1984; LaBerge & Samuels, 1974; Samuels, 2004). Goodman (1969) and Smith (1978) conceptualized reading as a top-down process, whereby word perception and passage meaning are heavily dependent on the reader's predictions of content. Information processing models describe reading as a highly interactive process involving phonological, orthographic, syntactic, lexical, and semantic components that interact as needed to achieve comprehension (Adams, 2004; Rumelhart, 2004; Stanovich, 1980). Still other theorists see reading as a constructive process that is heavily dependent upon reader schema or prior knowledge (Anderson, 2004; Bransford, 2004; Bransford, Brown, & Cocking, 2000) as well as socio-cultural influences (Brice Heath, 2004; Gee, 2004). In reality, all of these definitions and models have some validity, and regardless of the model we adopt, there is agreement that reading is a unified and highly complex act with the ultimate aim of attaining meaningful comprehension (Kintsch, 1998; Kintsch & Kintsch, 2005).

Reading may not be an innate cognitive activity (Wolf, 2007). While human beings are genetically programmed to develop oral language, they may not be similarly programmed to develop reading, and some societies never develop a written language. When reading was invented in response to cultural, economic, and political needs, the brain was forced to use existing structures originally designated for other activities. However, the plasticity of the human brain allowed it "to be shaped by experience" (Wolf, p. 3). Present-day non-invasive brain scans are beginning to identify which areas of the brain are involved in reading. Some children who find learning to read extremely difficult show different brain patterns than those who learn to read with seemingly little effort, and emerging evidence suggests that reading impairment may be familial and heritable (Gilger & Wise, 2004).

Reading achievement is strongly tied to and dependent on oral language development. This makes sense. If children are to learn to read and write their language, they must first acquire that language. They must develop the awareness that sounds stand for meaning and learn to string them together to form words and then sentences (Troia, 2004). They must also understand the morphological system represented by compound words, inflections, and derivations (Carlisle, 2004) and the underlying concepts represented by words (McGregor, 2004; Scott, 2004).

At all age levels, strong correlations exist between listening comprehension and reading comprehension; good readers tend to be good listeners, and poor readers are generally poor listeners (Daneman, 1991). All components of oral language communication contribute to reading performance, and children with specific communication difficulties are singularly at risk for not reaching their potential as readers.

To complicate matters further, the quality and amount of oral language interactions in the home have a profound effect on children's linguistic development (Hart & Risley, 1995; Wasik & Henderson, 2004). Hart and Risley suggested that children of poverty do not have opportunities to engage in the kind of interactive exchanges that foster language development and mimic the language of written text. As a result, they enter school already far behind their more fortunate peers in the sheer number of words that they have heard. Wolf (2007) estimated that such children know 15,000 fewer words than peers who do not live in poverty!

Another predictor of reading achievement is the extent of early literacy activities provided by caregivers (Caldwell, 2008a; Wolf, 2007), and "the single most important activity for building the knowledge and skills eventually required for reading appears to be reading aloud to children" (Adams, 1990, p. 46). Children learn a lot about language from such experiences: new concepts, new vocabulary words, and new sentence structures. Wolf noted that being read to involves more than learning concepts and syntax. "When story forms are never known, there is less ability to infer and to predict. When cultural traditions and the feelings of others are never experienced, there is less understanding of what other people feel" (p. 102).

How Is Reading Achievement Assessed?

Reading assessments fall into two general categories: formal and informal. Formal tests are generally standardized and norm-referenced; they are administered to all children in the same way, and a child's score is compared to the average score of the norm group. Some formal instruments are individual in nature and take the form of test batteries that assess a variety of component skills, such as the Woodcock Reading Mastery Test-Revised (WRMT-R) (Woodcock, Mather, & Schrank, 2004). Others are group instruments comprised of short passages followed by multiple-choice questions. Given the importance of the 2001 No Child Left Behind Act, group tests have taken on increased importance.

In contrast to formal instruments, informal assessments allow diagnosticians and teachers to adapt the instrument to the needs of the child and the context of the classroom. This type of assessment takes many forms (Leslie & Caldwell, 2009). One commonly used informal assessment is the informal reading inventory (IRI), which is composed of word lists and passages at a variety of levels from preprimer to high school. An IRI can identify a student's reading level and can provide valuable information about word identification, fluency, and comprehension in both oral and silent reading.

Although some questions exist regarding the validity and reliability of informal reading inventories in general (Fuchs, Fuchs, & Deno, 1982; Klesius & Homan, 1985; Spector, 2005), the Qualitative Reading Inventory 5 has been used to successfully document growth in reading after program or intervention implementation (Leslie & Caldwell, 2011). Another popular informal assessment in the primary grades is the running record, whereby the teacher listens to a child read orally and creates an ongoing record of his/her performance (Caldwell, 2008a). A running record can indicate if a text is easy, difficult, or appropriate for a child as well as suggest the strategies the child is using to identify words.

When faced with the necessity of understanding a complex entity, it helps to break it down into smaller and more manageable parts. And so it is with reading. The National Reading Panel (2000) described reading as primarily involving five factors: phonological awareness, word identification, fluency, vocabulary, and comprehension. These factors provide a workable structure for examining an extremely complex and interrelated process. However, successful reading instruction involves an integrated approach as opposed to the fragmented "skill and drill" lessons that were popular some years ago but have been found to be ineffective. Successful literacy interventions address all components of reading (see Table 4.1) within the context of focusing on both the strengths and needs of the students (Caldwell & Leslie, 2009; Jennings, Caldwell, & Lerner, 2006).

Table 4.1
The Reading Process Defined

Theories of the Reading Process
Bottom-Up Process: Readers move from letters to words to comprehension
Top-Down Process: Reader prediction influences word identification and comprehension
Interactive Process: Knowledge of letter sounds, word parts, sentence syntax, word meaning, and reader knowledge interact to achieve comprehension
Constructive Process: Reader prior knowledge and socio-cultural influences interact to influence comprehension
Predictors of Reading Achievement
Oral language development
Quality and extent of oral language interaction in the home
Extent of early language activities
Components of the Reading Process
Phonological Awareness
Word Identification/Phonics
Fluency
Vocabulary
Comprehension

The purpose of this chapter is to describe the reading process for typically developing learners. Following chapters discuss each of the components of the reading process in greater detail and with specific links to autism spectrum disorders (ASD). Though the components are presented in separate chapters, we advocate an integrated approach to instruction that includes attention to the entire reading process every day.

Phonological Awareness

Table 4.2 presents the components of phonological awareness. *Phonological awareness* refers to the awareness of sound; that is, the ability to perceive words, syllables, and phonemes as discrete units. The first level of such awareness is the ability to distinguish words in a sentence as separate entities. This seems obvious to an adult, but it is not so obvious to the young child. When speaking, we generally do not pause between words. We string words together in an uninterrupted stream of speech, and our perception of single words is based on our understanding of their meaning. Think of how you feel when listening to someone speak a language that you do not know. You cannot really tell how many words were spoken. They all seem to run together. In order to transfer oral language knowledge to learning to read, children must be able to distinguish words as distinct sounds within a sentence.

Children must also be able to distinguish syllables (Caldwell & Leslie, 2009; Goswami, 2000), the second level of phonemic awareness. A syllable contains a single vowel sound. The word *top* forms one syllable, with the vowel sound represented by the letter *o*. Most words contain more than one syllable, and recognition of the written word is extremely difficult for children who do not perceive syllables as discrete units.

The final level of phonological awareness is the phonemic level; that is, the awareness of component sounds in words. The ability to perceive and manipulate individual sounds within syllables and words is critical if children are to apply letter and sound relationships for word identification. Sound perception is not easy. Let me offer an example. Suppose you hear two chords played on the piano, but you cannot see the placement of the pianist's fingers. You will probably be able to tell if the chords are the same or different, but you may find it difficult to distinguish how many notes are in each chord. Most syllables contain consonant sounds as well as the required vowel sound. The consonant sound/s that precede/s the vowel is the onset. The sound/s that includes and follows the vowel represents the rime. In the word *splash*, *sp* is the onset and *ash* is the rime. Perception of onsets and rimes allows the reader to break a word into smaller and more manageable sections than individual sounds.

Table 4.2
Units of Phonological Awareness

- Awareness of discrete words in a sentence: *Mary saw John* contains three words
- Awareness of syllables in a word: *happy* contains two syllables
- Awareness of sounds within syllables: *hap* contains the sounds represented by *h* (the onset) and *ap* (the rime)

A child's ability to identify and manipulate sounds is strongly related to later reading and spelling achievement (Ehri et al., 2001; National Reading Panel, 2000; Stanovich, 1988;

Troia, 2004). Researchers measure young children's ability in sound-related tasks and then correlate their scores with later achievement scores in reading and spelling. Preschoolers who attain high scores on phonological tasks demonstrate strong reading achievement in first and second grade. Stanovich (2004) suggested that for children who find learning to read difficult, the core deficit may lie in the area of phonology. Because the child experiences difficulty in perceiving component sounds in words, and thus in attaching these sounds to letter configurations, learning to read becomes challenging and problematic. Further, because reading is uncomfortable, the child avoids it.

Unfortunately, avoiding reading has a detrimental effect on learning new concepts, understanding new genres, and acquiring new information. Stanovich (2004) called this the Matthew Effect. Those who read a lot learn more and become better readers … the rich get richer. Those who avoid reading miss the opportunity to expand their cognitive horizons … the poor get poorer.

Assessment of Phonological Awareness

Phonological awareness is assessed by a variety of activities. *Segmentation tasks* ask children to tap or push tokens forward to indicate how many sounds they hear in a spoken word or to repeat a word by breaking it into its component sounds. *Phoneme deletion* involves saying a word without a certain sound. For *blending tasks*, children listen to a series of sounds and blend them into a word. *Phoneme substitution* requires the child to change a sound within a word. In addition, some assessments present the child with a series of spoken words, and the child is to indicate which word is different in the beginning, middle, or ending position. Yopp (1988) warned that all phonological assessment tasks are not equal. Some, like rhyme detection, are relatively easy; others, like sound deletion or substitution, are more difficult (see Table 4.3).

A variety of phonological assessment tasks are part of early reading assessment batteries. Popular examples of such batteries include the Dynamic Indicators of Basic Early Literacy Skills (DIBELS) (Good & Kaminski, 2002); the Phonological Awareness Literacy Screening (PALs) (Invernizzi, Meier, Sullivan & Swank, 2004; Invernizzi, Meier, Swank, & Juel, 2005; Invernizzi, Meier, & Juel, 2005); and the Early Reading Diagnostic Assessment (ERDA) (Jordan, Kirk, & King, 2003). These assessment batteries and many others are included in the Southwest Educational Development Laboratory (SEDL) database (SEDL, 2007). The Yopp-Singer Test of Phonemic Segmentation (Yopp, 1999) is a user-friendly and quick measure of phonemic awareness that may be downloaded for free from the International Reading Association web site (http://www.reading.org).

Table 4.3

***Level of Difficulty of Phonological Assessment Tasks* (Easiest Task Listed First)**

- Rhyme: Indicate if two words rhyme
- Auditory discrimination: Indicate if two words are the same or different
- Phoneme blending: Blend isolated sounds into a word
- Word-to-word matching: Indicate if two words sound the same or different in the beginning, middle, or end
- Sound isolation: Identify beginning, middle, or ending sounds
- Phoneme counting: Tap the number of sounds heard
- Phoneme segmentation: Repeat a word by segmenting the phonemes or syllables
- Phoneme deletion: Delete sounds and/or syllables in a word

From Yopp, H. (1988). The validity and reliability of phonemic awareness tests. *Reading Research Quarterly, 21*, 253-266. Used with permission.

Instructional Implications of Phonological Awareness

Phonological awareness can be taught (Ball & Blachman, 1991; Bradley & Bryant, 1983; Byrne & Fielding-Barnsley, 1991; Lundberg, Frost, & Peterson, 1988) and seems to have a reciprocal relationship with reading. That is, while children need a certain measure of phonological awareness to begin the journey toward learning to read, as they learn to read, they acquire higher levels of phonological skill. Programs for developing phonological awareness all involve similar activities, such as focusing on rhyme, noting how words sound alike or different, and omitting or substituting sounds in words. Yopp and Yopp (2000) suggested that instruction begin with larger sound units, moving from an emphasis on rhyme detection to a focus on syllables, then onsets and rimes, and finally to phonemes.

Word Identification

There are basically four ways to identify a word (Ehri, 1991; Ehri & McCormick, 2004).

1. **Recognizing the word by sight.** The word is so familiar and has been seen so often that it is recognized without the necessity of "sounding out." The term *sight word* comes from the mistaken belief that readers access such words visually by connecting the shape of the word to its meaning. However, research (Wolf, 2007) suggests that the word s*ight* may be a misnomer. Even if a word is

recognized immediately without overt attention to letter and sound matching, there is still a strong auditory component. At a level below conscious awareness, the brain connects sounds to the perceived letters, and it is sound that unlocks our mental dictionary and calls up meaning. A large sight word vocabulary allows the reader to direct attention to comprehension.

2. **Guessing or predicting what it might be by using initial letters, preceding words, pictures, and topic knowledge.** Consider the reader who encounters the following sentence: "At the zoo, I fed peanuts to the big grey _____." The reader can probably predict that the word is *elephant*. Goodman (1969) hypothesized that good readers do not look at every word but primarily use prediction to identify words. However, this view has been seriously questioned by research on eye movements (Just & Carpenter, 2004). Such research indicates that readers look at or fixate on every word – even those that are highly predictable. Prediction is often overused by poor readers who, experiencing difficulties in word pronunciation, resort to prediction in an effort to attain meaning. Prediction only works in very familiar text, and most content words do not lend themselves to accurate guessing.

3. **Decoding.** Decoding involves matching sounds to individual letters and letter patterns, holding these in memory, and then blending them into a recognizable word. Decoding letter by letter has limitations when the reader meets a multi-syllabic word such as *revolutionary*. Holding each sound in memory so that all the sounds can be blended is not easy and often exceeds the boundaries of short-term memory. Decoding works best if it involves usage of syllables, common affixes, and onset-rime configurations.

4. **Through analogy.** The reader identifies already known words that contain the same sound elements as the unfamiliar word and uses this knowledge to pronounce the unknown word. Let's use a nonsense word to illustrate how this works: *plussfoomagraph*.

As a good reader you probably had no difficulty pronouncing this word. Why? We can assume that you know the consonant pattern *pl,* because you know the word *plan*. You know *fuss,* so the vowel pattern *uss* is not a problem. You know many words that contain the sound of *f,* and your knowledge of *room* allows you to quickly pronounce the second syllable. The letter *a* is no problem. You know many words that contain this letter in a within-word position, and you quickly assign the schwa sound. Finally, *graph* is a common root as well as a word in itself, so you apply the sound and blend all together. This is much more efficient than going letter by letter. Of course, because this is a nonsense word, your accurate pronunciation does not result in any meaning. This process is called decoding by analogy. The sounds you already knew (*plan*, *room*, etc.) are called analogues, and skilled readers pronounce an amazing number of unfamiliar words using this process.

Learning to pronounce words occurs by stages, which provide useful benchmarks for describing a child's progress in word identification.

The first stage is the **logographic stage** (Ehri, 1991; Ehri & McCormick, 2004), or the stage of visual cue reading (Spear-Swirling, 2004; Spear-Swirling & Sternberg, 1996). While children are aware that written words stand for meaning, they don't understand the role of letters and sounds as clearly. As a result, they assign meaning based on context or on the visual aspects of the word. They recognize *McDonald's* but only in the context of the double arches. A child may recognize *monkey* because the word has a tail at the end (the letter *y*). As a result, she probably reads any word ending with the letter *y* as *monkey*.

The next stage is called the **alphabetic stage**, or the stage of phonetic cue recoding. At this point, children recognize that letters stand for specific sounds. After focusing first on initial letters, they gradually come to realize that all letters are important. They attempt to match letters and sounds but do so slowly and laboriously. Children in this stage often skip words they cannot decode, because they understand that different letter patterns make different sounds, and they cannot just say anything.

Eventually, children move to the **stage of automatic word identification**, or controlled word reading. They know many words and word parts by sight, and they use onset rimes and vowel phonograms as analogues to pronounce unknown words. A child who knows *club* probably also knows *pub, flub, nub,* and *grub,* even if he has never seen those words in print before. If the child has heard a word before encountering it in print, that is, if the word is a part of the child's listening or meaning vocabulary, this knowledge can influence choice of pronunciation as well as result in meaning.

Consider the child who encounters the word *motel* in print for the first time. The child knows what a motel is but first pronounces the word as *mot el*. His meaning vocabulary contains no word that is pronounced that way. The child then tries *mo tel* and arrives at the correct pronunciation. The reciprocal relationship between decoding skill and listening vocabulary suggests that vocabulary development should be an important component of word identification instruction.

Assessment of Word Identification

How is word identification assessed? Listening to students read orally can suggest proficiency or difficulty in word identification. The child reads graded word lists usually found in published IRIs, and her performance is scored according to guidelines provided by the IRI. The usual practice is to ask the child to read successively higher word lists in an attempt to find the highest instructional or independent level.

The Qualitative Reading Inventory 5 (Leslie & Caldwell, 2011) uses the following scoring system for lists of 20 words.

- **90% to 100%** – independent level, the level at which a child can read words with ease
- **70% to 85%** – instructional level, or the level at which a child can function with assistance
- **below 70%** – frustration level

Word identification may also be assessed through oral reading of graded passages on an IRI.

- **98% to 100%** – independent level
- **90% to 97%** – instructional level
- **below 90%** – frustration level

Many IRIs also provide a system called miscue analysis for describing the nature of oral reading errors by asking questions such as: Is the error or miscue similar to the original word? Does it involve consonants or vowels? Does it retain meaning? Was it spontaneously corrected?

Early reading assessment batteries also contain subtests for measuring knowledge of individual consonants and consonant blends, vowel phonograms, and common onset-rime patterns (SEDL, 2007). Many assessments use phonetically regular words to assess phonics knowledge, but there is a problem with such instruments. If a child correctly pronounces a word, it is impossible to determine if this is because he has previously memorized the word without overt attention to letter and sound matching, or because he has actually decoded it. In order to avoid this diagnostic dilemma, some assessments include nonsense words such as *trat* and *clumb,* which force the child to apply knowledge of letter and sound patterns. However, because nonsense words do not result in meaning, some educators frown upon their usage. Another strategy is to use low-frequency phonetically regular words such as *slat* as opposed to *cat*. Because the child has probably not encountered the words previously, they present a viable alternative for assessing the ability to match letters and sounds.

As mentioned, readers must learn to decode using larger units of sound than a single letter by dividing syllables into onset and rimes and by focusing on vowel phonograms. Assessment should focus on meaningful letter-sound patterns. While single vowel sounds can be variable, in phonograms, they display much more regularity. Of the approximately 286 vowel phonograms that appear in primary-grade texts, 95% are pronounced the same way in a variety of words (Caldwell & Leslie, 2009). Evaluating an assessment of decoding ability should involve the extent to which it focuses on common vowel phonograms (see Table 4.4).

Table 4.4
Common Vowel Phonograms

ad, ag, am, an, ap, ar, at, aw, ay, ax, ack, age, ail, ain, air, ake, ale, all, alk, ame, and, ane, ang, ank, are, ash (*wash* and *smash*), ast, ate, ave, aught

e (*me*), ed, ee, en, et, er, ew, ear (*bear* and *dear*), eal, eat, een, eep, eet, eck, ell, end, ent, ess, est, each

id, ig, in, im, ip, it, ice, ick, ide, ife, ike, ile, ill, ine, ing, ink, ire, irt, ish, ite, ight

o (*go* and *do*), og, op, or, ot, ow (*how* and *blow*), oy, oat, ock, oil, oin, oke, old, ole, one, ong, oil, ook, ool, oom, ore, out, oast, ould, ound

ug, ue, un, up, uck, ull, ump, unk, ure, use

Instructional Implications of Word Identification

Word identification instruction has been and continues to be an area of controversy. Unfortunately, some types of phonics instruction have acquired a bad name, often being associated with uninteresting worksheets involving isolated drill in letter and sounds. Nevertheless, extensive research reviews by Chall (1967, 1989) indicated that children who receive explicit phonics instruction do better than those who do not. In explicit instruction, the teacher directly demonstrates the match between sounds and letters and usually follows a set sequence for presenting the consonants, consonant blends, and vowel sounds. Others advocate teaching phonics as needed and are opposed to following an established sequence. Given that successful decoding depends on application of larger units than single sounds (syllables and onset rimes), it makes sense to emphasize such units in instruction.

Exemplary phonics instruction (Stahl, 1990) (a) stresses reading words, not learning rules; (b) directs attention to the internal structure of words; and (c) includes a focus on vowel phonograms and/or decoding by analogy. The Benchmark Program (Gaskins, Downer, et al., 1988; Gaskins et al., 1997) is an effective program that incorporates these recommendations. Children are taught words that contain frequent sound patterns and use them as analogues to pronounce unfamiliar words.

Fluency

Fluency is a "hot" topic in literacy instruction today because of its prominence in government-funded Reading First grants. Fluency involves three components: accuracy, automaticity, and prosody. A fluent reader pronounces both familiar and unfamiliar words accurately and quickly. A fluent reader also reads with expression, stopping at punctuation marks, and changing voice tone in an attempt to convey meaning.

The importance of fluency rests on the theory of attention proposed by LaBerge and Samuels (1974) and Samuels (2004). We can only pay attention to one thing at a time, but if we become automatic in certain skills, we can perform these skills without conscious attention, thus freeing our mind for other things. Within the context of literacy, when letter perception and sound perception become automatic, the child can move to matching these components. When letter and sound matching become automatic, the child can direct her attention to comprehension. **Fluent reading is regarded as a signal that decoding is relatively automatic and that the child has the cognitive space to attend to meaning.**

Much research has indicated significant correlations between fluency and comprehension and, as a result, fluency is often used as a proxy for comprehension (Caldwell, 2008b). Correlation is a statistic that establishes the existence of a relationship; however, that relationship is not necessarily causal. Many who forget or fail to recognize this leap to the conclusion that fluency causes comprehension and accept the results of fluency assessments as indicative of adequate or inadequate comprehension. While fluency suggests that the student has achieved the necessary automaticity in word identification for comprehension to occur, comprehension involves additional processing operations. In other words, the ability to fluently read a segment of text does not guarantee comprehension. Consider your comprehension after reading income tax directions. Comprehension can also occur in the absence of fluency when we significantly slow our reading rate and reread in order to comprehend.

Assessment of Fluency

Fluency is usually assessed by measuring reading rate; that is, by listening to an individual read orally and measuring how long it takes him to read a certain passage. When measuring silent reading rate, the reader indicates when he has finished reading. Reading rate is calculated by determining the number of words read per minute (WPM) or the number of correct words read per minute (CWPM) (Jennings et al., 2006).

However, reading rates must be interpreted with caution. Typical readers demonstrate a wide range of reading rates even within the same grade level (Carver, 1990). For example, oral reading rates for third graders ranged from 51 to 97 WPM (Leslie & Caldwell, 2011). Rates also vary depending upon the text. Seventh and eighth graders demonstrated silent WPM ranges of 119 to 233 for narrative selections but 105 to 189 for expository text. Individuals read easy selections, familiar selections, and narratives faster than difficult, unfamiliar, and expository text. Therefore, a reading rate established in one selection may or may not be indicative of overall fluency. **Fluency assessment should never completely substitute for comprehension assessment, and a reading rate must always be interpreted in relation to the passage that was read.**

Instructional Implications of Fluency

Fluency is developed by wide reading of easy, independent-level text. As children read for enjoyment or information, they see familiar words repeated over and over, and these words soon become words that no longer need overt decoding strategies. Other classroom practices such as repeated and assisted reading can help develop fluency (Caldwell & Leslie, 2009). However, teachers should not focus on fluency instruction under the naïve assumption that if fluency increases, comprehension will do so as well. It may or it may not, and a misguided emphasis on fluency may deny students "what they most need, instruction in strategies for comprehension" (Caldwell, 2008b, p. 152).

Vocabulary

Vocabulary knowledge and reading proficiency are closely related. Individuals who know more word meanings are better readers. Paris, Carpenter, Paris, and Hamilton (2005) described vocabulary knowledge as a "genuine predictor of reading comprehension" (p. 151). Not only does a large store of word meanings help in decoding (as we illustrated with the word *motel*), but word knowledge is also important factor in text comprehension.

Most words represent more than one meaning, and individuals with strong vocabularies comprehend these multiple meanings (Stahl & Nagy, 2006). Consider the possible meanings of the word *court,* such as *judge's court, king's court, tennis court, courtyard,* and *court a girl*. Words also represent variations of similar meaning. For example, we can describe an individual as *thin, slim, scrawny, bony, emaciated, willowy, wiry,* and so on. Further, many words represent derivations of other words, constructed through an extensive system of prefixes, suffixes, and roots, such as *phone, phoned, telephone, phonograph, phoneme; phonetic, phonics, phonology, phonological,* and so on.

Our meaning vocabulary has often been described as involving receptive and productive components (Caldwell, 2008b; Johnson, 2001). Our **receptive vocabulary** is composed of words whose meaning we recognize when we hear them (listening vocabulary) and words we recognize in print (reading vocabulary). Our **productive vocabulary** includes words we normally use in speech (speaking vocabulary) and words we can spell and tend to use while writing (writing vocabulary).

Vocabulary knowledge has often been described as a mental lexicon or dictionary. Unlike the typical dictionary that is arranged in alphabetical order, our mental lexicon is organized in semantic networks; that is, words with similar meanings are stored together in general categories (Johnson, 2001; Stahl & Nagy, 2006). If we learn the meaning of *unicycle* or *moped*, for example, we will unconsciously store it with words that represent other wheeled vehicles.

What does it mean to know a word? Many people naively believe that knowing a word means being able to provide a definition or a synonym. However, this represents a limited view. Words stand for concepts, and concepts are much richer and more extensive entities than definitions or synonyms.

There are three types of concepts that readers must grapple with (Caldwell, 2008b; Stahl & Nagy, 2006):

1. Matching print to words that are already in a student's speaking vocabulary, such as recognizing the print counterparts of *home* or *cat*
2. Learning a new word for a familiar concept, such as understanding that *lope, meander,* and *scuttle* all represent variations of the basic meaning attached to the verbs *move* or *run*
3. Learning a new word for a new or unfamiliar concept such as *organelle, oligarchy,* and *replicate*. This is the most difficult concept.

Assessment of Vocabulary

How is vocabulary knowledge assessed? Standardized tests usually employ a selected-response, multiple-choice format. That is, the reader chooses which of four definitions best represents the meaning of a word. However, the reader may answer incorrectly even if she knows the meaning of the target word because of unfamiliarity with one or more of the four choices. The best that can be said about large-scale standardized measures is that they provide a general or rough estimate of vocabulary knowledge (Beck, McKeown, & Kucan, 2002).

Classroom vocabulary assessments often employ a constructed response format. The reader supplies a missing word in a sentence, provides a definition or synonym, constructs a sentence containing the target word, or matches a column of words with a column of possible meanings. However, it is important to recognize that vocabulary knowledge is not an "all or nothing proposition" (Beck et al., 2002), and individuals may have very different levels of knowledge about a single word. Some may have heard or seen the word but not know what it means. Some may know its meaning in context but be unable to apply it to a different situation. Finally, some possess "a rich, decontextualized knowledge of a word's meaning, its relationship to other words and its extension to metaphorical uses" (Beck et al., p. 10).

Unfortunately, vocabulary assessment has not moved beyond typical paradigms, which fail to distinguish between the above levels. In addition, vocabulary assessment, especially in the classroom, tends to be short term in nature. That is, it assesses word knowledge usually after an instructional unit, and seldom returns to the words at a later date to assess long-term retention of meaning.

Caldwell (2008b) suggested assessing vocabulary knowledge in the classroom using the same activities designed to teach word meaning (see Comprehension).

- *literal level* – assesses students' ability to provide definitions, synonyms, and antonyms, a level that is perhaps overemphasized in the classroom
- *inferential level* – assesses students' ability to compare and contrast words, sort and categorize words, provide examples and non-examples of words, and create word maps or webs
- *application level* – assesses students' ability to create sentences using targeted words and connect words to their personal lives

Instructional Implications of Vocabulary

We learn the majority of word meanings from context during reading and listening. For example, Nagy and Scott (2004) estimated than many children learn 2,000 or more new words each year "through immersion in massive amounts of rich written and oral language" (pp. 587-588). While direct instruction of word meaning can increase vocabulary learning, Stahl (1986) and Stahl and Fairbanks (1986) suggested that such instruction should focus on comprehension and generation activities.

Comprehension involves knowing the more common meanings of a word; for example, *meander* means *wander* or *roam.* Generation means that the reader can use a word in a new or novel context, such as *the river meandered through the plain*. Beck et al. (2002) described rich vocabulary instruction as engaging students in thinking about word meanings, discussing how they may be used in different situations, and describing the relationships between them.

Comprehension

Reading comprehension is "the process of simultaneously extracting and constructing meaning through interaction and involvement with written language" (RAND Reading Study Group, 2002, p. 11). Comprehension is not a unitary entity; the reader engages in a variety of simultaneous processes (Kintsch, 1998; Kintsch & Kintsch, 2005).

The reader first attaches meaning to letters and sounds, comprehends individual words, and then moves beyond by chunking words into idea units or propositions. For example, consider the following sentence: *The small boy hid behind a tall bush in the yard.* This short sentence contains five idea units or propositions: the boy hid; the boy was small; the hiding was behind a bush; the bush was tall; and the bush was in a yard. The reader connects propositions from the first sentence to succeeding sentences, and this network of meaning forms the microstructure. Eventually, the reader distills all propositions into the macrostructure or overall gist of the paragraph or passage. The microstructure (details) and the macrostructure (main ideas) form the text base, the "mental representation that the reader constructs of the text" (Kintsch & Kintsch, 2005, p. 73). While the text base remains close to the author's intended meaning, much more goes into the comprehension process. The reader integrates her prior knowledge with the text base and, as a result, readers encountering the same selection may construct very different interpretations. This final meaning construction is the situation model (see page 22).

It is important to distinguish comprehension from learning. Kintsch and Kintsch (2005) described learning as remembering what was initially comprehended and using it when the information is needed at a later date. Remembering and applying are integral parts of learning; they are not always part of comprehension. We comprehend many things that we do not necessarily remember or use, such as a conversation on a certain topic or the directions for assembling a toy or an appliance. In many cases, comprehension is a relatively automatic and unconscious process, whereas learning requires a high level of intention and consciousness, particularly if focused on unfamiliar content.

Comprehension is influenced either positively or negatively by a variety of factors that should be taken into account in assessment.

Impact of Reader

With regard to the reader, word-level skills play a role, and the skill, accuracy, and fluency of the reader in recognizing printed words is important. Prior knowledge is another reader component. If the reader knows a lot about the topic, he comprehends more easily and completely than in unfamiliar content. Contrast understanding an account of a football game with attempting to comprehend an insurance agreement. A third reader component involves the conscious processes that readers use when dealing with unfamiliar and conceptually dense text (Kintsch & Kintsch, 2005; Pressley & Afflerbach, 1995). Such processes include overviewing, paraphrasing, summarizing, rereading, notetaking, questioning, constructing diagrams, and drawing analogies. Comprehension is also influenced by the reader's motivation for reading (Caldwell, 2008b). Does the reader see the text as important or useful? Is the topic one of interest? Finally, anxiety can play a role. When faced with a high-stakes form of assessment, comprehension may suffer, for example.

Impact of Nature of Text

The nature of the text also plays an important role in comprehension. Perhaps most important is the structure of the text. Narratives follow a very predictable structure: setting, character, goal/problem, events, and resolution. As a result, they are generally easier to comprehend and remember (Grasser, Golding, & Long, 1991; Leslie & Caldwell, 1989). The structure of expository text is much less uniform. It is generally organized around five main patterns: listing or description, sequence or time order, cause/effect, problem/solution, and compare/contrast (Jennings et al., 2006). These patterns are not always clearly signaled by the author, so what one reader perceives as description may be perceived by another as sequence. However, skilled readers recognize these patterns and use them to facilitate comprehension (Goldman & Rakestraw, 2000; Meyer, 2003). When comprehending expository text, good readers seldom worry about finding the "right" pattern; they choose a likely pattern and use it to structure their comprehension and recall.

Impact of Text Difficulty

Text difficulty is a third factor that impacts comprehension. Vocabulary knowledge is a powerful predictor of comprehension (RAND Reading Study Group, 2002). Much expository material not only contains many new and unfamiliar terms such as *nanometer* and *mitochondria,* but also uses familiar words in new ways such as *envelope* defined as a protective coating of viruses that infect animal cells. The syntax of the text can also contribute to its difficulty, with long and complex sentences presenting a "high load on working memory" (RAND Reading Study Group, p. 95). Text coherence involves the organization or top-level structure of the text (Meyer, 2003). Coherent texts are well organized. That is, the authors signal the introduction of new topics and organize their ideas according to importance. Headings, charts, graphs, and illustrations add to the explanation of unfamiliar concepts. Coherent texts are easier to read and are recalled more successfully (Loxterman, Beck, & McKeown, 1994).

Impact of Readability

When discussing factors that can affect comprehension, it is important to also address the concept of readability levels. Text used for assessment is generally divided into levels of difficulty. For example, IRIs contain passages that represent difficulty levels appropriate for various grades. Passage levels are determined through the use of readability formulas based on the premise that longer words and sentences and the presence of unfamiliar words increase text difficulty. Readability formulas, therefore, count the number of syllables in words, the number of words in sentences, and the number of low-frequency words present in a passage. Some formulas describe text difficulty in terms of grade levels; others use descriptors. The popular Lexile formula (MetaMetrics, 2001) reports difficulty on a scale from 200 to 2,000.

While readability methods predict 49-85% of the variance in comprehension (Meyer, 2003), they still represent a limited view that does not take into account the possible effects of prior knowledge, text structure, text coherence, and reader strategies (Zakaluk & Samuels, 1988).

Assessment of Comprehension

Use of Questions

Comprehension is primarily assessed by asking questions. Questions take many forms. A popular format is **selected response**, such as multiple-choice or true/false items. **Constructed-response** formats involve open-ended questions that require short-answer or essay rejoinders. However, because comprehension is not a unitary activity, the format of the question is less important than the level of comprehension it assesses.

Various question categories all identify literal questions as one form of questioning; all pay attention to the inferential level; and all differentiate between inferences that are tied to text content and inferences that ask the reader to apply what was understood (Applegate, Quinn, & Applegate, 2002; Bloom & Krathwohl, 1956; Ciardiello, 1998). If assessment of comprehension is to be valid, literal comprehension must be differentiated from inferential (Caldwell, 2008b). In an ideal world, literal and inferential comprehension should also be differentiated from application-level questions, which are perhaps the true indices of learning. Unfortunately, literal questioning is primarily emphasized in the classroom, probably because of the ease in correcting written work or reacting to students' oral answers.

In assessing comprehension, it is important to consider the nature of the testing passage. Seldom do students possess a single reading level. Extensive piloting through five editions of the Qualitative Reading Inventory (Leslie & Caldwell, 2011) has demonstrated that students attain higher reading levels in narrative and familiar text than in unfamiliar expository selections. Because of the powerful effect of prior reader knowledge, all five editions assess a student's knowledge of key concepts in the passage in order to determine if performance is related to topic familiarity. If a student attains a certain reading level in narrative text, it is important to also administer an expository selection and contrast performance on the two passages.

Another issue must be addressed with regard to the use of questions in assessing comprehension. For example, should the student be allowed to look back in the text to find the answer? Standardized group tests allow the student to refer back to the text. In the classroom, however, many students believe that looking in the text is a form of cheating, and classroom tests often take a "closed-book" format. Basically, looking back distinguishes between understanding and memory (Leslie & Caldwell, 2011). The student may have understood the text while reading but forgot the specific item needed to answer a question. Successfully looking back to find an answer suggests that some comprehension was in place during reading. Leslie and Caldwell found that students above third grade were able to increase their reading level on an informal reading inventory when looking back, and they suggested that closed-book formats may seriously underestimate a student's comprehension.

Retelling

Asking students to retell what they read and analyzing their retelling is another way of assessing comprehension. Retelling may or may not assess a different construct than answering questions. Leslie and Caldwell (2011) found few significant correlations between retelling and comprehension as measured by questions. Amount of retelling is related to the type of text read, and students recall narrative texts more extensively (Leslie & Caldwell, 2011). Caldwell and Leslie (2007) analyzed student retellings after reading expository text. Retellings included several components: paraphrases of literal content; explanatory, predictive, and associative inferences (Trabasso & Magliano, 1996); gist or topic statements; and comments totally unrelated to text content. The importance of retelling as an assessment tool is signaled by the fact that retelling grids are present in many published informal reading inventories. Suggestions for evaluation focus on the completeness, accuracy, sequence, and/or coherence of the retelling (Leslie & Caldwell, 2009).

Thinking Aloud

Thinking aloud is another form of comprehension assessment. The student reads a selection divided into short sections marked with signals to stop reading. When the student meets the signal (usually the word *Stop*), she describes her thoughts while reading the text segment. Think-aloud statements are analyzed according to the type of comments made and what it suggests about the reader's thought patterns. Leslie and Caldwell (2011) divided think-aloud statements into the following categories: paraphrasing/summarizing, making new meaning (inferring), noting understanding or lack of understanding, reporting prior knowledge, identifying personally, and questioning that indicates understanding or lack of it. Leslie and Caldwell found that for fifth through eighth graders reading expository text, the most common form of think-aloud was paraphrasing/summarizing, and the next most frequent type was making new meaning. The number and type of think-aloud statements were positively correlated with the number of inferences made during retelling.

Cloze Procedure

The cloze procedure is a comprehension assessment that is part of some standardized tests and early reading assessments (Caldwell, 2008b). The student reads a text with every fifth, seventh, or ninth word deleted and supplies the missing word. The score is based upon the number of words that represent exact matches to the original text word. Cloze has been criticized as a true measure of comprehension. It tends to assess comprehension of single sentences, is strongly affected by grammatical constraints, and lacks sensitivity to comprehension across sentences or to paragraph integration. Therefore, if the purpose of the task is to assess understanding and recall of ideas and information, the cloze procedure may not be a wise choice (Carlisle & Rice, 2004).

Classroom comprehension assessment has long been driven by a focus on underlying skills assumed to differ on "some dimensions of cognitive complexity": finding and inferring details, selecting or inferring main ideas, making judgments or drawing conclusions, and so on (Pearson & Hamm, 2005, p. 23). Unfortunately, this often resulted in lengthy scope-and-sequence charts that were difficult, if not impossible, for teachers to keep track of with regard to individual students. In addition, the distinction between separate items was not always clear. Basically, what is the difference between making an inference, arriving at a conclusion, or forming a judgment?

Scope-and-sequence charts have been recycled to fit state standards and are now called target behaviors or performance expectations. However, they are still too unwieldy and imprecise to serve as a guideline for comprehension assessment. An alternative comes from verbal protocol analysis (Pressley & Afflerbach, 1995). Using the previously mentioned think-aloud process, students are asked to read a selection and think aloud as they do so. This process has identified a group of reader behaviors that can be used as a more manageable framework for classroom comprehension assessment (Caldwell, 2008a). See Table 4.5.

Table 4.5
Reader Behaviors

- Learn new words and refine the meanings of known ones
- Connect what is known with information in the text
- Determine what is important
- Recognize text structure
- Summarize and reorganize ideas in the text
- Make inferences and predictions
- Construct visual images
- Ask questions
- Synthesize information
- Form and support opinions on ideas in the text
- Recognize the author's purpose/point of view/style
- Monitor comprehension and repair comprehension breakdowns

There is a dismal lack of landmark studies involving informal assessment (Leslie & Caldwell, 2009). Articles on assessment tend to focus on purposes for and descriptions of assessment techniques and seldom address the validity and reliability of such methods. The National Research Council (2001) described the limitations of classroom assessment as not addressing student organization of knowledge, student use of strategies, and student self-monitoring.

Instructional Implications of Comprehension

A classic study by Durkin in 1979 revealed that classroom comprehension instruction at that time primarily focused on telling students to comprehend without showing them how to do it. Since then, suggestions for instruction have focused on four components of explicit comprehension strategy instruction (Harvey & Goudvis, 2000): teacher modeling, guided practice, independent practice, and application to real reading situations.

1. The teacher explains the strategy, tells why it is important, and demonstrates how to apply it by using the think-aloud technique to model his or her own mental processes.

2. In guided practice, the teacher and students practice the strategy together, with the teacher providing feedback and additional modeling if needed. Students share their thinking processes with peers and offer suggestions to each other.

3. The students practice the strategy independently, again receiving teacher and peer feedback.

4. Students apply the strategy to a new genre or to more difficult text.

A quasi-experimental study of strategy instruction for second graders (Brown, Pressley, Van Meter, & Schuder, 2004) showed that long-term strategy instruction can positively affect student recall, the quality of individual think-alouds, and standardized test scores. While the importance of teaching comprehension strategies is generally accepted, and many published materials now include strategy instruction in their teacher manuals, Durkin's 1979 study has not been replicated, and the extent to which teachers actually model such strategies and provide practice guided by thoughtful feedback is unknown. It may be that, like Durkin's teachers, today's educators simply tell students what to do without showing them how to do it.

Diversity

There is a growing and disturbing gap between minority and nonminority students with regard to reading achievement. This gap extends to children of poverty versus children from more affluent families. It also extends to those whose first language is not English (Silliman, Wilkinson, & Brea-Spahn, 2004). Results from the 2002 administration of the National Assessment of Educational Progress (NAEP) revealed that 70-75% of Caucasian and Asian-American students read at or above a basic level. In dismal contrast, only 40-44% of Hispanic and African-American students did so (U.S. Department of Education, National Center for Education Statistics, 2003).

Children of diversity bring different language backgrounds to the act of reading. Some English language learners (ELLs) can read in their native language; others cannot. Their command of English varies, and they represent different levels of exposure to English, different educational histories, and different family practices with regard to literacy and language. Some African-American children speak African-American English (AAE); some do not. Some spontaneously engage in code-switching, or moving from their familiar dialect to the more standard form of "school talk"; others do not. In addition, the form of AAE varies (Craig & Washington, 2004) depending upon the geographic area and the context in which it is used. In order to read formal English, AAE speakers may first read the text as AAE and then translate it into standard English, a process that may be more time-consuming and cognitively complex than that engaged in by children who come to the classroom already using the language of school.

This widening achievement gap is evident at the preschool and kindergarten level. Some children come to school already reading and well on their way to developing higher-level literacy skills. They come with basic rudiments in place. They value books, and they enjoy the process of being read to. They know some letters and sounds, and they recognize that print stands for meaning. They have a large store of word meanings and an adequate oral language base to apply to written text. Unfortunately, too many children of poverty enter our schools lacking these skills and experiences. They have not been read to, their experience with written text is limited, and their store of known word meanings is woefully below that of their more fortunate peers.

The No Child Left Behind Act (2001) seems to assume that problems associated with diversity will be eliminated by application of "research-based" instructional practices. This is a simplistic and overly optimistic view that does not take into account the value and extent of socio-cultural diversity present in our society. Unfortunately, too little research exists "on how educators can effectively manage the wide range of variation inherent in every classroom" in order to teach all children to read (Silliman et al., 2004, p. 74).

Technology

Reviews of research involving technology suggest a positive association between the use of educational software and reading achievement; however, such research is somewhat ambiguous in that many studies involved older technology, not the hardware and software presently available. Kamil and Chou (2009) suggested that "application of new technologies to reading instruction may provide unique opportunities" (p. 295). They specifically mentioned podcasts, online chats, collaboratively developed wiki's, computer games, and adaptive agents that adjust computer instruction to the responses of the student.

Conclusion

Literacy is a complex process, and teaching children to read is equally complex. In an age that frantically seeks fast answers and one-size-fits-all solutions, reading instruction remains one of the more difficult tasks faced by the teacher. Most research on effective instruction has focused on struggling readers. A review of successful interventions reveals that, despite very different formats, they exhibit many similarities (Caldwell & Leslie, 2009; Jennings et al., 2006). They involve some form of integrated instruction and emphasize reading as opposed to "skill and drill." Teachers read to students as an effective vehicle for modeling good reader behaviors. The teacher and students read together and stop at various parts to discuss the content. The students read independently and become involved with text that they find interesting and can handle successfully.

Instead of worksheets, successful literacy interventions focus on understanding and practicing the strategies that good readers use. They emphasize and integrate three forms of knowledge: local, global, and affective (Fitzgerald, 1999). Local knowledge includes phonological awareness, sight word knowledge, strategies for word identification, and understanding of word meanings. Global knowledge centers on the understanding and use of good reader strategies. Finally, affective knowledge is perhaps the most important of all. It is a love of reading.

It is crucial that all children learn to read in order to function in our digital and verbal society. But reading is more than a skill for ensuring an adequate level of economic independence. Reading has important cognitive consequences. Cunningham and Stanovich (1998) strongly suggested that the volume of reading engaged in by an individual is an important contributor to vocabulary knowledge, growth in verbal skills, and depth of general knowledge. "The dynamic interaction between text and life experiences is bidirectional: we bring our life experiences to the text, and the text changes our experience of life. ... Sometimes we emerge after this immersion into other worlds of thought ... with an expansion of our capacity to think, feel and act in new and courageous ways; but wherever we are led, we are not the same" (Wolf, 2007, p. 160).

Chapter Highlights

- Many different theories attempt to describe the reading process. There is agreement that reading is a unified and highly complex act with the ultimate aim of attaining meaningful comprehension.

- Reading achievement is strongly tied to and dependent on oral language development.

- There is strong correlation between listening comprehension and reading comprehension at all age levels.

- The quality and amount of oral language interactions in the home have a profound effect on children's linguistic development.

- Children learn a lot about language from early literacy experiences provided by caregivers: new concepts, new vocabulary words, and new sentence structures.

- Reading assessments fall into two general categories: formal and informal. Formal tests are generally standardized and norm-referenced. Informal assessments allow diagnosticians and teachers to adapt the instrument to the needs of the child and the context of the classroom.

- The National Reading Panel (2000) has described reading as primarily involving five factors: phonological awareness, word identification, fluency, vocabulary, and comprehension.

- Successful literacy interventions address all components of reading within the context of focusing both on the strengths and the needs of the students.

Phonological Awareness

- Phonological awareness refers to the awareness of sound: the ability to perceive words, syllables, and phonemes as discrete units.

- A child's ability to identify and manipulate sounds is strongly related to later reading and spelling achievement.

- Phonological awareness is assessed by a variety of activities:
  - ✔ Segmentation tasks – children tap or push tokens forward to indicate how many sounds they hear in a spoken word, or repeat a word by breaking it into its component sounds
  - ✔ Phoneme deletion – saying a word without a certain sound
  - ✔ Blending tasks – children listen to a series of sounds and blend them into a word
  - ✔ Phoneme substitution – changing the sound within a word

- Phonological awareness can be taught and seems to have a reciprocal relationship with reading.

Word Identification

- There are four basic ways to identify a word:
  - ✔ Recognize the word by *sight* (the word is so familiar and has been seen so often that it is recognized without the necessity of "sounding out")
  - ✔ *Guess or predict* what a word might be (by using initial letters, preceding words, pictures, and topic knowledge)
  - ✔ *Decoding* (matching sounds to individual letters and letter patterns, holding these in memory, and then blending them into a recognizable word)
  - ✔ *Analogy* (the reader identifies already known words that contain the same sound elements as the unfamiliar word and uses this knowledge to pronounce the unknown word)

- Learning to pronounce words occurs by stages:
  - ✔ Logographic stage: visual cue reading (assigning meaning based on context or on the visual aspects of words)
  - ✔ Alphabetic stage: phonetic cue recording (recognizing that letters stand for specific sounds)
  - ✔ Automatic word identification: controlled word reading (knowing words and word parts by sight, using onset rimes and vowel phonograms as analogues to pronounce unknown words)

- Word identification is assessed using a variety of strategies:
  - ✔ Oral reading of graded words lists from published reading inventories
  - ✔ Oral reading of graded passages from published reading inventories
  - ✔ Early reading assessment batteries

- Exemplary phonics instruction stresses reading words not learning rules, directs attention to the internal structure of words, and includes a focus on vowel phonograms and/or decoding by analogy.

Fluency

- Fluency involves three components: accuracy, automaticity, and prosody.

- When letter perception and sound perception become automatic, the student can move to matching these components; when letter and sound matching becomes automatic, the student can direct her attention to comprehension.

- Fluency suggests that the student has achieved the necessary automaticity in word identification for comprehension to occur, but it is only one of many components of comprehension.

- Fluency is assessed by measuring reading rate (listening to an individual read orally and measuring how long it takes to read a certain passage)
  - ✔ Reading rate is calculated by determining the number of words read per minute (WPM) or the number of correct words read per minute (CWPM)
  - ✔ Reading rates must be interpreted in relation to the passage that was read

- Classroom practices such as repeated and assisted reading can help develop fluency.

- Fluency instruction should never be used as a replacement for instruction on comprehension strategies.

Vocabulary

- Individuals who know more words are better readers. A large store of word meanings can help in decoding and in text comprehension.

- Individuals with strong vocabularies comprehend the multiple meanings of words.

- Meaning vocabulary is generally described as having four components:
  ✔ Receptive meaning vocabulary
    – Listening vocabulary (words whose meaning is recognized when we hear them)
    – Reading vocabulary (words we recognize in print)
  ✔ Productive vocabulary
    – Speaking vocabulary (words we normally use in speech)
    – Reading vocabulary (words we can spell and tend to use while writing)

- Understanding meaning involves knowledge of definitions, synonyms, and concepts.

- There are three types of concepts:
  ✔ Matching print to words that are already in a student's speaking vocabulary
  ✔ Learning a new word for a familiar concept
  ✔ Learning a new word for a new or unfamiliar concept

- Large-scale standardized measures provide only a general or rough estimate of vocabulary knowledge.

- Assessment of vocabulary knowledge can take place in the classroom using the same activities used to teach meaning.
  - ✔ Literal level: assesses students' ability to provide definitions, synonyms, and antonyms
  - ✔ Inferential level: assesses students' ability to compare and contrast words, sort and categorize words, provide examples and non-examples of words, and create word maps
  - ✔ Application level: assesses students' ability to create sentences using targeted words and connect words to their personal lives

- Vocabulary instruction should focus on comprehension and generation activities.
  - ✔ Comprehension: involves knowing the more common meanings of a word
  - ✔ Generation: means the reader can use the word in a new or novel context

Comprehension

- Comprehension involves a variety of simultaneous processes: attaching meaning to letters and sounds, comprehending individual words, then moving beyond by chunking words into idea units or propositions.

- Microstructure (details) and macrostructure (main ideas) form the text base. The reader integrates her prior knowledge with the text base, thereby constructing an independent interpretation. This interpretation is called the situation model.

- Comprehension is a relatively automatic and unconscious process, while learning requires a high level of intention and consciousness.

- Comprehension is influenced either positively or negatively by a variety of factors:
  - ✔ Reader components: word-level skills, prior knowledge, conscious processes (overviewing, paraphrasing, summarizing, rereading, notetaking, questioning, constructing diagrams, and drawing analogies), motivation, and anxiety
  - ✔ Text components: text structure (i.e., narrative structure vs. expository structure), text difficulty (i.e., vocabulary and syntax), and text coherence
  - ✔ Readability levels

- Comprehension is assessed in a number of ways:
  - ✔ Asking questions (literal, inferential, and application level)
  - ✔ Asking students to retell what they have read and analyzing their responses
  - ✔ Analyzing think-aloud statements made by students
  - ✔ Using cloze procedures (for comprehension of single sentences)

- Suggestions for instruction in comprehension focus on four components of explicit comprehension strategy instruction:
  - ✔ Teacher modeling
  - ✔ Guided practice
  - ✔ Independent practice
  - ✔ Application to real reading situations

- Successful literacy interventions focuses on three forms of reading: local, global, and affective.

Chapter Review Questions

1. What are the five components of the reading process identified by the Reading Panel?

2. What are the three levels of phonological awareness?

3. How is phonological awareness assessed?

4. What are the four ways to identify a word?

5. What are the stages of learning to pronounce words?

6. How is word identification assessed?

7. Define fluency.

8. How is fluency assessed?

9. Differentiate between receptive and productive vocabulary.

10. Describe Kintsch's definition of comprehension.

11. List factors that influence comprehension.

12. How is comprehension assessed?

References

Adams, M. J. (1990). *Beginning to read: Thinking and learning about print.* Cambridge, MA: MIT Press.

Adams, M. J. (2004). Modeling the connections between word recognition and reading. In R. B. Ruddell & N. J. Unrau (Eds.), *Theoretical models and processes of reading* (pp. 1219-1243). Newark, DE: International Reading Association.

Anderson, R. C. (2004). Role of the reader's schema in comprehension, learning and memory. In R. B. Ruddell & N. J. Unrau (Eds.), *Theoretical models and processes of reading* (pp. 594-606). Newark, DE: International Reading Association.

Applegate, M. D., Quinn, K. B., & Applegate, A. (2002). Levels of thinking required by comprehension questions in informal reading inventories. *The Reading Teacher, 56,* 174-180.

Ball, E. W., & Blachman, B. A. (1991). Does phoneme awareness training in kindergarten make a difference in early word recognition and spelling? *Reading Research Quarterly, 26,* 49-66.

Beck, I. L., McKeown, M. G., & Kucan, L. (2002). *Bringing words to life: Robust vocabulary instruction.* New York: The Guilford Press.

Bloom, B., & Krathwohl, D. (1956). *Taxonomy of educational objectives: The classification of educational goals.* New York: Longmans Green.

Bradley, L., & Bryant, P. (1983). Categorizing sounds and learning to read: A causal connection. *Nature, 30,* 419-421.

Bransford, J. D. (2004). Schema activation and schema acquisition: Comments on Richard C. Anderson's remarks. In R. B. Ruddell & N. J. Unrau (Eds.), *Theoretical models and processes of reading* (pp. 607-619). Newark, DE: International Reading Association.

Bransford, J. D., Brown, A. L., & Cocking, R. R. (Eds.). (2000). *How people learn: Brain, mind, experience and school.* Washington, DC: National Academy Press.

Brice Heath, S. (2004). The children of Trackton's children: Spoken and written language in social change. In R. B. Ruddell & N. J. Unrau (Eds.), *Theoretical models and processes of reading* (pp. 187-211). Newark, DE: International Reading Association.

Brown, R., Pressley, M., Van Meter, P., & Schuder, T. (2004). A quasi-experimental validation of transactional strategies instruction with low-achieving second grade readers. In R. B. Ruddell & N. J. Unrau (Eds.), *Theoretical models and processes of reading* (pp. 998-1039). Newark, DE: International Reading Association.

Byrne, B., & Fielding-Barnsley, R. (1991). Evaluation of a program to teach phonemic awareness to young children. *Journal of Educational Psychology, 83,* 451-455.

Caldwell, J. (2008a). *Reading assessment: A primer for teachers and coaches.* New York: The Guilford Press.

Caldwell, J. (2008b). *Comprehension assessment: A classroom guide.* New York: The Guilford Press.

Caldwell, J., & Leslie, L. (2007). *The effects of thinking aloud in expository text on recall and comprehension.* Unpublished manuscript.

Caldwell, J., & Leslie, L. (2009). *Intervention strategies to follow informal reading inventory assessment: So what do I do now?* Boston: Allyn & Bacon.

Carlisle, J. F. (2004). Morphological processes that influence learning to read. In C. A. Stone, E. R. Silliman, B. J. Ehren, & K. Apel (Eds.), *Handbook of language and literacy: Development and disorders* (pp. 318-339). New York: The Guilford Press.

Carlisle, J. F., & Rice, M. S. (2004). Assessment of reading comprehension. In C. A. Stone, E. R. Silliman, B. J. Ehren, & K. Apel (Eds.), *Handbook of language and literacy: Development and disorders* (pp. 521-540). New York: The Guilford Press.

Carver, R. B. (1990). *Reading rate: A review of research and theory*. San Diego, CA: Academic.

Chall, J. S. (1967). *Learning to read: The great debate.* New York: McGraw-Hill.

Chall, J. S. (1989). Learning to read: The great debate 20 years later. *Phi Delta Kappan, 70*, 521-538.

Ciardiello, A. V. (1998). Did you ask a good question today? Alternative cognitive and metacognitive strategies. *Journal of Adolescent and Adult Literacy, 42*, 210-219.

Craig, H. K., & Washington, J.A. (2004). Language variation and literacy learning. In C. A. Stone, E. R. Silliman, B. J. Ehren, & K. Apel (Eds.), *Handbook of language and literacy: Development and disorders* (pp. 228-247). New York: The Guilford Press.

Cunningham, A. E., & Stanovich, K. E. (1998, Spring/Summer). What reading does for the mind. *American Educator/American Federation of Teachers*, 1-8.

Daneman, M. (1991). Individual differences in reading skills. In R. Barr, M. L. Kamil, P. B. Mosenthal & P. D. Pearson (Eds.), *Handbook of reading research* (Vol. II, pp. 512-538). White Plains, NY: Longman.

Durkin, D. (1978-79). What classroom observations reveal about reading comprehension instruction. *Reading Research Quarterly, 15*, 481-533.

Ehri, L. C. (1991). Development of the ability to read words. In R. Barr, M. L. Kamil, P. Mosenthal, & P. D. Pearson (Eds.), *Handbook of reading research* (Vol. II, pp. 383-417). White Plains, NY: Longman.

Ehri, L. C., & McCormick, S. (2004). Phases of word learning: Implications for instruction with delayed and disabled readers. In R. B. Ruddell & N. J. Unrau (Eds.), *Theoretical models and processes of reading* (pp. 365-389). Newark, DE: International Reading Association.

Ehri, L. C., Nunes, S. R., Willows, D. M., Schuster, B. V., Yaghoub-Zadeh, Z., & Shanahan. T. (2001). Phonemic awareness instruction helps children learn to read: Evidence from the National Reading Panel's meta-analysis. *Reading Research Quarterly, 36*, 250-287.

Fitzgerald, J. (1999). What is this thing called balance? *The Reading Teacher, 53*, 672-689.

Fuchs, L. S., Fuchs, D., & Deno, S. L. (1982). Reliability and validity of curriculum-based Informal Reading Inventories. *Reading Research Quarterly, XVIII*, 6-25.

Gaskins, I., Downer, M., and the teachers of Benchmark School. (1997). *The Benchmark word identification and vocabulary development program.* Media, PA: The Benchmark Press.

Gaskins, I., Downer, M., Anderson, R., Cunningham, P., Gaskins, R., & Schommer, M. (1988). A metacognitive approach to phonics: Using what you know to decode what you don't know. *Remedial and Special Education, 27*, 36-41.

Gee, J. P. (2004). Reading as situated language: A sociocognitive perspective. In R. B. Ruddell & N. J. Unrau (Eds.), *Theoretical models and processes of reading* (pp. 116-132). Newark, DE: International Reading Association.

Gilger, J. W., & Wise, S. E. (2004). Genetic correlates of language and literacy impairments, In C. A. Stone, E. R. Silliman, B. J. Ehren, & K. Apel (Eds.), *Handbook of language and literacy: Development and disorders* (pp. 25-48). New York: The Guilford Press.

Goldman, S. G., & Rakestraw, J. A. (2000). Structural aspects of constructing meaning from text. In M. L. Kamil, P. B. Mosenthal, P. D. Pearson, & R. Barr (Eds.), *Handbook of reading research* (Vol. III, pp. 311-336). White Plains, NY: Longman.

Good, R. H., & Kaminski, R. A. (2002). *Dynamic indicators of early literacy achievement*. Eugene: University of Oregon.

Goodman, K. S. (1969). Analysis of reading miscues: Applied psycholinguistics. *Reading Research Quarterly, 5*, 9-30.

Goswami, I. (2000). Phonological and lexical processes. In M. L. Kamil, P. B. Mosenthal, P. D. Pearson, & R. Barr (Eds.), *Handbook of reading research* (Vol. III, pp. 251-267). Mahwah, NJ: Lawrence Erlbaum.

Gough, P. (1984). Word recognition. In P. D. Pearson, R. Barr, M. L. Kamil, & P. Mosenthal (Eds.), *Handbook of reading research.* (Vol. III, pp. 225-253). New York: Longman.

Grasser, A., Golding, J. M., & Long. D. L. (1991). Narrative representation and comprehension. In R. Barr, M. L. Kamil, P. B. Mosenthal & P. D. Pearson (Eds.), *Handbook of reading research* (Vol. II, pp. 171-205). White Plains, NY: Longman.

Hart, B., & Risley, T. R. (1995). *Meaningful differences in the everyday experiences of young American children.* Baltimore: Brookes Publishers.

Harvey, S., & Goudvis, A. (2000). *Strategies that work: Teaching comprehension to enhance understanding.* York, MA: Stenhouse Publishers.

Invernizzi, M., Meier, J., Sullivan. A., & Swank, L. (2004). *Phonological awareness literacy screening PALS PK.* Charlottesville: University of Virginia Press.

Invernizzi, M., Meier, J. D., & Juel, C. (2005). *Phonological awareness literacy screening PALS 1-3.* Charlottesville: University of Virginia Press.

Invernizzi, M., Meier, J. D., Swank, A., & Juel, C. (2005). *Phonological awareness literacy screening PALS K.* Charlottesville: University of Virginia Press.

Jennings, J., Caldwell, J. S., & Lerner, J. (2006). *Reading problems: Assessment and teaching strategies.* Boston: Pearson Education, Inc.

Johnson, D. D. (2001). *Vocabulary in the elementary and middle school.* Boston: Allyn and Bacon.

Jordan, R. R., Kirk, D. J., & King, K. (2005). *Early reading diagnostic assessment* (2nd ed.). San Antonio, TX: Harcourt Assessment.

Just, M. A., & Carpenter, P. A. (2004). A theory of reading: From eye fixations to comprehension. In R. B. Ruddell & N. J. Unrau (Eds.), *Theoretical models and processes of reading* (pp. 1182-1218). Newark, DE: International Reading Association.

Kamil, M. I., & Chou, H. K. (2009). Comprehension and computer technology: Past results, current knowledge, and future promises. In S. Israel & G. Duffy (Eds.), *Handbook of research on reading comprehension* (pp. 289-30). New York: Routledge.

Kintsch, W. (1998). *Comprehension: A paradigm for cognition.* Cambridge, UK: Cambridge University Press.

Kintsch, W., & Kintsch, E. (2005). Comprehension. In S. G. Paris & S. A. Stahl (Eds.), *Children's reading comprehension and assessment* (pp. 71-92). Mahwah, NJ: Lawrence Erlbaum Associates.

Klesius, J. P., & Homan, S. P. (1985). A validity and reliability update on the informal reading inventory with suggestions for improvement. *Journal of Learning Disabilities, 18,* 71-76.

LaBerge, D., & Samuels, S. M. (1974). Toward a theory of automatic information processing in reading. *Cognitive Psychology, 6,* 293-323.

Leslie, L., & Caldwell. J. (1989). The qualitative reading inventory: Issues in the development of a diagnostic reading test. In S. McCormick & J. Zutell (Eds.), *Cognitive and social perspectives for literacy: Research and instruction* (pp. 413-419). Chicago: National Reading Conference.

Leslie, L., & Caldwell, J. (2011). *The qualitative reading inventory 5.* Boston: Allyn & Bacon.

Leslie, L., & Caldwell, J. (2009). Formal and informal measures of reading comprehension. In S. Israel & G. Duffy (Eds.), *Handbook of research on reading comprehension* (pp. 403-427). New York: Routledge.

Loxterman, J. A., Beck, L. L., & McKeown, M. G. (1994). The effects of thinking aloud during reading on students' comprehension of more or less coherent text. *Reading Research Quarterly, 29,* 353-368.

Lundberg, I., Frost, J., & Peterson, O. (1988). Effects of an extensive program for stimulating phonological awareness in preschool children. *Reading Research Quarterly, 23*, 263-284.

McGregor, K. K. (2004). Developmental dependencies between lexical semantics and reading. In C. A. Stone, E. R. Silliman, B. J. Ehren, & K. Apel (Eds.), *Handbook of language and literacy: Development and disorders* (pp. 302-317). New York: The Guilford Press.

MetaMetrics, Inc. (2001). *How is readability determined within the Lexile Framework for reading?* Durham, NC: MetaMetrics.

Meyer, B.J.F. (2003). Text coherence and readability. *Topics in Language Disorders, 23*, 204-225. Retrieved from http://0-proquest.umi.com.topcat.switchline.org/pqdweb?index=624&did=288780701&Srch

Morris, D. (2008). *Diagnosis and correction of reading problems.* New York: The Guilford Press.

Nagy, W. E., & Scott, J. A. (2004). Vocabulary processes. In R. B. Ruddell & N. J. Unrau (Eds.), *Theoretical models and processes of reading* (pp. 574-593). Newark, DE: International Reading Association.

National Reading Panel. (2000). *Report of the National Reading Panel – Teaching children to read: An evidence-based assessment of scientific-based literature on reading and its implications for reading instruction.* Washington, DC: National Institute of Child Health and Human Development.

National Research Council. (2001). *Knowing what students know: The science and design of educational assessment.* J. Pelligrino, N. Chudowsky, & R. Glaser (Eds.). Washington, DC: National Academy Press.

No Child Left Behind Act of 2001, Pub. L. No.107-110 .

Paris, S. G., Carpenter, R. D., Paris, A. H., & Hamilton, E. E. (2005). TITLE? In S. G. Paris & S. A. Stahl (Eds.), *Children's reading comprehension and assessment* (pp. 131-160). Mahwah, NJ: Lawrence Erlbaum Associates.

Pearson, P. D., & Hamm, D. N. (2005). The assessment of reading comprehension: A review of practices – past, present, and future. In S .G. Paris & S. A. Stahl (Eds.), *Children's reading comprehension and assessment* (pp. 13-69). Mahwah, NJ: Lawrence Erlbaum Associates.

Pressley, M., & Afflerbach, P. (1995). *Verbal protocols of reading: The nature of constructively responsive reading.* Hillsdale, NJ: Lawrence Erlbaum Associates.

RAND Reading Study Group. (2002). *Reading for understanding: Toward an R&D program in reading comprehension.* Retrieved from http://www.rand.org.publications/MR/MR1465/

Rumelhart, D. E. (2004). Toward an interactive model of reading. In R. B. Ruddell & N. J. Unrau (Eds.), *Theoretical models and processes of reading* (pp. 1149-1179). Newark, DE: International Reading Association.

Samuels, S. J. (2004). Toward a theory of automatic information processing in reading, revisited. In R. B. Ruddell & N. J. Unrau (Eds.), *Theoretical models and processes of reading* (pp. 1127-1148). Newark, DE: International Reading Association.

Scott, C. M. (2004). Syntactic contributions to literacy learning. In C. A. Stone, E. R. Silliman, B. J. Ehren, & K. Apel (Eds.), *Handbook of language and literacy: Development and disorders* (pp. 340-362). New York: The Guilford Press.

Silliman, E. R., Wilkinson, L. C., & Brea-Spahn, M. R. (2004). Policy and practice imperatives for language and literacy learning: Who will be left behind? In C. A. Stone, E. R. Silliman, B. J. Ehren, & K. Apel (Eds.), *Handbook of language and literacy: Development and disorders* (pp. 97-129). New York: The Guilford Press.

Smith, F. (1978). *Understanding reading.* New York: Holt, Rinehart and Winston.

Southwest Educational Development Laboratory (SEDL). (2007). *Reading assessment database.* Available from http://www.sedl.org/reading/rad/list.html

Spear-Swirling, L. (2004). A road map for understanding reading disability and other reading problems: Origins, prevention and intervention. In R. B. Ruddell & N. J. Unrau (Eds.), *Theoretical models and processes of reading* (pp. 517-573). Newark, DE: International Reading Association.

Spear-Swirling, L., & Sternberg, R. J. (1996). *Off track: When poor readers become "learning disabled."* Boulder, CO: Westview Press.

Spector, J. E. (2005). How reliable are informal reading inventories? *Psychology in the Schools, 42,* 593-603.

Stahl, S. A. (1986). Three principles of effective vocabulary instruction. *Journal of Reading, 29,* 662-668.

Stahl, S. A. (1990). Saying the "p" word: Nine guidelines for exemplary phonics instruction. *The Reading Teacher, 45,* 618-125.

Stahl, S. A., & Fairbanks, M. M. (1986). The effects of vocabulary instruction: A model-based meta-analysis. *Review of Educational Research, 56,* 72-110.

Stahl, S. A., & Nagy, W. E. (2006). *Teaching word meanings,* Mahwah, NJ: Lawrence Erlbaum Associates.

Stanovich, K. E. (1980). Toward an interactive-compensatory model of individual differences in the development of reading fluency. *Reading Research Quarterly, 16,* 32-71.

Stanovich, K. (1988). *Children's reading and the development of phonological awareness.* Detroit, MI: Wayne State University Press.

Stanovich, K. E. (2004). Matthew effects in reading: Some consequences of individual differences in the acquisition of literacy. In R. B. Ruddell & N. J. Unrau (Eds.), *Theoretical models and processes of reading* (pp. 454-516). Newark, DE: International Reading Association.

Trabasso, T., & Magliano, J. P. (1996). Conscious understanding during reading. *Discourse Processes, 21,* 255-287.

Troia, G. A. (2004). Phonological processing and its influence on learning. In C. A. Stone, E. R. Silliman, B. J. Ehren, & K. Apel (Eds.), *Handbook of language and literacy: Development and disorders* (pp. 271-301). New York: The Guilford Press.

U.S. Department of Education, National Center for Educational Statistics. (2003) *The condition of education 2003.* Retrieved from http://nces.ed.gov.

Wasik, B. H., & Hendrickson, J. S. (2004). Family literacy practices. In C. A. Stone, E. R. Silliman, B. J. Ehren, & K. Apel (Eds.), *Handbook of language and literacy: Development and disorders* (pp. 154-174). New York: The Guilford Press.

Wolf, M. (2007). *Proust and the squid: The story and science of the reading brain.* New York: HarperCollins Publisher.

Woodcock, R. W., Mather, N., & Schrank, F. A. (2004). *WJIII® Diagnostic reading battery.* Ithaca, IL: Riverside Publishing.

Yopp, H. (1988). The validity and reliability of phonemic awareness tests. *Reading Research Quarterly, 21,* 253-266.

Yopp, H. K. (1999). A test for assessing phonemic awareness in young children. In S. J. Barrentine (Ed.), *Reading assessment: Principles and practices for elementary teachers* (2nd ed., pp. 166-176). Newark, DE: International Reading Association. (Original work published 1995)

Zakaluk, B. L., & Samuels, S. J. (1988). *Readability: Its past, present and future.* Newark, DE: International Reading Association.

Chapter 5
Linking Communication and Literacy

Sandra M. Grether, Ph.D., Cincinnati Children's Hospital Medical Center, and Communication Sciences and Disorders, University of Cincinnati

Christina Yeager Pelatti, M.A., Cincinnati Children's Hospital Medical Center

Learner Objectives

After reading this chapter, the learner should be able to:

- Define "language" and describe important components of language acquisition

- Discuss the link between language development and literacy acquisition

- Describe the core deficits of ASD and explain potential areas of difficulty for children with ASD

- Explain how technology may assist with language and literacy learning for children with ASD

■ ■ ■

For several months, I have been working with a school-aged child with ASD. Kate is not only very intelligent, she also has excellent literacy skills. On standardized IQ tests, Kate demonstrates cognitive abilities as well as language scores that are moderately above the average range for her age. She loves using words for reading, writing, and speaking. Frequently, she asks if she can complete activities and play games that incorporate reading and writing. Recently, when asked about reading and writing, Kate responded, "I love reading, and I wish that I could do it all day, every day."

Despite her impressive testing skills and understanding of the components of language – phonology, morphology, semantics, syntax – and literacy, Kate has difficulty using these skills for effective social **communication**. *Her deficit is described as pragmatic in nature. Kate's family became very concerned at the beginning of this school year. She entered fourth grade in a small school, and her social deficits became apparent immediately. Her teachers and principal described "disrespectful" actions that Kate does at school. For example, in class, Kate asks questions without raising her hand, and she interrupts both teachers and peers while they are talking. She does not establish or maintain eye contact, and she frequently looks around the room while talking, giving the impression that she is bored and uninterested in the conversation. Also, she tends to dominate conversations while answering questions, describing events, and telling stories.*

Last week, I asked Kate to tell me about her weekend, and she talked for 7 minutes straight without once asking me a question. She told me about watching her younger brother's basketball game and going to lunch at her favorite local deli. Then she described a new web site that she found on the Internet as well as the ending to the book that she was reading.

Kate's mother described her as being "weird" and just "not getting it." Several weeks ago, Kate's family hosted a dinner party. In preparation for the party, Kate's mom accidentally dropped a potato on the floor. She quickly picked it up, wiped it off, and continued cooking the food. Much to her mother's surprise, Kate brought up this story while sitting at the dinner table with several other couples and their children. Kate's mother was mortified that Kate brought up the story, but Kate continued to tell the story, despite significant attempts by her mother to get her to stop talking.

In contrast, I have known Zach since his preschool years, first professionally as I consulted with his school team, and now more personally, with opportunities to join in community activities with Zach and his family. Besides school, Zach attends activities at church and the "Y," and he is well known at many community restaurants. Zach is nonverbal, has autism, and has a mild to moderate intellectual disability. He does not establish or maintain eye contact. He is in the third grade, and although he spends part of his day in an autism supportive classroom, he is included with his peers throughout the day for morning routine, group work, computer class, library, lunch, art, and gym. He has peer buddies who walk with him between classes, and he joins in activities throughout the day, including learning games and computer tasks – and he loves to laugh and has a great giggle that is contagious (often getting him in trouble in class!).

For most of his communications, Zach uses a dynamic screen speech-generating augmentative communication device that he calls his "talker." He began learning to communicate requests by using the Picture Exchange Communication System (PECS).

When his PECS binder became so full of pictures that it was difficult to manage and carry, his team looked for other ways for Zach to communicate more effectively. Using his talker, he is now generating three- and four-word basic sentences and recently began adding morphological markers to mark tense, plurals, and possession. When Zach gets upset, he may scream and run from the situation and needs to be prompted to use his talker to communicate the problem. Otherwise, he uses his talker to share information from home and from school and often verbalizes a key word in the message. He has opportunities to play games with his peers, but he needs cues to participate in social interactions. Although Zach is highly motivated by having his requests and needs met, he is spending more time with peers and learning to interact using social phrases.

■ ■ ■

K ate and Zach are on opposite ends of the autism spectrum. They both represent challenges that individuals with autism spectrum disorders (ASD) face with regard to communication and literacy. The purpose of this chapter is to provide a greater understanding about communication and language. The underlying premise of the chapter is that language is the foundation for literacy, and reading and writing are forms of communication. The goals for all individuals should be the acquisition of literacy skills.

If an individual is literate, he or she can communicate any message to anyone (Sturm & Clendon, 2004). This is especially important for Zach, who is dependent on his speech-generating device (SGD) to communicate with both familiar and unfamiliar communication partners. He is dependent on the vocabulary that is preprogrammed into his device by adults. To be an effective communicator, he must know which words are in the device and where they are located. He has an onscreen keyboard to use for spelling as his literacy skills increase. Literacy is the key for Zach to be able to communicate anything to anyone at any time.

What Is Communication?

Communication is the sending and receiving of messages. It takes a minimum of two individuals (a sender and a receiver) and a message that is expressed either in verbal or written forms. Messages are used to regulate behavior, to interact socially, and to establish joint attention (Wetherby, Cain, Yonclas, & Walker, 1988).

Humans regulate the behavior of others by requesting objects or actions and by protesting. The speaker and listener may interact socially by greeting and saying goodbye, showing off by telling jokes, requesting social routines (e.g., playing pat-a-cake, singing a song), and calling attention to others or themselves (e.g., pointing, vocalizing, calling someone's name). In addition, joint attention is essential for sharing events with others by commenting and by requesting and clarifying information (Wetherby & Prizant, 1992). For example, a child may vocalize and point to an object of interest, such as an animal in the yard, to get his communication partner to look at or notice it. The communication partner may then comment (e.g., That animal is really big!), request more information (e.g., Are you pointing to the dog?), or clarify (e.g., I think it's a black lab.).

Communication is essential to attaining quality of life, allowing humans to connect with each other, touching others' lives, and having others touch our lives (Light, 2003). To be competent communicators, we need to understand the multifaceted components of the language system. Reading, writing, listening, and speaking are interconnected yet independent language systems that develop in overlapping, parallel waves (Berninger, 2000). Since language is the cornerstone of literacy learning, a solid foundation in language and communication is essential to active literacy learning across all grades.

What Is Language?

Language is a system of abstract symbols and rule-governed structures with specific conventions that need to be learned. The content of a message is not just spoken; it may also be written. Spoken and written forms of communication involve both a receptive (understanding) and an expressive (production) component. Individuals must understand all the important aspects of language – phonology, semantics, morphology, and syntax – as well as the social rules, or pragmatics – and use this information to be competent communicators (Bryant, 2009).

Receptive language is the comprehension of words, sentences, and stories. We generally receive receptive input through hearing; however, we can also receive information through pictures, symbols, and signs, as well as the printed word. If language is received by hearing, it is perceived at the sound level (auditory perception) and then decoded for meaning (auditory processing). For example, the sounds b + a + l are perceived individually, decoded as *ball*, and then matched to the stored memory of the object, ball. Receptively, a child must be able to decode at the single-word level before being able to understand multiword utterances. Understanding longer phrases is essential to following directions and understanding a story.

Similarly, learning language through pictures, symbols, and/or signs requires a visual perception and processing component. Pictures, symbols, and signs that are more concrete, such as objects or nouns (e.g., *ball*), are easier to understand than pictures, symbols, or signs of actions (e.g., *throw* or *kick*). Concepts such as big/little and in/out are more difficult to represent than actions because they represent even more abstract ideas that cannot be seen or acted out (see Figure 5.1).

Figure 5.1. Note the visual complexity of the symbols as the concepts become more complex. These symbols were generated using Boardmaker™. The Picture Communication Symbols © 1981-2009 by Mayer-Johnson LLC. All Rights Reserved Worldwide. Used with permission. Boardmaker™ is a trademark of Mayer-Johnson LLC.

Expressive language refers to how we share our thoughts, ideas, and feelings. It begins in infancy as the baby vocalizes pleasure and displeasure, and it continues through the preschool years as the child begins to speak words and tell stories. Typically, expressive language occurs verbally; however, some individuals have difficulty in this area. They express their needs, wants, and ideas through writing, gesturing, signing, or using communication boards or speech-generating devices.

Pragmatics refers to how language is used to express intentions. An individual, such as Kate, may demonstrate average receptive and expressive language skills but have deficits in pragmatic language. Because she has poor pragmatic language skills, Kate has difficulty getting her needs met and socializing with others in her world.

Pragmatically, goal-directed, intentional communication behaviors begin preverbally and move through the linguistic stages of development (Bates, 1976). Intentional communication criteria generally include the following:

- The child makes eye contact with his communication partner while gesturing or vocalizing, usually alternating his eye gaze between the partner and object.
- The child uses gestures that are consistent and ritualized (occur over and over).
- The child uses vocalizations that are consistent and ritualized.
- After the gesture or vocalization, the child pauses to wait for a response from his communication partner.
- The child persists in attempting to communicate until his goal has been met (Sugarman, 1984).

Joint attention, which occurs when two people attend to the same object, activity, or topic, is a key pragmatic skill needed for early language development (Tomasello, 1995). A child can respond to a joint attention act by following the direction of an adult's gaze or point, or initiate a joint attention act by pointing or showing an object. One study found that the time spent maintaining joint attention is positively related to vocabulary acquisition, frequency of communicative utterances, length of conversation, and rate of language development (Kaiser, Hemmeter, & Hester, 1997). Establishing joint attention allows individuals to play interactively, respond emotionally, and interact appropriately with peers and adults.

This is an area in which the social interactions of a child with ASD can falter. For example, Zach's friend Nathan invited him to play Connect Four during morning recess the other day. Zach didn't understand that the game was about turn-taking and competition. Instead, he frustrated his opponent because he was more interested in making a pattern with the checkers than strategically placing them in order to win the game. He couldn't read Nathan's frustration, and didn't understand why his classmates didn't invite him to play the next round. Zach and Nathan were not attending to the same thing. Nathan was trying to play the game, while Zach, although participating, was more interested in making patterns.

Eye gaze is also an important nonverbal aspect of a successful conversational exchange. By establishing eye gaze, speakers convey to their conversational partners (listeners) that the message is shared and requires their attention and interaction, and it lets speakers know whether listeners are attending. It alerts listeners that their conversational partners (speakers) are directing information to them to hear and understand (Prelock, 2006). Zach does not have an effective eye gaze. He has difficulty alerting his communication partners that he is attempting to convey an important message. Therefore, his communication partners often do not know that his message is intended for them, leading to frustration on both sides.

Children learn many of their pragmatic skills through play, which lays the foundation for later use in conversations. As such, play provides children with opportunities for learning. For example, through play, they learn about the things and people in their world, as well as basic concepts such as colors, numbers, simple prepositions (e.g., *in* and *on*), and more complex concepts (e.g., sharing and the rules of social interactions) (Hulit & Howard, 2006).

An important component of learning language through play is symbolic play, an activity where one object represents another. If children have difficulty with symbolic play, they will most likely struggle with learning to use words to represent the same object. A research study by Bates and colleagues reported that children who utilized symbolic play acquired language faster than children who were more rigid in their object use (Bates, Bretherton, Snyder, Shore, & Volterra, 1980).

Zach is beginning to use symbolic play. Recently, an army helicopter landed in the soccer field at his school. During center time today, he used a large block to represent a helicopter and zoomed it through the air, making a chopper sound. Later, he will have an easier time connecting the word *helicopter* to the actual object.

By the time a typical child is 18 months old, he or she demonstrates some of the basic rules of turn-taking in conversations with others (Bloom, Rocissano, & Hood, 1976). To participate effectively in a conversation/dialogue, children need to learn that communication partners fill and exchange multiple roles throughout the conversation.

Consider the following scenario: Evan speaks and Sydney listens, and then Sydney speaks and Evan listens. When Evan speaks, Sydney can (a) respond to his message, (b) simply acknowledge his message, (c) add more information, (d) agree with him, or (e) disagree with him. Sometimes Evan is the questioner, and Sydney is the responder (Hulit & Howard, 2006). It is essential that children learn ALL of these roles of communication to ensure that they are effective communicators.

At the most complex level of language development, children develop metalinguistic abilities, which means that they have the capacity to use language to analyze, study, and understand language. The development of metalinguistic awareness is related to cognitive development, intellectual capacity, scholastic achievement, reading skills, and environmental factors, including play experiences and parental input (Saywitz & Cherry-Wilkinson, 1982). In addition, metalinguistic abilities are important in understanding humor, metaphors, and ironies.

At times, Kate has difficulty understanding all three of these aspects. Because she tends to be a concrete learner, she often has difficulty understanding the underlying meanings of humor, metaphors, and ironies. For example, several weeks ago, Kate and I were talking about types of jokes. Kate had difficulty producing possible responses to the jokes, and she did not think that they were funny because she did not understand the connections between the jokes and the responses. For example, when Kate was told the joke "Why do elephants wear purple toenail polish?," she was unable to come up with possible humorous reasons, only giving the answer, "because I like purple." She missed the absurdity of the punch line, "so they can hide behind grape vines," and didn't think the joke was funny.

Components of Receptive and Expressive Language

The key components and building blocks of receptive and expressive language are semantic, morphological, and syntactic development. Semantic development is learning the meanings of words (vocabulary). Professionals specializing in language development generally think of a child's vocabulary *breadth* (the number of words that he knows) as the primary measure of vocabulary; however, vocabulary *depth* (the complexity of the words the child knows) is an important component as well.

As we discuss vocabulary breadth and depth, we must keep in mind that they overlap with the other areas of language. These may include "(a) the sound and spelling of the word (phonology); (b) the morphological structure (morphology); (c) the types of sentences in which words may occur; (d) multiple meanings and word associations; (e) the situations in which use is appropriate; and (f) the origin of its form and meaning(s)" (Pan & Uccelli, 2009, p. 121). Children have a vocabulary set that they understand (receptive) as well as one that they can use (expressive). The receptive vocabulary is usually larger than the expressive.

Morphemes are the smallest meaningful units of language. Morphemes can be simple content or open-class words, such as *cat, play, read, blue,* and *big*. This group of morphemes includes nouns, verbs, and adjectives. Function, or closed-class words, such as *in, and, the, you, is,* and *no*, include prepositions, conjunctions, articles, pronouns, auxiliaries, and inflections. Examples of morphemes at the beginning of words (prefixes) include *un-* and *re-*, and morphemes at the end of words (suffixes) include *-s* and *-ed*.

As children's language becomes more complex, the number and type of morphemes become more complex as well. If a child cannot attach tense markers, such as *-ing* or *-ed*, to verbs, it is difficult for her to talk about present- versus past-tense events.

Morphological development also has receptive and expressive components. For example, when we hear *-s* added to the word *girl*, we need to reference the context of the sentence to know if we are talking about more than one girl (indicating plurality) or something that belongs to the girl (indicating possession). Expressively, children who do not have age-appropriate morphological development sound immature. For example, both of the following sentences describe the same event:

1. Girl kick ball.
2. The girl is kicking the ball.

Your perception of the speaker saying the first sentence is likely that he is much younger or intellectually less competent than the second speaker because of the lack of function words (e.g., *the*) and morphology (e.g., *-ing*). Because Zach is at a three- to four-word utterance level and is just beginning to use morphological markers, the first example is representative of sentences that he produces. One of his language goals is to produce a sentence with the complexity of the second example so that his communication partners will naturally converse with him on a level that is more consistent with his intellectual functioning. An added benefit to achieving this goal is increased modeling of more complex sentences by Zach's communication partners, including his classmates.

Syntactic development (grammar) refers to how children combine words in a systematic way to create sentences that follow the linguistic rules of their native language. The production of sentences does not occur in random fashion. As children get older, their sentences become longer and more complex. Sentence length and complexity is measured by calculating the mean length of utterance (MLU), the number of morphemes in a sentence. Syntactical development is an important component of creating simple sentences, questions (e.g., *yes/no, who, what, where, when, why*), negative statements, and imperatives.

As children acquire additional skills, they move towards mastery of more complex sentence constructions, such as passives (e.g., The ball was kicked by the boy.), coordinations (e.g., The girl went to the store and bought some milk.), and relative clauses (e.g., The cat that is under the table is eating the food.). The ability to understand syntax is as important as the ability to produce it. For example, if children do not comprehend passive sentences, they may easily reverse the meaning of "The dog was chased by the cat." In this example, the child may think that the dog chased the cat, especially since a cat chasing a dog is an atypical situation.

Speech

Speech is also an important component of communication. Children must clearly articulate words and sentences while speaking in order to be understood by unfamiliar communication partners. Speech consists of articulation (how speech sounds are made), phonological processes (sound patterns), voice (use of the vocal folds and breathing to produce sound), and fluency (the rhythm of speech). Anatomically, to produce any sound, children must first initiate air or a breath from the lungs, which is sent through the vocal folds in the trachea, where either vibration produces a voiced sound or lack of vibration produces a voiceless sound. This "sound" then moves through the oronasal cavity, where it is further shaped by the articulators (jaw, tongue, teeth, lips) to produce the sound. This sound is called a phoneme (see Figure 5.2).

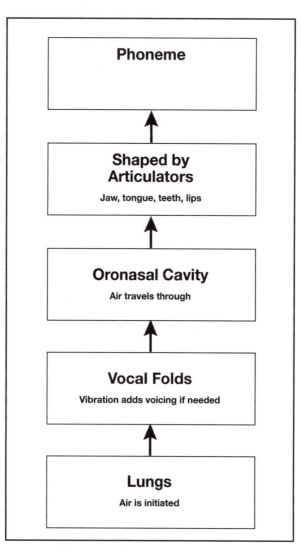

Figure 5.2. Phoneme production.

Sounds are classified by how they are produced and include both vowels and consonants. This classification includes the place of articulation (where the articulators in the oral mechanism move); the manner of articulation (air flow is stopped, released, forced through the oral or nasal cavity); and whether it is voiced (vocal fold vibration) or unvoiced (no vocal fold vibration). For example, the phoneme /b/ is made by closing the lips, forcing air through the oral cavity, and then stopping and releasing it. Because the vocal folds vibrate as air is passed through, /b/ is a voiced sound. The phoneme /p/ is made in the same way, except that it is unvoiced with no vocal fold vibration.

Children typically develop speech according to a developmental pattern or stage, referred to as phonological development. Most children begin speech development around 18 months of age, and it is typically complete between the ages of 4 and 8 years, depending on the individual child (Hulit & Howard, 2006). Children who have persistent difficulties with speech development may receive services by a certified speech-language pathologist.

Fluency refers to the rhythm of speech. An individual who stutters has a fluency disorder, or has dysfluent speech, which may include prolongations, repetitions, and/or interjections. Frequently, a person who stutters also demonstrates struggling behavior, such as eye blinks or throat tremors. Young children often go through a period of dysfluent speech as they develop their language skills, because their speech and language skills are not able to meet their verbal demands.

A number of suprasegmental aspects to speech add more communicative information to words and phrases. Important components include pitch (how high or low the voice is), stress, intonation, rhythm, loudness, rate, and timing. The terms *intonation* and *prosody* describe the variations in pitch or stress that speakers use to clarify the intent of their message. For example, American English speakers use a final rise in pitch to indicate a question rather than a statement, and add stress and loudness to a word to emphasize a point (e.g., I want to go NOW!).

The Assessment Process

A combination of approaches is typically used to determine if a child has a communication deficit in any of the areas described above. Standardized and norm-referenced assessments are common. In addition, parent and teacher interviews as well as observations of the child in natural settings (e.g., during play or in the classroom) are often combined to get the best picture of a child's speech and language skills.

Standardized Tests

Standardized tests are norm-referenced to compare the individual with a suspected communication delay/disorder with others of the same age. In making such comparisons, speech-language pathologists are able to determine if the child's skills are the same, below, or above average in relation to his peers. These assessment tools make the assumption that all students display comparable skills at similar ages and in a specific developmental order (Siegel & Allinder, 2005).

Frequently, it is valuable to use standardized tests to document skills and areas of concern and to compare the results with the student's performance in a more authentic setting. Because the former are generally administered in a quiet area with the test administrator, the child, and sometimes the parent/caregiver, there are usually fewer distractions, allowing the child to maintain attention to the testing materials. This may provide the speech-language pathologist with a better picture of the child's strengths. In contrast, the natural setting of the classroom may be more distracting and may prohibit some children from demonstrating their skills because of distractions and inability to focus on the presented tasks.

When using standardized tests, assumptions are made about students based on their performance on the diagnostic assessment tool. Because students with ASD may have difficulty manipulating materials, communicating, and responding to directions in typical ways, they may not be able to reliably demonstrate their knowledge for the evaluator. For example, a student with ASD may not have the ability to accurately point to a test item or picture to indicate his response, so even if the student knew the correct answer, he may not be able to demonstrate his knowledge appropriately. Further, many students with ASD use few or no spoken words; therefore, assessments that require verbal responses may not generate accurate information regarding their language skills. In addition, individuals who have a deep or perseverative interest in a topic may be unable to proceed further in an assessment because a particular test item or picture on the test page attracts their attention. For example, during a standardized language assessment, Zach had significant difficulty proceeding to the next test item because he was obsessed (i.e., perseverated) with identifying the page numbers on each test page and could not attend to the pictures in order to respond to a question or directive.

Standardized tests also require a student to respond to most test items out of context, which may be difficult for some students, especially students with ASD. For example, speech-language pathologists may be assessing the student's ability to create a grammatically correct sentence by providing her with a word and showing her a picture for context. Because the student may not be familiar with the picture scene, she may not be able to generate the sentence, even though she is capable of creating grammatically correct sentences.

During a recent assessment, one of the authors showed a student with ASD a picture of a girl and boy on the playground and asked her to create a sentence using the word *playing*. The student initially said, "The slide is big." When the author prompted her to look at the picture again and asked her to use the word *playing*, the child said, "The boy has a bat." This example demonstrates the difficulty the child was having not just with appropriately understanding the context but also with the unfamiliar assessment task.

Other Types of Assessments

To accurately assess the language skills of a student with ASD, it is extremely important to observe the student's communication and social interactions during spontaneous exchanges in the natural setting of the classroom and other school environments with familiar communication partners (children and adults) to validate their language skills within a familiar context.

Commonly, authentic assessments are used in the classroom and are integrated with classroom instruction. These may be formal assessments where the teacher, in a systematic way, evaluates how well the student is progressing in a particular instructional program. Or, this type of assessment may be more informal and include special activities, such as group or individual projects, experiments, oral presentations, demonstrations, or performances. Generally, authentic assessments are taken from typical classroom activities, such as assignments, journals, essays, reports, literature discussion groups, or reading logs, to determine if the child demonstrates delays or difficulties during these activities within an authentic environment, the classroom.

A functional-ecological approach to assessment provides an alternative method of assessment, which is strength-based and recommended for determining a student's learning needs, especially for students with severe and multiple disabilities (Cosden, Koegel, Koegel, Greenwell, & Klein, 2006; Snell, 2002). This assessment process determines what is expected and needed by the student to be able to complete specific activities for the setting. Once the assessment process is complete, intervention strategies are identified that will occur in natural contexts at natural times of the day that will help the student acquire the skills needed to be as successful as possible within meaningful activities. This approach to assessment is dynamic and ongoing, requiring revisions as the student's abilities, needs, and desires change (Downing & Demchak, 2008).

For example, our IEP team identified asking questions as an important communication need for Zach across all environments. Zach is in the third grade, and all students in the third grade go weekly to the school library to choose a book to read. The team identified this as an important activity that will allow Zach to participate and provide an opportunity for him to ask questions in a natural setting. To determine the steps of the task, Zach's classmate was observed. He entered the library, found the appropriate book section, looked at a few books, chose his book, took it to the librarian, and checked it out. The next step was to observe Zach in this situation to see what he could and could not do. When Zach entered the library, he just wandered around the room. He did not ask where the third-grade books were located or for a favorite book.

The team then set goals and objectives for asking questions in the library that included locating the question words on his SGD, identifying the correct question word, adding the name of the book, and then speaking the message to the librarian. The instruction would subsequently be implemented using natural cues (e.g., walking with a peer partner to the appropriate area in the library), appropriate adaptations (e.g., using his SGD to ask for the specific book), and effective teaching strategies (e.g., peer modeling of the behavior; teacher/librarian/aide providing visual/verbal cues). In this approach, reassessment could occur in one of two situations: either when Zach was successfully asking appropriate questions in this setting, or if the current strategies did not result in successfully asking questions and new strategies needed to be developed.

Impact of Communication on Literacy Development

Understanding language and language learning plays an important role in the acquisition of literacy development. Spoken language, also referred to as expressive language, is, as previously discussed, the foundation of reading and writing, and the development of speaking, reading, and writing occurs concurrently. Individuals with difficulties with spoken language tend to have deficits in written language or literacy acquisition, and vice versa. Therefore, it is essential that professionals working with individuals with language and literacy learning deficits, including children with ASD, understand language development and its impact on literacy acquisition.

The following subsections discuss the specific areas of language and their impact on literacy. As described with speech and language development, it is important to note that none of the following areas exists in a vacuum: **Proficient skills within each are required to gain meaning from the text. Mastery of a single skill does not automatically mean that a child can read well.**

Phonological Awareness and Phonics

Phonological awareness is the ability to manipulate sounds. This general term includes skills such as initial phonemic awareness, sound isolation, rhyming, blending, segmentation, and syllable deletion. Phonological awareness is an important skill needed for reading, especially decoding, and children who demonstrate difficulties in this area are at risk for poor reading achievement (Schuele & Boudreau, 2008).

The meanings of the terms *phonological awareness* and *phonics* are often confused by teachers and practitioners. While phonological awareness includes the manipulation of the sound structures of oral language, phonics typically includes the written print, or letters, that represent sounds of oral language. The essential link is that children understand that spoken words are composed of sounds (phonological awareness) and that letters make up written words (phonics).

Morphology

As with the other important aspects of spoken language that have been described in this chapter, understanding morphology (the study of word structure, or morphemes) plays an integral part of language and literacy acquisition. Thus, morphology is important to spelling and decoding as well as to gaining meaning from the text. Morphemes are the smallest element of linguistic processing that carry meaning.

Readers must have an understanding of derivations and inflections. For example, the words *knitted, hugged,* and *leaped* all have the same morphological ending, *-ed*, to indicate the regular past tense form; however, all three words end with different phonemes (*knitted* ends with the sound "ed," *hugged* ends with the sound "d," and *leaped* ends with the sound "t"). Therefore, readers and writers must not only be aware that *-ed* indicates that something happened in the past, they must also know how to correctly produce the word.

In addition, the ability to comprehend morphologically complex words relies on semantic and syntactic information. In the sentence, "The *reorganization* of the classroom allowed the class to be more efficient," the word *organize* is the base form and provides the core meaning, "to form a cohesive group." The prefix *re-* carries semantic information and indicates "again," and the suffix *-tion* provides semantic and syntactic information, stating "the state or condition of," which marks the word *reorganization* as a noun.

Syntax

Syntax, or grammar, plays a key role in language development, and a thorough understanding of grammar is required for literacy comprehension. Syntax development for typically developing children begins in the preschool years with rapid growth of the ability to combine words to produce longer utterances. It continues into the school-age and adolescent years at a slower pace. Whereas rapid growth during the preschool years is focused on increasing the length of utterances and adding complex structures, growth during the older years includes production of longer, complex, multi-embedded structures (Nippold, 1993).

As described, syntax is an essential component of both oral and written language. That is, information is conveyed through the use of a systematic order to get the overall gist of a message. For example, the simple sentence "Jeff ran." is composed of a subject and a verb. The sentence becomes more complex when information is added: "Jeff ran to the playground." Typical users of English have a general understanding that a subject comes before a verb, and that a verb tends to come before the prepositional phrase. The above sentence may become even more complex when other words and ideas are added. For example, "Jeff ran to the playground at recess to be the first on the swings."

Semantics

Research supports the notion that vocabulary, or semantics, plays an important role in reading, especially in comprehension (Davis, 1968; McGregor, 2004). Individuals who have a greater lexical breadth and depth during spoken language are more likely to comprehend texts than those who know fewer words (Thorndike, 1973).

Children learn the meanings of words through meaningful linguistic experiences, creating semantic networks based upon prior knowledge and previous experiences that form associations or schemas in the mind. As the reader goes through a series of new experiences, the schema adjusts and expands as new information is acquired. For example, a young child may represent "vehicle" by the toy car that he plays with at home. However, after attending the Indianapolis 500, the child's schema expands to include race cars. Similarly, the child's schema continues to increase after experiences on the farm with a tractor, in a big-rig semi, and during his first airplane ride.

This process never stops, and schemata continue to change throughout life. For readers, information from the text is assigned a specific schema, including the most inclusive information to decipher meaning. If the child is reading a book about race cars, his schema will adjust based on his past experience at the Indy 500. The pertinent characteristics of "vehicle" will include "race car" and not "tractor." Schemata provide temporary, yet useful information that may be modified or discarded if not used. Therefore, the reader integrates new knowledge with pre-existing knowledge, and the schema is constantly evolving over time (Weaver, 2002).

Because all individuals have distinct life experiences, cultural, educational, social, and personal differences may affect vocabulary acquisition. For example, a child raised on a farm in Kansas has a certain set of experiences surrounding a farm, such as milking a cow and baling hay. In contrast, a child growing up in a large, metropolitan city, such as New York or Chicago, may not have any of these life experiences, but has different experiences, such as riding on the subway or in a taxi. Because the child raised in the city does not have experiences living on a farm, he or she may not have a cognitive schema for specific topics related to life on a farm, unless there has been some kind of prior exposure to this vocabulary. Therefore, this child may not have a thorough understanding and recall of this information until a cognitive schema has been developed (Weaver, 2002).

Metalinguistic Skills

As described, metalinguistic skills refer to the act of "thinking about language." This plays an important role in the reading process, and is especially important during the later elementary and intermediate school years when children move from "learning to read" to "reading to learn." Several aspects of metalinguistic skills are essential to reading, and are a culmination of previously discussed topics: phonological awareness, syntax, vocabulary and morphological awareness, and pragmatics.

In general, proficient readers perform many metalinguistic activities before, during, and after reading. Good readers are aware that the purpose of reading is to gain meaning, and they incorporate strategies that allow them to comprehend. For example, they look over the text before they begin reading and trigger prior knowledge and background information. They read the title, flip through the pages, and look at the pictures and diagrams, if any. While reading, they make inferences about the information in the book, think about the author's message, and form hypotheses (Westby, 2004). In summary, good readers actively engage with the text to understand the author's intended message.

Overall, Kate demonstrates excellent literacy skills. She enjoys reading, and she continually seeks opportunities and experiences that incorporate literacy-based activities. However, at times, Kate has difficulty with the pragmatic and metalinguistic components that ultimately affect comprehension. Specifically, she has difficulty understanding that the writer, or author, has an intended message. She is very literal in her understanding of the text, and it is hard for her to incorporate strategies, such as inferring, predicting, and integrating, while reading. This was especially evident when watching Kate read *The Mysterious Tadpole*, by Stephen Kellogg, with her sister, who is in second grade. Although Kate was able to decode the text and read it fluently, she had trouble making predictions about why the tadpole was not turning into an ordinary frog and missed the author's humorous message.

Transaction

Reading involves transaction, whereby both the text and the reader are changed through the process (Goodman, 1994; Rosenblatt, 1994). "Every reading act is an event, or a transaction involving a particular reader and a particular pattern of signs, a text, and occurring at a particular time in a particular context" (Rosenblatt, p. 1063). This quotation emphasizes several key components of the process of reading: social, linguistic, time, and context. Meaning from the text results from the transaction that occurs between the reader and the text. It does not reside strictly in the text or in the reader. Ultimately, meaning is the end product of the transaction. Although the words on the page are the same, each reader interprets the text in different ways for a variety of reasons, including expectations, prior experience, background knowledge, and stance.

Stance

The reader's stance and purpose for reading are two important components of the reading process that are closely related. According to Rosenblatt (1994), the stance mirrors the purpose. As the reader and text transact, the reader chooses a stance, whereby specific elements are brought into consideration while others are pushed aside. The idea of stance occurs along a continuum with **efferent** and **aesthetic** on the two poles. The efferent stance focuses on facts from the text that are utilized following the reading event, whereas the aesthetic stance emphasizes feelings and ideas, which include past psychological events. Therefore, readers frequently take an efferent stance while reading a textbook to learn facts, such as names and dates, but approach poems or personal letters from an aesthetic stance. Overall, the concept of stance refers to the reader's selected attitude about the presented text. Because stance occurs along a continuum, most readers fall close to the center of the continuum.

The same text may be read from either an aesthetic or an efferent stance (Rosenblatt, 1994). Because of specific cues presented in the text, the author, at times, automatically accepts a stance. However, the reader's purpose for reading and previous experiences may activate a stance that is different from the author's intended stance (Rosenblatt). For example, a book about Blue Jacket, a famous Ohio Native American, might have an aesthetic component for a child who has an interest in Native Americans, in addition to the efferent component for a class that is learning about American history.

Communication and Literacy Skills of Children With Autism Spectrum Disorders

Communication is often a core deficit associated with ASD. As such, it includes the following: (a) delay in or lack of development of spoken language or gestures; (b) impairment in the ability to initiate or maintain conversation; (c) repetitive and idiosyncratic use of language; and (d) lack of pretend play (*Diagnostic and Statistical Manual of Mental Disorders*, fourth edition, text revision [DSM-IV-TR]; American Psychiatric Association, 2000). In addition, frequently there is a failure to acquire and use joint attentional skills, symbol use (Woods & Wetherby, 2003), and theory of mind (Walenski, Tager-Flusberg, & Ullman, 2006).

Functional speech fails to develop in one third to one half of all individuals diagnosed with ASD (Lord & Bailey, 2002). Landa (2007) noted that approximately 20% of children with ASD do not achieve more than a five-word spoken vocabulary. Two thirds of children who do not achieve this minimum level have substantial deficits in both receptive and expressive language skills. The remaining third of the ASD population appears to have age-appropriate structural language or grammatical abilities but significant difficulties with pragmatic/social use of language.

Joint Attention

Osterling and Dawson (1994) analyzed first-birthday videotapes of children later diagnosed with ASD. At that young age, these children demonstrated a noticeable lack of pointing and showing activity. In addition, they did not look at the faces of others or respond as frequently when people called their names compared to their typically developing peers. This lack of joint attention at an early age may impact language development, specifically vocabulary acquisition, as well as the frequency and length of conversational turns.

Symbol Use

Because language is an inherently symbolic behavior, children with ASD have significantly more difficulty learning both verbal labels for concepts and conventionalized gestures, such as waving and pointing. Children with ASD also demonstrate deficits understanding and using conventional meanings for words as well as using objects functionally and in symbolic play. Gestures are typically primitive motoric gestures, such as the contact gestures of leading, pulling, or manipulating another's hand (Woods & Wetherby, 2003).

Theory of Mind

It has been suggested that individuals with ASD lack a "theory of mind," or the ability to recognize the mental states of others as well as their own mental state. Therefore, their predictions and explanations of actions are commonly incorrect (Baron-Cohen, Leslie, & Frith, 1985). The ability to make inferences about what others are thinking, feeling, or believing about particular objects, actions, or events, in turn, is affected (Prelock & Ducker, 2006).

For example, one day while working with Kate, I appeared to be upset, did not make eye contact, and only talked, when asked, in one- or two-word phrases. Kate did not understand that I was nonverbally communicating to her that I was having a bad day. Once prompted, she appeared to understand how I was feeling; however, she was not able to do this on her own because of her difficulties with theory of mind.

Language and Literacy Development

Children with ASD diagnoses demonstrate many different and often uneven characteristics, including variations in language and literacy development. Because of the heterogeneity of language skills in these children, there is still a lot we do not know about their language and literacy development. However, researchers have attempted to make generalizations about individuals with ASD based on what is expected for children who are typically developing. The specific results are based on the population studied and the measurements used to determine similarities and differences. If a child has difficulty with specific aspects of language, such as morphology, similar deficits will be observed while reading.

We have described two very different children with ASD in our vignettes. Zach has significant language delays, and he uses various forms of augmented speech to communicate functionally. On the other hand, Kate is verbal and does not have any identifiable language difficulties, with the exception of a pragmatic disorder, or the way she uses language. Therefore, Zach and Kate are at two very different levels in their literacy development based on age and language skills.

All children with ASD are unique and have varied strengths and areas of deficit with regard to language and literacy development. As professionals, we want to meet the child at his current level of development and encourage him to achieve his fullest potential with adequate and appropriate language and literacy intervention.

Vocabulary. In general, although vocabulary may appear to be relatively well developed in children with ASD, typically they use object words and nouns more commonly than other types of vocabulary words such as actions or emotions (Walenski et al., 2006). For example, vocabulary, such as mental state verbs (e.g., *think*, *feel*, *believe*), which assist with understanding abstract mental processes, may be absent. While syntactic development is typically delayed, when acquired, it is usually normative, showing a reliance on a relatively narrow range of grammatical constructions and reduced use of forms that initiate social interaction, such as questions. Further, reversal of personal pronouns (e.g., using *you* rather than *I*) may reflect the difficulty the child with ASD has in conceptualizing roles and perspectives in conversation (Tager-Flusberg, Paul, & Lord, 2005).

Echolalia. Immediate or delayed echolalia, the imitation of the speech of others, has been reported in about 75% of children with ASD (Loveland & Tunali-Kotoski, 2005). Researchers have noted that a great portion of children with ASD demonstrate echolalia that is mitigated in nature; that is, it may contain minor changes in structure from the original model. It has been proposed that this may be representative of the child's grammatical capacity (Bernstein Ratner, 2000). For example, one January day while I was working with Zach, he spontaneously said to me, "Put it where the Christmas tree was," a statement that had no relevance to the topic at hand. I came to learn later that his mother bought him a new train night light the day before. When she showed it to him, she told him she would "put it where the Christmas tree was" in his room.

Pragmatics. As discussed, pragmatics, or the ability to use language in social contexts, is an area of significant difficulty for many children with ASD. Research has shown that the appropriate use of language is important to gain entry into social groups. Pragmatics affects self-esteem, pride, and happiness. Because of deficits with pragmatics, children with ASD may be separated from peers and may have difficulty entering and exiting conversation (Nippold, 1993).

This is a significant area of difficulty for Kate. For example. Kate says, "The kids in my class think I'm weird." Her teachers tell us that this is because she walks up to a group of students, makes a statement or asks a question, waits for an answer but doesn't respond, and then walks away. She does not use a greeting (e.g., "hi") to enter the conversation or a closing (e.g., "Ok, thanks, bye.") to leave. Kate commented the other day that her peers do not even acknowledge her when she makes a statement or asks a question in class. This shows that Kate is aware that her pragmatic difficulties affect her social relationships with her peers.

Hyperlexia

Children with ASD tend to be concrete learners, so it is common for them to have difficulty with abstract concepts as well as words/ideas that have multiple meanings. As a result, many children have hyperlexia. That is, they demonstrate the ability to decode or recognize words, but are not able to describe the meaning of the words, sentences, or paragraphs.

Several years ago, I met a child in a local school district who had dyslexia with a hyperlexic component. As I was observing in his classroom, I was amazed at how well this second grader could read. He read fluently and with ease; however, when he finished, he did not demonstrate any understanding of the text (i.e., lack of reading comprehension).

Transaction and Stance

Transaction involves the interaction between the reader and the text, resulting in meaning. Frequently, individuals with ASD interpret text literally and have difficulty understanding that other people have different thoughts, ideas, and opinions about the meaning of the words on the page. In addition, stance is an important component of the reading process. Based on my experience with children with ASD who can read, these individuals tend to always fall near the efferent, or factual, end of the continuum when compared to typically developing children, who fall more near the middle.

Although Kate fluently reads and easily comprehends the material, she has difficulty with the transaction and perspective-taking components of literacy. For example, while reading *The Incredible Journey,* by Sheila Burnford, Kate did not have any difficulty answering questions about the facts: setting, main characters, or events that occur in the book (factual information). However, she had significant difficulty answering questions that focused on aesthetic dimensions of the characters, such as their emotions. In this example, she could not understand why the three animals wanted to go home or how and why they survived. In addition, it is difficult for her to respond with empathy in real-life, personal situations.

Supporting Children With Augmentative Communication

Augmentative communication strategies, whether low-tech communication boards, computer software, or high-tech, speech-generating devices, can be used to support literacy. To be most successful, the communication set needs to be word-based with keyboard access. This gives the child a choice of single words and word parts (morphological markers) instead of preprogrammed phrases and sentences. The child should also have access to a keyboard feature to spell new words.

In order to use augmentative communication strategies effectively, the child needs to know how to search the word-based system by category – whether the words are encoded syntactically (e.g., question words, pronouns, verbs, adjectives, adverbs, object words) or semantically (e.g., foods, places, transportation). Because understanding and use of morphology is important, the child also needs access to tense (e.g., *-ing, -ed, -s*); plurality (e.g., *-s*); possession (e.g., *-'s*); adjective (e.g., *-er, -est*); and adverb (e.g., *-ly*) markers.

Students with more advanced language skills need communication tools that will allow them to communicate in a precise and grammatically correct fashion. Students should be allowed to experiment with the grammatically correct form and not be forced to communicate telegraphically, imprecisely, or incorrectly, which may lead to a negative perception of themselves and others (Zangari & Van Tatenhove, 2009).

Table 5.1 lists important core vocabulary categories and morphological variations to which students need quick and easy access when developing language and literacy skills using augmentative communication.

Table 5.1

Access to Core Vocabulary and Morphological Variations When Using Augmentative Communication

Core Vocabulary Are high-frequency, multipurpose, commonly occurring words drawn from all word classes	Examples
1. Pronouns	I, me, you, him
2. Verbs	Go, want, put, get, let
3. Helping verbs	Is, can, could, will, was, did
4. Adjectives	Good, bad, more
5. Adverbs	Again, now, here, there
6. Prepositions	In, on, with, of, for
7. Determiners	This, that, the
8. Conjunctions	And, or, because
9. Interjections	Yes, no, please, sorry
10. Question words	Who, when, where, what
11. Nouns	Idea, way, thing, stuff
Morphological Variations Permit productions of mature, grammatically correct forms	**Examples**
1. Present progressive	Writing
2. Regular plural -s	Books, legs, glasses
3. Irregular past	Went, said, came, told
5. Possessive -'s	Teacher's, boy's
6. Regular past -ed	Needed, worked, believed
7. Regular third-person -s	Gives, knows, helps
8. Irregular third person	Has, does
9. Adverbs -ly	Quickly, slowly
10. Adjectives -er, -est	Smaller, fastest

Note. AAC systems must be linguistically based with access to core vocabulary and morphological variations. Adapted from Zangari and Van Tatenhove (2009).

Children can effectively learn the location of the vocabulary in their communication systems through the use of aided language stimulation. This strategy occurs where the communication partner assists the child in learning how to access the communication system most effectively by touching the appropriate word and adding morphological markers while talking with them (Cafiero, 2005; Drager et al., 2006).

When a word is not easily accessed via the communication system, semantic webbing strategies may be used to identify features of the word that can help in locating it (i.e., activating schema). In order to find words such as *train* and *tractor*, Zach first had to learn that they were in the category of vehicles, which is located in the category of things, versus school and playground, which are located under the category of places. In order to put together the sentence "I played with my tractor on the playground," Zach had to look in both categories to find his words.

Also, it is important to allow the child to have access to the keyboard, whether on the computer or on an SGD. This encourages the child to practice phonemic awareness skills such as segmenting and blending by copying words or by generating his own words or nonsense words. For example, Zach is using the Edmark Reading Program (2001) as part of his reading instruction. He is able to match words to pictures using the word set in his device as well as copy words using his keyboard page.

Zach uses his SGD to locate vocabulary words so he can use them to communicate. Because Zach knows the location of these words, reading comprehension is easier to assess. His teacher can ask him basic questions regarding the main idea and characters in the story, which he can answer using his SGD. Also, he is beginning to sequence events and to predict what might happen next with familiar stories. For writing, Zach is using the program Writing with Symbols Version 2 (2000). His Edmark words are added to writing environments so that he can directly use them to produce written text. In addition, he uses the keyboard on his SGD to spell his Edmark words, which gives him additional practice with both reading and writing. See Figure 5.3.

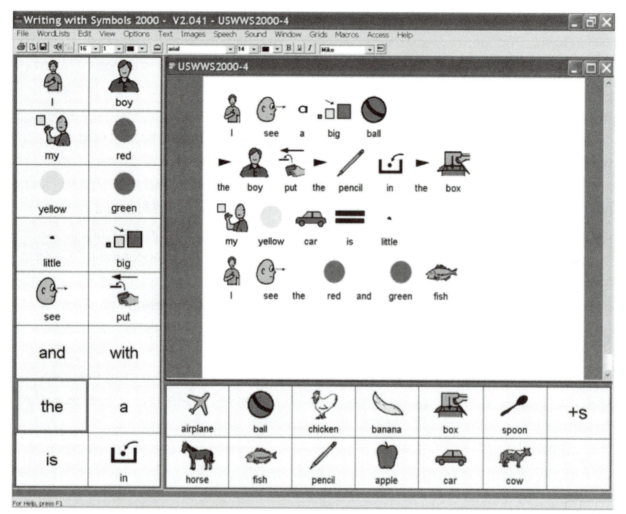

Figure 5.3. Writing with Symbols 2000™ with Edmark Words 1 through 29 in writing environment. These symbols were generated using Boardmaker™. The Picture Communication Symbols © 1981-2009 by Mayer-Johnson LLC. All Rights Reserved Worldwide. Used with permission. Boardmaker™ is a trademark of Mayer-Johnson LLC.

Last week, Zach spelled *sky* when he was with his grandmother. She was excited to see him spell what seemed like a novel word for him, and she began commenting on things in the sky. Zach then went to a food category page and found the symbol "hot dog." At that point, Zach's grandmother was confused. But luckily his mother entered the room and shared with her that Zach's new favorite restaurant was Skyline, a restaurant famous for its chili. He gets a cheese coney, a hot dog topped with chili and cheese, at Skyline. In this example, when Zach spelled *sky*, he was indicating to his grandmother that he wanted to eat a cheese coney from Skyline! This example illustrates how Zach was able to navigate his SGD and use literacy-based information to communicate this intended message.

Diversity and Multicultural Education

In this chapter, we have described typical language and literacy acquisition as well as the development of children with ASD. There are many other children who demonstrate differences in language and literacy development, such as children who are second-language learners, speakers of African-American English, and those raised in poverty. These children present with differences because of the impact of culture, but they are not considered to be disordered or delayed.

Speakers of African-American English (AAE) demonstrate systematic differences in morphosyntax and phonology compared to speakers of Standard American English (SAE) (Connor & Craig, 2006). For example, AAE speakers may include or exclude copulas or auxiliaries and say "This how I do it." instead of "This *is* how I do it." (Craig, Thompson, Washington, & Potter, 2003). Additionally, children who are bilingual or learning two languages may use features of one language to affect the other. For example, Spanish speakers may use some of the Spanish rules while talking in English.

These are only two brief examples, but children who are second-language learners or those who speak AAE often enter school at a disadvantage compared to children who are speakers of SAE because assessments, interventions, and curriculum use SAE. It is important to remember that these differences may also have an impact on the children with ASD who are in your classroom.

Conclusion

This chapter has focused on the link between language and literacy skills in children with ASD. Because language and reading are interconnected processes, we have described, in detail, important components of both. Throughout the chapter, we highlighted Kate and Zach – two children who have very different skills. Because of the variability of skills in children with ASD, language and literacy development – as well as intervention – may be significantly different depending on where they fall on the spectrum. As professionals working with children with ASD, we must strive to provide them with strategies and techniques that facilitate language and literacy skills so that they can achieve their highest potential.

Chapter Highlights

- Communication is the sending and receiving of messages. It takes a minimum of two (a sender and a receiver) and a message that is expressed in either verbal or written form.

- Language is the cornerstone of literacy learning, and a solid foundation in language and communication is essential in active literacy learning across all grades. Language is a system of abstract symbols and rule-governed structures with specific conventions that need to be learned. The content of a message is either spoken or written.

- Receptive language is the comprehension of words, sentences, and stories. We generally receive receptive input through hearing; however, we can also receive information through pictures, symbols, and signs, as well as the printed word.

- Typically, expressive language is communicated verbally. However, other methods, such as SGDs, may be used when verbal output is not possible.

- Pragmatics refers to how language is used in social contexts.

- Intentional communication behaviors begin preverbally and move through the linguistic stages of development. Criteria include the following: (a) child makes eye contact, (b) child uses gestures, (c) child uses vocalization, and (d) child attempts to communicate until his goal has been met.

- Joint attention occurs when two people attend to the same object, activity, or topic. Establishing joint attention allows individuals to play interactively, respond emotionally, and interact appropriately with peers and adults.

- Children learn many of their pragmatic skills through play, which lays the foundation for later use in conversations. An important component of learning language through play is symbolic play, an activity where one object represents another.

- At the most complex level of language development, children develop metalinguistic abilities, which means they have the capacity to use language to analyze, study, and understand language.

- The key components and building blocks of receptive and expressive language are semantic, morphological, pragmatic, and syntactic development.

- Semantic development is learning the meanings of words (i.e., vocabulary).

- Morphemes are the smallest meaningful units of language.

- Syntactic development (grammar) refers to how children combine words in a systematic way to create sentences that follow the linguistic rules of their native language.

- Speech is an important component of communication. Speech consists of articulation, phonological processes, voice, and fluency.

- Fluency refers to the rhythm of speech.

- A number of suprasegmental aspects of speech add more communicative information to words and phrases, including pitch, stress, intonation, rhythm, loudness, rate, and timing.

- Standardized and norm-referenced assessments are commonly used to determine if a child has a communication deficit. Standardized tests are norm-referenced in order to be able to compare the individual with a suspected communication delay/disorder to other individuals of the same age.

- Frequently, authentic assessments are used in the classroom and are integrated with classroom instruction.

- A functional-ecological approach is strength-based and, therefore, is recommended for determining a student's learning needs.

- Phonological awareness includes manipulation of the sound structures of oral language; phonics typically includes the written print, or letters, that represents the sound of oral language.

- Morphology is the study of word structure or morphemes.

- Syntax, or grammar, plays a key role in language development, and a thorough understanding of grammar is required for literacy comprehension.

- Metalinguistics refers to the act of "thinking about language."

- It has been suggested that individuals with ASD lack a "theory of mind," or the ability to recognize the mental states of others as well as their own mental state.

- Many children with ASD have hyperlexia. That is, they demonstrate the ability to decode or recognize words but are not able to describe the meaning.

- Transaction involves the interaction between the reader and text, resulting in meaning. Frequently, children with ASD interpret text literally.

- Augmentative communication strategies, whether low-tech communication boards, computer software, or high-tech speech-generating devices, can be used to support literacy.

- Language differences should be given multicultural consideration when working with children from other cultural backgrounds.

Chapter Review Questions

1. What are the important components of language and literacy development, and how are they interrelated in the process of gaining meaning from text?

2. Although children with ASD demonstrate varied language and literacy skills, what are the primary deficits, and what is the impact on reading?

3. What are some possible therapeutic techniques that may help children with ASD learn how to read?

References

American Psychiatric Association. (2000). *Diagnostic and statistical manual of mental disorder* (4th ed., text rev.). Washington, DC: American Psychiatric Association.

Baron-Cohen, S., Leslie, A. M., & Frith, U. (1985). Does the autistic child have a theory of mind? *Cognition, 21,* 37-46.

Bates, E. (1976). *Language and context: The acquisition of pragmatics.* San Diego: Academic Press.

Bates, E., Bretherton, I., Snyder, L., Shore, C., & Volterra, V. (1980). Vocal and gestural symbols at 13 months. *Merrill-Palmer Quarterly, 26,* 407-423.

Berninger, V. (2000). Development of language by hand and its connections with language by ear, mouth, and eye. *Topics in Language Disorders, 20,* 65-84.

Bernstein Ratner, N. (2000). Elicited imitation and other methods for the analysis of trade-offs between speech and language skills in children. In L. Menn & N. Berstein Ratner (Eds.), *Methods for studying language production* (pp. 291-312). Mahwah, NJ: Erlbaum.

Bloom, L., Rocissano, L., & Hood, L. (1976). Adult-child discourse: Developmental interaction between information processing and linguistic interaction. *Cognitive Psychology, 8,* 521-522.

Boardmaker. (2001). Solana Beach, CA: Mayer-Johnson, Inc.

Bryant, J. B. (2009). Language in social contexts: Communicative competence in the preschool years. In J. B. Gleason & N. B. Ratner (Eds.), *The development of language* (7th ed., pp. 192-226). Boston: Pearson.

Burnford, S. (1960). *The incredible journey.* New York: Bantam Doubleday Books for Young Readers.

Cafiero, J. M. (2005). *Meaningful exchanges for people with autism: An introduction to augmentative and alternative communication* (pp. 35-45). Bethesda, MD: Woodbine House.

Connor, C. D., & Craig, H. K. (2006). African American preschoolers' language, emergent literacy skills, and use of African American English: A complex relation. *Journal of Speech, Language, and Hearing Research, 49,* 771-792.

Cosden, M., Koegel, L. K., Koegel, R. L., Greenwell, A., & Klein, E. (2006). Strength based assessment for children with autism spectrum disorder. *Research and Practice for Persons with Severe Disabilities, 31,* 134-143.

Craig, H. K., Thompson, C. A., Washington, J. A., & Potter, S. L. (2003). Phonological features of child African American English. *Journal of Speech, Language, and Hearing Research, 46,* 623-635.

Davis, F. (1968). Research in comprehension in reading. *Reading Research Quarterly, 3,* 499-545.

Downing, J. E., & Demchak, M. A. (2008). First steps: Determining individual abilities and how best to support students. In J. E. Downing (Ed.), *Including students with severe and multiple disabilities in typical classrooms: Practical strategies for teachers* (3rd ed., pp. 49-90). Baltimore: Paul H. Brookes Publishing Company.

Drager, K.D.R., Postal, V. J., Carrolus, L., Castellano, M., Gagliano, C., & Glynn, J. (2006). The effect of aided language modeling on symbol comprehension and production in two preschoolers with autism. *American Journal of Speech-Language Pathology, 15,* 112-125.

Edmark Reading Program Level I. School version. (2001). Austin, TX: Pro-Ed.

Goodman, K. S. (1994). Reading, writing, and written texts: A transactional sociopsycholinguistic view. In R. B. Ruddell, M. R. Ruddell, & H. Singer (Eds.), *Theoretical models and processes of reading* (4th ed., pp. 1093-1130). Newark, DE: International Reading Association.

Hulit, L. M., & Howard, M. R. (2006). Cognitive development: Building a foundation for language. In L. M. Hulit & M. R. Howard (Eds.), *Born to talk: An introduction to speech and language development* (4th ed., pp. 55-108). Boston: Allyn & Bacon.

Kaiser, A., Hemmeter, L., & Hester, P. (1997). The facilitative effects of input on children's language development: Contributions from studies of enhanced milieu teaching. In L. Adamson & M. A. Romski (Eds.), *Communication and language acquisition: Discoveries from atypical development* (pp. 267-294). Baltimore: Paul H. Brookes Publishing Company.

Kellogg, S. (2001). *The mysterious tadpole.* New York: Penguin Putnam, Inc.

Landa, R. (2007). Early communication development and intervention for children with autism. *Mental Retardation and Developmental Disabilities Research Reviews, 13,* 16-25.

Light, J. C. (2003). Shattering the silence: Development of communicative competence by individuals who use AAC. In J. C. Light, D. R. Beukelman, & J. Reichle (Eds.), *Communicative competence for individuals who use AAC: From research to effective practice* (pp. 3-38). Baltimore: Paul H. Brookes Publishing Company.

Lord, C., & Bailey, A. (2002). Autism spectrum disorders. In. M. Rutter & E. Taylor (Eds.), *Child and adolescent psychiatry* (3rd ed., pp. 636-663). Oxford, UK: Blackwell.

Loveland, K., & Tunali-Kotoski, B. (2005). The school-aged child with an autism spectrum disorder. In F. Volkmar, R. Paul, A. Klin, D. Cohen, & D. Hoboken (Eds.), *Handbook of autism and pervasive developmental disorders* (Vol. 1, 3rd ed., pp. 24-287). Hoboken, NJ: John Wiley & Sons.

McGregor, K. K. (2004). Developmental dependencies between lexical semantics and reading. In C. A. Stone, E. R. Silliman, B. J. Ehren, & K. Apel (Eds.), *Handbook of language and literacy: Development and disorders* (pp. 395-427). New York: The Guilford Press.

Nippold, M. (1993). Clinical forum: Adolescent language developmental markers in adolescent language: Syntax, semantics, and pragmatics. *Language, Speech, and Hearing Services in the Schools, 24,* 21-28.

Osterling, J., & Dawson, G. (1994). Early recognition of children with autism: A study of first birthday home videotapes. *Journal of Autism and Developmental Disorders, 24,* 247-257.

Pan, B., & Uccelli, P. (2009). Semantic development: Learning the meanings of words. In J. R. Berko & N. B. Gleason (Eds.), *The development of language* (7th ed., pp. 104-138). Boston: Pearson.

Prelock, P. (2006). Understanding and assessing communication. In P. Prelock (Ed.), *Autism spectrum disorders: Issues in assessment and intervention* (pp. 167-219). Austin, TX: Pro-Ed.

Prelock, P., & Ducker, A. (2006). Understanding and assessing the social-emotional development of children with ASD. In P. Prelock (Ed.), *Autism spectrum disorders: Issues in assessment and intervention* (pp. 251-302). Austin, TX: Pro-Ed.

Rosenblatt, L. M. (1994). The transactional theory of reading and writing. In R. B. Ruddell, M. R. Ruddell, & H. Singer (Eds.), *Theoretical models and processes of reading* (4th ed., pp. 1057-1092). Newark, DE: International Reading Association.

Saywitz, K., & Cherry-Wilkinson, L. (1982). Age-related differences in metalinguistic awareness. In S. Kuczaj (Ed.), *Language development: Language, thought, and culture* (Vol. 2, pp. 229-248). Hillsdale, NJ: Lawrence Erlbaum Associates.

Schuele, C. M., & Boudreau, D. (2008). Phonological awareness intervention: Beyond the basics. *Language, Speech, and Hearing Services in the Schools, 39,* 3-20.

Siegel, E., & Allinder R. M. (2005). Review of assessment procedures for students with moderate and severe disabilities. *Education and Training in Developmental Disabilities, 40,* 343-351.

Snell, M. E. (2002). Using dynamic assessment with learners who communicate non-symbolically. *Augmentative and Alternative Communication, 18,* 163-176.

Sturm, J. M., & Clendon, S. A. (2004). Augmentative and alternative communication, language, and literacy: Fostering the relationship. *Topics in Language Disorders, 24*(1), 76-91.

Sugarman, S. (1984). The development of preverbal communication. In R. Schiefelbusch & J. Pickar (Eds.), *The acquisition of communicative competence* (pp. 23-67). Baltimore: University Park Press.

Tager-Flusberg, H., Paul, R., & Lord, C. (2005). Language and communication in autism. In F. G. Volkmar, R. Paul, A. Klin, & D. Cohen (Eds.), *Handbook of autism and pervasive developmental disorders* (Vol. 1, pp. 335-364). Hoboken, NJ: John Wiley & Sons.

Thomasello, M. (1995). Pragmatic contexts for early verb learning. In M. Tomasello & W. Meriman (Eds.), *Beyond names for things: Young children's acquisition of verbs* (pp. 115-146). Mahwah, NJ: Lawrence Erlbaum Associates.

Thorndike, R. L. (1973). Reading as reasoning. *Reading Research Quarterly, 9*, 135-147.

Walenski, M., Tager-Flusberg, H., & Ullman, M. (2006). Language in autism. In S. Moldin & J. Rubenstein (Eds.), *Understanding autism: From basic neuroscience to treatment* (pp. 175-204). Boca Raton, FL: Taylor & Francis.

Weaver, C. (2002). Schema and transactions in the reading process. In C. Weaver (Ed.), *Reading process and practice* (3rd ed., pp. 14-40). Portsmouth, NH: Heinemann.

Westby, C. (2004). A language perspective on executive functioning, metacognition, and self-regulation in reading. In C. A. Stone, E. R. Silliman, B. J. Ehren, & K. Apel (Eds.), *Handbook of language and literacy: Development and disorders* (pp. 395-427). New York: The Guilford Press.

Wetherby, A., Cain, D., Yonclas, D., & Walker, V. (1988). Analysis of intentional communication of normal children from the prelinguistic to the multiword stage. *Journal of Speech and Hearing Research, 31*, 240-252.

Wetherby, A. M., & Prizant, B. M. (1992). Profiling young children's communicative competence. In S. F. Warren & J. Reichle (Eds.), *Causes and effects in communication and language intervention* (pp. 217-253). Baltimore: Paul H. Brookes Publishing Company.

Woods, J., & Wetherby, A. (2003). Early identification of and intervention for infants and toddlers who are at risk for autism spectrum disorder. *Language, Speech, and Hearing Services in Schools, 34*, 180-193.

Writing with Symbols. (2000). Solana Beach, CA: Mayer-Johnson, Inc.

Zangari, C., & Van Tatenhove, G. (2009). Supporting more advanced linguistic communications. In G. Soto & C. Zangari (Eds.), *Practically speaking: Language, literacy, & academic development for students with AAC needs* (pp. 176-177). Baltimore: Paul H. Brookes Publishing Company.

Language and Literacy Resources

Language Resources

- http://www.asha.org/publications/literacy: This web site by the American Speech-Language-Hearing Association provides information about the role of speech-language pathologists with regard to language and literacy.

- http://www.asha.org/public/speech/: This web site by the American Speech-Language-Hearing Association provides general information about speech, language, and swallowing.

- http://www.asha.org/about/leadership-projects/multicultural/: This web site by the American Speech-Language-Hearing Association's Multicultural Affairs and Resources provides information about cultural and linguistic diversity.

Literacy Resources

- http://www.readingrockets.org/: This web site provides information and resources, including lessons and activities, for parents and teachers to assist young children who require additional help in reading fundamentals and comprehension skills development learn how to read and read better.

- http://www.starfall.com: This web site provides ideas and strategies to help teach children of all ages and abilities learn how to read using a phonics approach in conjunction with phonemic awareness practice.

- http://www.nationalreadingpanel.org: This web site by the National Reading Panel provides information about research-based knowledge on reading instruction.

Augmentative Communication Resources

- http://www.mayer-johnson.com: This web site by Mayer-Johnson provides information about symbol-based resources for individuals with special needs. Picture Communication Symbols™ (PCS) are the base for their Boardmaker® software products and are available in 44 languages.

- http://www.news-2-you.com/index.aspx: This web site provides a weekly current-events newspaper with symbol-supported text at four different reading levels for children learning how to read. It includes news, activities, computer games, and storybooks, all related to the feature story of the week.

- http://www.aac.unl.edu/yaack: This web site, Augmentative and Alternative Communication (AAC) Connecting Young Kids (YAACK), provides resources for parents and professionals interested in augmentative communication for children at various ages and stages of communication ability, and with different strengths, disabilities and learning characteristics.

- http://www.aacintervention.com: This web site, created by Dr. Caroline Musselwhite and Julie Maro, provides a wealth of information and ideas for reading and writing with students with AAC needs. There are Tips of the Month and instructions on creating your own literature based communication boards.

- http://www.isaac-online.org/en/aac/index.html: This web site, created by the International Society of Augmentative and Alternative Communication, provides information about augmentative and alternative communication for individuals of all ages.

Chapter 6
Creating Print-Rich Environments to Support Literacy Instruction

Elizabeth B. Keefe, Ph.D., University of New Mexico

Susan R. Copeland, Ph.D., University of New Mexico

Heather DiLuzio, M. A., Albuquerque Public Schools

Learner Objectives

After reading this chapter, the learner should be able to:

- Understand basic elements of brain-friendly learning and how it may relate to print-rich classroom environments for students with ASD

- Discuss the research supporting the importance of print-rich learning environments for literacy learning

- Identify the unique learning styles of students on the autism spectrum and relate them to the development of appropriate print-rich environments

- Modify literacy materials within a print-rich classroom to take into account the unique sensory needs of students with ASD

- Discuss ways in which print-rich classroom environments can help connect school and home settings

- Design instruction linked to print-rich classroom environments in order to facilitate literacy learning for students with ASD

■ ■ ■

Ryan is a 7-year-old boy who has autism. Ryan's school day is split between an inclusion setting and a self-contained classroom specifically designed to meet the unique learning needs of children with ASD. Within his segregated setting, Ryan's teachers use teaching methods such as repeated storybook readings, high-interest leveled readers, highly structured teaching routines, and naturally reinforcing materials and subject matter as part of his daily reading instruction.

While Ryan's teachers use a variety of research-based strategies to increase his positive behaviors, Ryan's highest level reinforcers are books. As part of Ryan's classroom modifications, he has access to a variety of high-interest leveled readers and books that have been used during repeated storybook readings.

Frequently Ryan has difficulty transitioning from one activity to another, especially from a highly preferred activity such as physical therapy to a less preferred or nonpreferred activity such as toileting routines. The importance of having a print-rich classroom environment for Ryan became apparent.

One day Ryan had a particularly difficult time transitioning from library, one of his favorite activities, back to his segregated classroom. His behavior escalated such that by the time he reached his classroom, he was screaming, crying, throwing himself on the floor, as well as throwing objects, including his shoes. Indeed, Ryan's behavior had escalated to such a level that the school nurse came to see what was going on. At this point, Ryan's teachers were able to move Ryan to an area of the room where he could calm himself down without the risk of harm to himself and/or other students. Near this area of the classroom, a set of leveled readers were stored. The students have access to this area during free-choice times. All the books are displayed on a choice board (see Figure 6.1).

Once he was moved to this area of the classroom, the school nurse sat with Ryan, patting his back encouraging him to calm down. Ryan suddenly stopped crying and looked up at the choice board. He then looked over at the nurse and requested one of the leveled readers. After checking with one of the classroom teachers to make sure it was okay, the nurse located the level reader Ryan had requested and handed it to him. Ryan then asked to sit on the nurse's lap and proceeded to read the book to her.

After Ryan had read the book to the nurse, the teacher asked Ryan if he was ready to check his schedule and come to the next activity. He indicated that he was, got up, and moved on to the next activity with no negative behavior during the transition. From that point on, any time the school nurse entered the classroom, Ryan would go over to the leveled readers. He would look at the choice board, make a choice, ask the school nurse for a book, and then sit and read to her.

■ ■ ■

Figure 6.1. Choice board.

The story of Ryan highlights the critical importance of making sure that all students, including those with autism spectrum disorders (ASD), have access to print-rich classrooms. In Ryan's case, the print-rich environment not only encouraged his love of reading and his literacy skill development, it also provided positive behavioral supports and helped him manage transitions.

This chapter presents a clear rationale for print-rich environments, along with general and specific strategies for teachers who want to create print-rich classroom environments for their students. The evidence base will be examined through a brief review of what we know about brain-friendly teaching and a discussion of the research of the impact of print-rich environments on literacy learning for all students, including those with disabilities and ASD. General considerations for designing print-rich environments for students with ASD will also be presented. Finally, the chapter describes specific instructional strategies using aspects of the classroom environment.

Brain-Friendly Learning and Print-Rich Environments

Recent advances in imaging technologies such as magnetic resonance imaging (MRI), functional magnetic resonance imaging (fMRI), and positron emission tomography (PET) are giving direction to educators who want to provide environments that are "brain friendly" to their students. Specifically, these imaging technologies demonstrate ways in which real-time neuronal activity may be associated with the perception of environmental stimuli, how that sensory input is processed, and how information is stored in memory. While a complete biological understanding of the functioning of the brain is not yet possible, useful models of brain functioning have been developed (see Brinkerhoff & Keefe, 2007, for a more complete discussion of this topic).

One of the most useful frameworks for describing the brain and learning relevant to print-rich classrooms is the **information processing** model offered by Gagne and Driscol (1988). Figure 6.2 shows a modification of this basic model applied to classroom environments.

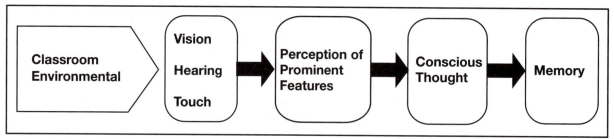

Figure 6.2. Information processing model.

This model proposes that all learning begins with the perception of environmental stimuli through activation of the body's sensory receptors. Thus, the environment may be experienced through any of the senses, which then transmit information to the sensory register through neurons to be stored in short- and/or long-term memory for immediate or future use. Brinkerhoff and Keefe (2007) described how this process works for letter recognition:

> For example, the visual stimulus generated by looking at the letter X would be recognized as two crossed lines. This process takes the merest fraction of a second before the information is transferred to the short-term or conscious memory. Here the information is coded into a meaningful concept, i.e., the crossed line pattern is associated with a stored memory of the letter X retrieved from long-term memory. The consciousness is now aware that the letter X has been seen. This information will reside in short-term or conscious memory for at most a few seconds unless it is actively dealt with. Conscious memory might actively consider some aspect of the X or its meaning as part of a word within a sentence, which would result in its retention for a longer period. If information in conscious memory is to be remembered, it is sent to the long-term memory where it is stored for later retrieval. (p. 9)

One of the challenges for educators working with students with ASD is taking into account potential deficits and differences in sensory processing and integration (Heflin & Alaimo, 2007; Kluth & Chandler-Olcott, 2008). These may influence the way in which neurons transmit stimuli to the brain and sensory register, and thus how these environmental stimuli are perceived. In turn, this may impact the ability to store and retrieve information in short- and long-term memory.

Research into brain-friendly learning provides general recommendations for enhancing information processing (Brinkerhoff & Keefe, 2007). Here are some ideas to think about when considering how to develop print-rich classroom environments:

1. **Novelty.** When something is new, we are more likely to pay attention and notice. For example, something as simple as putting up a new bulletin board, a word wall, or a choice board can capture students' interest. Students with ASD may not react positively to novelty without scaffolds and visual supports.

2. **Intensity.** People pay greater attention to stimuli that are more intense. For students with ASD, teachers need to be aware of sensory issues that may interrupt students' ability to perceive environmental stimuli in areas where they may have hypersensitivity.

3. **Emotion.** When students have an emotional connection to the materials in the environment, they are more likely to remember and use the information. This applies equally to students with ASD, even though it may be challenging to recognize the unique ways in which each student expresses his or her emotions. Teachers may even think it is necessary to avoid emotional preferences for students with ASD for fear they will lead to obsessive behavior (Kluth & Schwartz, 2008). We believe that it is critical for the classroom environment to reflect the unique nature of the group of students in the room. The classroom environment should enable a visitor to know something about the students' special interests or favorite books. The classroom environment should include linguistic and cultural differences.

4. **Use of images and graphics.** Another strategy for lessening the demands on short-term memory resources is to use images and graphics as scaffolds and models. This may be of particular importance to students with ASD, who often benefit greatly from the use of visual supports in the classroom and other environments (Downing, 2005; Kluth & Chandler-Olcott, 2008).

5. **Connecting to prior learning.** There is much teachers can do to support students in linking new learning to existing knowledge through the ways in which we design print-rich classroom environments.

The next section examines what the research says about print-rich environments and literacy learning for student with and without ASD. As you read this research, think about what we discussed about brain-friendly learning in this section. How does this relate to the research presented below?

What Does the Research Say About Print-Rich Environments and ASD?

Print-Rich Environments and Early Literacy Skills

One way that young children construct knowledge is by interacting with their environments (Roskos & Neuman, 2002). Research on how children acquire early literacy skills has demonstrated that children gain crucial understandings about print (written language) and how it relates to oral language by being immersed in "literacy-rich environments" (Katims, 1994; Kuby, Goodstadt-Killoran, Aldridge, & Kirkland, 1999).

What constitutes a literacy-rich environment? Such environments display text, pictures, and graphics that are meaningful to the children in that setting. Literacy-rich environments offer recurring opportunities for the children to interact with books and other engaging printed materials individually and in group play (Katims, 1994; Neuman, 2004). Mirenda (2003) added that these environments must be "rich in meaningful communication opportunities" (p. 275).

This perspective on how children begin the process of becoming readers and writers is based on the notion that literacy development begins well before children start school and are introduced to formal skill-based literacy instruction. In other words, children's literacy knowledge and understandings emerge as they have meaningful and sustained interactions within literacy-rich environments with other individuals who are what Kluth and Chandler-Olcott (2008) call "literate models" (p. 49).

Neuman and Celano (2004, as cited in Neuman, 2004) conducted one of several studies supporting the belief that early interaction with literacy-rich environments facilitates the development of literacy skills. For example, they examined the literacy skills of over 4,000 preschoolers living in high-poverty neighborhoods and identified 43 who had reading skills exceeding what would be expected for their ages. After extensive individual testing (e.g., assessing vocabulary, intelligence, and specific reading skills), the authors concluded that the "children's ability to read was related to skill development, not aptitude" (Neuman & Celano, p. 90). Further investigation revealed that these "precocious early readers" (p. 90) had had regular, repeated experiences, often facilitated by adults, within print-rich environments that facilitated their development of literacy skills.

Additional evidence supporting the importance of print-rich environments in the development of literacy skills comes from research on **environmental print**. Environmental print refers to the print that is found all around us in our homes and communities. It includes items such as road signs, food wrappers, logos on soft drink cans, or the print on common household items like toothpaste. Environmental print commonly has visual and contextual cues in combination with text. For example, the logo for the soft drink Sprite contains letters paired with a graphic design and a representation of a lemon and a lime. However, environmental print can also be simply a printed word (e.g., EXIT on a sign) or a picture or other visual representation of an object or place (e.g., the grocery store ads in the newspaper that contain pictures of products or produce).

From birth, children typically have repeated exposure to and experience with a variety of environmental print, even if they do not have many opportunities to interact with books or other forms of literacy materials. These early experiences with environmental print help children to begin developing basic understandings about written language and its relationship to oral language. Thus, almost all children come to school with at least some understanding that print represents meaning (Kuby & Aldridge, 2004). Mirenda (2003) noted that even children who do not use speech often react to familiar environmental print, demonstrating recognition. It has been suggested that as many as 35-40% of children with ASD will not develop spoken language (Heflin & Alaimo, 2007).

Several researchers have determined that even very young children can correctly recognize logos of familiar objects or places. For example, Masonheimer, Drum, and Ehri (1984) found that children as young as 2 years old could recognize the McDonald's restaurant logo when it was presented in full color (i.e., with all the visual and contextual cues).

However, simply being exposed to environmental print is not sufficient for children to acquire the ability to read words (Masonheimer et al., 1984; Reutzel, Fawson, Young, Morrison, & Wilcox, 2003). Without explicit instruction that calls attention to the text, children may rely more on the visual cues in environmental print to identify an item than focusing on the print itself and applying their knowledge about letters and sounds to recognize words.

Kuby, Aldridge, and Snyder (1994) studied kindergarten students' ability to read environmental print when the visual/contextual cues in the item were faded until only the word in the logo written in manuscript remained. Participating students in five classrooms received environmental print instruction in somewhat varied ways within each classroom. The researchers found that, except in one classroom, the students' ability to recognize the words in each logo decreased as the visual and contextual cues were faded. In this classroom, the teacher had systematically used the words from environmental print items written in manuscript as a part of the environmental print instruction, thus focusing the students' attention on the print itself. This finding supports the importance of directing environmental print instruction explicitly on the print features to build early literacy skills.

Print-Rich Environments and Students With Disabilities

The influence of print-rich environments on the literacy skill development of students with disabilities has not been examined as closely as it has with typically developing children. This is the case for children with ASD.

Some researchers have suggested that children with disabilities of all types have fewer opportunities to engage in early literacy activities and less exposure to print-rich environments than their typically developing peers (e.g., Weikle & Hadadian, 2004). An absence of these important experiences with print may adversely affect students' acquisition of foundational literacy understandings.

Among available studies, a few researchers have examined the use of environmental print to enhance the early literacy skills of children with disabilities. Aldridge and Rust (1987), for example, described the effects of an environmental print reading program on the literacy skills of elementary-school students "identified as high-risk based on referrals for special education and IQ scores" (p. 324), who received reading instruction for one period a day within a resource room setting. The teacher used an environmental print reading program with the following steps.

First, students were asked to bring environmental print from their homes and communities. The teacher used these items during reading instruction by showing an item and asking the children to identify it and orally describe and make up a sentence about it. During the next step, the teacher photocopied the items and asked students to identify each item, match the original item to the copy, and describe/make up sentences (orally) about the items. In the third step, the teacher copied items and removed the visual cues, leaving only the photocopied word. The teacher asked students to identify the words, match the words to the original item, and describe/make up sentences (orally) about the item. In step four, the teacher showed the students the original items and wrote the word from the item in manuscript. Students then practiced writing these words in manuscript and reading the words written in manuscript. Finally, the teacher created sentences on the board that used the item words (written in manuscript) and asked students to practice reading them.

Although the researchers did not present formal assessment data, they described positive changes in participating students' attitudes toward reading. In particular, by the end of the school year, students who had initially verbalized that they could not read stated that they could read, thus seeing themselves as readers for the first time. Students also demonstrated more awareness of environmental print and began to attempt to read environmental print in the community.

Alberto and colleagues (2007) employed an intervention to increase the visual literacy skills of six elementary and middle school students with moderate or severe disabilities. The authors defined visual literacy as "the ability to discern meaning conveyed through images" (p. 234). One aspect of visual literacy is the ability to obtain information from environmental print.

In this study the researchers used a constant time delay procedure to teach participating students to name a store when shown an environmental print item (logo) depicting that store and to name a product that could be obtained in the store. Students participated in both individual instruction three times per week and in a small-group activity in which they played games using the logos from their individual instructional sessions once a week. The researchers selected for instruction environmental print logos that represented businesses in the students' neighborhoods that students' parents indicated they had visited in the last six months.

Using a multiple-probe design across sets of logos, both maintenance and generalization of students' logo recognition skills after intervention were assessed. After intervention, all students were able to successfully identify all logos and name a product found in each of the businesses represented by the logos. Students maintained these skills across the intervention and generalized them when out in the community during two generalization probes.

Further, several descriptive studies have depicted the outcomes of immersing young children with disabilities in a print-rich environment. Cooley and Cooley (1994), for example, described the use of a print-rich environment combined with active participation in multiple literacy activities on the literacy skills of elementary school students with a range of disabilities, including four students with ASD. The teacher in this self-contained special education classroom put numerous literacy materials and texts (e.g., poems, wall charts, pictures, labels on objects, students' literacy work) up around the room. Further, he embedded literacy experiences across the school day in both structured (e.g., shared reading) and unstructured ways (e.g., opportunities to interact with books during free-choice time). In addition, he included literacy-based music activities and a variety of literacy centers in the classroom as well as providing individual and small-group instruction in literacy.

The researchers used videotaped and anecdotal observations to document student progress. Results indicated that students' engagement in and enjoyment of literacy activities increased, their knowledge about print improved, and their language skills increased. For some students, conventional reading skills developed or improved (e.g., ability to decode unfamiliar words, acquisition of sight words).

Katims (1991) examined the effect of immersion in a literacy-rich environment on the early literacy skills of 14 preschool children with a range of disabilities, comparing their performance on several early literacy measures to that of 10 children in a control group. Children in the literacy-rich environment received daily active and engaging storybook readings and opportunities to participate in writing activities using a variety of materials. They were also allowed free access to a wide range of children's books (e.g., picture books, poems, alphabet books).

At the end of the school year, the mean gain scores on Clay's Concepts About Print Test (1979) of the children in the experimental group were significantly higher than those of children in the control group. Coding of the children's interactions with books across the year also showed that the children in the experimental group demonstrated more sophisticated book handling skills at the end of the school year.

Koppenhaver and Erickson (2003) described the effect of a five-month emergent literacy intervention on three, 3-year-old children with ASD who had severe communication disorders and did not use speech to communicate. After collecting baseline measures (i.e., direct observation of the children's participation in literacy activities, interviews with the classroom teachers and support staff, and review of IEPs and lesson plans), the researchers brought a broad assortment of literacy materials into the classroom and structured opportunities for the children to explore these reading and writing materials across the school day using existing classroom routines and adding time for the children to explore materials independently. They encouraged the children to explore the materials and then followed the children's lead to model a conventional literacy skill or extend a literacy skill a child was already using. To create a print-rich setting, they labeled items in the room with word cards and added words to picture symbol cards.

As a result of the intervention, all three children demonstrated increased engagement in literacy activities and displayed new early literacy skills. In addition, some of the children acquired conventional reading skills, such as verbally identifying letter names. The researchers concluded that based on these outcomes, it seems clear that young children with ASD who have significant communication challenges can benefit from a literacy-rich environment and instructional strategies that in many ways are similar to high-quality literacy instruction for typically developing children.

Summary

Although additional research is needed, evidence from the few existing studies suggests that immersion in a print-rich environment that offers repeated opportunities for active engagement in meaningful literacy activities can facilitate acquisition of early literacy skills in children with ASD. In fact, experts have recommended that children with significant disabilities, including those with ASD, have access to high-quality early literacy instruction in a print-rich environment, since positive outcomes have been found with typically developing children (de Valenzuela & Tracey, 2007; Lanter & Watson, 2008).

No two children are exactly alike; however, some of the general learning characteristics of individuals with ASD seem to be a good match for instruction within a print-rich environment. Specifically, many children with ASD are strong visual learners. Meaningful text, graphics, and pictures in the classroom can provide the visual cues and support these children need to develop deeper understanding of the forms and functions of written language.

Using familiar materials for literacy instruction, such as environmental print, can also be an effective approach for these learners, because these recognizable materials provide a meaningful context for learning an abstract skill (e.g., learning that letters represent sounds). Although not referring specifically to individuals with ASD, Reutzel et al. (2003) stated that "using environmental print to teach children to read may not only help them learn to read but may form a bridge from the known to the new that helps them more readily involve the entire contents of their knowledge of printed language and word analysis strategies to read in a variety of new situations and contexts" (p. 160).

Kluth and Chandler-Olcott (2008) illustrated this point. They described a student with ASD whose favorite reading material was cereal boxes. His wise teacher incorporated these high-interest materials into his daily instruction and was successful in broadening and expanding his literacy skills and knowledge.

Creating classroom environments in which literacy is a part of all aspects of the daily routines is another way to assist students with ASD in understanding the purposes of literacy and the way in which written and oral language are related. Doing so allows children to experience first-hand how print and other literacy materials and activities convey meaning and provide opportunities for communication.

Setting up Print-Rich Environments: General Considerations

This section discusses how to carefully incorporate print into the classroom environment to meet the specific needs of students with ASD.

Classroom Structure

When creating a print-rich environment for students with ASD, it is important to first establish a classroom environment that is conducive to learning. Classroom environments that best support children with ASD include a variety of visual supports, such as visual schedules and augmentative/alternative communication (AAC) systems to allow for easy communication across the child's school environment.

Students with ASD also benefit from classrooms that are visually salient; that is, areas of the classroom have clearly defined boundaries and support natural transitions from one activity to another. An example would be setting up the entrance area of the room so that the natural progression of events from entering the room, walking in, hanging jacket and backpack up, checking schedule, and transitioning to the next activity, is supported by the physical arrangement of the room.

In addition, visually salient classrooms have specifically designated areas for different activities, which allow the students to better anticipate what activity is going to occur (Kluth, 2003). Students with ASD also benefit from classrooms where materials, toys, areas, and other classroom items the student may need to access or want to access are clearly labeled, and easily accessible during daily routines.

By implementing these strategies, teachers are helping to create print-rich environments that also support the unique learning needs of children with ASD. Teachers must be careful to balance the importance of having a print-rich environment with the specific learning needs of their students with ASD. Specifically, these students can become overwhelmed if visual supports are not carefully designed and delimited.

Incorporating Print Into the Classroom Structure

Once the learning environment is set up to support students with ASD, incorporating print throughout the classroom can be easily achieved. One of the simpler ways to do so is to label materials, toys, areas of the room, and activities throughout the classroom. When labeling materials, it is important to consider the individual students who will be accessing them. Students with ASD are typically considered strong visual learners, thus incorporating pictorial labels such as pictures or symbols in addition to written labels provides additional information for them (Downing, 2005).

When using pictures or symbols to label materials, toys, activities, and areas of the room, it is important to consider the communication systems being used by students in the class – if possible, use the same picture or symbol set the student uses. If more than one picture or symbol set is used within the classroom, more than one system may be used to label.

Another option for labeling the environment is to provide tactile labels (Downing, 2005). Tactile labels can provide additional support for students who need more concrete labels to establish meaning. By pairing written and visual labels (see Figure 6.3) throughout the classroom environment, we are not only building print-rich environments, we support and expand students' communicative abilities.

Figure 6.3. Pictorial and written labels.

Schedules and Other Communication Systems

The classroom structure can also support the development of print-rich environments through the use of visual schedules and AAC systems and devices. Visual schedules provide students support in anticipating the events of the day and changes in typically occurring routines. They also offer an additional opportunity to label the room and activities and incorporate print into the classroom.

When creating visual schedules, it is important to consider individual student skill levels to ensure that the visual schedule is meaningful (see Figure 6.4).

Figure 6.4. Examples of visual schedules.

Augmentative and alternative communication systems and devices provide another opportunity to build a print-rich learning environment while also enhancing communication. One way of building communication systems into the classroom environment is to provide students with choice boards. Choice boards can provide choices for particular activities or areas of the classroom or school environment. For example, a choice board may be used in the reading area for students to select books that are no longer displayed but are of high interest to the students. Choice boards offer another effective means of labeling the classroom and increasing communication opportunities and abilities within the student's school day.

Technology to Increase Access to Print in the Classroom Environment

We recommend providing low-, medium-, and high-technology options to enhance student access literacy in the classroom. Low-technology strategies could include communication/ schedule boards using pictures or photos, pencil grips, word walls, modifying text size, spacing, and color, labels, and choice boards. Medium-technology strategies could include adapted paper and books, electronic books, voice-output devices, digital recorders, switches, and text readers. High-technology strategies might be provided by a computer-based AAC system, voice-recognition software, multimedia software, and portable word processor. See Foley and Staples (2007) for a more extensive discussion of the use of assistive technology to support literacy development in general.

Visual Modifications

It is important to remember that each student with ASD is an individual and may require different modifications to his/her learning environment. One area that impacts many students with ASD is sensory sensitivity. Students may be sensitive to colors, textures, auditory input (talking, singing, loud noises), visual input (lights, computer screens, background color of materials), and particular materials (glue, markers, paint) (Kluth & Chandler-Olcott, 2008).

Examples of modifying the classroom to incorporate sensory sensitivity include printing pictures, symbols, or words on a background other than white, using a material other than Velcro to make visual schedules, placing books that contain pictures a child finds aversive in a safe area where other students can access them but the child does not have to see them, scanning books into the computer to create a computer-based classroom library (if a student finds the feel of paper aversive), or placing a sheet/paper over the word wall during certain activities (for students who may be too distracted by it to engage in another classroom activity).

While it is necessary to provide modifications to accommodate for some students' sensory needs, it is also necessary to provide modifications that build on students' strengths. This may include pairing a picture with the words on the word wall, making an interactive word wall where students can match words, pictures, or symbols, placing books used in classroom instruction in the class library so students can continue to access them, visually modifying books in the class library so students can engage with adults and peers with a book, or providing access to computer-based "sight word walls." Table 6.1 offers a convenient worksheet for developing strengths-based modifications.

Assessing Areas of Student Strength

Find out as much as you can about the strengths and interests of your students from family, peers, and previous teachers, as well as your own observations. These strengths and interests can become an important tool in planning effective print-rich environments for students with ASD. Using the Strengths-Based Modifications Worksheet can also be an effective strategy to connect literacy at school and home.

Table 6.1
Strengths-Based Modifications Worksheet

Student: _____ Teacher(s): _____ Date: _____

Strengths and Interests: _____

_____

_____

_____

Student Strength/Interest	Literacy Focus	Environmental Modifications
Strong visual learner	Sight words	Pair a picture with the word on the word wall
Love of books	Fluency	Provide access to book choice board

Setting up Print-Rich Environments: Specific Instructional Strategies

When teachers develop print-rich classrooms, the environment becomes a critical tool that can be used to support and implement literacy instruction.

Reading the Room

The importance of pictorial, tactile, and written labeling of the classroom was described earlier. Such labels can form the basis for a sight word program. Typical sight word programs are based on frequently used word lists that consist of words that may be abstract or have no meaning to a student with ASD. The advantage of using words of objects and people found in the classroom environment is that they are connected to a concrete object that holds meaning and connects to prior knowledge for the student.

Reading the room can be used for both incidental and direct instruction. The hope is that the students will see the sight words with high frequency and come to associate them with the object. The words can then be incorporated into direct instruction in a number of ways. For example, the doors, desks, sink, window, and chairs in the room can be labeled. Written, pictorial, and tactile labels can be used as appropriate for students.

Here are some ideas for teaching and assessing sight word acquisition and expand their use into connected text:

- Place Velcro or a library pocket next to each classroom label. The student can now match a set of classroom sight words to the items labeled in the room. This has the advantage of building movement into the task. You also have a clear assessment of how many words were matched correctly. Students can progress to reading and possibly spelling the words.

- Make folder tasks where the student matches classroom sight words to written, tactile, or pictorial cues. This can also serve as an assessment.

- Ask the student to read the sight word labels and progress to reading the sight words away from the concrete object. Keep a running tally of which words the student has acquired.

- Make sentence strips that require one of the classroom sight words to complete the sentence. For example, "I look out of the _____."

- Move beyond sight words into connected text. This may be a challenge because not many books use your classroom's sight words! One great idea we got from one of our students is to make a class book using the classroom sight words in the story. Here is a sample.

Where Is the Silly Spider?

Is the spider in the sink?
No the spider is not in the sink.
Is the spider on the door?
No, the spider is not on the door.
Is the spider looking out of the window?
No, the spider is not looking out of the window.
Is the spider on my desk?
No, the spider is not on my desk.
Is the spider on the chair?
No the spider is not on the chair.
Look under the chair.
Yes, here is the silly spider!

This idea can be implemented in many ways to meet the individual needs of your students. For example, the book may be written and illustrated as a language experience story or be written by the teacher. Each sentence could be one page of a book. A cheap, easy, and effective way to make classroom books is to put each page in a plastic sheet protector and use book rings to connect the pages. Prior to reading the story, the teacher could hide a plastic or plush spider under the chair and the students could take turns looking for the spider as each page is read aloud or silently. This enables teachers to observe whether the student comprehends the story – this is especially important for students who struggle with demonstrating comprehension through verbal language. With repeated readings, the students could learn to read part of or the whole story themselves. A connection between home and school can be made by encouraging students to take the book home and read it to their families.

A digital camera is a great tool and can be used to photograph people and objects in the room, school, home, and community. The photographs can then be labeled, and sentences and stories can be written about them. We recommend expanding these ideas to incorporate the wider school, community, and home as appropriate.

Environmental Print Ideas

The concept of print richness should not be confined to the classroom or the school environment. Environmental print consists of high-frequency print found in school, home, and community environments. Naturally occurring environmental print is a great source of literacy instruction that is supported by the research (Alberto et al., 2007; Aldridge & Rust, 1987). Environmental print may include common signs (e.g., stop, exit), business signs (e.g., K-Mart, Wendy's), and products (e.g., Coke, Pepsi, Cheerios, Starburst).

Using environmental print builds upon students' prior knowledge about the world around them and their ability to associate symbols consistently with an object. The use of environmental print has many advantages, as outlined in Table 6.2.

Table 6.2
Advantages of Environmental Print

- By definition, environmental print builds on prior knowledge because the print is found in the student's own environment and is familiar.

- Environmental print connects words to concrete objects for students who might have difficulty with words out of context.

- Environmental print uses multiple senses, including olfactory and gustatory.

- Environmental print has meaning for students and connects with home and personal interests.

- Environmental print is highly motivating and can be intrinsically rewarding. Often teachers tell us a student is not capable of learning literacy skills but then relate how that same student is able to tell the difference between Coke and Dr. Pepper.

- Environmental print can form the basis for instruction that addresses all areas of reading.

- Environmental print is age appropriate.

- Environmental print encompasses cultural and linguistic diversity.

- Environmental print is cheap! Bringing print from home can be a homework assignment for the students and a lesson in recycling.

Environmental print can be incorporated into all areas of reading instruction – oral language, phonemic awareness, phonics, vocabulary, comprehension, and writing. Table 6.3 lists ideas for literacy instruction in these areas.

Table 6.3

Literacy Instruction in Reading

- Sharing environmental print with classmates through oral language, sign, or AAC device
- Including environmental print words on the word wall
- Classifying and sorting environmental print words (e.g., drinks, foods, toys)
- Making a poster out of words beginning with certain letters or sounds
- Putting environmental print words on flashcards and teaching them as sight words
- Making sentences out of environmental print words
- Finishing sentences with environment print words (e.g., I like to drink Coke)
- Matching environmental print to flashcards of the same word
- Cutting up the individual letters in environmental print and asking the student to put them back in order
- Making word families out of the letters in environmental print
- Making an alphabet chart or alphabet book with an environmental print word for each letter
- Using environmental print to help with instructions for class activities such as cooking
- Making individual or class books using environmental print

Think about ways in which environmental print can have potential beyond the classroom and be used in the wider school environment, home, and the community. For example, by teaching common signs such as stop, poison, and exit, you are not only increasing students' vocabulary but also helping to make them become safer and more independent.

Diversity Enhances the Classroom Environment

What better way to make sure you are respecting diversity in your classroom than to encourage students to share environmental print from their home and community? By using this type of print as part of your classroom environment, you are providing a concrete connection between home, school, and community. This will enable you to learn more about your students and their unique background. It will also enhance learning in the classroom by building on your students' prior knowledge. Today's classrooms are increasingly diverse, and we encourage you to approach this as an opportunity for learning – not as a problem!

Word Walls

Word walls (see Figure 6.5) are a common feature of elementary classrooms. Word walls are a systematically organized collection of words displayed in large letters on a wall (e.g., on a shower curtain, a rolling cabinet, folding cardboard, or even individual word walls for each student). They are designed to promote group learning and provide visual support for targeted vocabulary. Sight words from reading the room and environmental print can be incorporated into word walls. In addition to supporting sight word, phonemic, and vocabulary instruction, word walls can also target specific content areas such as science or social studies. One way that word walls can be incorporated into literacy instruction is to introduce a new word wall word every day. As a group, students can see the word, say the word, chant the word (i.e., *snap, clap, stomp*), and write the word.

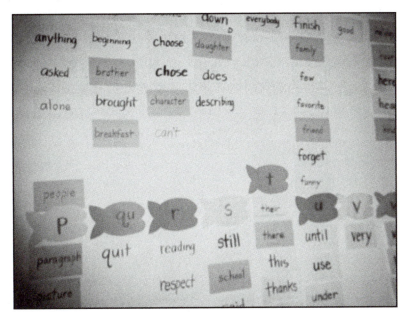

Figure 6.5. Word wall.

Conclusion

A print-rich environment is characterized by easy access to the printed word in multiple formats and genres together with ways to engage actively with the printed word. Every classroom should have plenty of books, magazines, posters, and other printed material at various reading levels. Every classroom should also have a variety of literacy tools, including computers and other technology, so that students can make and interact with printed materials.

Teachers must be thoughtful about the print in their classrooms and organize the classroom environment so students know how to access and use the materials (Copeland & Keefe, 2007; Reutzel & Cooter, 2006). This may require direct instruction about how to use specific technology or learning centers. Teachers also need to think about ways in which the print in the classroom can reinforce IEP goals and expose students to additional literacy in meaningful ways. Finally, print-rich environments have the potential to create connections between literacy in school and home environments.

Like any student, students with ASD require access to literacy opportunities (Kluth & Chandler-Olcott, 2008). However, it is important to remember that for students with ASD to engage in meaningful learning within a print-rich environment, it may be necessary to provide them with individualized modifications and visual supports such as those discussed in this chapter.

Finally, when creating a print-rich environment for students with ASD, always remember to make it brain-friendly, functional, meaningful, motivating, and fun. By setting up a learning environment that is easy to access and engaging, you enable students to utilize the classroom tools around them to build functional and meaningful literacy skills.

Chapter Highlights

- Recent advances in imaging technologies are providing direction to educators who want to provide environments that are "brain friendly."

- One of the most useful frameworks for describing the brain and learning relevant to print-rich classrooms is the information processing model.

- One of the challenges for educators is to consider potential deficits and differences in students' sensory processing and integration.

- In order to develop print-rich classroom environments, the following aspects should be considered: novelty, intensity, emotion, use of images and graphics, and connecting to prior learning.

- A literacy-rich environment displays text, pictures, and graphics that are meaningful to the children in the given setting.

- Literacy development begins well before children start school, and early interaction with literacy-rich environments facilitates the development of literacy skills.

- Environmental print refers to the print that is found all around us in our homes and communities. Environmental print may include common signs, business signs, and commercial products.

- Environmental environment print builds on prior knowledge because the print is found in the student's own environment and is familiar.

- Few studies have examined the influence of print-rich environments on the literacy skill development of students with disabilities. Children with disabilities generally have fewer opportunities to engage in early literacy activities and less exposure to print-rich environments than their typically developing peers.

- Young children with ASD who have significant communication challenges can benefit from a literacy-rich environment and instructional strategies.

- Many children with ASD are strong visual learners. Meaningful text, graphics, and pictures in the classroom can provide the visual cues and support these children need to develop deeper understandings of the forms and functions of the written language.

- When creating a print-rich environment for students with ASD, it is important to first establish a classroom environment that is conducive to learning for children with ASD.

- While modifications to accommodate for some students' sensory needs are necessary, it is also necessary to provide modifications that build on student strengths.

- Word walls are a common feature in elementary classes; they are a systematically organized collection of words.

- A print-rich environment is characterized by easy access to the printed word in multiple formats and genres, together with ways to engage actively with the printed word.

- Teachers must be thoughtful about the print in their classrooms, and organize the classroom environment so students get direct instruction on how to access and use classroom materials.

- When creating a print-rich environment for students with ASD, it is important to remember to make it brain friendly, functional, meaningful, motivating, and fun.

Chapter Review Questions

1. In what ways might a literacy-rich environment for students with ASD differ from literacy-rich environments for typically developing students?

2. In what ways might a literacy-rich environment for students with ASD be similar to literacy-rich environments for typically developing students?

3. Write a sample paragraph for your class newsletter explaining to families why a print-rich environment is so important for students with ASD.

4. Give three examples of how can you set up the classroom environment so it supports students' ability to learn specific literacy skills.

5. Write a lesson plan that incorporates environmental print to teach a targeted literacy skill.

References

Alberto, P. A., Fredrick, L., Hughes, M., McIntosh, L., & Cihak, D. (2007). Components of visual literacy: Teaching logos. *Focus on Autism and Other Developmental Disabilities, 22,* 234-243.

Aldridge, J. T., & Rust, D. (1987). A beginning reading strategy. *Academic Therapy, 22, 323-326.*

Brinkerhoff, J. D., & Keefe, E. B. (2007). Creating rich literacy learning environments for all students. In S. R. Copeland & E. B. Keefe (Eds.), *Effective literacy instruction for individuals with moderate or severe disabilities* (pp. 23-40). Baltimore: Paul H. Brookes.

Clay, M. M. (1979). *The early detection of reading difficulties.* Auckland, New Zealand: Heinemann Educational Books.

Cooley, N., & Cooley, J. (1994). Great expectations: Using an early childhood whole language curriculum to teach 6- through 11-year-old students in a TMI classroom. *Focus on Autistic Behavior, 9*(1), 1-18.

Copeland, S. C., & Keefe, E. B. (Eds.). (2007). *Effective literacy instruction for individuals with moderate or severe disabilities.* Baltimore: Paul H. Brookes.

de Valenzuela, J. S., & Tracey, M. M. (2007). The role of language and communication as a basis for literacy. In S. R. Copeland & E. B. Keefe (Eds.), *Effective literacy instruction for individuals with moderate or severe disabilities* (pp. 23-40). Baltimore: Paul H. Brookes.

Downing, J. E. (2005). *Teaching literacy to students with significant disabilities.* Thousand Oaks, CA: Corwin Press.

Foley, B. E., & Staples, A. (2007). Supporting literacy development with assistive technology. In S. R. Copeland & E. B. Keefe (Eds.), *Effective literacy instruction for individuals with moderate or severe disabilities* (pp. 127-148). Baltimore: Paul H. Brookes.

Gagne, R. M., & Driscol, M. P. (1988). *Essentials of learning for instruction* (2nd ed.). Englewood Cliffs, NJ: Prentice Hall.

Heflin, L. J., & Alaimo, D. F. (2007). *Students with autism spectrum disorder.* Upper Saddle River, NJ: Pearson.

Katims, D. S. (1991). Emergent literacy in early childhood special education: Curriculum and instruction. *Topics in Early Childhood Special Education, 11,* 69-84.

Katims, D. S. (1994). Emergence of literacy in preschool children with disabilities. *Learning Disability Quarterly, 17,* 100-111.

Kluth, P. (2003). *"You're going to love this kid!": Teaching students with autism in the inclusive classroom.* Baltimore: Paul H. Brookes.

Kluth, P., & Chandler-Olcott, K. (2008). *"A land we can share": Teaching literacy to students with autism.* Baltimore: Paul H. Brookes.

Kluth, P., & Schwarz, P. (2008). *"Just give him the whale!"* Baltimore: Paul H. Brookes.

Koppenhaver, D. A., & Erickson, K. A. (2003). Natural emergent literacy supports for preschoolers with autism and severe communication impairments. *Topics in Language Disorders, 23,* 283-292.

Kuby, P., & Aldridge, J. (2004). The impact of environmental print instruction on early reading ability. *Journal of Instructional Psychology, 31,* 106-114.

Kuby, P., Aldridge, J., & Snyder, S. (1994). Developmental progression of environmental print recognition in kindergarten children. *Reading Psychology, 15,* 1-9.

Kuby, P., Goodstadt-Killoran, I., Aldridge, J., & Kirkland, L. (1999). A review of research on environmental print. *Journal of Instructional Psychology, 26,* 173-182.

Lanter, E., & Watson, L. R. (2008). Promoting literacy in students with ASD: The basics for the SLP. *Language, Speech, and Hearing Services in the Schools, 39*, 33-43.

Masonheimer, P. E., Drum, P. A., & Ehri, L. C. (1984). Does environmental print identification lead children into word reading? *Journal of Reading Behavior, 16*, 257-271.

Mirenda, P. (2003). "He's not really a reader . . ." Perspectives on supporting literacy development in individuals with autism. *Topics in Language Disorders, 23*, 21-282.

Neuman, S. B. (2004). The effect of print-rich classroom environments on early literacy growth. *The Reading Teacher, 58*, 89-91.

Reutzel, D. R., & Cooter, R. B. (2006). *Strategies for reading assessment and instruction* (3rd ed.). Upper Saddle River, NJ: Merrill Prentice Hall.

Reutzel, D. R., Fawson, P. C., Young, J. R., Morrison, T. G., & Wilcox, B. (2003). Reading environmental print: What is the role of concepts about print in discriminating young readers' responses? *Reading Psychology, 24*, 123-162.

Roskos, K., & Neuman, S. B. (2002). Environment and its influences for early literacy teaching and learning. In S. B. Neuman & D. K. Dickinson (Eds.), *Handbook of early literacy research* (pp. 281-292). New York: Guilford Press.

Weikle, B., & Haddian, A. (2004). Literacy, development and disabilities: Are we moving in the right direction? *Early Child Development and Care, 174*, 651-666.

Recommended Web Sites

- http://www.pre-kpages.com/environmental_print.html: Mrs. Levin's PreK Pages: Environmental Print. This web page features basic information about using environmental print in the early literacy classroom. It includes descriptions of literacy activities using environmental print as well as links to additional relevant resources.

- http://www.sharonmacdonald.com/environmental-print.aspx: Sharon's McDonald.com. This web page contains dozens of ideas for using environmental print in literacy instruction, including downloadable pictures of activities.

- http://www.starfall.com: Starfall is a web site with multiple early reading instruction resources. Many of the resources are free (e.g., activities, leveled readers, even short videos).

- http://www.mrsperkins.com/: Mrs. Perkin's Dolch Words web site features numerous ideas for teaching Dolch sight words as well as links to downloadable materials.

- http://www.readinga-z.com/: ReadingA-Z is a subscription-based web site that features hundreds of reading activities and materials. Topics cover all essential components of reading instruction and more.

Chapter 7
Exemplary and Balanced Literacy Instruction

Lesley Mandel Morrow, Ph.D., Rutgers, The State University of New Jersey

Christina Carnahan, Ph.D., University of Cincinnati

Learning Objectives

After reading this chapter, the learner should be able to:

- Describe balanced literacy instruction

- Describe the elements of balanced literacy instruction

- Discuss the implications of balanced literacy for instructing students with ASD

- Define differentiated instruction

- Write a plan for a balanced literacy day

When asked to talk about her philosophy of literacy instruction, Ms. Jonas said:

"Our classroom encourages students to function as a community of learners. The atmosphere is one of acceptance of differences in cultures, ability levels, and abilities. I encourage children to be academic risk-takers; their ideas are shared and valued. Students are given and accept responsibility for their learning and contribute as members of a family. In our classroom all students are viewed as capable learners who progress at their own developmental level.

As much as possible, I devote extended, uninterrupted periods to language arts instruction. Literacy instruction in my classroom involves integrating language arts into content-area themes. Skills are taught within a meaningful context and in an explicit manner, when necessary. I use assessment-guided instruction. Therefore, I meet in small groups and teach based on the specific needs of the children. I teach to learning style and ability as well. This works for my students if I provide them with a positive and supportive attitude. I guess I want to provide what has been referred to as a comprehensive or balanced approach to literacy instruction."

What Is Balanced Literacy Instruction?

Over the years, literacy development has moved in many directions – from a constructivist, open-ended approach in which students generate their own knowledge to a very direct approach with behavioral objectives for students to achieve. A position statement by the International Reading Association (IRA) entitled *Using Multiple Methods of Beginning Reading Instruction* (1999) suggests that no method or combination of methods can teach children to read. Exemplary teachers teach children to read by knowing the social, emotional, physical, and intellectual status of their students. Exemplary teachers know how to select from the many methods of reading instruction to meet the individual needs of students and then develop a comprehensive plan for teaching reading.

This perspective on literacy instruction is referred to as a balanced approach. A balanced perspective includes careful selection from the best theories available and using different learning strategies to match the learning styles of individual children. Skill-based explicit instruction and holistic/constructivist ideas such as problem-solving activities complement each other in this model. Explicit teaching strategies often serve as the foundation for constructivist activities (Pressley, 1998). One does not preclude the other.

A balanced perspective is neither a random combination nor an orderly sequence of strategies. Rather, teachers use assessment data to select strategies from different learning theories to provide appropriate instruction to meet the needs of each individual learner. To ensure instruction meets the varied reading and writing levels of students, teachers spend considerable time assessing students using formal and informal measures, including daily informal assessments. For example, in September, January, and June, teachers might formally assess students' knowledge about phonics, the ability to read sight words, and their reading comprehension, fluency, and writing ability. They use the results of such assessment to identify individual learning needs and guide instruction. Teachers then do running records for each child. Running records help identify the types of errors children make, decoding strategies they use, and their comprehension and reading levels. A comparison between current and previous running records indicates student progress or lack thereof. In addition, anecdotal notes provide insight about student behavior, indicating both achievement and challenges.

Table 7.1 offers general assessment guidelines for use within a balanced literacy approach. The balanced approach is thoughtful, student centered, focused on the individual learner rather than the latest trends in literacy instruction.

Table 7.1
Assessment Guides – Balanced Literacy Instruction

The following general guidelines support the assessment process:

- Assess students using a variety of tools, including observation and evaluation, rather than relying on one assessment approach. Include observations of children engaged in authentic daily performance samples of classroom reading and writing tasks.

- Use formal standards and standardized tests as one means of assessment.

- Use assessment to drive instruction. Assessments should be based on curriculum goals, state standards, and IEPs.

- Make sure assessment is ongoing and continuous throughout the year.

- Design assessments to meet students' cultural diversity, language, and learning needs.

- Remember that assessment is collaborative and includes the active participation from children, parents, teachers, and related service professionals.

Balanced instruction is grounded in a rich model of literacy learning that encompasses both the elegance and complexity of reading and language arts processes (Morrow, 2005). Such a model acknowledges the importance of both the form (phonics, mechanics, etc.) and the function (comprehension, purpose, meaning) of the literacy processes, and recognizes that learning occurs most effectively in a whole-part-whole context. A balanced literacy program is characterized by meaningful literacy activities that provide children with both the skill and motivation to become proficient and lifelong literacy learners. Specifically, balanced program literacy programs include:

- Daily reading, writing, listening, speaking, spelling, and viewing activities
- Literacy instruction that occurs within a block of uninterrupted time
- Instruction embedded across the school day. Literacy instruction occurs during social studies, music, art, science, math, etc.
- Thematic instruction based on student interests (theme-based instruction increases student motivation and interest in reading and writing activities)

Special Considerations for Students With Autism Spectrum Disorders

For students with autism spectrum disorders (ASD), balanced, meaning-centered instruction is especially important. Previous chapters have discussed the characteristics of learners with ASD in the context of reading. In this chapter, a focus on the cognitive style, especially differences in attention, meaning making, motivation, and generalization, helps highlight the importance of contextualized, balanced instruction.

Motivation/interest. Students with ASD often appear unmotivated or uninterested in traditional learning activities, especially when presented with skills taught in isolation (Koegel, Koegel, Harrower, & Carter, 1999; Mesibov, Shea, & Schopler, 2005). These students have difficulty identifying and connecting information or experiences to make meaning (Happé & Frith, 2006; for additional discussion see Carnahan & Williamson, this text, Chapter 1). Even when students with ASD acquire specific skills or concepts, they often have difficulty generalizing skills from one setting or environment to another (Hume & Odom, 2007; Koegel et al.).

Many teachers feel frustrated when students with ASD fail to learn discrete skills such as letter naming, letter-sound correspondence, or writing individual letters. However, as mentioned, a whole-part-whole model helps set the context and purpose for learning new skills. Like most learners, students with ASD need to understand the purpose for learning. They need to understand the function of letters, both for writing and reading. Once students have experiences with words, sentences, and meaningful stories, they may demonstrate increased attention to individual letters and sounds. Identifying a particular theme or special interest and using that interest to guide instruction increases the likelihood that the student will demonstrate independent engagement and attention to learning activities (Boyd, Conroy, Mancil, Nakao, & Alter, 2007; Hume & Odom, 2007; Mesibov et al., 2005).

Instructional group. Designing balanced literacy programs also includes attention to instructional grouping and material selection. Such instruction incorporates whole-group, small-group, and one-to-one teaching. Well-structured centers (e.g., reading) provide opportunities for independent and social learning. During whole-group instruction, teachers set the thematic unit and introduce and teach new concepts. Priming is an effective strategy for preparing students with ASD to participate in these groups (Hume, this text, Chapter 3). If students are going to choose an aspect of the theme to explore, the student(s) with ASD may identify a specific topic in advance. This provides opportunities to link to the individual's special interests, make connections to relevant background knowledge, and connect to previous experiences or texts, all crucial for building comprehension (Mirenda, 2003).

Many students with ASD also need instruction in small-group or one-on-one settings because of difficulties with change, transition, as well as attention. This is especially true when presented with new or challenging skills and content. For example, higher-functioning students may learn comprehension strategies (e.g., inference, prediction) in a small group to expose or prime them for whole-group instruction. A student with more complex communication needs may receive individualized vocabulary instruction in a one-on-one setting and then practice the new vocabulary during small-group activities. All students have opportunities to independently practice their new skills in well-organized stations and in small groups.

Materials selection. When planning balanced instruction, teachers ensure that students have access to a variety of well-organized materials that support literacy development. Using the principles of universal design for learning, teachers incorporate materials to meet the needs of each child, promote uniqueness rather than conformity, and actively engage all students in the learning process (Council for Exceptional Children [CEC], 2005).

There are materials for reading and writing that include narrative and informational texts, instructional texts, pencil and paper, technology, and manipulatives. The teacher uses a systematic, explicit curriculum, including differentiated tasks or activities that allow students to demonstrate their knowledge in many different ways. These differentiated activities are scaffolded to meet the individualized needs of all students. That is, students receive support that allows them to complete activities they would not be able to accomplish on their own. In the daily routine, the teacher includes shared reading and writing, guided reading and writing for skill development, oral and silent reading and writing, independent reading and writing, collaborative reading and writing, content-area reading and writing, and performance of reading and writing.

When choosing materials, it is important to pay special attention to the social communication and cognitive style demonstrated by students with ASD. Engagement is one important aspect of social communication that influences learning. Classrooms are inherently busy social, verbal places. For students with ASD, the verbal language and social interactions can be overwhelming. These students often demonstrate levels of engagement that are qualitatively and quantitatively different from those of their peers (Mundy & Burnette, 2005), which in turn influence their learning.

Related to engagement is the issue of attention. Students with ASD attend to a limited number of environmental cues at one time. For example, they may attend to specific parts of a situation without regard for the context within which the situation occurs (Happé & Frith, 2006; Quill, 2000). Such focus on details makes it difficult for students with ASD to understand the big picture or attend to details deemed important by others.

Similar to the social aspects of the classroom, traditionally designed learning activities may be overwhelming to students with ASD (Mesibov et al., 2005). For example, handing a student with ASD a blank graphic organizer or an entire book chapter to read, or setting him free in a writing center without specific guidelines could cause tremendous challenges. The student may feel overwhelmed and not know where to begin, which often results in the student shutting down with little or no learning accomplished. It is crucial to remember that the student is not lazy or defiant. Rather, she needs external support to accomplish tasks. A better approach is to expect independent performance after instruction.

Given their inherent challenges with expressive communication, it is not surprising that many students with ASD are not able to communicate their learning through traditional paper-pencil tasks or verbal reports. Integrating technology is not just good practice (CEC, 2005), it also supports the learning and active participation of students with ASD in educational settings (Gal et al., 2009). Table 7.2 lists a variety of technology resources that support students with ASD as they engage in literacy activities.

Table 7.2

Technology and Online Resources

An abundance of resources are available to support a balanced approach to quality literacy instruction. The following web sites offer software and hardware for increasing student participation in literacy experiences:

- Intellitools – Software and hardware (e.g., adapted keyboard) to help students actively engage in a variety of learning activities. http://www.intellitools.com/

- Mayer-Johnson Company – Offers software such as Boardmaker and Speaking Dynamically Pro. http://www.mayer-johnson.com/

- Don Johnston Write Out Loud – Talking word processor. http://www.donjohnston.com/products/write_outloud/index.html

- Crick Software – Software (e.g., Clicker 5) to support both reading and writing for students with significant communication challenges. http://www.cricksoft.com/us/default.asp

The following web sites provide additional information to support instructional design:

- Center for Applied Special Technology – Offers an overview and resources related to universal design for learning. http://www.cast.org/index.html

- International Reading Association – Offers lessons and web resources in reading and language arts instruction. http://readwritethink.org/

In summary, well-organized learning materials support the active engagement and meaningful learning and participation of students with ASD (Aspy & Grossman, 2007). Each child's strengths, needs, and interests must guide the instructional planning process. Table 7.3 presents considerations that are key to designing instructional materials.

Table 7.3

Key Considerations for Designing Instructional Materials

1. Attend to the organization and structure of materials. Provide clear guidelines and structures to communicate expectations.
2. Use student interest. Gradually expand experiences to include a variety of topics.
3. Incorporate technology whenever possible. Provide students with alternate ways of learning and expressing their knowledge.
4. Address task demand considerations (Aspy & Grossman, 2007). If a student does not engage or seems to know more than he shows, carefully consider the instructional materials. The following questions may help in problem solving:
   a. Are the materials organized in a way the student can understand?
   b. Does the student need explicit instruction to use the materials?
   c. Has the student been taught the skills necessary for completing the activity?
   d. Do the materials align with the skills the student is to demonstrate?

When seeking the best way to teach, we often look for a silver bullet, the best program, or the latest trend. In 2000, the National Reading Panel Report (NRP) (National Institute of Child Health and Human Development, 2000) discussed research-based strategies that predict reading success. The NRP suggests teachers, not methods or programs, are the key for successful literacy development. In the following, we will look at exemplary teaching.

Exemplary Teaching as the Foundation of Balanced Instruction

Given the role educators play in literacy development, it is important to understand exemplary teaching. The research on exemplary teaching looks at effective practices, teacher behavior, and classroom dynamics, including student-teacher interactions, routines and schedules, environmental design, and classroom community (Coker, 1985; Duffy & Hoffman, 1999; Genishi, Ryan, Ochsner, & Yarnall, 2001; Haigh & Katterns, 1984; Roehler & Duffy, 1984; Shulman, 1986).

In an attempt to build a universal model of effective instruction, researchers in one large-scale study questioned students in grades K-12 about the characteristics of their influential literacy teachers (Ruddell, 1995; Ruddell & Harris, 1989; Ruddell & Kern, 1986). The results of the study indicated that influential teachers (a) motivate learners, (b) build strong affective relationships with students, (c) create excitement about content, (d) adjust instruction to meet individual needs, (e) create literacy-rich physical environments, and (f) have strong organizational and management skills (Ruddell).

Building on the work on effective teaching, investigators examined exemplary language arts instruction. The research shed light on how excellent teachers organized reading as well as writing and their instructional decision making (e.g., deciding how and what to teach, materials to use, environmental organization, and structuring social interactions to meet individual needs). Table 7.4 summarizes these studies (Metsala & Wharton-McDonald, 1997; Morrow, Tracey, Woo, & Pressley, 1999; Taylor, Pearson, & Clark, 2000). A synthesis of investigations about exemplary literacy practice in the elementary grades identified several common characteristics of excellent literacy instruction. Table 7.5 details the synthesis and the application to ASD.

Table 7.4
Research on Exemplary Teachers

Study	Participants	Data Collection	Findings
Taylor et al. (2000)	– 26 teachers in grades K-3 across the U.S.A.	– Five observations per teacher – Teacher interviews – Activity logs and written survey for each teacher	Effective teachers: – Focus on small-group instruction – Provide time for independent reading – Monitor on-task behavior – Provide explicit phonics instruction within the context of reading and writing activities – Ask high-level comprehension questions – Ask students to respond in writing to written text
Morrow et al. (1999)	– Six exemplary teachers from three different school districts	– 25 hours of observation per teacher – Teacher interviews	Effective teachers: – Design literacy-rich learning environments – Incorporate many different groupings, including whole group, small group, one on one, teacher directed, centers, and social interactions with adults and peers – Engage children on a daily basis in shared, guided, oral, silent, independent, collaborative, and performance reading and writing. – Offer regular writing, word analysis, and comprehension instruction – Consistently connect reading and writing instruction to content using themes – Use individual assessment as the basis of instruction – Design organized, well-managed, and predictable routines
Metsala et al. (1997)	– 89 K-3 teachers – 10 special education teachers	– Teacher interviews and surveys	Effective teachers: – Are "masterful" classroom managers – Attend to and manage time – Organize and structure learning materials – Manage student behavior with finesse

Table 7.5

What Do Exemplary Teachers Do?

Exemplary Teachers	Description	Application to ASD
1. Motivate learners and create excitement about learning	Teachers use student interests to identify themes or increase involvement in theme-based lessons. They consistently monitor students' engagement and literacy progress through data collection. They collect daily performance samples, observe and record behavior, conduct informal assessments such as running records, and administer standardized tests as well.	*Active engagement* is one of the strongest predictors of learning for students with ASD (Iovannone, Dunlap, Huber, & Kincaid, 2003; Koegel, Koegel, & McNerney, 2001). Students with ASD often lack the motivation or skill to engage in traditional learning activities (Hume & Odom, 2007; Koegel, Carter, & Koegel, 2003; Mesibov et al., 2005). However, when presented with learning materials that incorporate their special interests, they demonstrate increased attention, social engagement, independent initiation, and learning (Boyd et al., 2007; Mancil & Pearl, 2008; Vismara & Lyons, 2007). When instructing students with ASD, educators should collect information to understand the child's skills, strengths, needs, and interests and use the special interests to begin instruction (Carnahan & Borders, in press). Gradually, teachers can expand instruction to include new concepts, skills, and topics.
2. Build strong relationships	Excellent teachers are always building good relationships with students, especially during learning. Discussions expand student knowledge and allow children to do as much talking, if not more, than the teacher. These teachers create supportive, encouraging, and friendly atmospheres. Children in classrooms with excellent teachers understand that their questions and comments are both valuable and important. There are times for fun, jokes, and play.	According to the diagnostic criteria, social differences are inherent in ASD (American Psychiatric Association, 2000). These differences influence how students with ASD interact and build relationships with adults and peers. Additionally, social communication differences often result in challenging behavior in the classroom (Lord et al., 2005). Given these challenges, students with ASD may need explicit instruction in how to engage in social interactions around the classroom. Social behaviors that may need to be taught include turn taking, sharing, conversation skills (including listening), game playing, telling, giving and receiving compliments, etc. The key is to recognize that inappropriate behavior is often related to skill deficit or lack of understanding, not "acting out."

Table 7.5 (cont.)

Exemplary Teachers	Description	Application to ASD
3. Link instructional strategies to individual learning needs	These teachers teach to individual needs using a variety of instructional groupings. Frequent assessments allow them to design differentiated instruction (Tomlinson, 2000) and select appropriate materials and instructional strategies for each child.	The learning needs of students with ASD do not align with the teaching styles in most traditional classrooms (Carnahan, 2006; Mesibov et al., 2005). Traditional teaching methods often rely on verbal communication, a challenge for students with ASD. When information is well structured and incorporates a variety of visual supports, students with ASD are more likely to understand and demonstrate active and independent engagement. Understanding the unique learning needs of each individual and developing individualized instruction that meets these learning needs maximizes instruction time.
4. Engage in both explicit and holistic literacy instruction	Exemplary teachers clearly state the learning objectives. These teachers model explicitly the behavior they want students to acquire, provide guidance as students practice the skill, and design many opportunities for independent practice.	The whole-part-whole model described in this chapter helps set the context for teaching students with ASD. Many individuals with ASD demonstrate differences related to attention and memory. Consequently, many students with ASD need explicit instruction based on the principles of discrete trial instruction to learn new skills (National Research Council, 2001). However, they also need many opportunities to practice skills in natural settings (Weiss, 2005). With thoughtful planning, teachers can do the following: 1. Develop the instructional context before teaching. Help students make connections between prior knowledge and experience and new learning material. 2. Use group instruction whenever possible to support new content. See Maurice, Green, and Luce (1996) and Munk and Van Laarhoven (2008) for discussions of embedded instruction and group instruction strategies. 3. Use systematic one-on-one teaching strategies when necessary to teach new context. 4. Design integrated lessons where reading and writing are developed simultaneously around the topic. Link skills taught during one-on-one instruction to the natural environment and the theme or concept being addressed. Plan opportunities to practice and generalize new skills in many different settings. Reinforce key social, behavioral, and academic concepts in every facet of the student's day.

Table 7.5 (cont.)

Exemplary Teachers	Description	Application to ASD
5. Organize literacy-rich physical environments	Access to materials is crucial. Excellent teachers know how to supply interesting materials that are not expensive. They print materials from the Internet, collect free materials, buy materials at flea markets, and ask for donations.	Access to materials is crucial. However, for individuals with ASD too many materials can be overwhelming. For students with ASD to truly "access" the materials, only necessary materials should be displayed, and they should be well organized. The case example in this chapter demonstrates how two teachers decide what is important to display and organize the materials in a way that promotes learning for two students with ASD.
6. Have strong organizational and management skills	There are consistent rules for behavior, and routines for work and play. Excellent teachers develop routines for both the adults and children in their classrooms. They recognize the important relationship between rules and routines and the need for explicit instruction of each (for more information, see Carnahan & Snyder, in press).	Rules and routines are important components of learning environments for individuals with ASD. The predictability of clearly defined rules and routines promotes understanding and participation. Rules and routines reduce confusion and help individuals with ASD make predictions about an event, and then to meet the expectations of the environment (Schuler, 1995). This frees individuals with ASD to shift attention to other information, such as instruction, work tasks, and/or environmental cues. When they can better attend to, organize, sequence, and store information, individuals with ASD can later access and apply that information for meaningful purposes.

Rules and routines are not the same. Each is a different strategy for establishing behavioral boundaries and expectations. Rules are statements defining behavior permissible in given situations or environments, whereas routines detail the steps required in carrying out certain actions. |

Table 7.5 (cont.)

Exemplary Teachers	Description	Application to ASD
7. Integrate instruction across the school day	Weaving reading and writing throughout the curriculum by integrating content-area themes is crucial. Exemplary teachers recognize the importance of integrating literacy instruction into interesting content material across the school day. They are thoughtful in how they organize instruction to teach both content concepts and strategies.	Individuals with ASD experience cognitive processing differences related to attention, memory, planning, and organizing information. These differences manifest in difficulty generalizing skills and connecting information or concepts across settings. For this reason, students with ASD often need explicit instruction to use new skills or concepts in each environment (i.e., at home, in the classroom, in the cafeteria). Integrated instruction is important for at least two reasons. First, integrated instruction helps highlight the connections between one concept or skill and another; such instruction may assist students with ASD in storing information in a way that allows for easier access later. Second, integrated instruction provides opportunities to generalize learning from one setting or activity to another. For example, a student with ASD may need explicit instruction related to emergent literacy skills such as how to turn the pages in a book. Though the skill may initially be taught using one-on-one instruction, opportunities to practice the skill throughout the rest of the school day may increase the effectiveness and efficiency of instruction. The student may also independently demonstrate the skill in other settings such as at home.
8. Develop strong home-school connections	Parents play a critical role in student success. Teachers help parents understand and support instructional goals (e.g., Allington & Johnston, 2002; Block, 2001; Cantrell, 1999a, 1999b; Morrow et al., 1999; Morrow & Casey, 2003; Pressley, Rankin, & Yokoi, 1996; Taylor, Pearson, Clark, & Walpole, 1999; Taylor, Peterson, Pearson, & Rodriguez, 2002; Wharton-McDonald, Pressley, Rankin, & Mistretta, 1997). These teachers recognize the value of the information parents provide about their children. They ask questions and listen thoughtfully as parents talk about the child's strengths, interests, and needs.	Home-school collaboration is especially important for supporting students with ASD (Heflin & Alberto, 2001; Iovannone et al., 2003; NRC, 2001). However, when working with students with complex social communication needs, true collaboration does not just involve teachers and families. Other agencies and support professional (e.g., home-based tutors, clinical therapists, respite care providers, and the list goes on) often have important insights. Communication between all of these individuals may increase teaching efficiency and effectiveness, increase generalization, and promote problem solving. Simple strategies such as creating email groups, monthly or quarterly team meetings, communication notebooks, home visits (or visits to therapy centers, etc.), and planned phone conferences support communication and problem solving.

Case Example

This section presents a case study demonstrating exemplary balanced instruction. We will follow two fourth-grade teachers, Mrs. Blackburn (special education) and Mr. Johnson (general education), as they work to design balanced literacy instruction for two students with ASD, Nicholas and Micha. The case study is based in the research previously presented as well as personal accounts from experts in the field (Morrow et al., 1999; Pressley, Rankin, & Yokoi, 1996). The purpose is to (a) describe exemplary teaching practices as demonstrated in the first and fourth grades; (b) gain insights about constructivist, explicit, and balanced instruction; and (c) enhance the education community's understanding of the application of these principles to students with ASD.

Meet Micha

Micha is an 11-year-old male in the fourth grade. He was diagnosed with ASD when he was 3 years old. He receives special education services and is in a special education classroom a majority of the school day. He participates in lunch, morning assembly, recess, and language arts with his general education class. Micha watches his peers, but moves away if they approach him. His parents and teachers describe him as a "sweetheart" who is always seeking hugs.

Micha spoke his first words at 11 months of age and then stopped speaking completely when he was 20 months old. Currently, Micha does not use any spoken language. He frequently grabs his teacher's or peers' hands to guide them to an item he wants.

Meet Nicholas

Nicholas is also 11 years old and in the fourth grade. He was diagnosed with ASD at the age of 4. He lives at home with his parents and twin sister, Jessica. Nicholas has several special interests, including maps and directions and things that move in the water (e.g., boats, fish).

Nicholas communicates primarily through spoken language. His expressive vocabulary is much higher than his receptive vocabulary, and he frequently misunderstands what others say to him. Nicholas is able to decode text at an eighth-grade level, but comprehends on a second-grade level.

Well-Organized Learning Environments

A well-organized learning environment is important for all learners, but especially for individuals with ASD for whom traditional teaching methods are often ineffective (Carnahan,

2006; Mesibov et al., 2005). Organizing the physical environment and learning materials to meet the learning style of students with ASD increases student engagement and learning.

Organizing the physical space. As they set out to organize their classroom before school starts, Mr. Johnson and Mrs. Blackburn work hard to ensure that they organize literacy-rich environments that meet the needs of all learners. They begin by reflecting on last year's design. There were many bookcases filled with over 200 books of all levels and genres. They labeled the shelves according to text type (e.g., Reference, Fiction, Nonfiction, and Science). The nonfiction shelves contained books on fossils, the rain forest, planets, and reptiles, to name a few. Popular books such as *Nighty Nightmare* (Howe, 1987) and *Runaway Ralph* (Cleary, 1970) were part of the collection. These books shared space with trendy series books such as *Sweet Valley Kids* (Pascal, 1989-1998) and R. L. Stine's *Horror Series* (1990-1999). The open shelves contained books grouped by current science and social studies topics. For example, the last science unit was natural disasters. There were 20 books on the shelf about volcanoes, tidal waves, hurricanes, and earthquakes. Most titles were single copies, but for several there were multiple copies, such as *The Magic School Bus Inside a Hurricane* (Cole & Degen, 1995) and *Earthquakes* (Simon, 1995).

Recognizing the need of some students with ASD for clearly defined spaces, they decide to use the classroom furniture, especially the bookshelves, to organize centers and create clear boundaries throughout the room. For example, in the reading center, they push the large carpet to the corner so there are walls on two sides. Mr. Johnson then slides two small bookshelves on the other side to outline the space. Finally, Mrs. Blackburn posts a sign with the words "Book Nook" paired with a picture of several students sitting on the floor reading. The space appears well defined with a clear entry and exit.

After designing the boundaries, Mrs. Blackburn and Mr. Johnson organize the learning materials. Previously, there was a lounge chair surrounded by numerous floor cushions and large bean bags for students to sit to read. Next to the lounge chair was a book cart with a variety of books from which the teachers or students could choose. The cart had many types of books, from light reading like *Squids Will Be Squids* (Scieszka, 1998), to more serious texts such as *When I Was Young in the Mountains* (Rylant, 1982).

Mrs. Blackburn reflects on her experiences observing Micha and Nicholas with this setup. She recalls that they both LOVE books, but sometimes appeared overwhelmed or distracted. For example, while observing Micha, she noticed that after walking to a reading center, he lay sprawled across all of the cushions for several minutes without a book. Several other students wanted to share the pillows but could not access them without finally asking the teacher to intervene. Nicholas, on the other hand, was able to manage the physical arrangement, but seemed overwhelmed by the number of choices available. After choosing a book and reading a page or two, he placed the book back on the shelf and grabbed another one. He repeated this process at least four times in 20 minutes.

Using their knowledge about ASD and specific information about their new students, Mrs. Blackburn and Mr. Johnson set up the learning materials. Using short curtains Mrs. Blackburn brought from home, they create screens for the books. Students can easily open and close the curtains to access books. Thus, after choosing one or two books, Nicholas can shut the curtains to limit the distractions. Along with the lounge chair and the cushions, they also place a traditional student chair and a small bench in the reading area. Before school starts, Mrs. Blackburn will create a video model demonstrating exactly how to participate in the reading center.

Next, Mr. Johnson and Mrs. Blackburn decide to design a writing/publishing center. They identify an area next to the computers and again use bookshelves to create the space. They stock the shelves with varied materials, including different styles and sizes of paper, computers with adapted keyboards, and software that meets different students' developmental needs. Students use the Internet frequently for research and/or entering information on the class web site, making PowerPoint® presentations, sending e-mails to pen pals, and so on. Mr. Johnson also organizes materials students can use when publishing final assignments. He then thinks back to a brief conversation with Micha's mother, who mentioned Micha's limited experience composing. Mr. Johnson jots himself a note to remember to look for additional resources related to composition for students with significant communication needs. He knows he will need to pay special attention to designing explicit instruction and activities for Micha.

The teachers continue organizing the other areas of the classroom. Recognizing that literacy skills develop across the school day, not just during language arts, they take care to ensure that each area encourages active, meaningful engagement in a variety of literacy activities. They incorporate tables and chairs for large- and small-group meetings, a place for the whole class to convene, and various hands-on learning materials and manipulatives. They group student desks in clusters of four or five near the front of the classroom. Mr. Johnson sets one desk against a wall in a corner of the classroom to create a structured work system (see Chapter 3). Micha can use the workspace for new activities or tasks that are especially challenging for him. Finally, Mrs. Blackburn creates a small teacher workspace near the back of the classroom. The space allows for individual meetings with students, brief conversations with parents, and organizing materials for volunteers to work on throughout the school day.

Decorating the walls. When it comes to decorating the walls, the teachers begin to feel challenged. Last year, they used almost every inch of wall space for important learning material. A word wall made of felt containing different parts of speech took up a good portion of the wall in the Book Nook. Posters of popular books such as *Harry Potter* (Rowling, 1998) covered the remainder of the wall. Next to the posters, they placed book reviews written by students. There were also posters, file cabinets, and bookcases. Chart paper with publishing guidelines (prewriting, drafting, revising, editing, and publishing) and definitions of literary terms such as *onomatopoeia* and *alliteration* hung from a rope strung diagonally across the room. Around the periphery of the blackboard were various smaller posters listings other literary terms, the class rules, and the bell schedule. The back wall of the classroom contained another word wall with commonly misspelled words. They had also placed easels and bulletin boards throughout the room. One easel contained a list with the titles "Said Is Dead" on the top half and "Fun Is Done" on the bottom half. Beneath the respective headings were synonyms students could use in their written work to replace the overused *said* and *fun*. Student-suggested synonyms for *said* included words such as *replied, uttered,* and *bellowed*. Synonyms for *fun* included *outstanding, excellent,* and *extraordinary*.

Both Mr. Johnson and Mrs. Blackburn feel these materials are important to student learning, but based on Mrs. Blackburn's observations and discussions with Nicholas's and Micha's teachers, they know that too many materials may overwhelm their students with ASD. They identified three strategies to mitigate this problem, while affording access to important materials.

The first strategy is to display only the most salient information needed for literacy instruction by students in the classroom. Rather than posting all of the materials, they decide to begin by posting the materials they believe are most important. For example, they post the writing checklists, a Question Answer Response (QAR) poster (Raphael, 1986), and a poster summarizing comprehension strategies. The second strategy involves putting up temporary course materials used for particular lessons. To do this, Mr. Johnson locates a whiteboard on wheels. He and Mrs. Blackburn put Velcro strips across the top of the whiteboard. During small- and large-group lessons, they hang lesson-relevant materials on the board. When the board is not in use, they take down the materials or turn the board so the side with the materials faces the wall. Finally, Mr. Johnson creates a folder for each student. He plans to put student-relevant references in the folders throughout the year.

A Look at the Language Arts Block

The two teachers understand the importance of classroom routines and procedures, communicating expectations and consequences of behavior, and designing meaningful learning experiences across the school day. Although they recognize that calendar changes may affect their schedule, they are committed to delivering 90 minutes of language arts instruction every day. Mr. Johnson and Mrs. Blackburn plan to divide their time between reading, writing, and word work or word study. They are integrating language arts across curricular areas, and the focus of the first language arts unit is the water cycle.

Although Mr. Johnson and Mrs. Blackburn are well versed in quality literacy instruction, they need additional supports and ideas to design meaningful literacy instruction for students with significant communication challenges. After a brief discussion about Micha's and Nicholas's needs, they set out to find more information. Mrs. Blackburn locates several resources from the Center for Literacy and Disability Studies at the University of North Carolina, http://www.med.unc.edu/ahs/clds. She finds case examples, teacher resources, and low-tech (e.g., tactual books) resources. Although the case examples do not include students with ASD, they help her visualize and plan instruction for her students with communication challenges. She also accesses Treatment and Education of Autistic and related Communication handicapped Children (TEACCH) from http://teacch.com/structuresuccess.html. For additional resources, see Table 7.5. Here she reads an article on organizing group instruction to support students with ASD and other communication differences.

Mr. Johnson and Mrs. Blackburn plan to split their 90-minute language arts block into two 45-minute sessions. During the first session, they will group the students homogeneously for reading and writing instruction. During the second session, they will group the students heterogeneously. Below is a brief description of the first unit Mr. Johnson and Mrs. Blackburn teach their fourth grade.

During the first 45-minute session, when students are grouped homogeneously in three different groups, one teacher teaches reading and the other leads a word work/word study lesson. The third group of students engages in independent work related to the theme. The teachers select reading materials appropriate for each group. During reading instruction, students partner read their assigned text and work through a variety of text-related questions together. Examples of activities that occur during word study include concept and word sorts, structural analysis activities (e.g., study the prefix *hydra-*), and vocabulary study of new concept words. The students then practice these activities during their independent work time.

Micha and Nicholas receive instruction in both the small group and individually. Mr. Johnson and Mrs. Blackburn use visual directions, rules and routines, and layered groups (i.e., groups in which a student attends the segments incorporating his needs) (Faherty, n.d.) to organize their group instruction. During small-group reading instruction, the teachers teach specific comprehension strategies. Nicholas always participates in strategies instruction. Micha, on the other hand, typically participates for the first 5 minutes. The teachers use embedded instruction to teach him discrete skills such as identifying words related to the unit by sight. When Micha is not participating in the small-group instruction, he works independently or with a paraprofessional on a literacy-related activity.

After strategy instruction, students engage in partner reading. Micha frequently partner reads with a peer from the class. At the start of each new book, the teachers choose a target word or concept for Micha. They put the word on an eight-cell voice output device he is beginning to use. Each cell (or button) on the device contains a picture or word. When Micha touches the picture or word, the device speaks the corresponding preprogrammed word. At the start of the unit on the water cycle, Micha's first word is *water*. The teachers realize that Micha may not press the button in the beginning. However, they hope that he will soon begin to use the voice output to indicate when he hears the word as his peers read. When Micha is not peer reading, one of the teachers works with him. They use an interactive, shared reading approach, focusing on communication and emergent literacy skills (e.g., holding a book, turning the pages). They frequently embed interactive materials (i.e., manipulatives) and music with the text to increase Micha's engagement (Carnahan, Musti-Rao, & Bailey, 2009).

Partner reading is challenging for Nicholas. Because he decodes at a higher level than his peers, he frequently becomes frustrated when they make mistakes. Mrs. Blackburn creates a specific rule for correcting peers' mistakes. She tells Nicholas that he can only correct mistakes at the end of the session. Because she knows this will be challenging for him, she develops a routine to support the rule. Nicholas will use a pencil to place a star next to the sentence in which the mistake occurred. At the end of the chapter or session, he will use a "nice" voice to reread the sentences to his peer. Mrs. Blackburn and Mr. Johnson then create a video model to demonstrate the correction procedure. They also develop a sheet of written directions to remind Nicholas of how to correct his peers.

During the second half of the language arts block, time is split between teacher read-aloud, writer's workshop, and reader's workshop. Mr. Johnson reads aloud to the whole class from a novel. The students then spend the remaining 40 minutes split between writer's workshop and reader's workshop. During writer's workshop, students work on a story related to the water cycle. They use various technologies at different stages in the writing process. For example, students use Kidspiration (2009), story grammar maps, and storyboards. Mr. Johnson and Mrs. Blackburn use strategies such as picture sequencing, computer-based fill-in stories, and picture-based graphic organizers during writing instruction, all focused on generation for Nicholas and Micha.

Writer's workshop is especially challenging for Nicholas, who is prone to meltdowns at the mere mention of writing. From idea generation to publishing, the process is hard for him. However, Nicholas is a technology genius. He loves working on the computer. Mrs. Blackburn creates a basic template that allows her to plug in a variety of closed- and open-ended questions to guide Nicholas to an idea. She then gives him a highly structured graphic organizer to assist him in brainstorming details about the topic. At the start of the year, Nicholas generates basic information such as who, what, when, and where. He will gradually increase the quantity and quality of what he produces. Additionally, Nicholas frequently creates PowerPoints® to accompany his story. He loads pictures from the Internet or his camera on individual slides. He then creates short captions and adds narration.

The teachers use three general activities to design writing instruction for Micha: (a) a highly structured writing task designed to teach Micha to type words he can already identify, (b) an open-ended typing task that frequently involves pictures, and (c) work with his communication system. When writing about theme-related text, Micha chooses two or three pictures from a stack. Mr. Johnson prints these from the Internet or assists Micha in taking photographs using a digital camera. After loading the pictures in the computer, Micha uses an Intelitools Keyboard (1994), an adapted keyboard that can be customized to meet individual students and include individual letters, words, and/or pictures to independently type letters or to select words paired with pictures to tell about the photograph.

Mr. Johnson develops a structured work system to teach Micha to type the words he is already able to identify by sight. They place a small plastic container on the left side of the keyboard. The container holds a small stack of note cards, each with one word. A small red star is drawn next to each word. Mr. Johnson places an identical star on the "enter" key on the keyboard and an empty plastic container to the right of the keyboard.

Micha takes a note card from the container on the left, places it at the top of the keyboard, types the word, presses the "enter" key, and puts the card in the plastic container. He repeats the process for each of the words. Finally, recognizing that writing is about more than just printed text, Mrs. Blackburn pays a great deal of attention to communication. She builds in many opportunities for Micha to interact with teachers and peers.

During reader's workshop, students choose books to read independently. Using individual contracts, students work with Mr. Johnson and Mrs. Blackburn to develop a project related to their reading. Micha and Nicholas choose their projects from a picture or written list. Some students create videos, others develop PowerPoints®, and still others write journals or research papers.

Conclusion

All children need access to quality literacy instruction to become independent, contributing community members. However, many individuals with ASD do not receive literacy instruction. Their experiences are frequently limited to drill-and-practice activities that lack meaning or context. For these students to develop the literacy skills necessary to communicate with others and interact with printed text, they need more than drill and practice. The balanced approach to literacy instruction presented in this chapter serves as a model for such instruction. Regardless of perceived cognitive and communication functioning, students with ASD deserve instruction that incorporates reading, writing, and word work across the school day. Although what constitutes reading, writing, and word work looks different for each learner, integrated instruction incorporating holistic and explicit teaching strategies across the school day is crucial.

Chapter Highlights

- A balanced approach to literacy instruction includes careful selection from the best theories available and use of different learning strategies to match the learning styles of individual children.

- Balanced instruction acknowledges the importance of both the form (phonics, mechanics, etc.) and the function (comprehension, purpose, and meaning) of the literacy processes and recognizes that learning occurs most effectively in a whole-part-whole context.

- Focusing on the cognitive style of students with ASD, especially differences in attention, meaning making, motivation, and generalization, helps highlight the importance of contextualized, balanced instruction.

- Students with ASD have difficulty identifying and connecting information or experiences to make meaning as well as generalizing skills from one setting to another.

- When planning balanced instruction, teachers incorporate materials to meet the needs of each individual child, promote uniqueness rather than conformity, and actively engage all students in the learning process.

- Students with ASD need instruction that incorporates reading and writing across the school day. Even if this may look different for each learner, integrated instruction incorporating holistic and explicit teaching strategies is crucial.

- Balanced literacy programs include:
  - Daily reading, writing, listening, speaking, spelling, and viewing activities
  - Literacy instruction that occurs within a block of uninterrupted time across the school day
  - Thematic instruction based on student interests (theme-based instruction increases student motivation and interest in reading and writing activities)

- Balanced literacy instruction includes attention to student interests, instructional grouping, and materials selection.

- Instructional grouping includes whole-group, small-group, and one-to-one teaching.

- A well-organized environment is important for all learners, especially for individuals with ASD. Organizing the physical environment and learning materials to meet the learning style of students with ASD increases engagement and learning.

- Exemplary teaching looks at effective practices, teacher behavior, and classroom dynamics, including student-teacher interaction, routines and schedules, environmental design, and classroom community.

- Teachers use ongoing formal and informal assessment measures to track student progress and inform their teaching. Assessment drives instruction.

Chapter Review Questions

1. What is balanced literacy instruction? Discuss the components of balanced literacy.

2. Describe the physical environment in a classroom organized to provide exemplary balanced literacy instruction to students with ASD.

3. List the characteristics of exemplary teachers. Provide a specific application or example of teaching students with ASD for each.

4. What is the purpose of assessment in balanced literacy classrooms?

5. Discuss the types of reading and writing experiences a student will encounter in a balanced literacy classroom.

6. Assume you are an exemplary teacher who uses a balanced literacy perspective. Describe the nature of your classroom, your philosophy, and what you are ultimately trying to achieve.

References

Allington, R. L., & Johnston, P. H. (2002). *Reading to learn: Lessons from exemplary fourth-grade classrooms.* New York: Guilford Press.

American Psychiatric Association. (2000). *Diagnostic and statistical manual of mental disorders* (4th ed., text revision). Washington, DC: Author.

Aspy, R., & Grossman, B. (2007). *The ziggurat model: A framework for designing comprehensive interventions for individuals with high-functioning autism and Asperger Syndrome.* Shawnee Mission, KS: Autism Asperger Publishing Company.

Block, C. C. (2001, December). *Distinctions between the expertise of literacy teachers preschool through grade 5.* Presentation at the annual meeting of the National Reading Conference, San Antonio, TX.

Boyd, B., Conroy, M., Mancil, G. R., Nakao, T., & Alter, P. (2007). Effects of circumscribed interests on the social behaviors of children with autism spectrum disorders. *Journal of Autism and Developmental Disorders, 15,* 1550-1561.

Cantrell, S. C. (1999a). The effects of literacy instruction on primary students' reading and writing achievement. *Reading and Research Instruction, 39*(1), 3-26.

Cantrell, S. C. (1999b). Effective teaching and literacy learning: A look inside primary classrooms. *The Reading Teacher, 52*(4), 370-379.

Carnahan, C. (2006). Photovoice: Increasing engagement for students with autism and their teachers. *Teaching Exceptional Children, 39*(2), 44-50.

Carnahan, C., & Borders, C. (in press). Language and communication in autism. In A. Boutot & B. S. Myles (Eds.), *Autism education and practice.* New York: Pearson.

Carnahan, C., Musti-Rao, S., & Bailey, J. (2009). Increasing academic engagement and literacy learning for students with autism. *Education and Treatment of Children, 32*(1), 37-61.

Carnahan, C., & Snyder, K. (in press). Rules and routines. In *Autism Internet Modules* (Ohio Center for Autism Low Incidence). Available from http://www.autisminternetmodules.org/

Coker, H. (1985). Consortium for the improvement of teacher evaluation. *Journal of Teacher Education, 36,* 12-17.

Council for Exceptional Children. (2005). *Universal design for learning: A guide for teachers and education professionals.* Arlington, VA: Pearson/Merrill/Prentice Hall.

Duffy, G. G., & Hoffman, J. (1999). In pursuit of an illusion: The flawed search for a perfect method. *The Reading Teacher, 53*(1), 10-16.

Faherty, C. (n.d.). *Group ideas for preschool and primary classrooms including students with autism: Structuring for success.* Retrieved October 24, 2009, from http://teacch.com/structuresuccess.html

Gal, E., Bauminger, N., Goren-Bar, D., Pianesi, F., Stock, O., Zancanaro, M., & Weiss, P. (2009). Enhancing social communication of children with high functioning autism through a co-located surface. *AI & Society, 24,* 75-84.

Genishi, C., Ryan, S., Ochsner, M., & Yarnall, M. M. (2001). Teaching in early childhood education: Understanding practices through research and theory. In V. Richardson (Ed.), *Handbook of research on teaching* (pp. 1175-1210). Washington, DC: American Education Research Association.

Haigh, N., & Katterns, B. (1984). Teacher effectiveness: Problem or goal for teacher education. *Journal of Teacher Education, 35*(5), 23-27.

Happé, F., & Frith, U. (2006). The weak coherence account: Detail-focused cognitive style in autism spectrum disorders. *Journal of Autism and Developmental Disorders, 36,* 5-25.

Heflin, L. J., & Alberto, P. (2001). Establishing a behavioral context for learning for students with autism. *Focus on Autism and Other Developmental Disabilities, 6*(2), 93-101.

Hume, K., & Odom, S. (2007). Effects of an individual work system on the independent engagement of students with autism. *Journal of Autism and Developmental Disorders, 37,* 1166-1180.

IntelliTools. (1994). *IntelliTools* [computer software]. Novato, CA: Author.

International Reading Association. (1999). *Using multiple methods of beginning reading instruction: A position statement of the international reading association.* Wilmington, DE: International Reading Association.

Iovannone, R., Dunlap, G., Huber, H., & Kincaid, D. (2003). Effective educational practices for students with autism spectrum disorders. *Focus on Autism and Other Developmental Disabilities, 18,* 150-165.

Inspiration Software, Inc. (2009). *Kidspiration* [computer software]. Beaverton, OR: Inspiration Software, Inc.

Koegel, L., Carter, C., & Koegel, R. (2003). Teaching children with autism self-initiations as a pivotal response. *Topics in Language Disorders, 23,* 134-145.

Koegel, L., Koegel, R., Harrower, J., & Carter, C. (1999). Pivotal response intervention I: Overview of approach. *The Journal of the Association for Persons with Severe Handicaps, 24*(3), 174-185.

Koegel, R., Koegel, L., & McNerney, E. (2001). Pivotal areas in intervention for autism. *Journal of Clinical Child Psychology, 30,* 19-32.

Leaf, R., & McEachin, J. (1999). *Work in progress: Behavior management strategies and a curriculum for intensive behavioral treatment information.* New York: DRL Book, LLC.

Lord, C. et al. (2005). Challenges in evaluating psychosocial interventions for autistic spectrum disorders. *Journal of Autism and Developmental Disorders, 35*(6), 695-708.

Mancil, G. R., & Pearl, C. (2008). Restricted interests as motivators: Improving academic engagement and outcomes of children on the autism spectrum. *Teaching Exceptional Children Plus, 4*(6), Article 7. Retrieved May 10, 2009, from http://escholarship.bc.edu/education/tecplus/vol4/iss6/art7

Maurice, C., Green, G., & Luce, S. (1996). *Behavioral interventions for young children with autism: A manual for parents and professionals.* Austin, TX: Pro-Ed.

Mesibov, G., Shea, V., & Schopler, E. (2005). *The TEACCH approach to autism spectrum disorders.* New York: Kluwer Academic/Plenum Publishers.

Metsala, J. L., & Wharton-McDonald, R. (1997). Effective primary-grades literacy instruction-balanced literacy instruction. *The Reading Teacher, 50*(6), 518-521.

Mirenda, P. (2003). "He's not really a reader …": Perspectives on supporting literacy development in individuals with autism. *Topics in Language Disorders, 23*(4), 271-282.

Morrow, L. (2005). *Literacy development in the early years: Helping children read and write.* New York: Pearson.

Morrow, L. M., & Casey, H. K. (2003). A comparison of exemplary characteristics in 1st and 4th grade teachers. *The California Reader, 36*(3), 5-17.

Morrow, L., Tracey, D., Woo, D. G., & Pressley, M. (1999). Characteristics of exemplary first-grade literacy instruction. *The Reading Teacher, 52*(5), 462-476.

Mundy, P., & Burnette, C. (2005). Joint attention and neural developmental models of autism. In F. Volkmar, R. Paul, A. Klin, & D. Cohen (Eds.), *Handbook of autism and pervasive developmental disorders* (3rd ed., pp. 650-681). Hoboken, NJ: John Wiley & Sons.

Munk, D., & Van Laarhoven, T. (2008). Grouping arrangements and delivery of instruction for students with developmental disabilities. In H. Parette & G. Peterspm-Karlan (Eds.), *Research-based practices in developmental disabilities* (2nd ed., pp. 269-290). Austin, TX: Pro-Ed.

National Institute of Child Health and Human Development. (2000). *Report of the national reading panel. Teaching children to read: An evidence-based assessment of the scientific research literature on reading and its implications for reading instruction* (NIH Publication No. 00-4769). Washington, DC: U.S. Government Printing Office.

National Research Council. (2001). *Educating children with autism.* Washington, DC: National Academy Press.

Pressley, M., Rankin, J., & Yokoi, L. (1996). A survey of instructional practices of primary teachers nominated as effective in promoting literacy. *The Elementary School Journal, 96*(4), 363-383.

Pressley, M. (1998). Comprehension strategies instruction. In J. Osborn & F. Lehr (Eds.), *Literacy for all, issues in teaching and learning* (pp. 113-133). New York: Guilford Press.

Quill, K. A. (2000). *Do-watch-listen-say: Social and communication intervention for children with autism.* Baltimore: Paul H. Brookes.

Raphael, T. (1986). Teaching question answer relationships, revisited. *Reading Teacher, 39,* 516-522.

Roehler, L. R., & Duffy, G. G. (1984). Direct explanation of comprehension process. In G. G. Duffy, L. R. Roehler, & J. Mason (Eds.), *Comprehension instruction: Perspectives and suggestions* (pp. 265-280). New York: Longman.

Ruddell, R. B. (1995). Those influential literacy teachers: Meaning negotiators and motivation builders. *The Reading Teacher, 48*(6), 454-463.

Ruddell, R. B., & Harris, P. (1989). A study of the relationship between influential teachers' prior knowledge and beliefs about teaching effectiveness: Developing higher order thinking in content areas. In S. McCormick & J. Zutell (Eds.), *Cognitive and social perspectives for literacy research and instruction* (pp. 461-472). Chicago: National Reading Conference.

Ruddell, R. B., & Kern, R. B. (1986). The development of belief systems and teaching effectiveness of influential teachers. In M. P. Douglas (Ed.), *Reading: The quest for meaning* (pp. 133-150). Claremont, CA: Claremont Graduate School Yearbook.

Schuler, A. (1995). Thinking in autism: Differences in learning and development. In K. Quill (Ed.), *Teaching children with autism: Strategies to enhance communication and socialization* (pp. 11-23). New York: Delmar Publishers.

Shulman, L. S. (1986). Paradigms and research programs in the study of teaching: A contemporary perspective. In M. C. Wittrock (Ed.), *Handbook of reading research on teaching* (pp. 3-36). New York: MacMillan.

Taylor, B. M., Pearson, P. D., & Clark, K. (2000). Effective schools and accomplished teachers: Lessons about primary-grade reading instruction in low-income schools. *The Elementary School Journal, 101*(2), 121-165.

Taylor, B. M., Pearson, P. D., Clark, K. E., & Walpole, S. (1999). *Beating the odds in teaching all children to read* (Ciera Report #2-006). Ann Arbor, MI: Center for the Improvement of Early Reading Achievement.

Taylor, B. M., Peterson, D. S., Pearson, P. D., & Rodriguez, M. C. (2002). Looking inside classrooms: Reflecting on the "how" as well as the "what" in effective reading instruction. *The Reading Teacher, 56*(3), 270-279.

Tomlinson, C. A. (2000). Differentiation of instruction in the elementary grades. *ERIC Digest.* ERIC_NO: EDO-PS-00-7. Retrieved October 24, 2009, from http://ceep.crc.uiuc.edu/eecearchive/digests/2000/tomlin00.pdf

Vismara, L., & Lyons, G. (2007). Using perseverative interests to elicit joint attention behaviors in young children with autism: Theoretical and clinical implications for understanding motivation. *Journal of Positive Behavior Interventions, 9*(4), 214-228.

Weiss, M. J. (2005). Comprehensive ABA programs: Integrating and evaluating the implementation of varied instructional approaches. *The Behavior Analyst Today, 6*(4), 249-256.

Wharton-McDonald, R., Pressley, M., Rankin, J., & Mistretta, J. (1997). Effective primary – grades literacy instruction equals balanced literacy instruction. *The Reading Teacher, 50*(6), 518-521.

Children's Books

Cleary, B. (1970). *Runaway Ralph.* New York: Morrow Junior Books.

Cole, J., & Degen, B. (1995). *The Magic School Bus Inside a Hurricane.* New York: Scholastic, Inc.

Howe, J. (1987). *Nighty Nightmare.* New York: Atheneum Books for Young Readers.

Pascal, F. (1989-98). *Sweet Valley Kids Series.* New York: Bantam Dell Publishing.

Rowling, J. K. (1998). *Harry Potter and the Sorcerer's Stone.* New York: Scholastic Press.

Rylant, C. (1982). *When I Was Young in the Mountains.* New York: Penguin Putnam, Inc.

Scieszka, J. (1998). *Squids Will Be Squids: Fresh Morals, Beastly Fables.* New York: Penguin Putnam, Inc.

Simon, S. (1995). *Earthquakes.* New York: Morrow.

Stine, R. L. (1990-1999). *Goosebumps series.* New York: Scholastic, Inc.

Part Three
Building Literacy Skills for Students With ASD

Chapter 8

Emergent Literacy Skills

Allison Breit-Smith, Ph.D., University of Cincinnati

Laura Justice, Ph.D., The Ohio State University

Learner Objectives

After reading this chapter, the learner should be able to:

- Define emergent literacy theory

- List emergent literacy skills

- Describe considerations in building emergent literacy skills in children with ASD

- Name strategies for promoting emergent literacy skills in children with ASD

- Explain contexts that support emergent literacy skills in children with ASD

■ ■ ■

Thomas, a 4-year old preschooler with ASD, strolls over to the kidney-shaped activity table in his classroom after **prompting** *from the teaching assistant to check his visual schedule. It is 10:00 a.m. and time for snack. Ms. Zigler, Thomas' teacher, has planned a special treat for the children based on a book about worms she read aloud to the whole group that morning. In small groups, Ms. Zigler arranges for the children to make a "dirt dessert" complete with gummy worms. As she presents the directions and each of the ingredients, Thomas sits quietly and watches – until she shows the children the milk. Within seconds of seeing the writing on the milk carton, Thomas says, "Trauth. That says Trauth. I drink Trauth milk in the morning." Ms. Zigler smiles, confirms Thomas' observation, and comments (while pointing) that the first letter of his name, "T," is the same as the first letter in the word "Trauth."*

■ ■ ■

Thomas does not yet read or write in the conventional sense. Nevertheless, he demonstrates an authentic interest in and awareness of print in his environment. He recognizes some words and understands that they carry meaning, and he relates those words to specific daily activities (e.g., morning breakfast). Had Ms. Zigler adopted a traditional perspective of reading, she might have dismissed Thomas' recognition of environmental print simply on the basis of his cognitive maturity and disability status. Instead, she places significant value on such examples of prereading and prewriting behaviors and adopts a more contemporary notion of how children come to read and write, known as the emergent literacy perspective.

Emergent literacy refers to the exploratory reading and writing behaviors children display long before they can read and write in the conventional sense and before formal schooling (Teale & Sulzby, 1986). Simply turning pages in a storybook, pretend reading, or scribbling the name of a friend on a piece of paper are examples of children's awareness and discovery of the function and meaning of print. Theoretically, the emergent literacy perspective suggests the importance of strong oral language skills as a foundation for developing strong literacy skills (Teale & Sulzby).

Empirically, longitudinal research findings show a consistently positive and moderate association between children's oral language abilities at a young age and reading abilities at an older age (e.g., Catts, Fey, Tomblin, & Zhang, 2002; Catts, Fey, Zhang, & Tomblin, 1999; Storch & Whitehurst, 2002). In particular, children who enter school with language skills that lag behind their peers' are at increased risk for later reading difficulties (e.g., Catts, Fey, Tomblin, & Zhang, 2001). Because children with autism spectrum disorders (ASD) often exhibit weaknesses or delays in oral language, their risk for reading difficulties is especially high. However, the relationship between oral language and literacy skills does not imply causality; nor does it propose that competence with oral language is a prerequisite for learning to read. Therefore, while oral language skills have important implications for reading skills, children's oral language status should not preclude them from literacy instruction.

Conceptualizations of emergent literacy also suggest that these behaviors originate early in life, specifically from birth to age 5. And research over the past 30 years on emergent literacy development has confirmed the use of age as a defining study parameter (Yaden, Rowe, & MacGillivray, 2000). However, practice and theory suggest that the broad development of literacy progresses along a continuum from basic to proficient knowledge, with children demonstrating certain levels of literacy achievement at any given point in time. Furthermore, such literacy knowledge is affected by environmental and developmental factors such as home environment (e.g., Roberts, Jurgens, & Burchinal, 2005; Storch & Whitehurst, 2001), classroom experiences (e.g., Mashburn et al., 2008), and child-level characteristics (e.g., McGinty & Justice, 2009).

Emergent literacy behaviors, therefore, may best be represented in terms of a fluid stage of development rather than a precise age. This is particularly important to consider for children with disabilities who may be emergent readers and writers long *after* the age of 5 and in spite of formal schooling. Thus, while the majority of the literature cited in this chapter reflects a younger population of children, the skills, concepts, and strategies described may be applied to any child of any age who is functioning within the emergent period of literacy development.

Emergent Literacy Skills

Emergent literacy skills may be defined as the skills, such as identifying the names of letters (alphabet knowledge) or analyzing the sound structure of words (phonological awareness), that lay the foundation for later fluent decoding (National Early Literacy Panel [NELP], 2008; Teale & Sulzby, 1986). Whitehurst and Lonigan (1998) suggested that children acquire literacy by using two separate but related processes of gathering information from print: (a) information obtained from the code-related aspects of the printed word (e.g., what is gleaned from alphabet knowledge and phonological awareness); and

(b) information obtained from understanding the meaning associated with the printed word (e.g., what is gleaned from vocabulary, background knowledge, context) (Storch & Whitehurst, 2002; Whitehurst & Lonigan). Code-related and meaning-based reading processes reflect two distinct yet codependent systems that draw on both common and unique skill sets to accomplish the task of reading (e.g., Berninger, Abbott, Thomson, & Raskind, 2001; Storch & Whitehurst). We discuss each of these processes and their components next.

Code-Related Reading Processes

Code-related reading processes refer to the reader's ability to understand the structure of print. These processes often first involve understanding the meaning and functions of print as well as recognizing print at the level of grapheme and phoneme. A grapheme refers to an individual unit of written language such as an alphabet letter, whereas a phoneme refers to the smallest unit of sound associated with one or more graphemes (e.g., /b/ for the letter *b* or /sh/ for the digraph *sh*). Therefore, understanding the structural aspects of print includes initially making sense of the purposes of print and becoming familiar with individually printed letters and words and linking sounds to letters and words. Code-related reading processes may be categorized into four domains: phonological awareness, alphabet knowledge, print concepts, and emergent writing.

Phonological awareness. Phonological awareness includes the ability to recognize and identify the sound properties of words. Because skills in this domain require an awareness of language and sound structure apart from meaning, phonological awareness tasks offer insight into children's underlying metalinguistic and metacognitive abilities. Acquisition of phonological awareness typically follows a developmental progression of attention to larger, then smaller units of sound (e.g., Anthony & Francis, 2005). At first, children may recognize that sentences consist of words and that words consist of syllables. They understand that words rhyme with one another and that some words start with the same letter. As they become more familiar with larger sound units, they begin to detect and recognize the smaller units of words such as individual sounds or phonemes. Instruction at this level involves activities related to isolating, blending, segmenting, and manipulating sounds in words.

Studies show a consistent and positive relationship between phonological awareness skills and later word reading ability (e.g., Vellutino, Fletcher, Snowling, & Scanlon, 2004; Vellutino & Scanlon, 1987). Research on phonological awareness abilities in children with disabilities, including ASD, while limited, has generally found that sound aware-ness skills in these children are less developed than in children with typical language skills (e.g., Koppenhaver, Hendrix, & Williams, 2007); however, studies also show that children with ASD respond favorably to phonological awareness intervention (Gabig, 2008; Newman et al., 2007).

Alphabet knowledge. Alphabet knowledge refers to familiarity with written symbols or graphemes. Knowledge about the alphabet encompasses three main skills: the ability to (a) receptively identify letters, (b) expressively name letters, and (c) match letters to sounds. Children with typical language skills come to know and learn the names and sounds of letters through direct and explicit teaching from parents within the home environment as well as from early school experiences (Senechal & Lefevre, 2002; Senechal, Pagan, Lever, & Ouellette, 2008). Alphabet letters that are most salient and important to children, such as those that make up their own names or those of family members, are often more readily learned than other letters (Treiman, Pennington, Shriberg, & Boada, 2008).

Alphabet knowledge is one of the most robust indicators of later literacy success (Hammill, 2004). Thus, children who know more letters upon school entry fare better with decoding than children who know fewer names of letters. For children with ASD, alpha-bet knowledge and a preoccupation with letters is among the first emergent literacy skills noted. In fact, observations of some children with ASD indicate precociousness with word reading long before formal schooling (i.e., hyperlexia). Yet not all children with ASD demonstrate such emergent reading patterns (Nation, Clarke, Wright, & Williams, 2006), and many struggle with alphabet knowledge skills well into the school-age years.

Print concepts. Print concept knowledge includes understanding the forms, func-tions, and features of print. This domain involves understanding the direction, organiza-tion, and meaning of print. Children in our culture who understand concepts about print know that print moves from left to right and top to bottom. They know where to begin and stop reading and understand that letters make up words and words make up sen-tences. Children who understand the meaning of print recognize that there are different genres of print and different purposes for reading (e.g., storybooks for entertainment, coupons for getting a discount at the store).

Knowledge of print concepts also includes an awareness of print in one's environ-ment. For example, many children first recognize the "M" (golden arches) in McDonald's and associate that letter with the fast-food restaurant. This type of logo and picture read-ing is particularly important for developing functional literacy skills in children with moderate to severe disabilities and is supported in recent research showing that logo reading taught to children with disabilities can be generalized to a community setting (Alberto, Fredrick, Hughes, McIntosh, & Cihak, 2007).

Emergent writing. Emergent writing refers to children's attempts to convey information through written symbols. That is, the development of writing progresses on a continuum from drawing and scribbling to letter-like representations and complete letter formations. When facilitating early writing skills, children should be encouraged to write creatively and use invented spelling. This allows them to devote cognitive and linguistic resources to the content and purpose of writing rather than to specific writing rules or mechanics such as punctuation and spelling.

For children with motor planning or sensory needs, writing often becomes a difficult and nonpreferred activity. However, there are many ways in which technology and adaptive equipment may be used to foster emergent writing in children with ASD, such as alternative and augmentative communication devices (Bedrosian, Lasker, Speidel, & Politsch, 2003).

Meaning-Based Reading Processes

While code-related processes reflect awareness of the structure of print, meaning-based processes refer to global understanding of printed words and sentences. Meaning-based processes are rooted in children's language comprehension of the semantic and syntactic relationships of and between words. Theoretically, three broad domains comprise meaning-based processes: vocabulary, grammatical understanding, and narrative production. For children with ASD, difficulties with meaning-based skills – both orally and in reading – tend to be defining child-level characteristics. That is, many children on the spectrum demonstrate relative strengths in word recognition (code-related reading processes) and significant weaknesses in reading comprehension (meaning-based reading processes).

Vocabulary. Vocabulary involves understanding the meanings of words. Studies of children's vocabularies show that the density with which parents use diverse and interesting words when talking with their children relates to the breadth and depth of children's oral vocabularies (Hart & Risley, 1995). In addition to language-rich interactions, factors such as home environment and language status have been found to affect children's understanding and use of vocabulary words. For example, children reared in homes of poverty tend to demonstrate more limited word knowledge than children from middle-class households (e.g., Pan, Rowe, Singer, & Snow, 2005). Research also shows that children with language impairments learn vocabulary words at a different rate than typically developing children (Skibbe et al., 2008).

Because children with ASD often demonstrate delays in language, they are at increased risk of delays in vocabulary development and subsequent reading difficulties. When it comes to understanding and using words, children diagnosed with high-functioning autism or Asperger Syndrome often score well on standardized measures of vocabulary skills (Jarrold, Boucher, & Russell, 1997; Kjelgaard & Tager-Flusberg, 2001). In fact, many professionals working with this population remark on what "rich vocabularies" children with high-functioning autism have. However, while these children on the surface demonstrate sometimes precocious semantic abilities, subtle difficulties with word use and meaning exist. In particular, observations of children with high-functioning autism indicate idiosyncrasies of word or phrase use during conversation, such as using a root word to make a new word (Capps, Kehres, & Sigman, 1998; Tager-Flusberg, Paul, & Lord, 2005; Volden & Lord, 1991). Although these new words are not necessarily obvious in conversation, they are slightly bizarre and are odd-sounding enough to distinguish the child with ASD from his typical peers.

On the other end of the spectrum are children for whom understanding and using vocabulary is severely limited. Yet, regardless of severity, difficulty with vocabulary development impacts children's reading comprehension skills (Nation, Snowling, & Clarke, 2007).

Grammatical understanding. Grammatical understanding entails the ability to understand the syntax of words and sentences. Children with a firm knowledge of grammar understand a variety of sentence types and clause structures, and when reading, they use this information for comprehension. In general, grammatical understanding relies heavily on intact receptive language skills. Empirical evidence suggests that children with disabilities, such as language impairments, who demonstrate delayed receptive language abilities perform more poorly on measures of grammatical morphology than children with typical language skills (Leonard & Deevy, 2004). Moreover, longitudinal studies of poor readers in second grade have noted persistent deficits in receptive language evident in prekindergarten (Catts et al., 1999, 2001).

The limited research available has systematically explored grammatical understanding and use in children with ASD. While existing studies in this area indicate a wide variety of abilities, generally, they have found weakness in the grammatical system (Fisher, Happé, & Dunn, 2005; Jarrold et al., 1997). For example, children with ASD have been found to expressively use less complex and less diverse grammatical forms when speaking (Fine, Bartolucci, Szatmari, & Ginsberg, 1994). In addition, they tend to use more unclear and unexpected references, as well as make fewer links to the preceding conversation. Such difficulty with syntactic cohesiveness and use of language may translate to difficulties with grammatical understanding when reading.

Narratives. Narratives refer to the oral or written description of an event. Narratives may be personal accounts or fictional retellings of stories. Their focus often includes one overarching topic presented by the speaker or writer as a sequence of events linked together using various linguistic devices. The production of oral narratives requires the use of decontextualized language (Snow, Burns, & Griffin, 1998); that is, talking about something that is not tangibly represented in the here and now. Familiarity with decontextualized language is important because reading and comprehending stories relies on this understanding (e.g., understanding that a carrot seed will produce a carrot).

Children who produce more syntactically complete and comprehensive oral narratives tend to demonstrate higher performance on measures of emergent literacy skills (Griffin, Hemphill, Camp, & Wolf, 2004). The growing research base on the oral narrative production of children with ASD in general shows that these children tend to relate fewer personal narratives during conversation than children without developmental delays (Capps et al., 1998; Losh & Capps, 2003). Furthermore, children with ASD typically use less complex syntax and diversity of clauses in narratives. This is important because these types of oral language skills are interrelated with literacy skills.

The Known and Unknown in Building Emergent Literacy Skills in Children With ASD

Few studies have explored the acquisition and development of emergent literacy skills in children with ASD, and even fewer have considered the effects of interventions with regard to this population of children. Furthermore, the studies that do examine emergent literacy interventions in children with ASD primarily consist of case study reports rather than experimental designs. This may be appropriate for the heterogeneous population of children with ASD, but leaves little room for drawing more general conclusions about intervention effectiveness.

Therefore, before presenting strategies and contexts for facilitating emergent literacy skills, we present and discuss what we currently know and do not know about the ways in which children with ASD acquire emergent literacy and respond to emergent literacy interventions. We have identified three factors that may impact the potential for building emergent literacy skills in children with ASD: variability, development, and applicability (Justice & Kaderavek, 2004).

Variability

■ ■ ■

Charlie is 9 years old, in third grade, and diagnosed with ASD. When asked to describe his level of literacy knowledge, Charlie's teachers describe him as a nonreader. Charlie knows the names of all of the alphabet letters and the sounds of every letter. He cannot perform phoneme deletion tasks or generate rhyming words. He can write his first name but not his last name. Charlie can hold a book upright, turn the pages, and point to words as someone else reads. He can also name objects pictured in books and can read approximately 20 sight words. He understands simple sentences, yet cannot provide a simple retelling of the beginning, middle, and end of a familiar story.

■ ■ ■

As illustrated, Charlie demonstrates significant variability in his emergent literacy skills. Some of his behaviors seem to be intact and congruent developmentally, whereas others appear to be significantly delayed. This inconsistent or fragmented representation of skills characterizes emergent literacy skills observed in children. However, variability is not unique to the population of children diagnosed with ASD. Considerable differences in emergent literacy skills also exist in typically developing children (e.g., Downer & Pianta, 2006; Duncan et al., 2007). For instance, some children know the names of all of the letters at kindergarten entry, whereas others can identify only a few letters despite school instruction.

Although there is general variability in skills within a population of children, overall, there are consistent group differences between populations. For example, children who are deemed at risk due to poverty or developmental delay tend to display less sophisticated literacy skill levels *overall* compared to children with typical language (e.g., Storch & Whitehurst, 2001). Despite these consistent skill weaknesses in literacy development, treatment research indicates that most at-risk children respond positively and favorably to intervention. What is not known for children with ASD is how profiles that reflect fragmentation of skills affect responsiveness to intervention, and if the type of variability noted within the ASD population is similar to the variability in literacy skills noted in other populations considered to be at risk.

Development

In typical populations, the trajectory for reading involves an explosive growth in reading abilities in the early years such as kindergarten and first grade (McCoach, O'Connell, Reis, & Levitt, 2006), followed by less dramatic increases in later school years (Skibbe et al., 2008). For children with disabilities such as language impairments, reading trajectories parallel those of children with typical language in that they develop along the same continuum but not at the same ability level (less developed reading abilities) (Catts et al., 2002; Skibbe et al.).

Given the overlap between features of language impairment and ASD (e.g., limited language abilities, social pragmatic difficulties, inconsistent understanding and use of grammar or syntax) (Whitehouse, Barry, & Bishop, 2007), it is possible that the reading trajectory for children with ASD follows the same path as that of language impairment, but few studies have examined this topic.

Hypothetically, for children with ASD, the shape of the reading growth curve is similar to that of children with language impairments in the early years of schooling when large achievement gains are noted, but then differ in the upper-elementary grades. For example, it is plausible that because, in the later schools years, there is more reliance on comprehension, children with ASD demonstrate a plateau in literacy skills rather than the slow rate of growth noted in the typical and language impaired populations. This similarity or difference in reading trajectories has potential implications for the effectiveness of interventions, particularly when the goal of literacy instruction is to close gaps in reading achievement.

Applicability

Many emergent literacy interventions have been shown to be effective when used with children with developmental disabilities, severe language impairments, children from backgrounds of economic disadvantage, and children learning English as a second language. Nevertheless, it is unclear whether these interventions are applicable to children with ASD.

First, applicability may be questioned because of the theoretical framework underlying emergent literacy theory. That is, emergent literacy interventions are grounded in the notion that reading and writing knowledge is built through social interactions with others. That is, social partners mediate the literacy experience and interaction with literacy-related materials and resources. Adult responsiveness, in particular, has been shown to be an effective strategy for promoting literacy skills in children, and forms the theoretical ground on which most emergent literacy interventions are based. Given the socio-cultural and social interaction framework from which literacy is theorized to develop, the applicability of such interventions may be questionable due to the inherent weaknesses in social behavior among children with ASD. On the other hand, implementing emergent literacy interventions from this framework may produce simultaneous or synergistic treatment effects of improving not only emergent literacy skills but also social skills.

Second, the applicability of such interventions may also be questionable given the differences in characteristics across vulnerable populations. For example, children with developmental disabilities such as Down syndrome often demonstrate mild to moderate intellectual impairments in the presence of sociability, whereas children with specific language impairment tend to demonstrate significant delays in verbal abilities in the presence of average intellectual achievement.

Given the strengths and weaknesses of particular populations, some interventions may be more suitable for certain children than for others. On the other hand, intervention studies including children with different backgrounds and diagnoses (e.g., language impairment, poverty) who received the same intervention have found positive effects for interventions across populations (e.g., Justice, Chow, Capellini, Flanigan, & Colton, 2003).

In summary, the general pool of scientifically based strategies and contexts of emergent literacy interventions have hypothetical merit, yet have not been empirically investigated or applied in large scale to the population of children diagnosed with ASD.

Strategies for Promoting Emergent Literacy Skills

Selecting a Target

Emergent literacy skill instruction begins with an intervention target. Intervention targets involve the specific skills or behaviors chosen to teach within a particular area (Justice, Sofka, & McGinty, 2007). Potential emergent literacy targets include skills associated with the code-related and meaning-based processes of reading (phonological awareness, alphabet knowledge, print concepts, writing, vocabulary, grammatical understanding, narrative). In addition, targets may include basic skills related to establishing and maintaining social interactions such as joint attention and turn taking. Selection of literacy targets depends on the needs of the child with ASD as well as severity of the disorder.

Kaderavek and Rabidoux (2004) described an excellent model for addressing the literacy needs of children with atypical or severe communication impairments along a dynamic continuum of participation, termed the interactive-to-independent model. The model provides five levels of literacy development and potential literacy targets within each level. For example, the first level of literacy development, termed Level I, describes one literacy target as "student maintains attention to a literacy artifact and the literacy partner for _____ minutes" (p. 246). Thus, for children with ASD, intervention target selection may include not only emergent literacy skills but also the social aspects of literacy learning.

Assessment. Target selection often begins with assessment. Assessment of emergent literacy skills includes formal and informal testing. Contemporary measures of emergent literacy skills may need to be adjusted depending on the needs of the child with ASD. For example, test administration may have to be modified in several ways, such as providing explicit examples, prompts, and feedback; allowing more time for task completion; or adapting the test format to include assistive technology.

Furthermore, children with ASD may be best evaluated using alternative methods of assessment such as dynamic assessment. Dynamic assessment, when delivered in a test-teach-retest format, is especially beneficial for gathering information about children's emergent literacy knowledge and learning potential. As an example, consider the case of Carson, a 5-year-old kindergartener with ASD. A teacher administers the Peabody Picture Vocabulary Test-IV (PPVT-IV; Dunn & Dunn, 2007) to Carson to estimate his vocabulary knowledge. Carson receives a very poor score. Knowing Carson as a student, his teacher suspects that he understands more words than the test shows. As a result, she goes through several of the words on the test, associates actions with the words, and shows him examples and pictures of the words around the room and in books. She then readministers the PPVT-IV and finds that Carson correctly identifies the words she taught him. Thus, the teacher now has a better idea of Carson's vocabulary knowledge and understanding.

In addition to adjusting assessments for children with ASD, teachers should consider evaluating precursor emergent literacy skills. For instance, many phonological awareness tests begin with the skill of rhyming, which for some children with ASD is too difficult. Therefore, teachers may want to design tasks that assess earlier phonological awareness skills in authentic ways, such as identifying different sounds in the environment (bell vs. rustling leaves). All in all, adjusting emergent literacy assessments in ways such as these will help teachers identify important targets for literacy instruction.

Authentic Assessments

For children who are "diverse" learners for environmental or developmental reasons, authentic assessments provide important opportunities to demonstrate what they know apart from norm-referenced or standardized tests. Authentic assessments require designing tasks representative of real-life challenges for children to perform. For example, a teacher who would like to know more about a child's understanding of story structure (fictional narrative) might conduct a small-group read-aloud and embed several questions related to the characters or problem of the story into the book reading (e.g., Who is this story about?). When creating authentic tasks, teachers identify the knowledge to be demonstrated, the criteria indicative of good performance of the task, and the method for recording children's actual achievements (e.g., rubric, checklist). One of the benefits of this type of assessment is that children rarely know they are being assessed.

Additional information about authentic assessments and how to design one may be found at the following helpful and useful web site: http://jonathan.mueller.faculty.noctrl.edu/toolbox/index.htm

Facilitative Techniques

Three adult-implemented strategies found to be effective in accelerating children's emergent literacy skills are (a) being explicit and systematic, (b) being responsive, and (c) scaffolding.

Being explicit and systematic. Being explicit refers to the direct and overt input provided. Contrasted with implicit learning, which occurs by means of exposures to activities, explicit instruction in emergent literacy behaviors has been shown to result in higher levels of learning (Justice et al., 2003). Many emergent literacy skills such as print concepts and phonological awareness are not learned implicitly through simply reading storybooks to children (Senechal & LeFevre, 2002), but require direct instruction. Therefore, while reading storybooks to children, teachers encourage emergent literacy skills by making direct comments and asking overt questions such as, "I hear two words that rhyme on this page: *mat* and *sat*. What's another word that rhymes with *mat* and *sat*?"

Systematicity refers to the planned and intentional ways in which teachers and other adults facilitate literacy. Adults who are systematic identify targets for emergent literacy instruction and create plans for addressing them sequentially. Systematic emergent literacy instruction is provided regularly with preparation rather than incidentally, or when the child appears "ready" for the interaction. For example, before a read-aloud to a group of children, a teacher may identify four to five vocabulary words to target and discuss explicitly during the book reading.

Being responsive. Adult responsiveness and warmth is another strategy shown to positively impact children's emergent literacy learning. Students of classroom teachers who demonstrate sensitivity to and empathy towards children's learning perform higher on measures of literacy and academics than those of less supportive teachers (e.g., Pianta & Stuhlman, 2004; Wilson, Pianta, & Stuhlman, 2007). Further, interactions that are reciprocal in nature improve children's oral language abilities compared to interactions that tend to be more directive or adult led. Responsiveness in adult-child interactions fosters secure and safe attachments. These secure attachments help the child feel confident to move forward and try new tasks.

As important as adult responsiveness is to child outcomes, child responsiveness to the adult and the task is equally significant. For example, research has shown that children who provide feedback and seek interaction from adults tend to elicit more adult responsiveness and warmth (e.g., Girolametto & Weitzman, 2002). This is particularly important to consider for children with ASD because, by nature, they tend to initiate less frequently and offer less explicit feedback during adult-child interactions compared to children with typical social skills. As a result, adults may have difficulty "reading" the subtle initiations and responses of the child with ASD and, therefore, miss important reactions and opportunities to continue the interaction (Girolametto, Hoaken, Weitzman, & van Lieshout, 2000).

Scaffolding. Scaffolding refers to the support adults provide to children that challenges them at a level just beyond what they are able to do independently (Vygotsky, 1978). As adults vary their level of guidance, children are encouraged to work at higher levels of performance. Scaffolds vary depending on the child's level of functioning. When scaffolding, adults must have a sense of the child's actual development or what the child can do alone or without assistance. Learning then takes place in the zone of proximal development, the "space" just beyond what children can do independently. Teaching that occurs at a level beyond a child's zone of proximal development may be too difficult, whereas teaching that occurs below this zone may be too easy.

Scaffolding to facilitate children's learning differs from other theories of learning, such as behaviorism. Whereas other strategies involve the adult managing or supervising tasks, scaffolding involves the adult creating opportunities for the child to be a collaborative participant (Wink & Putney, 2002). By its very nature, scaffolding implies a social approach to learning. In some ways, it seems contradictory to suggest that scaffolding be used with children with ASD to facilitate literacy skills given their inherent weaknesses in social interaction skills and need for structure. On the other hand, application of this facilitative strategy is not without structure; adults provide the necessary amount of support for learning and then gradually, as the child is ready, withdraw that support to help the child realize his/her independent potential.

Contexts for Building Emergent Literacy Skills

The following activities (see Table 8.1) have been found to be effective in increasing emergent literacy skills for children with typical language and vulnerable populations, including children with significant developmental disabilities (e.g., Browder, Mims, Spooner, Ahlgrim-Delzell, & Lee, 2008). Many of these contexts for improving emergent literacy skills have not been examined in the ASD population, and some have been examined only at the case study or descriptive level (e.g., Koppenhaver & Erickson, 2003). Nonetheless, the contexts we present next are grounded in strong theory and clinical practice and, therefore, possess potential applicability to children with ASD.

Table 8.1
Emergent Literacy Activities for Children With Autism Spectrum Disorders

Activity	Definition	Example
Shared book reading	Style of book reading in which the adult and child have rich conversations about the content and pictures in a text	Interactive or dialogic book reading
Dramatic storytelling and retelling	Activity in which children invent and act out stories or retell stories heard or read	Versions of popular stories or fairytales such as *Little Red Riding Hood*
Interactive routines	Predictable, repeated actions written down as a schedule or chart	Opening group or calendar
Music and movement	Enlarged-print versions of lyrics written as interactive charts	Good morning or welcome song
Language experience activities	Activity in which the teacher guides a discussion and written record of a shared experience (field trip)	Visit to the zoo
Signing-in and signing-up	Activity in which children write their name on a piece of paper when they come to school in the morning or for turn-taking purposes	Sign-up sheet to use the computer
Games	Type of play for targeting emergent literacy skills	Alphabet letter matching game

Shared Book Reading

Shared book reading refers to adult-child interactions surrounding text that involves conversations and discussions about the content as well as pictures and print in the book. For children with typical language skills, the frequency and quality with which adults and children engage in shared book reading interactions relate to children's reading and academic achievements (e.g., Bus, van Ijzendoorn, & Pellegrini, 1995; Senechal & LeFevre, 2002; Senechal et al., 2008). That is, children who have been read to on a regular basis and who have rich conversations about books tend to perform higher on measures of language and literacy than children who experience less frequent and interactive book reading sessions (e.g., Bingham, 2007).

As a group, children with severe language impairments and children with multiple disabilities have less access to literacy materials at home and demonstrate less engagement in adult-child book reading experiences than typically developing children (Koppenhaver et al., 2007; Light & Smith, 1993). Such lack of participation in literacy activities may be due in large part to the level of feedback they offer to keep the interaction going. For example, research exploring conversational participation between parents and children in terms of initiations and responses shows that children with disabilities, specifically language impairments, tend to ask and answer fewer questions during the shared book reading experience (e.g., Evans & Schmidt, 1991; Sulzby & Kaderavek, 1996). Therefore, the adult of a child with a disability tends to work harder during the interaction and bears more of the conversational load than the adult of a child without a disability. As a result, the adult may hypothetically engage the child with a disability in fewer shared book reading experiences. Despite these differences in shared book reading experiences for children with and without disabilities, shared book reading represents an authentic context for providing explicit literacy instruction given its frequent occurrence in home and classroom environments.

Scientific studies of interventions presented within shared book reading contexts have demonstrated positive effects on children's language and literacy skills through the use of various techniques (e.g., Wasik & Bond, 2001; Wasik, Bond, & Hindman, 2006; Zevenbergen, Whitehurst, & Zevenbergen, 2003). Interactive or dialogic book reading is one such technique, in which adults employ a range of prompts to facilitate interest and engagement in the reading experience (Lonigan & Whitehurst, 1998; Whitehurst et al., 1994). Prompts consist mainly of adult questions and comments that elicit responses, either verbal or nonverbal, from children and can range in difficulty from close- (e.g., show me the bear) to open-ended questions (e.g., why do you think the bear was so sad?) or statements. Interactive book reading studies show improvements in oral vocabulary and comprehension in children from a variety of backgrounds, such as economic disadvantage (Wasik & Bond) and language impairment (Crain-Thoreson & Dale, 1999; Crowe, Norris, & Hoffman, 2004). Further, Browder et al. (2008) used interactive book reading in combination with assistive technology to increase responsiveness and task completion in children with severe and multiple disabilities.

Code-related interventions embedded in shared book reading interactions have been shown to increase children's print and phonological awareness. Specifically, adults who read with a print-referencing style in which they focus children's attention on aspects of print positively affect children's knowledge about print (Justice & Ezell, 2000, 2002; Justice, Kaderavek, Fan, Sofka, & Hunt, 2009). While these interventions have been found to be effective for children with typical language and children with language impairments, few studies targeting the code-related aspects of print during shared book reading have been conducted with children with ASD. Theoretically, calling attention to print during interactive book reading makes sense for children with ASD due to their perceived strengths in visual-spatial skills. Alphabet knowledge and print concepts may be facilitated through explicitly referencing particular print aspects such as discussing specific letters in the book or the direction in which print is read.

Shared book reading is often associated with young children; however, children of all ages and abilities benefit from interactive reading. When conducting shared book reading, consider the interests and age of the child. Traditional storybooks are usually more appropriate for younger children, whereas comic books, newspapers, or weekly readers may be well suited for older children. Chapter books that reflect the interest, content, and literature read at middle and high school levels may be simplified, paired with pictures, and adapted for students who are emergent literacy learners with more significant special needs (Browder, Trela, & Jimenez, 2007). Indeed, the nature of shared book reading lends itself well to a range of emergent literacy targets across age levels. For example, for some children with ASD, the initial target of shared book reading may simply be to establish joint attention, whereas other children may be at the level of labeling objects in books. Yet, other children may read text fluently yet demonstrate poor comprehension. Therefore, shared book reading offers a flexible context for working on emergent literacy skills with children with a range of needs.

Large-group shared book reading may be difficult for some children with ASD. However, such settings may be structured in three ways to facilitate involvement.

1. **Give a smaller, adapted version of the same book to a child to hold during the large group.** These smaller books may include pictures and modified text for children to read along as the teacher reads (Browder, Ahlgrim-Delzell, Courtade, Gibbs, & Flowers, 2008). Using a smaller, adapted book encourages independence using various book-related skills such as holding the book upright or page turning, while at the same time encouraging participation and joint attention in the whole-group reading experience.

2. **Promote communication during the book reading experience by providing assistive technology or alternative and augmentative communication devices.** Such devices may be programmed with information such as repetitive text that the child recites with the teacher, or programmed with story information (e.g., characters, setting) for answering comprehension questions.

3. **Wait for a child's response before prompting, since children with ASD often require time to process information.** Furthermore, questions directed to specific children rather than the whole group may encourage participation in the book sharing interaction; however, caution is necessary to avoid singling out certain children.

While shared book reading is traditionally delivered using paper books, electronic storybooks may be particularly engaging for students with ASD. Also known as talking books or computer books, digital storybooks offer a different modality for children to listen to and read books. Many electronic storybooks include features such as highlighting the print while reading and rereading certain words. This type of digital and visual format plays to the strength and interest in computers often observed in children with ASD.

Many free web sites and software programs offer books in digital formats. Storybooks can also be invented and created on the computer using PowerPoint® (see Table 8.2). Children simply insert pictures and cohesive text into slides to generate a story. Interactive features of this technique include having the children record their own voices reading the book as well as programming or hyperlinking pictures and objects within the story to perform certain actions or to say certain things.

Table 8.2

Use of PowerPoint® to Create Storybooks

Microsoft PowerPoint® offers a creative and engaging format for children to create computer storybooks of different kinds, such as nursery rhymes, alphabet books, fairytales, simple stories, etc. The example below, based on the predictable text of *Brown Bear, Brown Bear, What Do You See?* (Martin, 1996), shows how books may be designed on the computer using the guide *How to Create Talking Books in PowerPoint® 97 and 2000* (Walter, 2002). The first slide shows how adding forward and backward action buttons to the bottom of each slide permits a child to "flip" to the next or previous page in the book. Children can also record and listen to themselves reading the book as indicated by the yellow speakers. The second slide shows how children might include animation of objects in the book as demonstrated by the blackbird appearing to fly off of the screen.

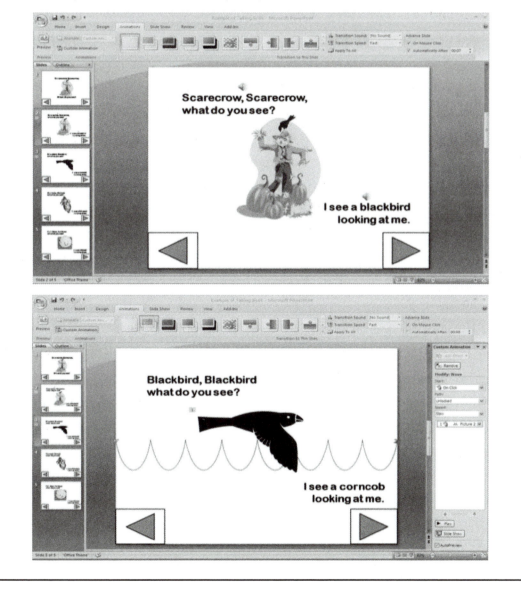

Dramatic Storytelling and Retelling

Acting out or retelling stories through drama is an important activity for building emergent literacy skills, particularly vocabulary and comprehension. When teachers provide encouragement and assistance for children to dramatize stories, children learn important elements of stories such as structure and dialogue. The more familiar children become with the literate features of stories, the more experience and understanding they gain with narrative texts.

Facilitation of dramatic retellings involves a scaffolded approach consisting of expressive storytelling, assisted retelling, and independent acting (McGee & Richgels, 2003).

1. Teachers first provide a model for how to tell stories; voices and simple props may be used to engage children in the dramatic aspects of stories. Dramatic storytelling is not just for young children. Stories that appeal to a variety of ages and interests might be selected for acting out and reenacting. Versions of popular stories such as the *Three Little Pigs* may also be dramatized to discuss different perspectives of characters and plot lines. For example, the adult might first tell the story of the three little pigs from one of the pigs' perspective and then tell the story form the wolf's perspective. For children with ASD, pretending to be different characters or the same character across stories encourages perspective taking – an important comprehension skill necessary for drawing inferences during reading.

2. Once children become engaged and familiar with the story, teachers assist them in a variety of story-related skills, including sequencing events using pictures or drawing events from the story. Teachers might also discuss elements of the story structure such as setting, characters, feelings of characters, and problems and solutions in the story. As teachers guide children in their retellings, dialogue that is important to the story is discussed. For children with ASD who demonstrate less sophisticated language use, sequencing pictures in a "first-then" format may be an initial step toward retelling. Teachers also guide the reenactment of stories read by providing children opportunities to create props and become characters. Character emotions are discussed, and children are encouraged to demonstrate those emotions during the dramatization. Teachers provide children feedback throughout this process. Video recordings may even be incorporated into story retellings and dramas.

3. As teachers gradually withdraw support, children are encouraged to reenact stories independently. In an emergent literacy classroom, children might act out stories in a book or puppet show center, complete with props brought in by the

teacher and/or props designed by the students (McGee & Richgels, 2003). Once a story is told, a retelling center may be created with scanned pictures of stories in pocket charts for children to put in sequence or flannel board cutouts for children to retell. For children who are older chronologically and are still emergent learners, reenactment of stories may be performed as part of a functional task of creating a video library for younger students, to include written scripts.

Interactive Routines

Predictable, repeated actions within the same daily routine may also facilitate emergent literacy development. The structure associated with these routines provides a good context for language and literacy learning to occur (McGee & Richgels, 2003). For example, opening group, which includes the calendar, weather, a song, and possibly large-group book reading, represents a typical start to the day in many preschool and elementary school classrooms. At first, the teacher teaches the children the routines and assigns roles or jobs and job descriptions. She then prompts and models the actions of each role and the associated language and vocabulary. As the children become more and more familiar with the routine, they assume more responsibility and independence in terms of participating in and leading the opening group activities.

Teachers facilitate literacy learning during these interactive routines by explicitly drawing children's attention to print. For example, during job assignments, the teacher might point to a child's name, encourage children to read it, and then discuss specific letters in the child's name and the names of other children who have the same letters in their names. This type of intentional discussion increases children's awareness of the alphabet, meaning, and function of print, and helps them relate print to daily activities.

Assistive technology

Assistive technology, including alternative and augmentative communication (ACC) devices, may be programmed with routines in mind so that children on the autism spectrum with fewer verbal language skills may participate in the routines. For example, during the weather routine, a child with ASD could select the word *cloudy* from a set of four pictures and words to tell the type of weather. In this manner, the child is working on various emergent literacy behaviors such as associating words with meaning as well as practicing sight word vocabulary. Higher-functioning students with ASD might act as the recorder of weather words or guide the students in days of the week to work on emergent writing and sight word recognition, respectively.

Music and Movement

Many classroom teachers play classical or soft background music while children work independently. Ideally, this type of music calms students and provides a peaceful atmosphere in the room. Some teachers ask children to bring in their favorite music to be played. A very small research base of descriptive studies as well as observations of children with ASD suggest that soft music, such as folk songs and classical music, can be a powerful tool for calming children and regulating their behavior (Boso, Emanuele, Minazzi, Abbamonte, & Politi, 2007; Wigram & Gold, 2006). Furthermore, music may stimulate play or communication in children with ASD, facilitating such skills as joint attention and turn taking. Teachers may also use music or sing songs to help children with ASD transition between activities or participate in everyday routines, such greeting each other at the start of a school day. In addition to teaching social communication skills with music, songs represent a potential context for fostering literacy skills in children with ASD.

Lyrics, when written down as an interactive chart, provide a meaningful and engaging context for facilitating emergent literacy skills. Teachers may write each word of a song on a card and place the words in the pockets of a chart (Moomaw & Hieronymous, 2002). As the teacher and children sing the song, the teacher tracks the print. A variety of phonological awareness and print awareness skill instruction might follow, using the interactive chart. For instance, the teacher might encourage children to sway with the words or the syllable structures. She might also point out sound-letter relationships or discuss the concept of words versus letters. Teachers may also intentionally select songs with rhyming words, such as nursery rhymes for younger children and raps for older children, and model how to change the meaning of the song depending on the rhyming word selected.

For children with ASD who have limited verbal abilities, songs may be recorded on audio or videotape for them to listen to or watch as they "read" the interactive chart. Children with higher-functioning skills may work on phonological awareness by generating rhyming words for songs or creating their own personal lyrics. Interactive charts that include song lyrics provide children an authentic and meaningful context for accessing and exploring print.

Caution: Not all children with ASD enjoy listening to music, and what may be enjoyable to listen to for one child may not be enjoyable for another. Therefore, special care must be taken when using music in the classroom to facilitate language and literacy skills.

Signing-In and Signing-Up

One strategy used to work on emergent writing includes name writing. Two authentic contexts for improving children's writing skills involve signing-in and signing-up procedures. With signing-in, children write their name on a piece of paper when they come to school in the morning. This serves as attendance for the teacher as well as practice for the children in writing their names. Signing-up involves directing children to write their names for turn-taking purposes. For example, teachers might use a sign-up procedure for using the computer during free time or indicating who is next to play with or use a certain item. Teachers simply place a sheet at each area and instruct children to write their names on the sheet in a list-style fashion.

Many children, including those with ASD, have difficulty with the formation and sequencing of letters in their name. Name writing may be scaffolded in three different ways.

1. **Write a child's name for him or her to trace or copy.** Tracing and copying provides a child with a high level of support, which is important for emergent writers who may lack confidence or have perfectionistic tendencies.

2. **Write a child's name or letters in his/her name as dots.** In this way, the child connects-the-dots to form letters, and ultimately write his/her name.

3. **Use chaining to foster name writing.** For example, a child may be encouraged to write the first letter of his/her name independently and then trace or copy the remaining letters. Then the child might progress to writing the second letter of his/her name independently, and so on.

While these scaffolds offer structure for name writing for the emergent writer, it is important to remember that emergent writing follows a developmental progression of scribbling to eventual letter-like formations. Therefore, all emergent writing, including name writing, should be encouraged and accepted unconditionally, with children given ample opportunities to write their names independently without restrictions.

Language Experience Activities

Language experience activities (LEAs) offer unique opportunities to use both code-related and meaning-based reading processes. Theoretically, LEAs help children connect, in their own words, what they know and have experienced with what they are presently learning. LEAs, in essence, involve some shared experiences. Examples of shared experiences include going on a field trip to the museum, performing a science experiment, making a recipe, building a model, or inviting a guest to the classroom.

After students have participated in such an experience, the teacher guides a discussion about the adventure and records the children's comments, thoughts, and questions. Teachers often guide this activity by beginning with a summary of the experience and pause along the way for children to offer bits of information. An LEA may consist of various genres such as summaries or recounts of what happened, lists of information, thank-you letters, or poems. This type of activity is particularly important for children with ASD because it addresses important meaning-based skills such as grammatical understanding, vocabulary, and narrative abilities. The product of such an activity may be a book or a chart that children can reread to themselves, read to parents or siblings, or use as a model for writing about their own adventures.

> The digital camera is an especially useful tool for recording and documenting language experience activities. For example, as a student is taking part in a shared experience, an adult can take pictures of the student and help her sequence the pictures. The pictures can be presented to the teacher for help in creating a summary of the experience.

■ ■ ■

It is 1:00 p.m. on Tuesday afternoon. Mrs. Kohl and her kindergarten children visited a recycling center earlier that day. They had been learning about the environment and the impact pollution has had on the earth. While at the recycling center, Mrs. Kohl gave Ryan, a 6-year boy diagnosed with ASD, a digital camera and told him and the teaching assistant to take pictures of the class visit. Upon returning from the center around 11:00 a.m., the teacher instructs Ryan and the teaching assistant to go to the computer to print out the pictures they took. She reviews the pictures with Ryan and sends the children to lunch.

After lunch, Mrs. Kohl calls the children to group and starts by writing a general statement on chart paper of what they did earlier that morning. "Today we went to the recycling center, and we saw and did many things (Mrs. Kohl stops writing and looks at Ryan). Ryan, you have some pictures from our visit. What did we see first?" Ryan looks at one of the pictures he is holding and says, "smashed cans." Mrs. Kohl smiles and says, "Yes, we saw a machine that smashed cans. Let's write that sentence together as a group. First we saw smashed cans." Once the story or sequence of events is completed, Mrs. Kohl reads the story back to the children and tracks the print with her finger as she goes. She draws attention to various letters and words in the story and points out any vocabulary words that might need reinforcing.

Using LEAs with English Language Learners (ELLs)

Language experience activities (LEAs) also support emergent literacy and language skills in children for whom English is not their native language (ELL). Because this type of approach allows flexibility in purpose (e.g., list, recount of experience, thank-you note), it also allows flexibility for children's responses. For example, children who are ELLs may initially be hesitant to offer their input due to their limited English proficiency; therefore, the teacher might pair the ELL child with another child in the classroom. The typically developing and the ELL child work together to generate a response. Teachers may also adjust LEAs to take grammatical errors into consideration for ELLs.

In a typical LEA, the teacher scribes exactly what the children say verbally, despite mistakes in English grammar. Teachers may adapt this experience and model for the child, without overtly correcting, the correct grammatical forms. This is especially important for literacy development in all children as they reread what has been written.

Games

Children learn through play. One type of play involves games. Children frequently play games at home and in school; therefore, games provide a meaningful context for teaching literacy skills. Children with ASD may struggle with the social aspects of playing games with others; however, with adult instruction and the structure of the game format, this type of activity can become enjoyable, especially when matched to the interests of the child. Furthermore, games are highly adaptable for the linguistic and cultural needs of children and capitalize on the relative visual-spatial learning strengths demonstrated by children with ASD.

Goals for literacy games may start with participation and joint attention in the activity and then progress to emergent literacy skills. Literacy games may be played between individuals or on a computer, and may focus on specific skills related to the code- or meaning-based aspects of print. Examples of games played between a child and adult or between two or more children include matching, memory, sorting, spinners, and Go Fish. These types of games may be adjusted according to the emergent literacy target intended for intervention. For instance, vocabulary words and examples or definitions associated with those words may form the basis for a matching or memory game. Go Fish provides the optimal opportunity to target letter identification and letter naming, especially when children are encouraged to ask each other in complete questions, "Do you have the letter A?" Thus, card games as well as file folder games (i.e., laminated manila file folder with specially designed game and game pieces inside) offer teachers unique opportunities in which to embed emergent literacy targets into instruction.

Computer Games

Many computer software games and many web sites target emergent literacy skills and educational learning. For example, in some games, children identify letters, match rhyming words, and recognize words that sound the same at the beginning. Computer and web site games are often particularly engaging and motivating for children with ASD, and thus represent an important context for improving emergent literacy skills in this population.

Computer games that might interest emergent literacy learners include *Bailey's Book House* (rhyming, alliteration) by Edmark and Kidspiration (prewriting, writing) by Inspiration Software, Inc. Web sites that may be particularly engaging for working on literacy skills include http://www.magpo.com/play.html (online magnetic poetry), http://www.funbrain.com/brain/ReadingBrain/ReadingBrain.html (Mad Libs Junior), and http://www.literacycenter.net/ (Early Childhood Education Network).

Conclusion

In this chapter we have discussed the concept of emergent literacy and the code-related and meaning-based processes employed in learning to read and write. We provided important considerations regarding building emergent literacy skills in children diagnosed with ASD and, based on the available research, presented specific contexts for promoting emergent literacy skills (e.g., shared book reading, music and movement, games). Throughout the chapter we also highlighted potential adjustments and adaptations to emergent literacy instruction for children with ASD.

While emergent literacy behaviors have traditionally been ignored in children diagnosed with ASD, the importance of these skills to later academic success cannot be overstated. By using the concepts and strategies presented in this chapter for facilitating emergent literacy skills, teachers can help children with ASD achieve reading and writing excellence.

Chapter Highlights

- Emergent literacy refers to the exploratory reading and writing behavior children display long before they can read and write in the conventional sense and before formal schooling.

- Theoretically, the emergent literacy perspective suggests the importance of language development for literacy.

- The emergent literacy stage may best be represented as a fluid period of development rather than a precise age.

- Emergent literacy skills may be defined as the skills, such as identifying the names of letters or understanding the meaning of words, that lay the foundation for later fluent decoding and comprehension of text.

- Code-related reading process refers to the reader's ability to understand the structure of print. These code-related processes consist of four domains: phonological awareness, alphabet knowledge, print concepts, and emergent writing.
  - ✔ *Phonological awareness:* the ability to recognize and identify the sound properties of words
  - ✔ *Alphabet knowledge:* familiarity with written symbols or graphemes
  - ✔ *Print concept knowledge:* understanding of the forms, functions, and features of print
  - ✔ *Emergent writing:* attempts to convey information through written symbols

- Meaning-based processes refer to a global understanding of printed words and sentences. Three broad domains comprise meaning-based processes: vocabulary, grammatic understanding, and narrative production.
  - ✔ *Vocabulary:* an understanding the meaning of words
  - ✔ *Grammatical understanding:* the ability to understand the syntax of words or sentences
  - ✔ *Narrative:* the oral or written description of an event

- Three factors impact the potential for building emergent literacy skills in children with ASD: variability, development, and applicability.
  - ✔ *Variability:* Some behaviors appear to be intact and congruent developmentally, whereas others appear to be significantly delayed. This results in a fragmented profile of emergent literacy skills.
  - ✔ *Development:* For children with ASD, the shape of the reading growth curve may be similar to that of children with language impairments in the early years of schooling, with large achievement gains noted in the early years and less gain in upper-elementary grades. More research is needed.
  - ✔ *Applicability:* Some interventions are more suitable for a certain child than for others.

- Several strategies are used to promote emergent literacy skills. They include:
  - ✔ *Selecting a target:* Intervention targets involve the specific skills or behaviors chosen to teach within a particular area.
  - ✔ *Facilitative techniques:* (a) Being explicit and systematic, (b) being responsive, and (c) scaffolding.

- Some activities have been shown to be effective in increasing emergent literacy skills:
  - ✔ *Shared book reading:* Refers to adult-child interactions surrounding text that involve conversations and discussions about the content as well as pictures and print in the book.
  - ✔ *Dramatic storytelling and retelling:* Acting out stories through drama is an important activity for building emergent literacy skills in children, particularly vocabulary and comprehension.
  - ✔ *Interactive routines:* Repeated actions with the same daily routine may also facilitate emergent literacy development.
  - ✔ *Music and movement:* Music helps calm students and provides a peaceful atmosphere in the room.
  - ✔ *Signing-in and signing-up:* With signing-in, children write their name on a piece of paper when they come to school. Signing-up involves directing children to write their names for turn-taking purposes.
  - ✔ *Language experience activities:* LEAs help children connect what they know and have experienced with what they are presently learning.
  - ✔ *Games:* Children learn through play. Children with ASD benefit from playing games if the games selected are adaptable to their linguistic and cultural needs.

Chapter Review Questions

1. How might emergent literacy theory be defined?

2. Which two interrelated but distinct processes are involved in reading?

3. Are all emergent literacy interventions effective with certain vulnerable populations of children also applicable to children with ASD?

4. In what ways is shared book reading a flexible context for targeting emergent literacy skills?

References

Alberto, P. A., Fredrick, L., Hughes, M., McIntosh, L., & Cihak, D. (2007). Components of visual literacy: Teaching logos. *Focus on Autism and Other Developmental Disabilities, 22*(4), 234-243.

Anthony, J. L., & Francis, D. J. (2005). Development of phonological awareness. *Current Directions in Psychological Science, 14*(5), 255-259.

Bedrosian, J., Lasker, J., Speidel, K., & Politsch, A. (2003). Enhancing the written narrative skills of an AAC student with autism: Evidence-based research issues. *Topics in Language Disorders, 23*(4), 305-324.

Berninger, V. W., Abbott, R. D., Thomson, J. B., & Raskind, W. H. (2001). Language phenotype for reading and writing disability: A family approach. *Scientific Studies of Reading, 15*(1), 59-106.

Bingham, G. E. (2007). Maternal literacy beliefs and the quality of mother-child book-reading interactions: Associations with children's early literacy development. *Early Education and Development, 18*(1), 23-49.

Boso, M., Emanuele, E., Minazzi, V., Abbamonte, M., & Politi, P. (2007). Effect of long-term interactive music therapy on behavior profile and musical skills in young adults with severe autism. *The Journal of Alternative and Complementary Medicine, 13*(7), 709-712.

Browder, D. M., Ahlgrim-Delzell, L., Courtrade, G., Gibbs, S. L., & Flowers, C. (2008). Evaluation of the effectiveness of an early literacy program for students with significant developmental disabilities. *Exceptional Children, 75*, 33-52.

Browder, D. M., Mims, P. J., Spooner, F., Ahlgrim-Delzell, L., & Lee, A. (2008). Teaching elementary students with multiple disabilities to participate in shared stories. *Research & Practice for Persons with Severe Disabilities, 33*(1), 3-12.

Browder, D. M., Trela, K., & Jimenez, B. (2007). Training teachers to follow a task analysis to engage middle school students with moderate and severe developmental disabilities in grade-appropriate literature. *Focus on Autism and Other Developmental Disabilities, 22*(4), 206-219.

Bus, A. G., van Ijzendoorn, M. H., & Pellegrini, A. D. (1995). Joint book reading makes for success in learning to read: A meta-analysis on intergenerational transmission of literacy. *Review of Educational Research, 65*(1), 1-21.

Capps, L., Kehres, J., & Sigman, M. (1998). Conversational abilities among children with autism and children with developmental delays. *Autism, 2*(4), 325-344.

Catts, H. W., Fey, M. E., Tomblin, J. B., & Zhang, X. (2002). A longitudinal investigation of reading outcomes in children with language impairments. *Journal of Speech, Language, and Hearing Research, 45*(6), 1142-1157.

Catts, H. W., Fey, M. E., Zhang, X., & Tomblin, J. B. (1999). Language basis of reading and reading disabilities: Evidence from a longitudinal investigation. *Scientific Studies of Reading, 3*(4), 331-361.

Catts, H. W., Fey, M. E., Zhang, X., & Tomblin, J. B. (2001). Estimating the risk of future reading difficulties in kindergarten children: A research-based model and its clinical implementation. *Language, Speech, and Hearing Services in Schools, 32*(1), 38-50.

Crain-Thoreson, C., & Dale, P. S. (1999). Enhancing linguistic performance: Parents and teachers as book reading partners for children with language delays. *Topics in Early Childhood Special Education, 19*(1), 28-39.

Crowe, L. K., Norris, J. A., & Hoffman, P. R. (2004). Training caregivers to facilitate communicative participation of preschool children with language impairment during storybook reading. *Journal of Communication Disorders, 37*(2), 177-196.

Downer, J. T., & Pianta, R. C. (2006). Academic and cognitive functioning in first grade: Associations with earlier home and child care predictors and with concurrent home and classroom experiences. *School Psychology Review, 35*(1), 11-30.

Duncan, G. J., Dowsett, C. J., Claessens, A., Magnuson, K., Huston, A. C., Klebanov, P., et al. (2007). School readiness and later achievement. *Developmental Psychology, 43*(6), 1428-1446.

Dunn, L. M., & Dunn, D. M. (2007). *Peabody Picture Vocabulary Test* (4th ed.). Bloomington, MN: Pearson Assessments.

Evans, M. A., & Schmidt, F. (1991). Repeated maternal book reading with two children: Language-normal and language impaired. *First Language, 11,* 269-287.

Fine, J., Bartolucci, G., Szatmari, P., & Ginsberg, G. (1994). Cohesive discourse in pervasive developmental disorders. *Journal of Autism and Developmental Disorders, 24*(3), 315-329.

Fisher, N., Happé, F., & Dunn, J. (2005). The relationship between vocabulary, grammar, and false belief task performance in children with autistic spectrum disorders and children with moderate learning difficulties. *Journal of Child Psychology and Psychiatry, 46*(4), 409-419.

Gabig, C. S. (2008). Verbal working memory and story retelling in school-age children with autism. *Language, Speech, and Hearing Services in Schools, 39*(4), 498-511.

Girolametto, L., Hoaken, L., Weitzman, E., & van Lieshout, R. (2000). Patterns of adult-child linguistic interaction in integrated day care groups. *Language, Speech, and Hearing Services in Schools, 31*(2), 155-168.

Girolametto, L., & Weitzman, E. (2002). Responsiveness of child care providers in interactions with toddlers and preschoolers. *Language, Speech, and Hearing Services in Schools, 33*(4), 268-281.

Griffin, T. M., Hemphill, L., Camp, L., & Wolf, D. P. (2004). Oral discourse in the preschool years and later literacy skills. *First Language, 24*(71), 123-147.

Hammill, D. D. (2004). What we know about correlates of reading. *Exceptional Children, 70*(4), 453-468.

Hart, B., & Risley, R. T. (1995). *Meaningful differences in the everyday experience of young American children.* Baltimore: Paul H. Brookes.

Jarrold, C., Boucher, J., & Russell, J. (1997). Language profiles in children with autism. *Autism, 1*(1), 57-76.

Justice, L. M., Chow, S., Capellini, C., Flanigan, K., & Colton, S. (2003). Emergent literacy intervention for vulnerable preschoolers: Relative effects of two approaches. *American Journal of Speech-Language Pathology, 12*(3), 320-332.

Justice, L. M., & Ezell, H. K. (2000). Enhancing children's print and word awareness through home-based parent intervention. *American Journal of Speech-Language Pathology, 9*(3), 257-269.

Justice, L. M., & Ezell, H. K. (2002). Use of storybook reading to increase print awareness in at-risk children. *American Journal of Speech-Language Pathology, 11*(1), 17-29.

Justice, L. M., & Kaderavek, J. (2004). Exploring the continuum of emergent to conventional literacy: Transitioning special learners. *Reading & Writing Quarterly: Overcoming Learning Difficulties, 20*(3), 231-236.

Justice, L. M., Kaderavek, J. N., Fan, X., Sofka, A., & Hunt, A. (2009). Accelerating preschoolers' early literacy development through classroom-based teacher-child storybook reading and explicit print referencing. *Language, Speech, and Hearing Services in Schools, 40*(1), 67-85.

Justice, L. M., Sofka, A. E., & McGinty, A. (2007). Targets, techniques, and treatment contexts in emergent literacy intervention. *Seminars in Speech & Language, 28*(1), 14-24.

Kaderavek, J. N., & Rabidoux, P. (2004). Interactive to independent literacy: A model for designing literacy goals for children with atypical communication. *Reading & Writing Quarterly: Overcoming Learning Difficulties, 20*(3), 237-260.

Kjelgaard, M. M., & Tager-Flusberg, H. (2001). An investigation of language impairment in autism: Implications for genetic subgroups. *Language and Cognitive Processes, 16*(2-3), 287-308.

Koppenhaver, D. A., & Erickson, K. A. (2003). Natural emergent literacy supports for preschoolers with autism and severe communication impairments. *Topics in Language Disorders, 23*(4), 283-292.

Koppenhaver, D. A., Hendrix, M. P., & Williams, A. R. (2007). Toward evidence-based literacy interventions for children with severe and multiple disabilities. *Seminars in Speech & Language, 28*(1), 79-90.

Leonard, L. B., & Deevy, P. (2004). Lexical deficits in specific language impairment. *Classification of developmental language disorders: Theoretical issues and clinical implications* (pp. 209-233). Mahwah, NJ: Lawrence Erlbaum Associates Publishers.

Light, J., & Smith, A. K. (1993). Home literacy experiences of preshoolers who use AAC systems and of their nondisabled peers. *AAC: Augmentative and Alternative Communication, 9*(1), 10-25.

Lonigan, C. J., & Whitehurst, G. J. (1998). Relative efficacy of parent and teacher involvement in a shared-reading intervention for preschool children from low-income backgrounds. *Early Childhood Research Quarterly, 13*(2), 263-290.

Losh, M., & Capps, L. (2003). Narrative ability in high-functioning children with autism or Asperger's syndrome. *Journal of Autism and Developmental Disorders, 33*(3), 239-251.

Martin, B. (1996). *Brown bear, brown bear, what do you see?* New York: Henry Holt and Company.

Mashburn, A. J., Pianta, R. C., Hamre, B. K., Downer, J. T., Barbarin, O. A., Bryant, D., et al. (2008). Measures of classroom quality in prekindergarten and children's development of academic, language, and social skills. *Child Development, 79*(3), 732-749.

McCoach, D. B., O'Connell, A. A., Reis, S. M., & Levitt, H. A. (2006). Growing readers: A hierarchical linear model of children's reading growth during the first 2 years of school. *Journal of Educational Psychology, 98*(1), 14-28.

McGee, L. M., & Richgels, D. J. (2003). *Designing early literacy programs.* New York: The Guilford Press.

McGinty, A. S., & Justice, L. M. (2009). Predictors of print knowledge in children with specific language impairment: Experiential and developmental factors. *Journal of Speech, Language, and Hearing Research, 52*(1), 81-97.

Moomaw, S., & Hieronymous, B. (2002). *More than letters: Literacy activities for preschool, kindergarten and first-grade.* St. Paul, MN: Redleaf Press.

Nation, K., Clarke, P., Wright, B., & Williams, C. (2006). Patterns of reading ability in children with autism spectrum disorder. *Journal of Autism and Developmental Disorders, 36*(7), 911-919.

Nation, K., Snowling, M. J., & Clarke, P. (2007). Dissecting the relationship between language skills and learning to read: Semantic and phonological contributions to new vocabulary learning in children with poor reading comprehension. *Advances in Speech Language Pathology, 9*(2), 131-139.

National Early Literacy Panel. (2008). *Developing early literacy: Report of the National Early Literacy Panel.* Washington, DC: National Institute for Literacy.

Newman, T. M., Macomber, D., Naples, A. J., Babitz, T., Volkmar, F., & Grigorenko, E. L. (2007). Hyperlexia in children with autism spectrum disorders. *Journal of Autism and Developmental Disorders, 37*(4), 760-774.

Pan, B. A., Rowe, M. L., Singer, J. D., & Snow, C. E. (2005). Maternal correlates of growth in toddler vocabulary production in low-income families. *Child Development, 76*(4), 763-782.

Pianta, R. C., & Stuhlman, M. W. (2004). Teacher-child relationships and children's success in the first years of school. *School Psychology Review, 33*(3), 444-458.

Roberts, J., Jurgens, J., & Burchinal, M. (2005). The role of home literacy practices in preschool children's language and emergent literacy skills. *Journal of Speech, Language, and Hearing Research, 48*(2), 345-359.

Senechal, M., & LeFevre, J. (2002). Parental involvement in the development of children's reading skill: A five-year longitudinal study. *Child Development, 73*(2), 445-460.

Senechal, M., Pagan, S., Lever, R., & Ouellette, G. P. (2008). Relations among the frequency of shared reading and 4-year-old children's vocabulary, morphological and syntax comprehension, and narrative skills. *Early Education and Development, 19*(1), 27-44.

Skibbe, L. E., Grimm, K. J., Stanton-Chapman, T., Justice, L. M., Pence, K. L., & Bowles, R. P. (2008). Reading trajectories of children with language difficulties from preschool through fifth grade. *Language, Speech, and Hearing Services in Schools, 39*(4), 475-486.

Snow, C., Burns, M., & Griffin, P. (1998). *Preventing reading difficulties in young children.* Washington, DC: National Academy Press.

Storch, S. A., & Whitehurst, G. J. (2001). The role of family and home in the literacy development of children from low-income backgrounds. *The role of family literacy environments in promoting young children's emerging literacy skills* (pp. 53-71). San Francisco: Jossey-Bass.

Storch, S. A., & Whitehurst, G. J. (2002). Oral language and code-related precursors to reading: Evidence from a longitudinal structural model. *Developmental Psychology, 38*(6), 934-947.

Sulzby, E., & Kaderavek, J. (1996). Parent-child language during storybook reading and toy play contexts: Case studies of normally developing and specific language impaired (SLI) children. *The National Reading Conference Yearbook, 45,* 257-269.

Tager-Flusberg, H., Paul, R., & Lord, C. (2005). Language and communication in autism. *Handbook of autism and pervasive developmental disorders, Vol. 1: Diagnosis, development, neurobiology, and behavior* (3rd ed., pp. 335-364). Hoboken, NJ: John Wiley & Sons, Inc.

Teale, W. H., & Sulzby, E. (1986). *Emergent literacy: Writing and reading.* Norwood, NJ: Ablex Pub. Corp.

Treiman, R., Pennington, B. F., Shriberg, L. D., & Boada, R. (2008). Which children benefit from letter names in learning letter sounds? *Cognition, 106*(3), 1322-1338.

Vellutino, F. R., Fletcher, J. M., Snowling, M. J., & Scanlon, D. M. (2004). Specific reading disability (dyslexia): What have we learned in the past four decades? *Journal of Child Psychology and Psychiatry, 45*(1), 2-40.

Vellutino, F. R., & Scanlon, D. M. (1987). Phonological coding, phonological awareness, and reading ability: Evidence from a longitudinal and experimental study. *Merrill-Palmer Quarterly, 33*(3), 321-363.

Volden, J., & Lord, C. (1991). Neologisms and idiosyncratic language in autistic speakers. *Journal of Autism and Developmental Disorders, 21*(2), 109-130.

Vygotsky, L. (1978). *Mind in society: The development of higher psychological processes.* Cambridge, MA: Harvard University Press.

Walter, R. (2002). *How to create talking books in PowerPoint® 97 and 2000.* Oxford, UK: ACE Centre Advisory Trust.

Wasik, B. A., & Bond, M. A. (2001). Beyond the pages of a book: Interactive book reading and language development in preschool classrooms. *Journal of Educational Psychology, 93*(2), 243-250.

Wasik, B. A., Bond, M. A., & Hindman, A. (2006). The effects of a language and literacy intervention on head start children and teachers. *Journal of Educational Psychology, 98*(1), 63-74.

Whitehouse, A.J.O., Barry, J. G., & Bishop, D.V.M. (2007). The broader language phenotype of autism: A comparison with specific language impairment. *Journal of Child Psychology and Psychiatry, 48*(8), 822-830.

Whitehurst, G. J., Epstein, J. N., Angell, A. L., Payne, A. C., Crone, D. A., & Fischel, J. E. (1994). Outcomes of an emergent literacy intervention in head start. *Journal of Educational Psychology, 86*(4), 542-555.

Whitehurst, G. J., & Lonigan, C. J. (1998). Child development and emergent literacy. *Child Development, 69*(3), 848-872.

Wigram, T., & Gold, C. (2006). Music therapy in the assessment and treatment of autistic spectrum disorder: Clinical application and research evidence. *Child: Care, Health and Development, 32*(5), 535-542.

Wilson, H. K., Pianta, R. C., & Stuhlman, M. (2007). Typical classroom experiences in first grade: The role of classroom climate and functional risk in the development of social competencies. *The Elementary School Journal, 108*(2), 81-96.

Wink, J., & Putney, L. G. (2001). *A vision of Vygotsky*. Upper Saddle River, NJ: Allyn & Bacon.

Yaden, D. B., Rowe, D. W., & MacGillivray, L. (2000). Emergent literacy: A matter (polphony) of perspectives. *Handbook of reading research, Vol. III* (pp. 425-454) Mahwah, NJ: Lawrence Erlbaum Associates Publishers.

Zevenbergen, A. A., Whitehurst, G. J., & Zevenbergen, J. A. (2003). Effects of a shared-reading intervention on the inclusion of evaluative devices in narratives of children from low-income families. *Journal of Applied Developmental Psychology, 24*(1), 1-15.

Online Resources

The following web sites provide abundant resources for online books, games, and puzzles:

- Collection of storybooks online: http://www.tumblebooks.com/library/asp/home_tumblebooks.asp

- Adapted books for elementary, middle, and high school students: http://www.tumblebooks.com/tumblereadable/

- Stories by Public Broadcasting Service (PBS): http://pbskids.org/lions/stories/

- Children's digital library: http://www.storyplace.org/

- Famous actors reading books: http://www.storylineonline.net/

Chapter 9
Word Recognition

Hope Smith Davis, Ed.D., Indiana University South Bend

Pamela Williamson, Ph.D., University of Cincinnati

Learner Objectives

After reading this chapter, the learner should be able to:

- Identify the phases and characteristics of students developing orthographic knowledge

- Assess students' orthographic knowledge for instruction in word recognition

- Implement instructional strategies that develop word knowledge within the context of a larger literacy instructional framework

■ ■ ■

Darius had a knack for reading printed words from an early age. At the age of 4, he was able to pronounce every word put in front of him from the word stop *on a stop sign to the words printed in the local newspaper. But, like many students on the autism spectrum, his ability to decode the words did not correspond with an understanding of word meanings. For example, although Darius could read the word* stop, *he walked right through a barrier with a stop sign on it intended to keep him from leaving his classroom. Darius' teacher is using his fascination with words to build his understanding that words have meanings. For example, Darius and his peers practice matching name cards with the student during circle time.*

In another classroom, Jose, a teenager diagnosed with ASD, and his teacher are writing a Social Story™ about being a good sport, as Jose got upset when peers won a classroom review game used to prepare for an exam. Since Jose's decoding skills are at the syllables and affixes phase, his teacher helped him include words using the prefixes un- *and* re- *in the social story they wrote together. She then created a word sort activity with the words, thereby integrating word work into a meaningful activity.*

In yet another classroom, Alicia, a 13-year-old emergent reader with ASD, is working on sorting two groups of picture cards – one group depicts the tools used to make her peanut-butter-and-jelly sandwich (plate, butter knife, and sponge); the other depicts the ingredients (bread, peanut butter, and jelly). The teacher gave Alicia a closed-concept sort with explicitly defined categories, because she understands that students with ASD typically have difficulty discerning categories independently. The picture cards in the sort consist of line drawings at the level of abstraction to which Alicia has progressed, with the word for the object printed beneath. She will later put the picture cards in the order in which Alicia uses them to make her sandwich. Her teacher hopes that by the end of this grading period, Alicia will be able to match picture cards to word cards.

■ ■ ■

Instruction in word recognition is only one aspect of balanced, integrated reading instruction for students with autism spectrum disorders (ASD). As the opening vignettes illustrate, students on the autism spectrum have differences in their abilities to recognize words. Word recognition can be defined as the process of converting print into speech, with the ultimate aim of being able to understand or comprehend the utterance.

Words may be recognized by sight (i.e., the student automatically recognizes the word) or be decoded (i.e., sounded out using knowledge of sound-symbol relationships).

Word recognition is important because of its relationship to comprehension, as skilled decoders perform better on reading comprehension tasks than less skilled decoders (Perfetti & Hogaboam, 1975). This may be because, in part, accurate and automatic decoding frees up cognitive processing resources so that more attention can be devoted to comprehending the text. However, adequate word recognition alone does not ensure reading comprehension, and instruction in this area should be approached with the understanding that word recognition is only one component, albeit an important one, of the skills and processes necessary for the ultimate goal of reading instruction: making meaning from text.

The goal of this chapter is to bridge research on phonics and word study with what we know about reading and instruction for students diagnosed with ASD, but there is much more to phonics instruction than can be covered in a single textbook chapter. Once you have a basic understanding of how phonics and words work to help students with ASD become more proficient readers, we suggest you continue to explore the relationship between word study and reading comprehension by consulting additional texts devoted entirely to word study techniques. Often these texts provide specific lesson plan strategies and materials for the general education classroom that, based on your knowledge of reading instruction for students on the autism spectrum learned in this text, may be modified for students with ASD (e.g., Bear, Invernizzi, Templeton, & Johnston, 2008; Marten, 2003; Rycik & Rycik, 2007). In this chapter, we will focus on building word recognition for students with ASD through knowledge of common English spelling patterns (orthography), phonics, and word attack skills as part of integrated, balanced literacy instruction aimed at facilitating meaning.

Word Recognition

Word recognition is one of the two basic information processing activities involved in reading. The other is comprehension. Much evidence suggests that word recognition is a relative strength for many students on the spectrum, whereas reading comprehension is a noted weakness (O'Connor & Klein, 2004).

Word recognition includes the ability to identify words through decoding (i.e., using knowledge of sound-symbol correspondences) or by sight (i.e., visual recognition of the whole word). In the world of cognitive psychology, these are referred to as the lexical route (sight word recognition) and the nonlexical route (decoding) to word recognition, respectively. While word recognition is often associated with the ability to accurately and fluently decode letter-sound relationships and/or recognize words by sight, the term *recognition* itself also implies the active use of a reader's semantic (or meaning-based) knowledge in order to supply accurate meanings at both the word and text level. As some of the research described in the following sections will show, the application of semantic knowledge during the reading process is an area of particular instructional significance for students on the autism spectrum.

Word Recognition in Children With ASD

While a great deal is known about word recognition in typically developing (TD) students, there is conflicting evidence regarding the word recognition skills of children with ASD (Gabig, in press). In their study of nine children with autism, Frith and Snowling (1983) found that the children with ASD were able to both recognize and decode unknown written words at the same levels as age-matched TD children. Similarly, Minshew, Goldstein, and Siegel (1994) studied the reading ability of 54 high-functioning adolescents with ASD and found they too performed similarly to TD children in word recognition, and did slightly better on decoding tasks than TD peers.

The results of these studies may lead to the assumption that all or most students with ASD have little difficulty with word recognition, and that many students with ASD are hyperlexic – a term that describes the troubling pairing of the ability of some students to precociously decode words and sentences with little or no comprehension (Craig & Telfer, 2005; Gately, 2008; Mirenda, 2003; O'Connor & Klein, 2004; Saldana & Frith, 2007).

However, as Nation, Clarke, Wright, and Williams (2006) suggested, there is great variability in patterns of reading ability among students with ASD. Variability in word reading and decoding ability is no exception. In their investigation of the reading skills of 41 children with ASD in which they assessed word recognition, these researchers found that while word recognition was in the average range, reading comprehension was impaired. This finding has been confirmed by numerous other studies (e.g., O'Connor & Hermelin, 1994; Patti & Lupinetti, 1993; Whitehouse & Harris, 1984).

Upon closer inspection of how individual students performed, Nation and her colleagues reported that of the 32 children who were able to read words at all, 42% scored one standard deviation below the norm group in decoding skills, and another 22% scored two standard deviations below the norm group. In addition, a smaller number of children ($n = 5$) had adequate levels of word reading abilities coupled with poor decoding skills.

Similarly, in a study investigating the role of phonological awareness and word recognition among 14 children with ASD, aged 5-7, Gabig (2010) found variability between the children's ability to decode nonwords and read real words; participants performed better when reading real words. (Please note that nonword reading is only one of several indicators that may be used to determine a student's ability to decode unknown words. Nonword reading proficiency should never be a goal for reading instruction. Instruction should focus strictly on learning to read real words in *meaningful* contexts.) In particular, nine children struggled in ways that were "characterized by slow and labored decoding attempts that were not accurate" (p. 10), two children were able to sound out words but were unable to blend sounds together to form the nonword, and two children "were able to decode the nonwords rapidly and efficiently" (p. 10).

Semantic awareness. Because autism is a spectrum disorder, as discussed throughout this text, students with ASD demonstrate a range of abilities, and this applies to word recognition as well. While some students will need word recognition instruction at the most basic decoding levels, others may already be fluent decoders who are unable to connect meaning to the words themselves (hyperlexic). Still others may be able to comprehend concrete words and texts once decoded, but tend to encounter difficulties making meaning from longer passages of text as specific word meanings become more subtle and abstract.

Researchers have investigated the semantic knowledge and processing systems of students on the spectrum for more than 25 years. As some similarities between students with ASD and typically developing students have been found in relation to reading growth and development, similar forms of instruction in this area are, in many cases, appropriate. However, there is still much to learn about how students on the spectrum process words semantically and how these processes (and, consequently, instructional needs) differ from those of their TD peers.

For example, Tager-Flusberg (1985) found that students with ASD and typically developing students were similarly able to categorize concrete words and concepts based on commonalities within conceptual groupings when the students were matched based on verbal mental age. Boucher (1988) determined that the students with ASD in her research also were able to respond similarly to their typically developing peers when asked to generate words in a global category (e.g., food or animals); however, when the students were asked to generate words based on a miscellaneous category (i.e., naming random words when they came to mind), the students with ASD were significantly less capable of coming up with words than their TD peers. Boucher's findings, along with the results of some neurobiological research (Dunn & Bates, 2005), suggest that semantic processing may occur differently for students with ASD than for their typically developing peers.

Taken together, this suggests that students with ASD may have as many as five different word recognition profiles:

- mostly high-functioning students with adequate word reading and decoding abilities
- students with adequate word recognition but poor decoding skills
- students with inadequate blending skills
- students with inadequate word recognition and poor decoding skills
- nonword readers

All of these profiles seem to exist against a backdrop of poor reading comprehension. This suggests that intervention specialists need a wide range of assessment tools and instructional methods to reach every student, and that word recognition work must always be done in ways that center around not just visual patterns but around meaning.

Influences on Word Recognition

Oral language deficits are widely documented in children on the spectrum. One aspect of language that appears to be unrelated to word reading in children with ASD is phonological awareness (PA). Gabig (2010) studied 14 school-age children with ASD and 10 age-matched TD peers and found that word reading was not related to PA. Due to the small sample size, additional research is needed to determine if this finding prevails.

Some evidence suggests that memory impairments, often associated with executive functioning (see Chapter 2), affect language acquisition of students on the spectrum (Hala, Rasmussen, & Henderson, 2005), while other evidence points to difficulties with pragmatic language, often associated with theory of the mind difficulties (see Chapter 2). Children with ASD have difficulties with joint attention, which scholars speculate causes mismatches between concepts and words (see McDuffie, Yoder, & Stone, 2006). For example, oral vocabulary is learned when adults draw attention to objects and name them. If children are not attending to the same object at the time of this naming, the wrong word and the wrong object may become paired.

Some case study evidence suggests that strength in word reading can be used to facilitate oral language skills (Craig & Telfer, 2005). Thus, while memory and word concept concerns are important considerations when planning word recognition instruction, at least some evidence supports the idea that text-rich environments and word recognition strengths can facilitate language development. For example, Koppenhaver and Erickson (2003) found that even very young students with ASD who had little or no oral communication benefited from rich-text environments that allowed them to explore books, letters, and other written materials on their own.

The Instructional Context for Word Study Work

Our work with students with ASD suggests that some approaches to helping students read words are more effective than others. Other scholars seem to agree (e.g., Mirenda, 2003). For example, Koppenhaver and Erickson (2003) recommended teachers "draw attention to forms, content, and use of written language" (p. 287) in everyday classroom interactions. In their study of natural emergent literacy supports, Koppenhaver and Erickson utilized various opportunistic interaction supports, such as engaging in writing activities (e.g., letter stamps and paper), oral interpretations of student drawings and scribblings, and parallel play using tools in novel ways, as teachers used think-alouds to describe their own actions. With these supports, students began exhibiting emergent literacy skills, such as engaging in emergent writing on chalkboards and "reading" to the researchers what was written. In addition, students began to understand that print carries meaning.

Further, reading and writing centers should be available to students to provide authentic, literacy-practice opportunities. For example, Kluth and Darmody-Latham (2003) described a student who was very interested in the weather and weather patterns. The student's teacher used this interest to introduce him to the daily weather in the local newspaper, and later to narrative books on weather-related topics.

Students should have access to a variety of print (e.g., age-appropriate books and magazines, newspaper stories, class-made books, books on tape) and writing materials (e.g., computers left open to word processing software, writing toys, crayons, pencils, paper, sticky notes, wipe-off markers, and white erase boards) for exploration (Koppenhaver & Erickson, 2003). See Table 9.1 for some thoughts about technology.

Table 9.1
Thoughts About Technology

Technology isn't always computer software or electronic equipment and devices that have to be plugged in for supplemental instruction. While several useful web sites like www.picturemereading.com (where word cards can be purchased that include pictorial representations for sight word recognition) are available for instruction in word work, in some cases, even the most basic tools and low-tech equipment offer the most appropriate accommodations for students with special needs.

For example, if a student has difficulty putting enough pressure on the page to form a mark, consider providing paint, markers, or a more high-tech option, keyboards, that require far less pressure. White boards, manipulatives for word sorts (e.g., affixing slips of paper to cardboard or blocks), or actual objects (like balls, or stuffed animals representing specific sounds and letter combinations) may also be used.

As a slightly more high-tech option, many publishers offer books on tape for students to read during independent reading time. For books that do not have such an option, Microsoft PowerPoint® offers a relatively easy interface for recording and narrating texts. Teachers can type or scan in copies of classroom-created books or materials, using any microphone with a standard USB connector to record his or her voice reading the text aloud. Classroom volunteers or the students themselves can also record their voices reading. Students can then call up the presentation, listen and read along at their leisure, or save a copy of the file and share student-created books with their parents at home.

Finally, although instruction will vary for individual students, it is important to have a conceptual framework to aid with the instructional decisions that need to be made. In other words, what are the guiding concepts that should be considered as phonics and word study instruction is crafted for all learners on the spectrum? From our review of the literature, as well as our own practice with students on the autism spectrum, we suggest that the following principles guide the decision-making process.

1. **Begin instruction where the student is.** This means that instruction begins with assessment. For example, in order to begin word study, teachers must first determine the student's present levels of understanding, beginning with the student's communication skills, all the way through individually administered spelling inventories (see p. 278). Instruction is individualized (where the student is academically) and personalized (accounts for **student interests**).

2. **Focus on meaning.** Since comprehension is a challenge for many students on the autism spectrum, all word-level instruction must be situated within a meaningful activity that requires thinking beyond rote memorization. Consider beginning instruction with students' interests. Since most students with ASD have strong visual cuing systems, think about how to exploit this strength to mitigate oral weaknesses (e.g., Craig & Telfer, 2005).

3. **Use a whole-part-whole approach.** Teaching students to read one word at a time through rote memory may take more instructional hours than students might have in their lifetime. Teaching children to use phonics to identify words affords students the ability to read more words more quickly than memorizing each word individually. However, not all students profit from phonics instruction that starts by teaching word parts or sound-symbol pairings. Many students, including students on the spectrum, learn these relationships better if instruction begins with whole words and then moves to sound-symbol instruction.

4. **Focus on encoding (spelling/writing) and decoding (reading) simultaneously.** These are reciprocal processes, and teachers would do well to pair them during instruction. For example, students might learn to read words and then use the same words in some kind of authentic writing activity, such as writing a class book or making a grocery list.

5. **Make word work an active, decision-making process.** Word work should encourage students to actively think about how groups of words are related. Attend to students' conceptual understandings along the way. Make sure patterns are both visually and aurally distinct enough to facilitate student classification. The level of sophistication required to make decisions should progress as students learn.

6. **Foster independence.** Consider moving literacy materials on which students have demonstrated mastery to independent learning centers. For example, favorite books could become books available for leisure reading in the classroom library space. Interactive charts and word sorts are excellent materials for work systems (see Chapter 3 for more information on work systems).

Word Study Instruction

In keeping with our principle of focusing on reading and writing simultaneously, we will describe characteristics of both throughout our discussion. Although the development of word recognition and spelling patterns among students with ASD has been little studied (Gabig, 2010), there is a large body of literature on typical skill development, which can be thoughtfully applied to instruction for students on the spectrum. As Mirenda (2003) noted, "It is increasingly clear that most – if not all – students with autism can benefit from literacy instruction that incorporates the use of multiple instructional strategies that are carefully matched to the stages or phases of development through which all readers pass on their way from emergent reading to skilled reading" (p. 275). Thus, development patterns among typically developing students offer instructional decision-making signposts, or points of comparison, that can inform instruction. Furthermore, we have selected word study as a predominant instructional practice for students on the spectrum because it supports two inclinations toward learning that typify these students – a propensity toward visual learning and a preference for routine.

Many literacy researchers have discussed taxonomic systems classifying the stages or phases of orthographic development for typically developing children (see Marten, 2003; Rycik & Rycik, 2007). These systems typically show a progression from beginning conceptualizations about print through understanding the complex meanings behind word origins, and they all seem to follow a similar pattern of development. For the purposes of this chapter, we have adopted categories of spelling development as defined by Bear et al. (2008), as we find them to be descriptive of each phase represented, including emergent, letter-name alphabetic, within-word pattern, syllables and affixes, and derivational relations. Although Bear et al. described these as developmental stages, we have adopted the term *phases* instead, since we can make no claim that students with ASD pass through the same spelling stages as typically developing students (Gabig, 2010). Phases should not be viewed as cut and dry, with finite beginnings and endings. Rather, students on the spectrum will likely display uneven development, perhaps sharing characteristics of multiple phases at once. We have summarized each phase, including characteristics, examples, instructional focus, and suggested instructional strategies, in Table 9.2.

Table 9.2
Phases of Word Recognition, Instructional Strategies, and Modifications for Students With ASD

	Characteristics	Examples	Instructional Focus	Instructional Strategies	Modification for Students With ASD
Emergent	**In the Beginning:** Students make seemingly random marks on paper; may look like letters or scribbles. Students may "read" or share the "stories" they have written, but the writing does not yet look like printed language.	Scribbles, lines, no visible pattern to the characters; may appear to be randomly placed at the top, bottom, or sides of a page	Concepts of word and print, letter-knowledge acquisition, and letter/sound correspondence	Word hunts focused on specific sounds; interactive writing; songs, rhymes, and read-aloud activities with repetitious sound patterns; opportunities to write using invented spelling; focus on letters in the students' own names and environmental print.	Because students with ASD are characterized as having difficulty attending to multiple tasks, concept sorts created for the emergent stage (and word sorts for all stages) should be based on a single, explicitly defined concept or category. Recall from the opening vignette the concept sort for making a sandwich that was used with Alicia.
	In the Middle: Students may make a few letters, often from hard consonant sounds found in their own names or environmental print.	Use of a single letter, or most vocalized letters in the student's own name; letters from environmental print; letters used do not yet correspond to sounds			
	At the End: Students have an emerging awareness of the conventions of print – left to right, top to bottom, that letters correspond to sounds, and that combinations of letters represent words.	Inconsistent use of letters to begin to represent sound			

Table 9.2 (cont.)

	Characteristics	Examples	Instructional Focus	Instructional Strategies	Modification for Students With ASD
Letter-Name Alphabetic	**In the Beginning:** Students begin to acquire concepts of print. They recognize that specific characters correspond with specific sounds and represent oral language or words. At this phase, students tend to recognize strong consonants and some vowels. Words are written as they sound to the students. Often the first letters understood are those whose names and sound representations are similar.	BD = bed DF = dog DN = down JP = drip	Continue to focus on initial and final consonants; letter-sound correspondence; short vowels, blends, digraphs, should be introduced and studied; *r*-influenced words; word families (onset and rime); Consonant-Vowel-Consonant (CVC), and Consonant-Vowel-Consonant-e (CVCe) patterns	Word hunts; word journals; word walls; interactive writing; independent writing; word sorts focusing on word families; open and closed picture and word sorts. Explicit teacher modeling of how letters blend to make specific sounds. Word sorts following whole-part-whole instruction should focus on similar spelling patterns and word families	Be on the lookout for hyperlexia. Students may be decoding the words effectively, but unable to come up with meaning; closed-concept sorts should be undertaken to aid in comprehension, as was the case with Darius in the opening vignette.
	In the Middle: Letters, digraphs, and blends are represented. Students represent sounds based on how they are physically produced in the mouth, or how they sound as interpreted by the student.	BAK = bake CHP = jump HED = had BRK = break			
	At the End: By the end of this phase, most common and single-syllable words are spelled correctly. Silent letters also emerge in common words. Still confusion over vowel blends and more complex onset-rime patterns				
Within-Word Pattern	Students begin to understand basic spelling patterns. Exploration of long-vowel patterns is marked by students' overuse of common patterns. High-frequency words and short-vowel words are consistently spelled correctly.	CREKE = creak PANE = pain RITE = right	Long-vowel combinations and patterns; silent letter patterns; ambiguous vowel patterns	Word hunts in trade books for interesting words and ambiguous patterns; word sorts for onset-rime patterns; word analogy strategies; word journals; word study for commonly confused homophones (*there, their, they're; to, too, two*). Word hunts in environmental print for misspelled words.	As with students in the Letter-Name Phase, teachers working with students on the spectrum should be sensitive to hyperlexia and conduct appropriate concept sorts if students demonstrate hyperlexic tendencies. Use texts based on student topics of interest for sources of words for study, sorts, and hunts.

Table 9.2 (cont.)

	Characteristics	Examples	Instructional Focus	Instructional Strategies	Modification for Students With ASD
Syllables and Affixes	Students correctly spell long and short vowel, ambiguous vowel and consonant patterns, and high-frequency words. Confusion in spelling affixes.	HOPING = hopping FLYES = flies PATERN = pattern STUDDENT = student	Doubling consonants; changing of *y* to *i* when adding *-es*, meanings and use of affixes; vowel patterns within multisyllabic words; compound and hyphenated words; syllable patterns	Increase vocabulary knowledge through activating student's prior knowledge and scaffolding; select words that are actively being used in class; word sorts focusing on syllable junctions and meaning/spelling changes with addition or removal of affixes; word journals for interesting words.	As with students like Jose, introduced at the beginning of this chapter, students on the spectrum who are in the Syllables and Affixes Phase should be given opportunities to explore patterns when affixes are added to words. Modifications for students with ASD should include opportunities to write stories and essays based on their areas of interest with explicit attention given to target affixes as well as specific prefix and suffix word-sort activities.
Derivational Relations	At this phase, students spell most words consistently and correctly. While some spelling issues remain, they deal mainly with lack of understanding word origins and derivational languages	DEFINESTRATE = defenestrate ORDERVES = hors d'oeuvres KEMOTHERAPY = chemotherapy	Understanding the linguistic origins (e.g., Norman French, Early German, Latin, Spanish, Japanese, Arabic) and a basic understanding of how words enter and impact the English language	Word sorts and study of linguistically related words, word origins; structural analysis of words and word parts; word journals for interesting and new words. Practice in this phase should consist of word sorts for similar words derived from the same language family. Teachers should explicitly model word hunts through classroom texts for the word families focused on.	Word work should also cover concept sorts that focus on degrees of meaning in synonymous words. For example, multiple words may be used to describe the state of being happy; for example, *happy, joyous, elated, ecstatic, thrilled,* but students with ASD may miss subtle degrees of meaning.

Skilled readers primarily use four strategies to recognize words: (a) sight, (b) decoding, (c) analogy, and (d) prediction. All four can be taught, depending upon individual instructional needs. Thus, to meet the ultimate goal of reading with comprehension, explicit teaching of these strategies must be thoughtfully integrated into balanced literacy instruction. See Table 9.3 for a list of phonics and linguistic terms.

Table 9.3
Additional Phonics and Linguistic Terms and Examples

Term	Definition	Example
Absorbed Prefix	Prefixes that, when added to some root words, lose letters or partial spelling due to difficult pronunciations, which would result if the prefix were to remain intact	In- + mobile = immobile In- + literate = illiterate
Affix	Morphemes added to the beginning or end of an already meaningful word, or root. Affixes may change or enhance the meaning of the root or change the original part of speech (see prefix, suffix)	-ed; jumped -ing; jumping -pre; preview -re; review -tion; revolution
Blend	Two or more letters that, when combined, produce a new sound that is influenced by each letter	bl; blend sh; ship
CVC Pattern	An English spelling pattern that is represented by a vowel enclosed by two consonants; typically this indicates a short vowel	bat; hit; let
CVCe Pattern	An English spelling pattern that is represented by a consonant-vowel-consonant plus the letter *e*. Typically this indicates a long vowel; however, many high-frequency words in the English language do not follow this pattern and must be taught by sight	Examples that follow the pattern: gave, kite, drive, write, dove Examples that do not follow the pattern: love, have Examples that may or may not follow the pattern depending on use: live (as an adjective), live (as a verb)
CVVC Pattern	An English spelling pattern that is represented by two vowels enclosed by consonants. Typically, this indicates the initial vowel is elongated, while the second vowel remains silent. However, there are high-frequency words in the English language that do not follow this pattern and must be taught by sight. In some cases, vowel blends also negate this pattern (e.g., *choice*)	Examples that follow the pattern: beat, meat, street, fries Examples that do not follow the pattern: neighbor, friend Examples that may or may not follow the pattern depending on use: read (in the present tense), read (in the past tense)
Digraph	Two or more letters that, when combined, create an entirely new sound not reflective of the individual sounds of each letter in the digraph	-ph: phone -ch: lunch
Diphthong	A vowel pattern characterized by an initial vowel sound blended into a second	-oi: toil, choice -ou: found, noun

Homographs	Words that are spelled the same way but carry different meanings and are pronounced differently	address (noun); address (verb) conflict (noun); conflict (verb) read (present tense); read (past tense)
Homophones	Words that sound similar but are spelled differently and carry different meanings	to, two, and too weigh and way there, their and they're
Onset	The beginning consonant sound in a syllable that comes before the initial vowel; may be a single letter, digraph, or blend	cat: onset = /c/ blue: onset = /bl/
Prefix	An affix (see above) that is written at the beginning of a word and somehow augments or alters the meaning of it	un- + happy = unhappy im + measurable = immeasurable
Rime	The final vowel sound of a word. Although often the rime does rhyme with the endings of other words, the two terms should not be confused	cat: rime = /at/ blue: rime = /oo/
Suffix	An affix added to the end of a word that enhances or changes the meaning of the original word, or changes its tense. Often adding a suffix will change the spelling of the root word	measure + able = measurable make + ing = making fly + es = flies flip + ing = flipping
Syllable	Parts of words that are separated during pronunciation. Each syllable contains as single vowel sound. Determination of syllables in oral reproduction of words is a component of phonemic awareness	de-scribe de-script-tion con-cen-trate in-voke mul-ti-ple

Emergent Phase

Learner characteristics. Emergent literacy learners, or prephonemic learners (Marten, 2003; Rycik & Rycik, 2007), like Alicia in one of the vignettes that opened this chapter, have not yet acquired a concept of print. (See Chapters 5 and 8 for discussions about communication and emergent literacy skills.) Regardless of age, students at this level do not understand alphabetics (i.e., written symbols), sound-symbol relationships, or that print conveys meaning. Their writing may be characterized by random scribbling, wavy lines, or letter-like symbols (Koppenhaver & Erickson, 2003). Students in this phase may just be beginning to explore writing but lack understandings of basic concepts, such as the fact that in English orthography written text moves from left to right, top to bottom, and front to back when texts are composed of multiple pages.

Instructional focus and strategies. At this phase, the instructional focus includes developing students' (a) concepts of word and print, (b) letter-name knowledge/recognition, (c) letter-sound correspondences, and (d) sight words, especially for older emergent readers. To facilitate development of concepts of word and print, small-group instruction should include read-alouds using engaging texts (e.g., big books, regular books, and interactive charts) that tell interesting stories, contain illustrations that reflect the content of the story, and are written using predictable prose.

Interactive charts are also meaningful instructional tools at the emergent phase (Hieronymous & Moomaw, 2001). Interactive charts are shorter pieces of text, perhaps a poem or a stanza from a children's song, that the teacher makes up using clearly written text. Designed to be read aloud with students, interactive charts may include other interactive elements, such as an open space to insert a student's name in the text. For older emergent readers, interactive charts can be used to illustrate a process, such as doing laundry or making a sandwich.

To work on concepts of print when texts are read aloud, teachers model where and how to begin reading (i.e., reading begins at the top left of the page, continues left to right, and top to bottom) and one-to-one correspondence (i.e., each written word represents one spoken word, and spaces represent word boundaries) by pointing to each word as it is read. After students are familiar with the text, they should be encouraged to "read" along with the teacher. Stories that provide sing-song, rhyming patterns, or that use the same phrasing with minor changes throughout the text allow students to verbally chant along with the teacher, as they begin to acquire knowledge of how texts work. If the student is apprehensive of this kind of public, choral reading, it may be done one on one with the teacher or paraprofessional instead of with the whole group.

Teachers can select read-alouds around letters of the alphabet being learned, pointing, for example, to the different forms of the letter *A* in the text. Read-alouds can also be used to model or think aloud about emerging sound-symbol correspondences students are beginning to make. For example, word hunts focused on finding words that begin with the /k/ sound might be the focus of the read-aloud. Finally, if books are used for read-alouds, concepts of books (e.g., how to hold the book, page turning) can also be modeled.

One-on-one instruction can facilitate joint attention and is ideal for introducing concept sorts. Concept sorting (Bear et al., 2008) is an instructional strategy that helps students conceptualize similarity and difference. In a concept sort, students are asked to organize a group of picture cards by category or attribute. For example, in the opening vignette, Alicia was provided a concept sort where she was asked to sort the tools for making a peanut-butter-and-jelly sandwich from the ingredients. The teacher should model how to put pictures into categories using think-alouds.

Student engaged in a concept sort.

Because of the unique cognitive differences of students with ASD, concept sorts should include (a) explicit rules for inclusion in categories (see Boucher, 1988; Dunn & Bates, 2005) and (b) concepts that are naturally static in nature. Students with ASD have difficulty generating categories on their own, but with explicit rules (i.e., closed sort with a category card at the top) about category formation, they are quite adept at the task. (There is evidence that students on the spectrum cannot make the conceptual leap to understand a picture card that depicts two people walking with an arrow pointing at their feet [Dunn & Bates]. Thus, movement-oriented words may not be good candidates for concept sorts and might better be taught using video models.)

Concept sorts should progress in sophistication as students master concepts. Beginning sorts should include two categories of objects or pictures given to the student as one group. More sophisticated sorts might include attribute work, such as items with wheels paired with items that are red in color. Beginning word sorts might be appropriate at this phase. Word sorts contain words rather than pictures. Students might classify word cards by grouping cards with the same initial sound together (see Table 9.2).

In the opening of this chapter, you were introduced to Darius, a student who could easily decode words but did not comprehend their meaning. Although the information provided in the vignette is not sufficient to determine what phase of English orthography would be the best instructional level for Darius, knowing that he does not connect words to meaning indicates that concept sorts that utilize both pictures and text would be beneficial as his teacher works to help him make the cognitive leap from print to meaning. Because Darius is an older student who will likely face transition in the near future, the pictures used in his sorts should relate directly to the people, objects, and places that matter to him in his daily life to facilitate concept generalization.

Related to concept sorts, as described for students like Darius, sight word instruction is another important strategy to work on during the emergent phase. Skilled readers recognize most, if not all, words by sight. For higher-functioning students who are beyond the emergent phase, sight word instruction is also useful, but should be focused on words that cannot be easily decoded based on recognizable English spelling patterns (e.g., *come, said,* and *went*) or other high-frequency words (i.e., decodable words that frequently appear in early reading). Such words could be put on word walls and reviewed each day as part of whole-group instruction. Consider starting with a few words (e.g., five or fewer), gradually adding new words as words are mastered.

For students who have very complex communication needs and for whom attention and focus are extremely challenging, one-on-one instruction is crucial. During one-on-one teaching sessions, these students receive instruction around authentic and functional sight words using systematic strategies (e.g., errorless teaching). For example, after the team develops a list of sight words for an individual student, the teacher may decide to begin with the word *water*, one of the student's most desired items.

1. The teacher begins with rote recognition (i.e., matching word to picture or object; receptive identification).

2. The teacher pairs the word to a real context using what might be termed a generalizing event. For instance, the teacher might place the word *water* on the student's schedule. When cued to check his schedule, the student removes the printed word from the schedule and walks to a water bottle across the room and takes a drink.

3. As the student learns to wash his hands, the teacher might create visual directions for hand washing, using sight words (e.g., *hands, soap, water*) rather than pictures whenever possible. The visual directions are displayed in the hand washing area, where the student independently uses the words to complete the process.

By following this process, the teacher creates a meaningful context to help students connect the printed word with the real object.

Letter-Name Phase

Learner characteristics. Characteristics of student writing in this phase of spelling development include (a) using beginning and final consonant sounds to represent letters, (b) understanding the basic conventions of print, and (c) understanding that letters correspond to sounds and words. During this period, students often represent words with the most easily recognized sounds within words, typically leaving out vowels. For example, the student may use the letters *ct* to represent the word *cat.* This practice, called invented spelling, provides educators with a window into students' conceptualizations of written language.

Instructional focus and instructional strategies. Since students with ASD tend to be visual thinkers, some learn to spell words conventionally with one exposure. For others, invented spelling should be encouraged as students move toward conventional writing. For example, by spelling the word *cat* with the letters *ct*, we know that the student has visually noticed that the word begins with the letter *c* instead of *k* (we know this because both letters can make the same sound), has processed the /k/ and /t/ sounds through auditory means, and missed the middle vowel sound, offering a clear indication that the student is in the letter-naming phase.

In addition, students often write letters that match the point of articulation in their mouths as they say the word they are attempting to write. For example, students may represent the sound made by the letters *dr* in *drip* as JP, as /j/ and /d/ are both articulated in the front of the mouth. They may write *Y* to represent /w/ as in *YT* for wait (Bear et al., 2008) for the same reason. As students progress through the phase, they begin to understand short vowels in single-syllable words, and to incorporate common blends like /st/, /bl/, /gr/, and digraphs like /ph/. (See Table 9.3 for specific phonics terms and examples.) Phonic Faces is a commercially available program that combines visual elements (i.e., graphemes) and auditory elements (i.e., phonemes) to help students with single word reading. (More information regarding these resources may be found at www.elementory. com.) Practicing word family sorts is a useful strategy for students in this phase. Table 9.4 presents how to do a word family sort.

Table 9.4
Word Family Sort

- Select two rimes that are distinct in terms of sound and visual pattern, such as *at* and *op*. Think of three words for each pattern (e.g., *cat, hat, fat* and *hop, cop, top*).
- Create picture cards for each word and rule cards for each category. Rule cards simply have the written representation of the two categories (i.e., *-at* and *-op*).
- Working with the student one on one, model how to sort the six pictures into two categories. For example, the teacher might say, "This is a picture of a cat. I have a cat at home. When I say the word *cat* slowly, I hear the /at/ sound at the end of the word. That means it goes in the -at column." Repeat this procedure for a picture of an *-op* word.
- Ask the student to try one. If she is successful, continue until all cards have been sorted. If the student is not successful, go back and model how to classify the word cards.
- Once the student is comfortable sorting picture cards, add words on the bottom of the cards, and repeat the sorting procedure.

Additional word and picture sorts during this phase should focus students' attention on beginning and ending consonants, gradually moving toward incorporating common short-vowel sounds, *r*-influenced pronunciations, blends, and digraphs, as student writing and assessments indicate students are shifting toward using these letters (Bear et al., 2008). At the beginning, word and picture sorts should be easily identifiable; for example, comparing words that start with the letter *b* to words that start with the letter *m*. It is also important to embed word study within meaningful contexts. For example, a word sort activity emphasizing short-vowel sounds could use words from a class book created from a shared language experience, such as going on a field trip, classroom procedures, or the individualized experiences of a particular student.

As students learn sound-symbol correspondences, it may be important to explicitly teach them to blend sounds together to produce words (Gabig, 2010). Explicit teaching should begin with modeling. See Table 9.5 for an example.

Table 9.5
Blending Words

1. Begin blending exercises with a known word, such as *cat*. Write *cat* on the board.
2. Model blending the word together by saying something like, "If I came to a word I didn't know, I could try figuring the word out like this. First, I look at the word to see if I know any parts of the word."
3. Continue modeling by saying something like this, while pointing to the letter c. "I know that the letter *c* makes the /k/ sound."
4. Next, point to the letters *at* and say, "I recognize *at*. So, I say, /k/at, *cat*. That makes sense. *Cat* is a real word. If I didn't know *at*, I could say (say each phoneme as you point to each word)."

If students have difficulty blending words, using a child's toy called a Slinky can illustrate what students are supposed to do. The Slinky may be stretched out as words are sounded out, as the teacher tells student to, "Say it slow," and collapsed as the whole word is pronounced, with the prompt to, "Say it fast."

Within-Word Pattern Phase

Learner characteristics. During this phase, students have taken a cognitive leap away from identifying the name of the letter with its corresponding sound and become aware of basic spelling patterns in the English language. Here they begin to experiment with long-vowel patterns, often demonstrated by a proclivity to overuse the silent *e*, as in spelling *braid* as BRADE, or to play with other long-vowel constructions, as in MEET for *meat*. Students in the within-word pattern phase are able to spell most frequently used words correctly, can recognize patterns in word families, and understand the use of blends and digraphs (Bear et al., 2008; Marten, 2003).

Instructional focus and instructional strategies. Marten (2003) emphasized that raising "spelling consciousness" (p. 75) is essential to learning how words work in the English language. This is especially true as students begin to explore multiple constructions for common spelling patterns. During the within-word pattern phase, spelling instruction should focus on (a) helping students see common long-vowel spelling patterns, diphthongs such as /oy/, /oi/, /oo/, homophones, and contractions (Marten); and (b) exploring silent letters and ambiguous vowel patterns (Bear et al., 2008). Only phonetic rules that are highly consistent, such as always following the letter *q* with the letter *u*, and soft *g* and *c* are usually followed by *i, y,* or *e,* are worth teaching explicitly (Fountas & Pinnell, 2001).

During the within-word pattern phase, closed word sorts continue to be an appropriate instructional method for helping students with ASD process word pattern differences. Similarly, word walls with sight words continue to be an appropriate method for working on sight words.

In addition, word-study journals are an instructional strategy that is amenable to raising word consciousness, while at the same time affording individualized experiences. A word journal is a student-maintained document in which students record interesting words, their meanings, and patterns discovered during class instruction and independent work, such as word hunts and other word-play activities. For example, current spelling lesson topics, such as the *-ight* rime family or different long-vowel patterns for /ā/, could form the basis of a word hunt where students might be asked to locate as many different *-ight* words or different long-vowel patterns for /ā/, as possible around their classroom (e.g., environmental print) or in a book they are reading during independent reading time, and record them in their journals. Journal words could be shared with peers or turned into word sorts. Word-study journals might also be a place for students to record unusual or interesting spelling patterns they have noticed for later discussion.

Syllables and Affixes Phase

Learner characteristics. Students in the syllables and affixes phase are competent with the features studied in the previous phases, including demonstrating the ability to recognize common English spelling patterns for long vowels, as well as many ambiguous vowels and digraphs. In this phase, students are using but confusing patterns when adding prefixes and/or suffixes. They may also demonstrate difficulties in spelling patterns at syllable junctures and in applying stress on the appropriate syllable, especially in relation to homophones. Confusion over when to change a *y* to an *i*, or consonant doubling when adding a suffix, is common, and explicit instruction in the spelling and development of compound words is needed (Bear et al., 2008; Marten, 2003).

Jose, described in the opening paragraphs of the chapter, demonstrates characteristics from the syllables and affixes phase. By incorporating his own writing about a lived experience into the word study instruction, his teacher is showing the importance of acquiring an understanding of how prefixes, suffixes, and roots combine to make meaning.

Instructional focus and instructional strategies. During this phase, students should learn (a) the meanings of affixes (i.e., prefixes and suffixes) and how adding affixes changes the meaning of words; (b) strategies for conducting structural analysis to determine the meanings of unknown, multisyllabic words; and (c) how adding affixes and inflectional endings influences the spelling of the root word. Instruction at the syllables and affixes phase should provide students with structural analysis methods; that is, methods for breaking down words into their constituent parts (i.e., compounds, affixes, and root words). See Table 9.6.

Kluth and Darmody-Latham (2003) indicated that students with ASD often have trouble understanding words with abstract concepts or meanings. Thus, it is important to emphasize meaning when teaching structural analysis. For example, concept sorts at this phase can be utilized to help students understand the meaning and spelling changes incurred by the use of inflectional endings (e.g., different sorts can be conducted to learn what happens to the meaning/tense and the spelling of words like *run, write,* and *eat* when *-ing* is added).

Table 9.6
Teaching Meaning Making With Structural Analysis

1. Start by writing a familiar word, preferably something concrete that can be paired with a picture that contains the target affix. For example, if the target suffix was *bi-*, the word *bicycle* could be used.
2. Underline the prefix and tell students that it means "two," as in a bicycle has two wheels.
3. Introduce a novel word that begins with the same prefix, such as *biplane,* along with a picture.
4. Model underlining the prefix. Model how to figure out what the word means using a think-aloud, such as, "I know what a plane is. It's something that flies in the sky filled with passengers, and I know that *bi* means 'two.' So, a *biplane* must be a plane with two of something. When I look at the picture, I see that it has two wings. A biplane is a plane with two wings."

During this phase, word sorts provide students with the opportunity to examine how individual words change and conform to spelling patterns. For example, students might be provided with a series of words ending with *-ing*. This list should include words ending with both consonants and vowels (e.g., *getting, loving, seeing, knowing, sharing, flying, running, teasing*). Ask students to write the root words of each word on one set of index cards (*get, love, see, know, share, fly, run, tease*) and the *-ing* form for each on another set. The first sort of the words should be based on whether the root ends with a vowel or a consonant. When using the second set of cards, draw students' attention to the fact that when the final letter is a consonant and *-ing* is added, the final consonant will be doubled, whereas in words that end with a vowel, the vowel is dropped before adding *-ing*. Similar sorts can be created with patterns of doubling consonants when endings are added or when changing nouns from singular to plural. Finally, the use of concept maps and other visual supports may help students with autism understand how different words connect to one another to understand meaning (see Chapter 11 for instructional strategies for vocabulary instruction).

Derivational Relations Phase

Learner characteristics. Students in the derivational relations phase of spelling development are likely to be advanced and avid readers, especially around topics of personal interest. In some cases, however, students at this level may still not communicate using speech. Mirenda (2003) wrote about a student who used a typewriter to communicate instead of speaking, noting that his involvement in advanced literacy activities led him to oral communication when he was 12 years old. Mirenda also described advanced readers with ASD, like their peers without ASD, using reading as a way to learn and further their own interests.

Generally, students operating within this phase, although able to comprehend explicit facts, especially around high-interest topics, are apt to miss more subtle concepts, often introduced through figurative language. In addition, comprehension may be less accurate when students read silently versus reading aloud (Myles et al., 2002). Although some evidence suggests that students do access background knowledge when reading to facilitate making inferences, they may need assistance determining what background information is relevant to the reading situation (Wahlberg & Magliano, 2004). Finally, in the derivational relations phase, students spell most words accurately. Misspellings at this phase "indicate an error in morphology [structure of word meaning] and etymology [word origin]" (Marten, 2003, p. 45).

Instructional focus and instructional strategies. In this phase, the focus of instruction should be on (a) reading and writing content-area vocabulary, (b) exploring word derivations, and (c) absorbed prefixes. Valuable instructional strategies continue to include word-study journals and word sorts. To facilitate integration among subject areas, content-area vocabulary words may form the context for word study instruction.

To study derivations, students could be provided with a common prefix derived from another language, for example, *poly-* from Greek, and asked to complete a word hunt within their social studies text to find examples of words that begin with *poly-.* It is also appropriate to study the consequence of absorbed prefixes. For example, when *in-* is added to some words, the result is the loss of part of the prefix in order to improve pronunciation. For example, when added to the root word *relevant,* the prefix *in-*, meaning not or without, the *n* is dropped from the prefix, and the beginning consonant of *relevant,* *r*, is doubled, resulting in the word *irrelevant* (Bear et al., 2008).

Because the goal of reading instruction should be independent practice of strategies and lessons taught, enabling students to transfer their reading skills to other areas, it is especially important that advanced readers be taught to monitor their comprehension. (See Chapter 12 for ideas on how to do this.) Thus, instruction during the derivational relations phase should continue to help students recognize and focus on layers of meaning, as well as figurative language. Use of strategies that encourage students with verbal communication skills to participate in think-alouds as they read may enable instructors to pinpoint areas of confusion or missed understanding.

Concept sorts in this phase can be used to help students understand degrees of meaning for synonymous words. For example, students may be divided into pairs and given a set of words all related to the concept happy (e.g., *joyous, content, excited, exuberant, ecstatic*) and asked to place the words in order from the weakest to the strongest forms. Because the students in this example would be working with a teacher or another student, the exact placement of the words on the scale is less important than the negotiations and thought processes required for completing the exercise. The value of the lesson itself lies in actively making students aware of the subtleties of meaning inherent in related words.

Assessment for Word Study

As emphasized earlier in this chapter, in order to begin instruction where students are, assessment must precede instruction. As with all students, assessment for students with ASD should include diagnostic assessments of word recognition during both reading and writing and continue with formative assessments along the way to monitor student progress and inform continued instruction. Summative assessments are given at the end of instruction to confirm that learning occurred. See Table 9.7 for some thoughts on assessment.

Table 9.7
Thoughts About Assessment

A major premise of this chapter is that instruction in word study for students with ASD (and all students) begins where the students are. Teachers have a variety of options for both formal and informal assessment at the onset and continuing through instructional phases in order to ensure that lessons and strategies remain situated within appropriate developmental phases. Spelling inventories and IRIs (informal reading inventories) are two methods of ensuring that instruction is on target.

Traditional summative assessments (i.e., the weekly spelling test) are not generally in line with the methods proposed in this chapter, as they are usually comprised of randomly generated words and inauthentic lists for rote memorization.

We recommend instead that summative assessments of orthographic knowledge be comprised of groups of words (including word families) that demonstrate similar features (e.g., similar blends, onsets, rimes, structural origins) as focused on in the previous lessons. In this instance, even new words not previously encountered but consistent with the target orthographic features may be included to determine concept mastery.

Reading Assessments

To assess word recognition while reading printed text, informal reading inventories (IRIs) and running records provide opportunities for diagnosing strengths and deficits in decoding. Evidence suggests that IRIs work well with students with ASD (Myles et al., 2002). Generally, IRIs include procedures to assess word recognition both out of context (i.e., lists of words) and in context (i.e., passages). Using IRIs, teachers can evaluate automaticity (i.e., identified by sight) and decoding skill, both in and out of context. Finally, IRIs contain procedures for conducting miscue analyses, a means to identify which systems (i.e., graphic, semantic, syntactic) students rely upon when encountering unknown words. There are many different IRIs on the market (e.g., Leslie & Caldwell, 2011).

Writing and Spelling Assessments

Bear and his colleagues (2008) noted that instruction in spelling should begin with what students are using and confusing. This suggests that there is recognition from the student that some kind of pattern exists between spoken and written words. There are two ways to determine this information – obtaining a student writing sample or conducting a spelling inventory.

Writing samples. This approach has the advantage of being unobtrusive. Essentially, teachers take samples of student writing and compare the writing to the phases of spelling described here. The drawback is that writing samples may not be comprehensive. Spelling inventories are available that are more comprehensive.

Spelling inventories. These are lists of words that represent sample features present in each phase of spelling development. They contain words that have not been targets of instruction during class. When students are given the test, they are told that they will not be graded on their performance, but that the test will be used to help the teacher figure out what the students need to learn. Word lists generally contain 5 words at each of the 5 levels, and are presented in order of increasing difficulty, with a total of 25 words on the test. Teachers ask students to write each word as best they can. Once five or more words are missed, the teacher should conclude the test. Points are awarded for each word, or feature (i.e., spelling pattern), spelled correctly. Results of these diagnostic assessments form the basis for instruction. Several commercially spelling inventories are available (e.g., Bear et al., 2008; Marten, 2003).

Jones (2001) provided another route for creating spelling inventories. In districts where spelling basals are used for instruction, Jones suggested that teachers list the features and skills addressed in each of the texts and then select five representative words from each leveled text for inclusion in the spelling inventory. This allows teachers to use classroom materials to create tests, pulling in words that will be addressed throughout the year. The potential problem with this method is that often spelling books are leveled by grade, and not developmental levels, as described in the research pertaining to word work.

Formative and summative methods. These assessment approaches should be chosen in accordance with instructional aims. The sorting activities described in this chapter are well suited as the basis of assessment.

Formative assessments during sorting activities might consist of completing data sheets regarding the number of words/concepts correctly classified. An important part of formative assessment is teacher reflection. In other words, if students struggle with the task, teachers must ask themselves if it is appropriate for the student.

In terms of a summative experience, if appropriate, a traditional spelling test can be given when the teacher is certain the student has been exposed to the target words for an appropriate length of time. For example, some students need to sort the same words for a week or more before appropriating targeted spelling patterns into their writing repertoire.

Conclusion

Word study is an important facet of reading instruction and meaning making, and should be strategically and systematically incorporated into the larger literacy context of the classroom based on student needs, determined through assessment, and student interests. Although students with ASD have not been adequately studied to determine specific developmental levels in relation to their typically developing peers, there is enough research available to support patterning word study instruction for students on the spectrum after stages identified for TD students.

As such, effective word study instruction for students with ASD begins with assessment, and then focuses word work around identified phases (emergent, letter-name, within-word pattern, syllables and affixes, and derivational relations). Methods include the use of closed-concept and word sorts through explicit modeling and demonstration of tasks by educators and individualized word walls and word-study journals. One specific concern for students with ASD is hyperlexia, or the tendency to be able to effectively and fluently decode words without understanding their meaning, at the word, sentence, or passage level. As a result, comprehension of the words in context must be an important component of word study instruction for these students.

Chapter Highlights

- Word recognition may be defined as the process of converting print into speech with the ultimate aim of being able to understand or comprehend the utterance.

- Word recognition and comprehension are the two basic information processing activities involved in reading.

- Word recognition includes the ability to identify words by sight (i.e., visual recognition of the whole word) and through decoding (i.e., using knowledge of sound/symbol correspondences).

Word Recognition in Children With ASD

- *Decoding:* There is great variability in patterns of reading ability in students with ASD.

- *Semantic awareness:* Some students need word recognition instruction at the decoding level, others may be fluent decoders but unable to connect meaning to the words themselves; still others may be able to comprehend concrete words once decoded, but encounter difficulties in understanding as word meanings become more subtle and abstract.

- *Influences on word recognition:* Strength in word reading may be used to facilitate oral language skills. Memory and word concept should be considered when planning word recognition instruction.

- The following principles should be used to guide the instructional decision-making process:
  - ✔ Begin instruction where the student is
  - ✔ Focus on meaning
  - ✔ Use a whole-part-whole approach
  - ✔ Focus on encoding (spelling/writing) and decoding (reading) simultaneously
  - ✔ Make word work an active, decision-making process
  - ✔ Foster independence

- Skilled readers use four strategies to recognize words: (a) sight, (b) decoding, (c) analogy, and (d) prediction.

Emergent Phase

- *Learner characteristics:* has not yet acquired a concept of print.

- *Instructional focus and strategies:* (a) concepts of word and print, (b) letter name knowledge/recognition, (c) letter-sound correspondences, and (d) sight word.

Letter-Naming Phase

- *Learner characteristics:* (a) uses beginning and final consonant sounds to represent word, (b) understands the basic conventions of print, and (c) understands that letters correspond to sounds and words.

- *Instructional focus and instructional strategies:* (a) students' emergent understandings of the correspondence between letter sounds and their written representation, and (b) word blending skill.

Within-Word Phase

- *Learner characteristics:* (a) identifies the name of the letter with its corresponding sound, and (b) becomes aware of basic spelling patterns in the English language.

- *Instructional focus and instructional strategies:* (a) helping students see common long-vowel spelling patterns, and (b) exploring silent letters and ambiguous vowel patterns.

Syllables and Affixes Phase

- *Learner characteristics:* demonstrates the ability to recognize common English spelling patterns for long-vowel patterns, as well as many ambiguous vowel and digraphs.

- *Instructional focus and instructional strategies:* (a) the meaning of affixes and how adding affixes changes the meaning of words; and (b) how adding affixes and inflectional endings influence the spelling of the root word.

Derivational Relations Phase

- *Learner characteristics:* is likely to be advanced and avid reader.

- *Instructional focus and instructional strategies:* (a) reading and writing content-area vocabulary, (b) exploring word derivations, and (c) absorbed prefixes.

- Assessment for students with ASD should include diagnostic assessments of word recognition during both reading and writing and continue with formative assessment. Summative assessments are given at the end of the instruction to confirm that learning occurred.

- *Reading assessment:* informal reading inventories (IRIs) and running records provide opportunities for diagnosing strengths and weakness in decoding.

- *Writing and spelling assessment:* obtaining student writing sample or conducting a spelling inventory.

- *Formative and summative methods of assessment:* both methods of assessment should be determined in accordance with instructional aims.

Review Questions

1. What is the purpose of phonics and word study instruction as described in this chapter, and how can it be used to improve reading comprehension for students with ASD?

2. Name and provide three characteristics for each of the five phases of spelling development.

3. What are three instructional strategies that may be used to facilitate phonics and word work? Provide a detailed example of how you might use one in your own classroom.

4. What are the advantages of using the developmental spelling model over traditional spelling methods for students with ASD?

5. What is a spelling inventory, and how can it be used to develop instruction for students with ASD?

References

Bear, D. R., Invernizzi, M., Templeton, S., & Johnston, F. (2008). *Words their way: Word study for phonics, vocabulary and spelling instruction* (4th ed.). Upper Saddle River, NJ: Pearson.

Boucher, J. (1988). Word fluency in high-functioning autistic children. *Journal of Autism and Developmental Disorders, 18*(4), 637-645.

Craig, H. K., & Telfer, A. S. (2005). Hyperlexia and autism spectrum disorder. *Topics in Language Disorders, 25*(4), 364-374.

Dunn, M. A., & Bates, J. C. (2005). Developmental change in neutral processing of words by children with autism. *Journal of Autism and Developmental Disorders, 35*(3), 361-376.

Fountas, I. C., & Pinnell, G. S. (2001). *Guiding readers and writers, grades 3-6: Teaching comprehension, genre, and content literacy*. Portsmouth, NH: Heinemann.

Frith, U., & Snowling, M. (1983). Reading for meaning and reading for sound in autistic dyslexic children. *British Journal of Developmental Psychology, 1,* 329-342.

Gabig, C. S. (2010). Phonological awareness and word recognition in reading in children with autism. *Communication Disorders Quarterly, 31* (2), 67-85.

Gately, S. E. (2008). Facilitating reading comprehension for students on the autism spectrum. *Teaching Exceptional Children, 40*(3), 40-45.

Goswami, U. (1993). Toward an interactive analogy of reading development: Decoding vowel graphemes in beginning reading. *Journal of Experimental Child Psychology, 56,* 443-475.

Graves, M. F., Juel, C., Graves, B. B. (2007). *Teaching reading in the 21st century* (4th ed.). Boston: Pearson.

Hala, S., Rasmussen, C., & Henderson, A.M.E. (2005). Three types of source monitoring by children with and without autism: The role of executive function. *Journal of Autism and Developmental Disorders, 35,* 75-89.

Hieronymous, B., & Moomaw, S. (2001). *More than letters: Literacy activities for preschool, kindergarten, and first grade.* St. Paul, MN: Redleaf Publishing Company.

Jones, C. T. (2001). Teacher-friendly curriculum-based assessment in spelling. *Teaching Exceptional Children, 34*(2), 32-38.

Kluth, P., & Darmody-Latham, J. (2003). Beyond sight words: Literacy opportunities for students with autism. *The Reading Teacher, 56*(6), 532-535.

Koppenhaver, D. A., & Erickson, K. A. (2003). Natural emergent literacy supports for preschoolers with autism and severe communication impairments. *Topics in Language Disorders, 23*(4), 283-292.

Leslie, L., & Caldwell, J. (2011). *Qualitative Reading Inventory: 5*. Upper Saddle River, NJ: Pearson.

Marten, C. (2003). *Word crafting: Teaching spelling, grades 1-6*. Portsmouth, NH: Heinemann.

McDuffie, A., Yoder, P. J., & Stone, W. L. (2006). Labels increase attention to novel objects in children with autism and comprehension matched children with typical development. *Autism, 10,* 257-279.

Minshew, N. J., Goldstein, G., & Siegel, D. J. (1994). Neuropsychological functioning in autism: Profiles of a complex information processing disorder. *Journal of the International Neuropsychological Society, 3,* 303-316.

Mirenda, P. (2003). He's not really a reader: Perspectives on supporting literacy development in individuals with autism. *Topics in Language Disorders, 23*(4), 271-282.

Myles, B. S., Hilgenfeld, T. D., Barnhill, G. P., Griswold, D. E., Hagiwara, T., & Simpson, R. L. (2002). Analysis of reading skills in individuals with Asperger Syndrome. *Focus on Autism and other Developmental Disorders, 17*(1), 44-47.

Nation, K., Clarke, P., Wright, B., & Williams, C. (2006). Patterns of reading ability in children with autism spectrum disorder. *Journal of Autism and Developmental Disorders, 36*, 911-919.

O'Connor, I., & Klein, P. D. (2004). Exploration of strategies for facilitating the reading comprehension of high-functioning students with autism spectrum disorders. *Journal of Autism and Developmental Disorders, 34*(2), 115-127.

O'Connor, N., & Hermelin, B. (1994). Two autistic savant readers. *Journal of Autism and Developmental Disorders, 24*, 501-515.

Patti, P., & Lupinetti, L. (1993). Brief report: Implications of hyperlexia in an autistic savant. *Journal of Autism and Developmental Disorders, 23*(2), 397-405.

Perfetti, C., & Hogaboam, T. (1975). Relationship between single word decoding and reading comprehension skill. *Journal of Educational Psychology, 67*(4), 461-469.

Rycik, M. T., & Rycik, J. A. (2007). *Phonics and word identification: Instruction and intervention, K-8.* Upper Saddle River, NJ: Pearson.

Saldana, D., & Frith, U. (2007). Do readers with autism make bridging inferences from world knowledge? *Journal of Experimental Child Psychology, 97*, 310-319.

Tager-Flusberg, H. (1985). The conceptual basis for referential word meaning in children with autism. *Child Development, 56*, 1167-1178.

Wahlberg, T., & Magliano, J. P. (2004). The ability of high function individuals with autism to comprehend written discourse. *Discourse Practices, 38*(1), 119-144.

Whitehouse, D., & Harris, J. C. (1984). Hyperlexia in infantile autism. *Journal of Autism and Developmental Disorders, 14*, 281-289.

Chapter 10

Reading Fluency

Pamela Williamson, Ph.D., University of Cincinnati

Christina Carnahan, Ed.D., University of Cincinnati

Learner Objectives

After reading this chapter, the learner should be able to:

- Define and describe reading fluency

- Define prosody and its implication for students with ASD

- Describe typical reading fluency difficulties of students with ASD

- Explain critical elements of reading fluency instruction

- List and describe research-based best practices in reading fluency instruction for typically developing students and for students with ASD

■ ■ ■

Ryan is a third-grade student with an ASD. As part of his school district's progress-monitoring policies, he was given the oral fluency measure of DIBELS (Dynamic Indicators of Basic Early Literacy; Good, Gruba, & Kaminski, 2002) – an early assessment tool. Since his correct words-per-minute fluency rate fell above the school's benchmark, his family received a letter from the school indicating that their son was on target for reading progress. However, his classroom teacher was not so sure. Although Ryan can quickly and accurately recognize words, he does not stop to pause for ending punctuation. In addition, his reading sounds almost robotic – his voice has little intonation or expression. When his teacher conducted a spelling inventory, she noted that he was in the middle of the Syllables and Affixes stage of development, which is consistent with his grade level. Ryan was using but confusing syllables that receive less stress (e.g., traped for trapped, crader for crater). The teacher thought this was interesting, as stress is one of the prosodic features (rhythmic) of language associated with reading fluency, and wondered if Ryan was not processing this aural difference. She also noticed that Ryan had difficulty answering even basic questions about what he read. For these reasons, the teacher is worried that the letter to Ryan's family overstated his ability to read. She felt that she needed to provide additional information to the family about Ryan's ability to comprehend text, so they had a clearer understanding of his reading abilities.

Over at the middle school, Jameka, a student with high-functioning autism, is included in social studies. The general education teacher and the special education teacher coteach the class, and, when possible, they use universal design principles during planning to meet the needs of all learners in their classroom. On this day, they are planning to have students work in small groups on projects related to the space race, an informal competition between the United States of America and the former Soviet Union to see who could make the greatest advances in space technology.

Some students are working on creating models of Sputnik, the first orbiting satellite launched by the Soviets, while others are creating radio scripts that delivered this news to the world. Janet, the special education teacher, decides that Jameka can make an excellent contribution to the radio scripts group, as she is very knowledgeable about space. She also knows that Jameka may benefit from performing the radio script aloud, as Jameka shows differences in translating the prosodic features of oral language to reading aloud. To support Jameka's work, Janet finds audio clips on the Internet of old-time radio news broadcasts. These clips, along with her typically developing peers, will provide models for Jameka of fluent oral reading as the group practices their radio newscast in preparation for sharing it with the class.

■ ■ ■

Comprehending is the overall goal of reading. Fluency is important, as there is a strong correlation between reading fluency and reading comprehension (Allington, 1983; Samuels, 1988). In particular, Hudson, Lane, and Pullen (2005) pointed out that increasing the rate of reading strongly correlates with improved comprehension for average and poor readers, as well as for students with reading disabilities. Some scholars have suggested that fluency is fast, accurate word recognition (Good et al., 2002), while others emphasize the cognitive processing implications of fluency for reading comprehension (e.g., LaBerge & Samuels, 1974; Samuels, 2006).

Although defining reading fluency remains controversial (Samuels & Farstrup, 2006), most scholars agree that the components of reading fluency include (a) accurate word decoding, (b) automaticity in word recognition, and (c) prosody (Kuhn & Stahl, 2000). Accurate word decoding refers to the ability to accurately apply sound-symbol knowledge to utter the text representation of a word. Automaticity in word recognition develops through practice, as readers are able to process words instantly, without the conscious attention required in decoding (LaBerge & Samuels, 1974). Finally, prosody is the ability to read with expression through proper understanding of stress (word emphasis), pitch (rise and fall of voice), and juncture (text phrasing) (Kuhn & Stahl). Through consideration of particular characteristics of these learners (i.e., reading comprehension difficulties, bottom-up processing strengths), we suggest that models that explain the relationship between fluency and comprehension fit with the cognitive profile of students on the spectrum. Thus, they will be reviewed here.

Automaticity Theory

The human brain has the capacity to process a finite number of things at one time, and since reading is a complex cognitive process, it puts heavy demands on our brains. Comprehending what is read is the goal of reading. Samuels (2006) conceptualized comprehension as a series of cognitive tasks (i.e., decoding, comprehension, and monitoring comprehension) that fluent readers attend to simultaneously. Attention is defined here as the cognitive energy expended in the effort to process a task. If one task takes up too much of the reader's attention, insufficient attention is left to process other tasks.

For example, beginning readers must attend to the surface-level features of words to decode words, which leaves little, if any, attention for comprehension or comprehension monitoring (Samuels, 2006). Since decoding is not automatic, beginning readers dip back into the text a second time to attend to comprehension. Next, beginning readers must stop and think about whether or not what they comprehended makes sense (i.e., monitor comprehension). Thus, beginning readers work slowly, cycling back multiple times to gain meaning from the text (Samuels).

As readers become more proficient, they gain automaticity; that is, they process these cognitive tasks simultaneously. When decoding is automatic, readers are capable of focusing on comprehending text. In addition, fluent readers monitor their reading comprehension. They continuously check their understanding, and if they detect a problem (e.g., something does not make sense), they employ a fix-up strategy, such as rereading, until they are certain that what is read makes sense.

In short, automaticity theory explains the importance of two components of reading fluency – word recognition and automaticity; however, it does not explain the last component – prosody (Kuhn & Stahl, 2000).

Prosody

Prosody includes the elements of intonation and phrasing present in fluent oral reading. Simply put, when fluent readers read aloud, it sounds like they are reading with expression. Prosody may be particularly important for students with autism spectrum disorders (ASD) by bridging surface word recognition to reading comprehension (Kuhn & Stahl, 2003). Prosody links written text to oral language (Kuhn & Stahl, 2000, 2003). Readers who read with proper prosody embed linguistic markers found in speech; in other words, they apply what they know about semantics, syntax, and pragmatics from oral language to written text. Thus, when reading aloud, proficient readers read like they speak.

Toward a Theory of Reading Fluency for Students With ASD

What does this mean for students with ASD? Students on the spectrum tend to be bottom-up processors who focus on minute details (Frith, 2008). In addition, they often possess strong rote memories. Taken together, these characteristics may explain the relative strength students on the spectrum have for word recognition. However, when it comes to simultaneously comprehending text, this strength may become a weakness. That is, these students may expend too much attention to the detail of individual words, even words they know by sight, leaving few cognitive resources for comprehension. Another possible explanation is found in emerging research on reading and ASD.

Williamson, Carnahan, and Jacobs (2009) conducted a study to better understand how students with ASD think about and process text. They asked students with high-functioning autism or Asperger Syndrome to read text aloud and pause to tell what they were thinking about as they read. Some students who demonstrated speed and accuracy in oral reading reported thinking about things unrelated to the text. For example, they were thinking about their favorite song or some special interest. So, even though these students had capacity left over, they did not attend to comprehension. Other students used reading comprehension strategies similar to those of typically developing peers, such as visualizing the text or asking questions related to the text. These findings suggest that while fast and accurate decoding affords capacity for comprehension, some students on the spectrum do not attend (i.e., expend cognitive energy in the effort to process a task) to comprehension, especially when the material is not directly related to their special interest.

In terms of prosody, students on the autism spectrum like Ryan in the opening vignette often read accurately, word by word, with little indication of appropriate phrasing and intonation. This may be explained by the connection between prosodic reading and oral language. The language differences of students on the spectrum are well documented in the literature (American Psychiatric Association, 2000; McCann, Peppe, Gibbon, O'Hare, & Rutherford, 2007). For example, scholars have suggested that students on the spectrum demonstrate differences in joint attention and miss language learning opportunities as a result (Carnahan & Borders, in press; Paul & Sutherland, 2005; Prizant & Wetherby, 2005; Quill, 2000). Typically developing children use prosodic features to derive meaning from language (Read & Schreiber, 1982). For students on the spectrum, who have cognitive and social communication differences, prosodic features may not function to facilitate meaning in the same way as they do for typically developing children. Thus, the fluency differences of students with ASD may be attributed to attention (i.e., cognitive energy expended in the effort to process a task) during the reading process and underlying language differences.

Other Factors That Influence Fluency

Characteristics of both the reader and the text contribute to fluent oral reading. First, the student's background knowledge, interest/motivation, and reading level all contribute to oral reading fluency. Background knowledge affords exposure to key content vocabulary words, making it likely that a text about a familiar topic is read more fluently. For example, if Ryan's special interest was baseball, he would likely read a passage about baseball more fluently than one about horticulture. In addition, since Ryan is interested in baseball, he is more likely to be motivated to read a text about baseball, and motivation translates to student engagement and effort. (For more on motivation and reading, see Guthrie, 2004; Guthrie & Humenick, 2004.) Related to motivation is the purpose for reading. If the purpose for reading is pleasure (e.g., reading a book at the beach), compared to reading a textbook to pass an exam, reading fluency will naturally differ, as the reader expends differing amounts of attention commensurate with the purpose for reading.

We refer to the text's influence on reading fluency as the readability of the text. The linguistic content of the text, such as the number of high-frequency words and spelling patterns, as well as the variety of linguistic content (i.e., the variety of words and spelling patterns) influence a text's readability. If a text contains too many unknown words, it increases the student's cognitive load (i.e., the number of words that are not automatically recognizable and, therefore, must be decoded) (Hiebert, 2006). A text with large numbers of multisyllabic words and complex sentence structure makes reading fluently a more challenging task. Hence, these factors are part of readability formulae (e.g., Flesch, 1948; Fry, 1977) that help determine the reading level of a text.

Assessing Fluency

As noted, the reading fluency of students on the autism spectrum varies widely, with most students showing some differences in prosody. As a result, it is important to gather diagnostic information, as well as to monitor student progress. Specifically, students should be assessed for accuracy, reading rate, and automaticity. Before giving any assessment, it is important to consider and mitigate potential stressors that accompany assessments such as changes in routine, or working with unfamiliar adults. The use of ongoing, routine assessment and systematic planning can help decrease these stresses.

There are multiple options for assessing fluency, including individual reading inventories (IRIs), running records, and curriculum-based measures. Commercially available IRIs contain leveled narrative and expository passages. Nilsson (2008) reviewed eight IRIs and found that aspects of particular IRIs are better suited for some students than for others. For example, some IRIs are useful for assessing students who read at higher levels. Because of the amount of time it takes to administer (as long as an hour for a skilled administrator), IRIs are generally used to obtain diagnostic (i.e., areas of strength and need) information about student abilities. Running records and curriculum-based measures generally use passages or parts of passages from instructional reading materials. They are typically quick to administer and are, therefore, suitable for progress monitoring.

The general procedure to assess reading fluency for all of these measures is to ask a student to read aloud a particular passage, during which the teacher records oral deviations from the text, times the reading with a stopwatch, and qualitatively assesses the student's prosody. It is helpful, particularly for teachers administering these kinds of assessments for the first time, to audio record each session. Clay (2000), however, argued against recording, believing that this detracts from teachers' attention to students' oral reading. Practically speaking, as teachers become proficient at listening for students' miscues, recordings become less necessary. Although all of these measures include procedures for assessing accuracy and rate, many of them omit measures for prosody since it cannot be "counted." Instead, it is rated using either a rubric or a checklist.

Accuracy

To assess the accuracy of student reading, the expected response (i.e., what the text says) is compared to the observed response (i.e., what the student utters), and miscues or deviations from print are recorded. Miscues can be recorded on an actual copy of the text, as with IRIs and Dynamic Indicators of Basic Early Literacy Skills (DIBELS; Goode et al., 2002), or on a blank sheet of paper, as is typical for a running record.

The comprehension/fluency mini-assessment (CFMA) shown in Figure 10.1 (blank forms may be found in the Appendix pp. 315-319) can be used with any passage, and is particularly useful to monitor student progress over time. The first portion of the form is based upon Clay's (2000) running record procedure. As the student reads a passage aloud for one minute, the teacher records a dot in each square of the grid for correct words uttered and records the actual miscue for each utterance that deviates from the text. Teachers can collect student miscues and analyze them to gather information about which cues (graphic, semantic, syntactic) students rely on to read unknown words. This information is useful when matching students to instructional strategies.

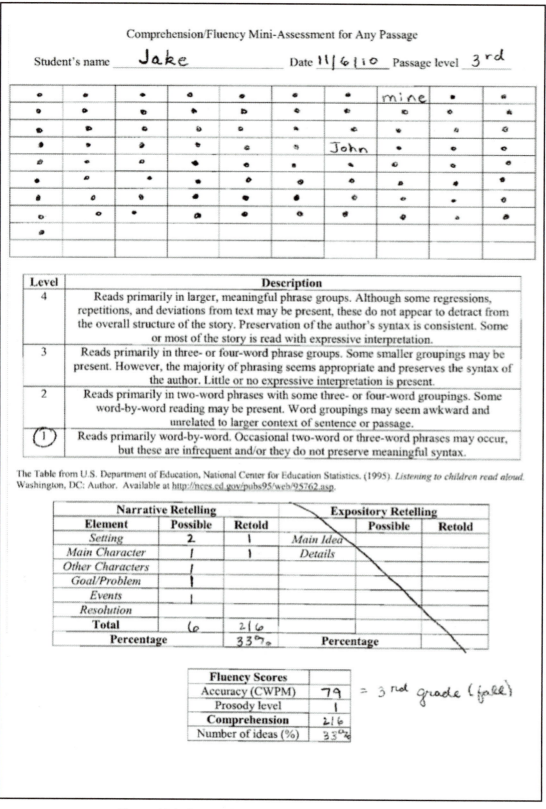

Comprehension/Fluency Mini-Assessment for Any Passage

Student's name __Jake__   Date 11/6/10   Passage level 3rd

Level	Description
4	Reads primarily in larger, meaningful phrase groups. Although some regressions, repetitions, and deviations from text may be present, these do not appear to detract from the overall structure of the story. Preservation of the author's syntax is consistent. Some or most of the story is read with expressive interpretation.
3	Reads primarily in three- or four-word phrase groups. Some smaller groupings may be present. However, the majority of phrasing seems appropriate and preserves the syntax of the author. Little or no expressive interpretation is present.
2	Reads primarily in two-word phrases with some three- or four-word groupings. Some word-by-word reading may be present. Word groupings may seem awkward and unrelated to larger context of sentence or passage.
(1)	Reads primarily word-by-word. Occasional two-word or three-word phrases may occur, but these are infrequent and/or they do not preserve meaningful syntax.

The Table from U.S. Department of Education, National Center for Education Statistics. (1995). *Listening to children read aloud.* Washington, DC: Author. Available at http://nces.ed.gov/pubs95/web/95762.asp.

Narrative Retelling			Expository Retelling		
Element	Possible	Retold		Possible	Retold
Setting	2	1	Main Idea		
Main Character	1	1	Details		
Other Characters	1				
Goal/Problem	1				
Events	1				
Resolution					
Total	6	2	6		
Percentage		33%	Percentage		

Fluency Scores	
Accuracy (CWPM)	79
Prosody level	1
Comprehension	2	6
Number of ideas (%)	33%

= 3rd grade (fall)

Figure 10.1. Comprehension/fluency mini-assessment.

If students obtain a sufficient number of miscues, a miscue analysis can be added to any fluency assessment (e.g., DIBELS, running record). For example, Leslie and Caldwell (2011) suggested that in order to determine a generalizable pattern, 15 or more miscues should be analyzed. Miscues can be collected across multiple passages and analyzed together. This has the advantage of providing instructionally relevant information beyond comparisons of improvements of reading rates over time and performance benchmarks (i.e., the rate at which other students performed on the passage). In Figure 10.2, we present a generic miscue analysis sheet that can be used for any passage.

Student Name: Jake   Date: 11/6/10

Expected Response	Observed Response	Graphic Cues			Syntax	Semantic
		Beginning	Middle	End		
visit	visited	✔	✔		✔	
for	from	✔				
the	a				✔	
hear	ears		✔			
senses	sense	✔	✔		✔	
though	thaw	✔				
birth	breathe	✔				
live	little	✔				
find	feed	✔		✔		
went	weren't	✔		✔		
aloud	out loudly		✔			✔
give	gave	✔		✔	✔	
I'm	I	✔				✔
taped	tapped	✔		✔	✔	
for	of				✔	
Total		11/15	4/15	4/15	6/15	2/15
%		73%	27%	27%	40%	13%

Figure 10.2. Miscue analysis worksheet.

To complete the miscue analysis, write the word from the text in the Expected Response column and what the student said in the Observed Response column. Next, compare the expected response with the observed response and place a checkmark in each column that applies. For example, if the expected word was *dog* and the observed word was *puppy*, both the Syntax column and the Semantic column are checked, as the miscue preserved both meaning (i.e., *dog* and *puppy* have similar meanings) and syntax (i.e., a noun was switched with another noun). For the Graphic Cues section, nothing would be checked, as the words have nothing in common visually (i.e., the same letters as the beginning, middle, and/or ending of the expected word). To complete the analysis, enter totals at the bottom of the chart. In addition, a percentage should be calculated, which represents the category total divided by the total number of miscues.

Once analysis is complete, it is important to interpret the data and use the interpretations to guide instruction. For example, if a student seems overly reliant on using graphic cues (i.e., visual cues), consider explicitly teaching her how to use context clues to determine unknown words, as context clues are dependent upon knowledge of syntax and semantics. Or, if the student's miscues show consistent use of beginning and end sound similarities to identify unknown words, perhaps explicitly teaching vowel sounds would improve accurate identification of unknown words.

Reading Rate

To determine a student's reading rate, a stopwatch is used. To decide how much text to have the student read, consider both the purpose of the timing and the student's needs. For example, if the goal is to obtain diagnostic information rather than simply monitoring progress, it is best to administer whole passages in order to get a more complete picture of student abilities. Another reason for administering an entire passage instead of part of a passage is that some students become stressed when asked to stop reading before they have finished the passage. (For these students, briefer passages used for progress monitoring may need to be typed onto a separate sheet instead of using the full text.)

To calculate the number of correct words read per minute (CWPM), multiply the number of words in the passage by 60, subtract 1 for each miscue, and then divide by the number of seconds it took for the student to read the passage. For example, if Ryan read a 250-word passage without any errors in 2 minutes and 10 seconds, or 130 seconds, he read a little more than 115 WPM (i.e., 250 X 60 = 15,000/130 seconds). To interpret this number, compare it to Figure 10.3. Thus, at the beginning of third grade, Ryan is reading slightly more CWPM than the average end-of-the-year third grader.

Another option is to have students read for 1 minute instead of reading an entire passage. The advantage is that is takes less time away from instruction; however, brief timings may provide less instructionally relevant information. When coupled with other measures, 1-minute timings may be useful for progress monitoring.

The comprehension/fluency mini-assessment shown in Figure 10.1 is designed to make calculating CWPM effortless. Notice that the grid is 10 squares by 10 squares. As noted earlier, a dot is marked in a square when a word is read accurately, and if the student miscues, the uttered word is written in the square. To determine WPM, simply count by 10s for each complete row, and then continue counting by 1 for the last partial row. To determine CWPM, subtract the total number of miscues.

Often, oral reading rates are compared to benchmarks. Benchmarks are established by taking the average reading rates of a particular population of students over time. It is important to remember that for students with ASD like Ryan, reading rates and comparisons to benchmarks offer an incomplete picture of their reading abilities. Since comparing individual students' reading rates to norms is a widely adopted practice, we include the information here.

As result of the widespread implementation of DIBELS, schools may have local benchmarks against which students can be compared. If no local benchmarks are available, in Table 10.1 we summarize mean fluency rates, as reported by Hasbrouck and Tindall (2006). These norms were established with large numbers of students (range = 3,496-20,128 scores) from schools and districts in 23 states (Hasbrouck & Tindall). Hasbrouck and Tindall report that the norm group included "a full range of students, from those identified as gifted or otherwise exceptionally skillful to those diagnosed with reading disabilities such as dyslexia" (p. 637).

Table 10.1
Mean Fluency Rates

Grade	Fall CWPM	Winter CWPM	Spring CWPM
1	--	23	53
2	51	72	89
3	71	92	107
4	94	112	123
5	110	127	139
6	127	140	150
7	128	136	150
8	133	146	151

From Hasbrouck, J., & Tindal, G. (2006, April). Oral reading fluency norms: A valuable assessment tool for reading teachers. *The Reading Teacher*, 59(7), 636–644. Copyright 2006 by the International Reading Association. Used with permission.

Prosody

The presence of prosodic features in oral reading is likely the link between fluency and reading comprehension. Reliably assessing prosody can be challenging, as it requires more than simply counting the number of words read and the number of miscues. Simply stated, assessing prosody requires a teacher to have a well-trained ear that can match student performance with either a rubric or a checklist. Figure 10.1 includes the prosody rubric developed by researchers in conjunction with the National Assessment of Educational Progress (U.S. Department of Education, n.d.), the only national assessment that looks at what students know and are able to do. Other researchers have developed checklists (e.g., Hudson et al., 2005) that also may be used.

Progress Monitoring Using the CFMA

As noted, the CFMA may be useful for monitoring student progress. To document student progress in both expository and narrative reading, 100-word passages are selected for assessment. In order to collect sufficient data without spending too much instructional time on assessment, data from expository and narrative passages are collected on alternating weeks. Since the CFMA has different scales for each component, each section should be charted on a separate line graph (see Figures 10.3-10.5). In addition, since it is important to monitor passage type (i.e., expositive, narrative), consider monitoring each separately. This means that for each student, six line graphs will be maintained.

To complete the reading rate accuracy progress monitoring tool, place a dot in the middle of the square that indicates the CWPM on the passage listed at the bottom of the CFMA. As new data points are added, simply connect the dots with a line.

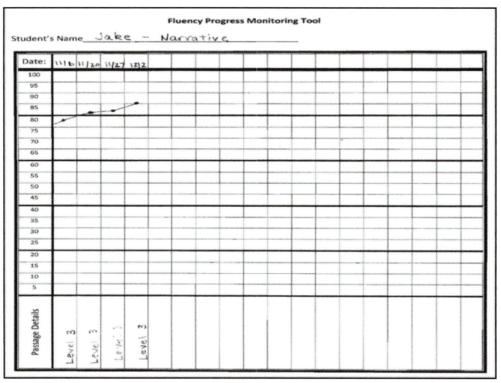

Figure 10.3. Monitoring the progress of reading rate.

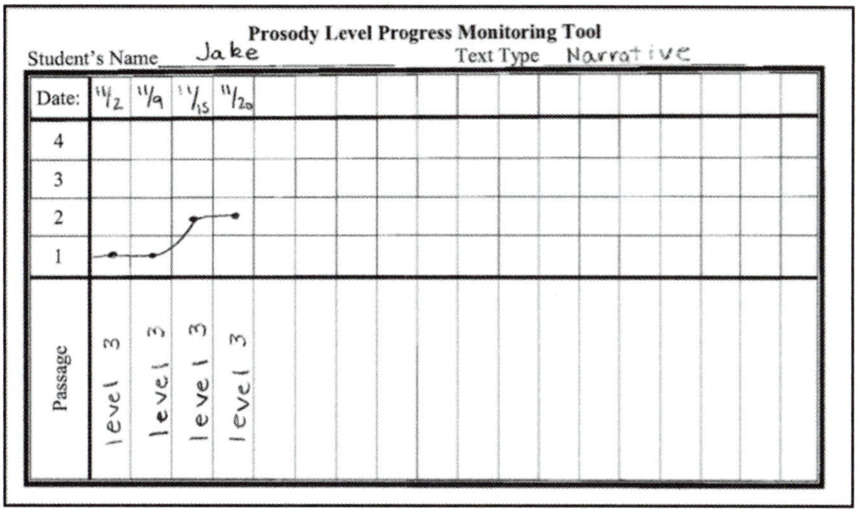

Prosody Level Progress Monitoring Tool

Student's Name ___Jake___   Text Type ___Narrative___

Date:	¹¹/₂	¹¹/₉	¹¹/₁₅	¹¹/₂₀															
4																			
3																			
2																			
1																			
Passage	level 3	level 3	level 3	level 3															

Figure 10.4. Monitoring the progress of prosody.

Retelling is frequently used to determine the extent to which individuals comprehend what is read (Morrow, 1986; Reutzel & Cooter, 2003). To monitor the progress of student retellings (see Figure 10.5), it is necessary for the teacher to read the passage to determine the number of elements that are possible for the student to retell. For narratives, story elements include the setting, such as where and when the story takes place, the main character, other characters, the goal or problem, events, and the resolution; one point is awarded for each of these elements. For expository passages, elements generally include a main idea and details about the main idea. Once again, one point is awarded for each main idea and detail present in the passage.

As the student retells the passage, he is awarded one point for each item from among the items possible told. The possible number of elements is compared to the student's performance (i.e., how many elements were included in the retelling) and converted to a percentage. The percentage is then charted, and as with other progress-monitoring graphs, data points are connected with a line to create a visual representation of student progress.

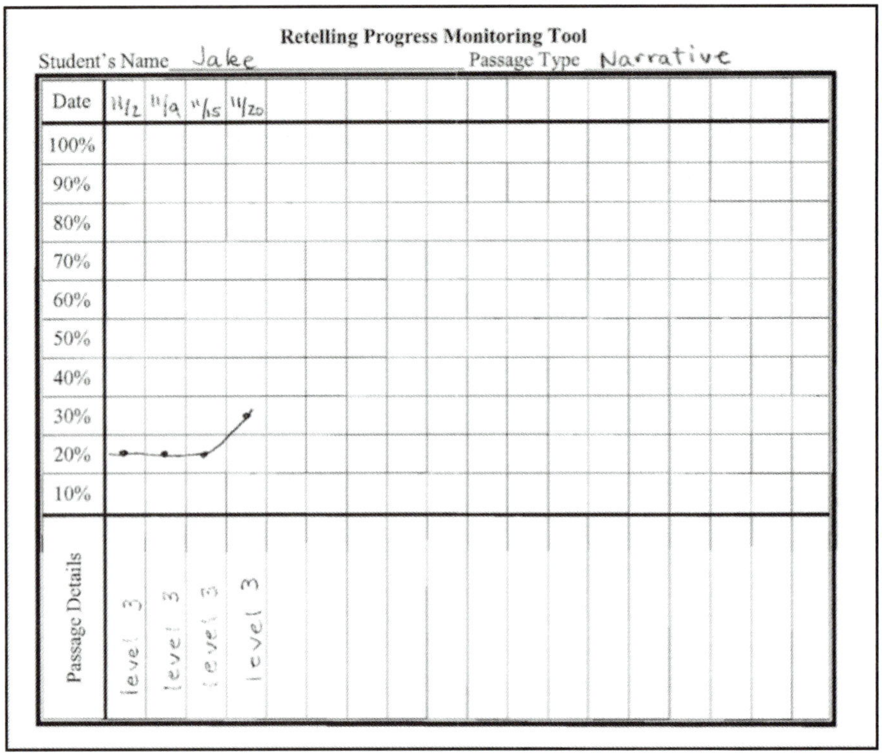

Figure 10.5. Monitoring the progress of retellings.

Final Thoughts on Assessment

Assessing literacy skills early in the instructional cycle is vital for ensuring students receive appropriate literacy instruction. It is important to have a thorough understanding of what students already know and are able to do, so that instructional time is maximized through individualized instruction. Commercially available IRIs are informal assessments that have been widely used in reading diagnosis by teachers, including for students with ASD (e.g., Myles et al., 2002). IRIs are flexible and provide rich information about reading abilities, including students' strengths and weaknesses in all areas of reading. Depending upon the IRI used, IRIs may be varied according to students' need for picture support and background knowledge on a topic related to comprehension. Teachers can also use IRIs to test students' use of comprehension strategies using think-aloud procedures (e.g., Leslie & Caldwell, 2011).

The CFMA and associated progress-monitoring tools are designed to offer a more comprehensive snapshot of reading abilities, not just reading fluency. Although we will discuss fluency instruction that aligns with the fluency part of these tools, readers are encouraged to consult other chapters throughout the book to determine how to meet the instructional needs of students.

Fluency Practice and Instruction

As part of balanced literacy instruction, all students should be widely exposed to connected text. For emergent readers, this includes listening to read-alouds, and for older students, it includes reading silently. One of the more controversial conclusions drawn by the National Reading Panel (NRP) (2000) was that there was not enough evidence to support the practice of reading in classrooms using such methods as Sustained Silent Reading or Drop Everything and Read (Jennings, Caldwell, & Lerner, 2011). Through these strategies, students are given an amount of time for independent reading equivalent to their independent reading abilities. Less skilled readers might be expected to read a book of their own choosing for 5 minutes, whereas more skilled readers might be expected to read for 15 minutes.

Leisure Reading

Barb teaches intermediate-aged students with ASD in a self-contained, multiage classroom. In one corner of the room, Barb visually signifies the reading area. On one wall, there is a small rack of books, and against the other wall, there is an old couch. There are also a couple of beanbag chairs on the floor. On the bookrack, Barb has carefully selected books for each of her students. For example, she knows that Jonathon loves trains and that his independent reading level is primer. With Jonathon in mind, she has placed a copy of *Freight Train* by Donald Crews on the rack. And for Lydia, a young lady who reads independently at the third-grade level and loves purses, she has placed a copy of *Lilly's Purple Plastic Purse*, by Kevin Henkes. Several of her students are interested in cooking, so she has placed small, well-illustrated cookbooks on the rack, too. Also included on the rack are several class books and other books she previously used for instruction.

Barb's students are well versed on the procedure for sustained silent reading. Immediately after lunch, students enter the classroom, select a book, and settle into their favorite spot in the reading corner. Barb finds that this eases students into the second half of their day. Barb joins students in the corner with her own book to model independent reading. Although she looks like she is reading, she carefully monitors student book selections, so that she can make changes in book offerings over time.

Instructional Considerations

As part of overall balanced literacy instruction, students who have some decoding skills or who have the ability to recognize words in isolation may be ready for fluency instruction. This would include students who are reading at the late preprimer level through late second-grade level (Kuhn & Stahl, 2003). Hasbrouk and Tindall (2006) also suggest that if students are 10 or more words below the mean on two cold passages from peer benchmarks (i.e., the passages have not been previously read), students are candidates for fluency instruction. For students on the spectrum, all facets of fluency should be considered, not just reading rate, as fluency instruction that focuses on improving reading rate only may not improve reading comprehension for these students as it does for students with other kinds of disabilities.

Texts used for instruction. Allington (2006) strongly suggests that matching students to text maximizes their learning opportunities. As noted earlier, IRIs can be used to establish each student's three reading levels – independent, instructional, and frustration. At the independent level, students can successfully read and understand the text. At the instructional level, students can read the text with appropriate support. Research examining which level of text is best used for fluency instruction is somewhat mixed. Clay (1993), the developer of Reading Recovery, has long argued for using independent-level texts, texts in which students read at least 95% of the words accurately, to practice reading fluency. However, in a review of fluency practices, Kuhn and Stahl (2003) concluded "more difficult materials would lead to greater gains in achievement" (p. 9). Thus, we suggest using instructional-level texts for students on the spectrum to potentially support academic growth, particularly when students are scaffolded using assisted reading strategies.

Repeated reading or wide reading. Repeated reading, or wide reading, is typically used to develop reading fluency. In repeated reading, students practice reading a text several times while teachers chart improvements in accuracy, speed, and sometimes prosody. In wide reading, the amount that is read is increased without the student reading the same text multiple times. Research exists to support both strategies.

For example, Dowhower (1987) found that repeated reading of the same text had positive effects on speech pauses and intonation; Herman (1985) noted that the same improvements transferred to other passages (as reported in Kuhn & Stahl, 2003). However, in comparing a repeated reading strategy with a wide reading strategy, Kuhn (2005) found that wide reading had the greatest effect on reading comprehension. Nevertheless, she concluded that both strategies were adequate to improve comprehension.

Priming. For students with ASD, it makes sense to use high-interest passages, perhaps around their favorite topic, to begin fluency work. As students become familiar with the process, introducing other topics with adequate priming may help extend their interests and build fluency. Since wide reading may have better effects on reading comprehension (Kuhn, 2004/2005), and exposing students to less familiar materials is part of the learning process, instruction must take a turn from the familiar to the unfamiliar. To meet their need for predictability, priming students on the spectrum for new materials and topics may facilitate the goal of wide reading.

Priming involves introducing students to new topics before they are incorporated into instruction (Wilde, Koegel, & Koegel, 1992). According to Myles and Adreon (2001), priming may improve the likelihood for success. It can be as simple as writing the details of the planned lesson on an index card (e.g., topic of the fluency passage, the length of the passage, and the planned method of instruction). The index card is presented to the student before the lesson, or assigned as a prereading homework assignment sent home the night before.

Instructional grouping. Fluency strategies are designed with differing group sizes in mind, including whole class, small groups, flexible grouping, and one on one. The instructional grouping of many strategies can be modified to account for students' social and behavioral needs. Essentially, the goal is to provide practice and support for reading fluently. (See Leaf & McEachin, 1999, and Maurice, Green, & Luce, 1996, for a discussion of embedded instruction and group instruction strategies.) For example, students might work in a pair with a reliable partner before working with a small group.

Focus on attention to meaning. Since improving comprehension is the goal of fluency instruction for students with ASD, it is important to orient their excess attention toward comprehension. Many strategies may not make this an overt goal of instruction. To start, use passages directly related to each student's special interest. Then employ a variety of strategies to direct student attention to comprehension. For example, ask students to represent what they read by drawing a picture, writing down key words, or composing a sentence about what was read.

Focus on language. Researchers are still unclear about whether prosody is the result of comprehension or if it facilitates comprehension (McCann et al., 2007). However, given the prevalence of language differences among students with ASD, to the maximum extent possible, fluency methods that focus on prosodic features should be used. Instructional methods that include a model – an adult, a peer, or even an audio file – are likely better than methods that do not include models.

Instructional Methods

Evidence-based instruction to develop fluency for average, struggling, and students with learning disabilities includes (a) models of fluent reading by teachers or peers; (b) direct instruction and feedback in decoding, prosody, and return eye sweep; (c) readily available independent-level reading materials; and (d) opportunities for practice (Hudson et al., 2005). All of this should take place in the context of reading for meaning (Hudson et al.). For students on the autism spectrum, interventions that provide models of fluent reading and explicit instruction in prosody within the context of reading for meaning seem most important. However, at least one researcher (Dowhower, 1987) found that repeated reading, typically considered an intervention to improve reading rate, also had measurable effects on speech pauses and intonation.

Repeated reading. Repeated reading is one of the most researched interventions for improving reading rate (Kuhn & Stahl, 2003). With the addition of a recorded model, repeated reading may also improve prosody (Dowhower, 1987). To conduct repeated readings, teachers select short passages of instructional-level text, typically from different genres of text (Hudson et al., 2005). Jennings and her colleagues (2006) noted that since the selection is read over and over, choosing a text of interest to the reader is crucial for sustaining interest. Next, teachers set a goal in CWPM that students must reach before moving to a different passage. The reading rate monitoring tool shown in Figure 10.3 may be used to chart student progress over time. As Ryan's case illustrates, however, improving only reading rate may not be helpful.

Dowhower (1987) varied this approach by supporting repeated readings with audiotapes. However, Hudson and her colleagues (2005) noted that the audiotapes found in listening centers are often not suitable for this purpose, as stories are read too fast and include music or other distracting elements along with the story. Instead, these authors recommend several commercially available products that are either audio recorded (e.g., Carbo Recorded Books, http://www.nrsi.com/carbo_recorded_books.php; Jamestown Timed Readings Plus, http://www.glencoe.com/gln/jamestown/) or computer software programs (e.g., Read Naturally, http://www.readnaturally.com/; Soliloquy Reading Assistant, http://www.connors.com/press/soliloquy-revamps-reading-assistant.html), which feature slower reading rates that maintain important prosodic features.

Other assisted reading strategies. Assisted reading is so named because these methods always include a reading model (e.g., classroom adults, typically developing peers). Thus, the reading-while-listening technique described above is an assisted reading strategy. Another strategy features the teacher simultaneously reading along with students at an appropriate pace. The teacher supplies unknown words quickly, so the pace of reading can be maintained (Jennings et al., 2006). While reading, the teacher may omit particular words, sometimes referred to as cloze-assisted reading (Hudson et al., 2005). He or she may also vary how loudly he or she reads, so that student voices become more prominent. This can be done with one or more students, as long as students are at the same reading level.

During **paired reading**, a student is paired with a more skilled, typically developing peer who serves as a tutor. Sessions are typically 15 to 30 minutes long. Selected texts should be at the student's instructional level (Jennings et al., 2010). The tutor and tutee begin by reading together at a reasonable pace. Using a predetermined signal, the tutee may start reading alone, as the tutor follows along. The tutor corrects mispronunciations, and the tutee repeats the word. If the tutee encounters an unknown word and stops reading, the tutor waits for 5 seconds and then supplies the word. When reading resumes, the tutor reads simultaneously with the tutee until signaled again to stop by the tutee.

Echo reading, another assisted reading method, pairs a skilled other with a struggling reader. During echo reading, the teacher or skilled peer reads a line of text, and then the tutee reads the same line of text. The tutor corrects the tutee for phrasing, inflection, and stress.

Performance reading. The idea behind performance reading is to practice reading a text so that it can be "performed." Variations include radio reading, talk show simulations, reader's theatre, and choral reading. In the opening vignette of this chapter, Jameka was participating in radio reading. Using an existing script or one written by students, students practice reading as though they are reading for a radio broadcast. Old-time radio shows (Hudson et al., 2005), talk radio, or broadcasts of sporting events are suitable for radio reading (Jennings et al., 2010).

Reader's Theatre Web Resources

The following web sites offer free downloads of scripts for reader's theatre. In other cases, there is a fee for scripts, so read sites carefully.

www.aaronshep.com/rt

www.playbooks.com

www.storycart.com

www.readinglady.com

Talk show reading is a variation on radio reading, the difference being the addition of a visual element. At a school where the first author worked, students prepared a morning news show that was broadcast on a closed-circuit television system. Students wrote the scripts, loaded them into a teleprompter, and then read them on camera.

Reader's theatre calls for dramatic readings of text. Students practice reading narrative scripts. Unlike talk shows or radio reading, reader's theatre uses narrative texts. Hudson and her colleagues (2005) suggested that teachers create scripts from stories that are rich in dialogue.

Choral reading is yet a different form of performance reading. During choral readings, students perform a written work chorally. Texts that are particularly well suited for choral reading include poetry or raps, although almost any text can be read aloud chorally. At a school where the first author taught, a creative special education teacher and her students wrote a rap about the termites that infested their classroom and displaced them to a different location in the building. She used this event as a teachable moment to work on her students' reading fluency.

Explicit methods to teach prosody. In addition to known language differences, prosody is challenging for students with ASD because there are few visual cues to alert readers to prosodic features (Rasinski, 1990). While commas and ending punctuation may alert readers to phrase boundaries, and ending punctuation alerts readers to intonation, not all intonation and phrase features are marked with these types of visual cues. Further, in English, there are no marks to emphasize stress. For students with ASD who are visually attuned, attention should be drawn to places where prosodic features should occur when text is read aloud to make this implicit knowledge of prosody explicit.

To draw attention to phrasing, Hudson and her colleagues (2005) proposed inserting a forward slash mark (/) after each phrase and a double forward slash mark at the end of each sentence. Students are explicitly taught to briefly pause for the single forward slash and pause longer for the double forward slash. For example, a text would be marked as follows:

When Will entered the house,/ he noticed/ the shadows hung over the foyer/ like cobwebs.// The picture/ of a young girl/ on the wall/ looked eerily/ like his sister/ when she was about four years old.//

As described in the Balanced Literacy Lesson box (see page 309), Mitchell marked a chapter in Alex's book using this method. Alex then echo read the chapter with a peer. This gave Alex both visual and aural cues for appropriate phrasing in the book he was reading.

Another way to increase student awareness of phrasing is to work with ambiguous sentences (Hudson et al., 2005). Take, for example, the following sentence: *The boy saw the teacher with binoculars.* The sentence can mean either (a) through a pair of binoculars, the boy spotted the teacher; or (b) the boy saw a teacher who was holding a pair of binoculars. The difference is whether or not the prepositional phrase *with binoculars* is grouped with *saw a teacher.* Parsing, questioning, and rephrasing (PQR), a comprehension strategy developed by Flood, Lapp, and Fisher (2002), chunks text into phrases that represent the ideas (meaning) found in the text. It uses syntax, a cue that is accessible to many students on the spectrum, to emphasize phrasing, which is an important facet of prosody.

Hudson and her colleagues (2005) offered several suggestions for working on intonation and stress. One strategy is for teachers to use the same sentence with different punctuation to explicitly explain how punctuation influences meaning. For example:

1. It's raining? For this sentence, a rising voice at the end signifies a question.
2. It's raining. The period at the end of this sentence signifies an exchange of information – a fact.
3. It's raining! This statement suggests that for some reason, the speaker is excited that it's raining.

Similarly, Hudson and her colleagues (2005) suggested an exercise to emphasize inflection, which can also change the meaning of the same sentence. In this case, words in italics are stressed.

1. *I* love broccoli.
2. I *love* broccoli.
3. I love *broccoli*.

In the first example, the pronoun *I* is emphasized. This sentence might be used in a playful back-and-forth among friends arguing over who loves broccoli the most. The second example would indicate a genuine enthusiasm for broccoli, and the third example is a stress pattern indicative of a response to the question, What's your favorite food?

Conclusion

Pressley, Gaskins, and Fingeret (2006) made an important point about reading instruction: Even methods supported by a strong research base do not work for every student. Consequently, they describe the "try and monitor" approach (p. 48). This suggests that teachers should select a method that appears to meet the needs of their students in their context, try the method for a while, monitor student progress, and, if the method improves student outcomes, continue. Otherwise, select a different approach and try again. This seems especially helpful advice for students with ASD whose reading abilities are known to vary widely.

For many students, fluency instruction can lead to improvements in reading comprehension. However, the needs of students on the spectrum have outpaced the research. Speech-language pathology researchers are beginning to scrutinize the role prosody plays in the language differences for students on the spectrum (e.g., McCannet al., 2007). In the meantime, our work with students on the spectrum leads us to believe that for these children, balanced literacy instruction that includes a fluency component focused on meaning is key.

Balanced Literacy Lesson

Sarah and Mitchell coteach using station teaching in a fifth-grade language arts class. During their 90-minute block, students are grouped by ability for 30 minutes of explicit reading instruction, 30 minutes of explicit writing instruction, and 30 minutes of heterogeneously grouped lessons that integrate reading and writing activities.

During the explicit reading group, Alex, a student with high-functioning autism, is grouped with four other students at his third-grade reading level. When students arrive at the kidney-shaped table, Mitchell has a blank semantic web for the word *mystery* and leads students through the web as they make meaningful connections to the word. Next, students do a character study from the mystery they began reading the day before. During yesterday's reading lesson, students were introduced to the main character. Today, they discuss the main character's attributes, searching the story for key words related to the main character. They create a group sketch of the character. To support Alex's social learning, Mitchell is sure to discuss the character's emotional state, which is then represented in the picture. Finally, Mitchell and his students read the story aloud simultaneously, beginning where they stopped the day before. Students then rotate to their writing lesson.

During writing, Sarah reminds students that they are writing a mystery story – the same genre they are reading. To support learning, students are given a story board with each element found in the mystery story labeled in a box. They begin filling in the box labeled Main Character, as Sarah asks them to visualize what the main character in their story looks like. Some students have trouble deciding what their main character might be like. Sarah suggests they model their main character after someone they know. After all, she explains, this is a technique used by many writers. This helps students begin writing key words down.

Alex still seems confused and leans over to look at his neighbor's list of key words. After seeing what his peer was doing, Alex writes some key words of his own. Based upon their key words, students make a quick sketch of their character. They share this with a partner in their group to make sure the key words and picture align. It's now time for whole-group work.

During whole-group instruction, students do partner reading. Alex is paired with a kind, funny girl named Jenni. Jenni understands that Alex learns differently, and over time, they have established rapport. To help Alex with prosody, Mitchell used a pencil to mark each phrase in one chapter of a short mystery written at Alex's instructional level. Jenni reads each sentence, modeling pauses and intonation, which Alex then echoes. Alex is getting better at pausing for the penciled-in slash marks after each phrase, and Jenni is quick to praise him. After they finish echo reading the passage Mitchell prepared, Jenni asks Alex to retell the story to her. She has a blank story map handy, which she uses to prompt Alex for any missing information.

With 10 minutes of the period remaining, the entire class is visually signaled that it is time for sustained silent reading, when Sarah places a picture of lots of books on the chalk tray in the front of the room. Alex pulls out a magazine filled with cars, one of his favorite topics. He flips through the magazine independently. When the timer goes off, he knows it is time for math.

Chapter Highlights

- Fluency is important because there is a strong link between reading comprehension and reading fluency.

- There are three components of fluency:
  - ✔ accurate word decoding
  - ✔ automaticity in word recognition
  - ✔ prosody

- Reader characteristics include background knowledge, reading level, and interest influence fluency.

- Text readability in terms of linguistic content, spelling patterns, unknown words, and multisyllabic words influence fluency.

- Reading fluency of students with ASD varies. Thus, it is important to gather diagnostic information as well as monitor student progress.

- Assessing accuracy includes:
  - ✔ Comparing expected student response with observed student response
  - ✔ Recording miscues with comprehension fluency mini-assessment (CFMA)
  - ✔ Analyzing responses to determine the cues on which students rely

- Assessing reading rate includes:
  - ✔ Calculating the correct words read per minute; multiply the number of words in the passage by 60, subtract 1 for each miscue, and divide by total seconds it took to read passage
  - ✔ Making a comparison between the reading rate and student norms
  - ✔ Student norms should include groups that range from students identified as gifted to those diagnosed with reading difficulties

- Assessing prosody can be challenging, and requires the use of a rubric or checklist.

- The comprehension fluency mini-assessment (CFMA) is a helpful tool in monitoring students' reading rate, prosody level, and retelling ability.

- There are eight strategies for practicing fluency:
  - ✔ Drop Everything and Read (i.e., time given for independent reading)
  - ✔ Wide Reading (amount and genre of text read is increased over a period of time)
  - ✔ Priming (preparing student for new material before the material is incorporated into instruction)
  - ✔ Instructional Grouping (peer groups are modified to provide fluency support)
  - ✔ Focus on Attention (directs students' attention towards the comprehension goal)
  - ✔ Focus on Language (focuses on prosody features due to language differences among students with ASD)
  - ✔ Assisted Reading Techniques (teacher models, student pairs, echo reading, and performance reading)
  - ✔ Teaching Prosody (physically inserting slashes to remind students to pause when reading, reviewing same phrase with different punctuation marks)

Chapter Review Questions

1. Which student factors influence fluent reading for students on the spectrum?

2. Which text features influence fluent reading?

3. How should fluency be assessed?

4. Under what circumstances would using a short piece of text to assess fluency be useful?

5. How should fluency be interpreted relative to a student's reading abilities?

References

Allington, R. L. (1983). Fluency: The neglected goal. *The Reading Teacher, 36*, 556-561.

American Psychiatric Association. (2000). *Diagnostic and statistical manual for mental disorders* (4th ed., text revision). Washington, DC: Author.

Carnahan, C. R., & Borders, C. (in press). Communication in students with autism spectrum disorder. In A. E. Boutot & B. S. Myles (Eds.), *Autism spectrum disorders: Foundations, characteristics, and effective strategies.* Upper Saddle River, NJ: Pearson.

Clay, M. (2000). *Running records for classroom teachers.* Portsmouth, NH: Heinemann.

Clay, M. M. (1993). *Reading recovery: A guidebook for teachers in training.* Portsmouth, NH: Heinemann.

Dowhower, S. L. (1987). Effects of repeated reading on second-grade transitional readers' fluency and comprehension. *Reading Research Quarterly, 22*, 389-406.

Flesch, R. (1948). A new readability yardstick, *Journal of Applied Psychology, 32*, 221-233.

Flood, J., Lapp, D., & Fisher, D. (2002). Parsing, questioning, and rephrasing (PQR): Building syntactic knowledge to improve reading comprehension. In C. C. Block, L. B. Grambrell, & M. Pressley (Eds.), *Improving comprehension instruction: Rethinking research, theory, and classroom practice* (pp. 181-198). San Francisco: Jossey-Bass.

Frith, U. (2008). *How cognitive theories can help us explain autism.* Retrieved August 22, 2008, from http://www.ucdmc.ucdavis.edu/mindinstitute/events/dls_recorded_events.html

Fry, E. (1977). Fry's readability graph: Clarifications, validity, and extension to level 17. *Journal of Reading, 21*, 242-252.

Good, R. H., Gruba, J., & Kaminski, R. A. (2002). *Best practices in using dynamic indicators of basic early literacy skills (DIBELS) in an outcomes-driven model.* Washington, DC: National Association of School Psychologists.

Good, R. H., & Kaminski, R. A. (Eds.). (2002). *Dynamic Indicators of Basic Early Literacy Skills* (6th ed.). Eugene, OR: Institute for the Development of Educational Achievement.

Guthrie, J. T. (2004). Teaching for literacy engagement. *Journal of Literacy Research, 36,* 1-28.

Guthrie, J. T., & Humenick, N. M. (2004). Motivating students to read: Evidence for classroom practices that increase motivation and achievement. In P. McCardle & V. Chhabra (Eds.), *The voice of evidence in reading research* (pp. 329-354). Baltimore: Paul H. Brookes.

Hasbrouck, J., & Tindall, G. A. (2006). Oral reading fluency norms: A valuable assessment tool for reading teachers. *The Reading Teacher, 59,* 636-644.

Herman, P. A. (1985). The effect of repeated readings on reading rate, speech pauses, and word recognition accuracy. *Reading Research Quarterly, 20,* 553-565.

Hiebert, E. H. (2006). Becoming fluent: Repeated reading with scaffolded texts. In S. J. Samuels & E. H. Farstrup (Eds.), *What research has to say about fluency instruction* (pp. 204-226). Newark, DE: International Reading Association.

Hudson, R., Lane, H., & Pullen, P. (2005). Reading fluency assessment and instruction: What, why, and how? *The Reading Teacher, 58*(8), 702-714.

Jennings, J. H., Caldwell, J., & Lerner, J. W. (2010). *Reading problems: Assessment and teaching strategies* (6th ed.). Upper Saddle River, NJ: Pearson Education, Inc.

Kuhn, M. R. (2004/2005). Helping students become accurate, expressive readers: Fluency instruction for small groups. *The Reading Teacher, 58,* 338-344.

Kuhn, M. R., & Stahl, S. A. (2000). *Fluency: A review of developmental and remedial practices.* Ann Arbor, MI: Center for Improvement in Early Reading Achievement.

Kuhn, M. R., & Stahl, S. A. (2003). Fluency: A review of developmental and remedial practices. *Journal of Educational Psychology, 95,* 3-21.

LaBerge, D., & Samuels, S. L. (1974). Toward a theory of automatic information processing in reading. *Cognitive Psychology, 6,* 293-323.

Leaf, R. B., & McEachin, J. J. (1999). *A work in progress: Behavior management strategies and a curriculum for intensive behavioral treatment of autism.* New York: DRL Books.

Leslie, L., & Caldwell, J. S. (2011). *Qualitative Reading Inventory-5.* New York: Allyn & Bacon.

Maurice, C. (Ed.), Green, G., & Luce, S. (Co-Eds.). (1996). *Behavioral intervention for young children with autism: A manual for parents and professionals.* Austin, TX: Pro-Ed.

McCann, J., Peppe, S., Gibbon, F. E., O'Hare, A., & Rutherford, M. (2007). Prosody and its relationship to language in school-aged children with high functioning autism. *International Journal of Language and Communication Disorders, 42,* 682-702.

Morrow, L. M. (1986). Effects of structural guidance in story retelling on children's dictation of original stories. *Journal of Reading Behavior, 18*(2), 135-152.

Myles, B. S., & Adreon, D. (2001). *Asperger Syndrome and adolescence: Practical solutions for school success.* Shawnee Mission, KS: Autism Asperger Publishing Company.

Myles, B. S., Hilgenfeld, T. D., Barnhill, G. P., Griswold, D. E., Hagiwara, T., & Simpson, R. L. (2002). Analysis of reading skills in individuals with Asperger Syndrome, *Focus on Autism and Other Developmental Disabilities, 17,* 44-47.

National Reading Panel. (2000). *Teaching children to read: An evidence-based assessment of the scientific research literature on reading and its implications for reading instruction: Reports of the subgroups.* Washington, DC: National Institute of Child Health and Human Development.

Nilsson, N. L. (2008). A critical analysis of eight informal reading inventories. *Reading Teacher, 61*, 526-536.

Paul, R., & Sutherland, D. (2005). Enhancing early language in children with autism spectrum disorders. In F. Volkmar, R. Paul, A. Klin, & D. Cohen (Eds.), *Handbook of autism and pervasive developmental disorders* (3rd ed., pp. 946-976). Hoboken, NJ: Wiley.

Pressley, M., Gaskins, I., & Fingeret, L. (2006). Instruction and development of reading fluency in struggling readers. In. S. J. Samuels & A. E. Farstrup (Eds.), *What research has to say about fluency instruction* (pp. 47-69). Newark, DE: International Reading Association.

Prizant, B. & Wetherby, A. (2005). Critical issues in enhancing communication abilities in persons with autism spectrum disorders. In F. Volkmar, R. Paul, A. Klin, & D. Cohen (Eds.), *Handbook of autism and pervasive developmental disorders* (3rd ed., pp. 925-945). Hobohen, NJ: Wiley.

Quill, K. A. (2000). *Do-watch-listen-say: Social and communication intervention for children with autism.* Baltimore: Paul H. Brookes Publishing Company.

Rasinski, T. V. (1990). Investigating measures of reading fluency. *Educational Research Quarterly, 14*, 37-44.

Read, C., & Schreiber, P. (1982). Why short subjects are harder to find than long ones. In E. Wanner & L. Gleitman (Eds.), *Language acquisition: The state of the art* (pp. 78-101). Cambridge, UK: Cambridge University Press.

Reutzel, D. R., & Cooter, R. B. (2003). *Strategies for reading assessment and instruction: Helping every child succeed.* Upper Saddle River, NJ: Merrill/Prentice Hall.

Samuels, S. J. (1988). Decoding and automaticity: Helping poor readers become automatic at word recognition. *Reading Teacher, 41*(8), 756-60.

Samuels, S. J. (2006). Toward a model of reading fluency. In. S. J. Samuels & A. E. Farstrup (Eds.), *What research has to say about fluency instruction* (pp. 24-46). Newark, DE: International Reading Association.

Samuels, S. J., & Farstrup, E. H. (Eds.). (2006). *What research has to say about fluency instruction.* Newark, DE: International Reading Association.

U.S. Department of Education, National Center for Education Statistics. (1995). *Listening to children read aloud.* Washington, DC: Author. Available at http://nces.ed.gov/pubs95/web/95762.asp.

U.S. Department of Education, National Center for Education Statistics. (n.d.). *National assessment of educational progress: the nation's report card.* Available at http://nces.ed.gov/nationsreportcard/

Wilde, L. D., Koegel, L. K., & Koegel, R. L. (1992). *Increasing success in school through priming: A training manual.* Santa Barbara: University of California.

Williamson, P., Carnahan, C., & Jacobs, J. (2009, April). *Increasing comprehension for students with autism: From research to practice.* Paper presented at the Council for Exceptional Children Conference, Seattle, Washington.

Appendix 10.1
Comprehension/Fluency Mini-Assessment

Student's name _____ Date _____ Passage level _____

Level	Description
4	Reads primarily in larger, meaningful phrase groups. Although some regressions, repetitions, and deviations from text may be present, these do not appear to detract from the overall structure of the story. Preservation of the author's syntax is consistent. Some or most of the story is read with expressive interpretation.
3	Reads primarily in three- or four-word phrase groups. Some smaller groupings may be present. However, the majority of phrasing seems appropriate and preserves the syntax of the author. Little or no expressive interpretation is present.
2	Reads primarily in two-word phrases with some three- or four-word groupings. Some word-by-word reading may be present. Word groupings may seem awkward and unrelated to larger context of sentence or passage.
1	Reads primarily word-by-word. Occasional two-word or three-word phrases may occur, but these are infrequent and/or they do not preserve meaningful syntax.

The Table from U.S. Department of Education, National Center for Education Statistics. (1995). Listening to children read aloud. Washington, DC: Author. Available at http://nces.ed.gov/pubs95/web/95762.asp.

Narrative Retelling				Expository Retelling		
Element	Possible	Retold			Possible	Retold
Setting				Main Idea		
Main Character				Details		
Other Characters						
Goal/Problem						
Events						
Resolution						
Total						
Percentage				Percentage		

Fluency Scores	
Accuracy (CWPM)	
Prosody level	
Comprehension	
Number of ideas (%)	

Appendix 10.2
Miscue Analysis Worksheet

Student Name _____   **Date** _____

Expected Response	Observed Response	Graphic Cues			Syntax	Semantic
		Beginning	Middle	End		
Total						
%						

Appendix 10.3
Reading Rate Accuracy Progress-Monitoring Tool

Student's Name_____   Text Type _____

Date:															
100															
95															
90															
85															
80															
75															
70															
65															
60															
55															
50															
45															
40															
35															
30															
25															
20															
15															
10															
5															
Passage															

Appendix 10.4
Prosody Level Progress-Monitoring Tool

Student's Name_____   Text Type _____

Date:														
4														
3														
2														
1														
Passage														

Appendix 10.5
Retelling Progress-Monitoring Tool

Student's Name_____   Text Type _____

Date																
100%																
90%																
80%																
70%																
60%																
50%																
40%																
30%																
20%																
10%																
Passage Details																

Chapter 11
Vocabulary

Jenni Jacobs, M.Ed., University of Cincinnati

Susan Watts-Taffe, Ph.D., University of Cincinnati

Learner Objectives

After reading this chapter, the learner should be able to:

- Explain what is meant by "levels of word knowledge" and the key characteristics of word learning

- Know what to consider when selecting words to teach

- Describe methods of teaching individual word meanings for deep understanding and lasting retention

- Describe approaches to teaching word learning strategies

- List techniques for assessing word knowledge

■ ■ ■

Snapshots of Jared

8:55 a.m.

In the few minutes before the school day officially begins, Jared sits at his desk reading about Burma. This country is his most recent fascination, and he has collected a pile of library books to learn more about its geography and its people. Jared is a 5th grader who decodes like a 10th grader, but he spends much of his time rereading single sentences in order to figure out what they mean. He has acquired much of the content-area vocabulary presented in social studies and uses it to piece together his understanding of the Burmese people, their land, and their economy. Out of nowhere, he says: "Hey, did you know that rice is the major export of Burma?" After his teacher responds, he repeats this idea three times: "Rice is the major export of Burma. Rice is the major export of Burma. Rice is the major export of Burma."

10:15 a.m.

Jared's teacher is leading a literature group discussion about the book Bridge to Terabithia, *(Paterson, 1977) – a story of the friendship between a boy and a girl and an imaginative world they create together. Jared is lost. He cannot remember any of what he read, and when the teacher asks students to discuss some of the vocabulary in the book, words like* monotonous, somber, *and* consequence, *Jared is stumped. When the teacher points to the word* mistreated, *Jared quickly raises his hand and says, "Mis. That means to do something wrong or bad."*

12:00 p.m.

Jared sits in the lunch room with a table full of kids, but he does not engage in conversation. At some point, he notices that other kids have chocolate pudding, but he does not. Jared looks up to the lunch line and sees that the food has been put away. Another child at the table notices this and teases, "Aw, I'm sorry. It looks like you missed the boat on the pudding. Jared stares blankly. "What boat?" he asks.

3:50 p.m.

Since it is Friday, Jared's teacher closes the day by drawing students' attention to the bulletin board labeled "Word Sightings." This is a classroom collection of words that students have been taught and then have seen or heard on their own. Its purpose is to encourage students to internalize meanings of new words by seeking them out in new contexts and then sharing these "sightings" with the class. Jared adds the word export. *"Rice is the major export of Burma," he says enthusiastically.*

■ ■ ■

ocabulary knowledge plays a vital role in children's reading success. Its strong correlation with reading comprehension has been recognized for nearly one hundred years (Beck, Perfetti, & McKeown, 1982; Davis, 1944; Terman, 1916). However, vocabulary knowledge affects much more than reading performance. It impacts social interaction, participation in academic routines, engagement in classroom learning communities, and content-area learning (Watts-Taffe, Blachowicz, & Fisher, 2009).

Vocabulary instruction is especially important for Jared and other students with autism spectrum disorders (ASD), who often struggle to understand, and be understood, both in school and social contexts. An integral part of this struggle is their understanding, or lack thereof, of the meanings and uses of specific words. A glimpse of Jared's day reveals not only the significance of word learning for students in school, but also the multidimensional nature of the task.

Although there is scant research on vocabulary instruction for students with ASD, it is clear that this curricular area is of great importance for these students. In this chapter, we address commonly asked questions about vocabulary instruction for students with ASD by considering the research on vocabulary teaching and learning among typically developing students alongside the research on the general learning characteristics of students with ASD. In particular, we focus on questions such as: What does the research say about the general nature of word learning? How might students with ASD approach the word learning task? Which words should be taught? Which word learning strategies should be taught? What are the characteristics of effective vocabulary instruction? How can vocabulary learning be assessed?

Vocabulary Development

Types of Vocabulary

We begin by distinguishing among four general types of vocabulary: listening, speaking, reading, and writing. Listening and reading vocabularies are receptive in nature. These are the collections of words whose meanings are understood when students hear them or read them. Speaking and writing vocabularies, on the other hand, are expressive. These are the collections of words that students know well enough to use in their own speech and writing. Generally speaking, our receptive language, whether written or oral, tends to be larger than our expressive language (Pearson, Hiebert, & Kamil, 2007), as evidenced by the fact that we understand the meanings of many spoken and written words but use far fewer of these words in our own speech or writing. This is particularly true of children with ASD, who typically understand more language than they are able to physically produce (Swensen, Kelley, Fein, & Naigles, 2007).

Historically, the term *reading vocabulary* has been understood by some to mean words that students can decode (i.e., word recognition vocabulary), regardless of their understanding of the meanings of these words. In this chapter, we use the term *vocabulary* to refer to words whose meanings are understood by students, whether or not they can decode or recognize them in print.

Levels of Word Knowledge and Characteristics of Word Learning

In the general population, word knowledge exists on a continuum, ranging from no knowledge, to partial knowledge, to rich knowledge (Dale, 1965). When teaching a new word, it is helpful to know where students' skills are on this continuum. If they have never heard the word before, your instructional approach will be different than if they have partial knowledge of the word that needs to be refined.

It is not uncommon for children with ASD to be able to decode words for which they have little or no knowledge of the associated meaning. For example, Jared appeared to be a "good reader" in his literature discussion group for just this reason. In addition, children with ASD may assign incorrect meanings to words they hear, even those they use in their own speech. Because of the cognitive inflexibility that many children with ASD display, once these meanings are assigned, they may persevere. Thus, it is useful to further clarify the continuum of word knowledge, with special focus on children with ASD.

The following is an adaptation of Beck, McKeown, and Kucan's (2002) levels of word knowledge:

- **No knowledge.** Student has never heard the word before.
- **Incorrect knowledge.** Student has an incorrect meaning for the word.
  - Example: *Anxious means confused.*
- **General knowledge.** Student has "a sense of the word," such as where you might hear the word, or whether the word has negative or positive connotation.
  - Example: *Anxious isn't a good thing.*
- **Narrow, context-bound knowledge.** Student knows the meaning of the word in a specific context, but does not recognize its meaning in other contexts.
  - Example*: Anxious is how you feel when you are going to take a test.*

- **Rich, decontextualized knowledge.** Student knows the word well enough to understand its meaning in a variety of contexts and to understand subtle differences in the meaning based on contextual differences.
  - Example: *When you're anxious, you're nervous or worried. Like when you are just about to take a really hard test or when you just found out that you're going to move to a new city.*

Whether a student "knows" a particular word is not simply a yes or no question. It is a matter of degree. Word learning is incremental. Students' understandings of words develop gradually, over time and with varied experiences (Nagy & Scott, 2000). Two other characteristics of words and word learning that are important for teachers to know are the following:

- **Multiple meanings.** Many words have multiple meanings that may be unrelated. The more common the word in the English language, the more likely it is to have more than one meaning. For example, the word *walk* has multiple meanings, including *to travel on foot* or *to receive a base on balls in the game of baseball*.
- **Interrelatedness.** Knowledge of one word is directly linked to knowledge of other words. We learn new words by relating them to familiar words or concepts. For example, a student may learn the word *cinema* by linking it with familiar words such as *movie, actor, theater,* or *film*.

Nagy and Scott (2000) recommended sharing these characteristics of word learning with students, so that they themselves better understand the word learning task.

Vocabulary Development and Students With ASD

Vocabulary instruction for students with ASD can be challenging due to the inconsistencies in their language abilities. Thus, students may display a variety of communication disorders that interfere with their ability to use language productively (Tager-Flusberg, Paul, & Lord, 2005). For example, they often exhibit echolalia, the repetition of words or phrases of another speaker (Eigsti, Bennetto, & Dadlani, 2007; Tager-Flusberg et al.), which can occur within the immediate conversation or within the context of a later, seemingly unrelated conversation. Although the function of these statements in children with ASD is still not well understood, research suggests that these types of utterances may serve very specific purposes, such as requesting an object or turn taking in a conversation, or serve as an aid to processing information (Prizant & Duchan, 1981).

More specific to vocabulary use, children with ASD may use jargon or nonsense words in their speech (Chomsky, 1957, as cited in Eigsti et al., 2007). Sometimes these nonsense words have been assigned specific, consistent meanings by the speaker. This is referred to as a neologism. At other times, children assign an atypical meaning to an existing word and use it consistently (Tager-Flusberg et al., 2005). This is often thought to occur due to poor referential abilities or an inability to update incorrect information in the brain (Eigsti et al.).

The speech of children with ASD can also be characterized by overly specific or proper words, as well as odd phrasings of words (Rutter, Mawhood, & Howlin, 1992). More verbal children with ASD may use advanced words consistently, even in appropriate contexts, without truly comprehending their meaning (Gerber, 2003; Prizant, 1983). Another interesting language characteristic of children with ASD is the literalness with which they sometimes interpret language (Eigsti et al., 2007). Students may have difficulty interpreting the figurative meaning of phrases such as "raining cats and dogs" or "skating on thin ice" that are common in everyday speech and classroom readings (Norbury, 2004).

Finally, a student's performance (see Table 11.1) at a specific moment may not be an accurate indicator of his understanding of language (Chomsky, 1957, as cited in Eigsti et al., 2007). Although the student may not be able to reproduce the language, he may understand the concepts being taught.

Table 11.1

Common Communication Disorders Among Students With ASD

- Echolalia
- Use of jargon/nonsense words – sometimes with specific, consistent meanings assigned by the student; sometimes with atypical meanings assigned by the student to an existing word and used consistently
- Use of overly specific or proper words
- Odd phrasings of words
- Literal interpretation of language

Given the challenges inherent in vocabulary instruction for students with ASD, we assume that a comprehensive, multidimensional approach, as recently advocated for typically developing children (Graves, 2006), is most effective. Within this approach, vocabulary instruction is not an isolated activity, but an integral part of the entire school day. Specifically, effective vocabulary instruction includes (a) teaching the meanings of individual words for deep understanding and lasting retention, (b) teaching strategies that students can use to learn word meanings on their own, and (c) maintaining a learning environment that is concept-rich, language-rich, and word-rich (Graves; Watts-Taffe et al., 2009).

Teaching the Meanings of Individual Words

Scholars agree that typically developing students learn most words in context (Stahl & Nagy, 2006). Nonetheless, teaching the meanings of specific words provides children with a collection of words that they can use to interact with their environment as they explore, understand, and explain various experiences. Written and oral communication skills improve because children have a wide base of vocabulary from which to choose as they communicate with others. In addition, preteaching vocabulary found in reading selections can lead to increased comprehension of those selections.

Teaching the meanings of specific words seems particularly important for students with ASD, as their language characteristics suggest that they may not learn words from naturally occurring contexts as readily as others and that their communication patterns may reduce the number of rich oral contexts they have for word learning.

Using Student Interest to Increase Motivation

Mrs. Scott had tried numerous ways to involve Cody in reading and learning new words using context to infer the meaning. She tried written texts that she had used with other students and using incentives to provide motivation, but Cody still showed no interest in the task. Feeling that she needed to try something different, Mrs. Scott decided to make up her own story to get Cody motivated to learn the meanings of new words. Cody was immensely interested in SpongeBob. He talked about him and drew him every chance that he got.

Mrs. Scott began to write stories about SpongeBob using unique vocabulary with which Cody was not familiar. The tools in her word processing program allowed her to determine the reading level for each passage, and the electronic thesaurus provided her with a method for choosing unique words. Because Cody loved SpongeBob, he was motivated to read the story. His motivation to read the story provided Mrs. Scott with an opportunity to talk about the unique words in the story and teach Cody how to determine the meaning of those words.

Selecting Words to Teach

Invariably, teachers want to know which words are most worthy of their valuable instructional time. Unfortunately, no single answer is applicable to all students across all instructional settings. Selecting the words to teach is a process of instructional decision making. However, it is helpful to consider the way words vary in type and function.

Blachowicz and Fisher (2009) suggested four different types of words to teach in school: comprehension words, useful words, academic words, and generative words. For students with ASD, we believe it is useful to add basic words and idiomatic words, as detailed in Table 11.2. Note that these word types are not mutually exclusive.

Table 11.2
Types of Words to Teach Explicitly

Word Type	Explanation	Examples
Basic Words	Essential to participating in daily life activities and routine social interactions	*Desk, paper, fast, slow*
Comprehension and Content-Area Words	Essential to understanding the selection and/or unit of study	From a novel: *agitate, extraordinary, worthwhile* From a social studies textbook: *geography, legislation, economics*
Useful Words	Not critical to comprehending a particular text or learning in a particular domain, but likely to be encountered in other contexts	From a picture book: *exciting, tumble, automatically, fancy*
Academic Words	Critical to understanding and participating in school routines and learning processes	*Compare, contrast, summarize, hypothesize*
Generative Words	Facilitate the learning of other words or a word learning strategy	*Disapprove.* A focus on the prefix *dis-* opens the door for learning the meanings of words such as *disrespect, disappear*
Idiomatic and Figurative Words/Expressions	Commonly used expressions that cannot be interpreted literally	"right on target," "missed the boat," "tip of the iceberg"

Adapted from *Teaching vocabulary in all classrooms* (4th ed.) by C.L.Z. Blachowicz and P. J. Fisher, 2009. Upper Saddle River, NJ: Pearson.

The optimal number of words to teach at one time is also highly situation-specific. When one or two words come up in the course of conversation or shared reading, it makes sense to spend time on them if their definitions are critical to making sense of the conversation or the reading selection. Though quite intentional, these instructional events are usually unplanned and require attention to the fact that a student is missing an important word meaning.

When planning to teach a set of words, it can be difficult to know how many to include. In general, we advocate teaching fewer words with more depth than teaching more words in a cursory way. This makes a good deal of sense for students with ASD. Since they very often need support in seeing semantic relationships among words and may have difficulty accessing prior knowledge to support learning the meanings of new words, in-depth instruction will be a benefit. In addition, it is depth of word knowledge that enhances future word learning (Nagy & Scott, 2000).

When determining how many words to teach, it is helpful to ask yourself the following questions:

- **Are any of the words semantically related?** Words with clear connections in meaning are usually easier to learn in combination than semantically unrelated words. Be aware that the connection may be one of contradiction – antonyms are semantically related, though not similar in meaning.

- **How much prior knowledge do students bring to the words being taught?** This is often tied to interest. In Jared's case, content-area vocabulary is much easier to learn than other types of vocabulary, as Jared is intensely interested in learning about countries.

- **Are the words concrete or abstract?** Words with concrete referents, such as *vehicle* and *photograph,* are easier to learn than words with abstract referents, such as *ideal* and *genuine*.

- **Are the words new labels for concepts that are already known or are the underlying concepts completely new as well?** New labels for known concepts (e.g., *joyous, conundrum*) are easier to learn than new concepts (e.g., *photosynthesis*).

Of course, the best guides to how many words to teach at one time are the students. Take note of how well they learn various types of words under varying conditions (e.g., number of words taught at one time, instructional approach), and you will develop a sense of the number of words, usually a range, to teach at one time.

Teaching Words Well

In-depth literature reviews and meta-analyses (Blachowicz, Fisher, Ogle, & Watts-Taffe, 2006; Mezynski, 1983; Stahl & Fairbanks, 1986), coupled with work by Beck, McKeown, and Kucan (2008), suggest five important components of teaching individual words: (a) provide a user-friendly definition, (b) create a meaningful context, (c) activate students' prior knowledge and help them build semantically related categories of words and concepts, (d) actively engage students, and (e) provide a lot of practice.

- **User-friendly definition.** Provide a definition using everyday language, including words like *you*, *something*, and *someone*. For example: "Eager means you can't wait to do something."
- **Meaningful context.** Share a situation in which the word has been or could be encountered. Be sure to select a situation that your students are familiar with. For example: "I can tell when you all are eager for lunch, because you keep asking me, When will it be time for lunch? When will it be time for lunch? I'm SO hungry!!!"
- **Prior knowledge and semantic relationships.** If you have not already done this with the **contextual information** you provided, be sure to help students connect the word's meaning to their own experiences and knowledge of other words. For example: "I've noticed that most of you are eager to go out and play when it's sunny. When it rains, you are disappointed." Providing this model of bridging the new word to prior knowledge is especially important for students with ASD, since research indicates that they often have difficulty applying their prior knowledge to the tasks of vocabulary learning and reading comprehension (Wahlberg & Magliano, 2004).

Additionally, semantic maps and word continua (Blachowicz & Fisher, 2009) allow for a visual representation of the relationships between words, as shown in Figures 11.1 and 11.2.

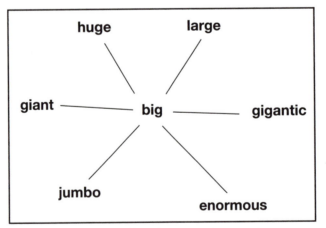

Figure 11.1. Simple semantic map.

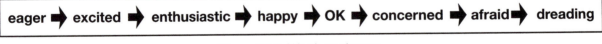

Figure 11.2. Word continuum.

Figure 11.1 shows a simple semantic map revolving around one word. More complex semantic maps allow for categorizing more than one cluster of words in the same map, thus showing relationships among categories (Stahl & Vancil, 1986). In general, students with ASD are more successful with visual than auditory processing (Myles & Simpson, 2003); therefore, semantic maps and word continua can be especially helpful. Whenever possible, add illustrations or photos. Venn diagrams are also powerful tools to enhance the word learning process, as they allow for a visual display of similarities and differences between concepts. Finally, T-charts, such as the one shown in Figure 11.3 that help students to see contrast between words/concepts, are very useful.

morose	joyous
Synonyms	
sad depressed unhappy	happy cheerful ecstatic
Looks Like	
crying screaming moving slowly with your head hanging down	smiling laughing hugging skipping
Sounds Like	
crying complaining	laughing giggling talking in a really high voice and really fast

Figure 11.3. T-chart contrasting concepts using synonyms and sensory characteristics.

- **Active engagement.** It is easy to make the mistake of providing so much information that the most cognitive engagement occurs on the part of the teacher. In order to shift engagement to students, require them to process the word in a new way. For example: "What are some things that you are eager for? What do you do when you are eager? How might you know that someone else is eager? Can anyone show me what someone might look like when they're eager?"

Knowing what someone looks like when she is eager may be difficult for children with ASD, since they often have a limited ability to recognize and understand the perspective of others (Baron-Cohen, 1995); therefore, guided practice is essential to further develop this skill. Toward this end, it is helpful to (a) show pictures, photographs, or video clips; (b) act out or let students act out; and/or (c) let students touch, feel, and interact with an object related to a new word of study.

- **Practice, practice, practice.** Most new words require multiple exposures in order to be fully learned. The best way to practice is to provide these many exposures over time and in a variety of contexts. This way, student understanding will move from being narrow and context-dependent to being rich and decontextualized. For example: "Throughout this week, I want each of you to be on the lookout for the word *eager*. If you see or hear the word, tell us about it. We will keep a tally of how many times we find this word."

Active engagement in word learning requires students to do the cognitive work of blending new information with prior knowledge, including expanding and/or altering current understanding. Quite commonly, students express misunderstandings along the way. Consider the student who hears his teacher use *eager* within the context of lunch and comes to understand that eager is something you feel before eating, with a meaning similar to *hungry*. These misunderstandings pave the way for swift and precise correction by the teacher. Engaging students provides the necessary window to their thinking for scaffolding on the part of the teacher.

Use of Technology

The teaching recommendations of the National Reading Panel (2000) suggest several ways in which technology can support vocabulary development, including the ability to:

- provide online, interactive vocabulary lessons with the technology features to engage students, provide feedback, individualize instruction, and keep records for teachers;
- provide online dictionaries, thesauri, and encyclopedias with speech capabilities to give students access to tools to use with their word learning strategies;
- provide online texts with hyperlinks that give students definitions of words and further information about key ideas in the text; and
- provide students with additional opportunities to extend their vocabularies by increasing the amount of reading and writing they do through the use of online materials and exchanges. Examples of such opportunities include web sites, discussions, online publishing, web logs, and other technology-enabled uses of text.

Vocabulary Instruction

Teaching Recommendation from National Reading Panel Report (2000)	Potential Uses of Technology to Support the Teaching Recommendation
Encourage a wide variety of experience with written and spoken language	Technology ranging from reading hypertext to exchanging emails to creating web logs
Teach key vocabulary words directly	Software to provide direct instruction and practice with vocabulary
Teach word learning strategies, such as the use of the dictionary and thesaurus; the use of suffixes, prefixes, and roots; and the use of context clues to figure out the meanings of words	Web-based and CD resources Software that provides direct instruction and practice using word learning strategies
Encourage students to make repeated use of new words in different contexts, including reading, discussions and their own writing	Technology used to provide a variety of opportunities for students to use new vocabulary words in both reading and writing

---

Integrating Vocabulary Instruction Into Read-Aloud Experiences

Reading aloud to students in general education settings positively affects vocabulary development among both native speakers of English and English language learners (Collins, 2005; Dickinson & Smith, 1994). Read-alouds provide students with more advanced words than they encounter in day-to-day conversation or in books written at their reading level. Knowledge of advanced, as opposed to basic, words is what propels future word learning (Beck & McKeown, 2002). In order to maximize vocabulary learning through read-alouds, both scaffolding and follow-up are needed (Biemiller & Boote, 2006; Robbins & Ehri, 1994; Senechal, Thomas, & Monker, 1995).

Interactive reading allows the adult reader to actively involve the student in the kinds of cognitively challenging tasks that enhance both vocabulary acquisition and retention (Neuman & Dickinson, 2001; Stahl & Fairbanks, 1986). There are several strategies for interactive reading, including dialogic reading (Whitehurst et al., 1994; Zevenbergen & Whitehurst 2003), direct and systematic instruction (Biemiller, 2001), text talk (Beck & McKeown, 2001), and anchored instruction (Juel & Deffes, 2004). Interactive reading can be done with picture books, poetry, and longer fiction or nonfiction texts.

Methods for interactive reading share several characteristics (Graves, 2006):

1. Books are carefully selected so that they are interesting to the students while also including challenging vocabulary words.

2. Teachers familiarize themselves with the text so that they read it fluently with appropriate expression, and so that they can preplan words to focus on and optimal places to stop for extended conversation.

3. Since most interactive reading strategies involve reading the book repeatedly, students hear the book or the passage once without interruption and then again with attention focused on specific concepts through questions, comments, or instruction.

Using PowerPoint® to Teach Vocabulary

Microsoft PowerPoint® allows teachers to enhance the vocabulary learning experience through the use of technology. Since PowerPoint® presentations can be designed to be interactive with the students, teachers can use PowerPoint® for a variety of vocabulary building exercises, including the following:

1. Teachers can create digital stories. The stories may parallel other readings in the classroom, or they may be created by the students. Each PowerPoint® slide would resemble a page of a book and include both text and illustrations or photographs. Since the stories can be created by students and teachers, they can be individualized to reflect student interests, making the activity more appealing to students.

2. Teachers can create interactive vocabulary games, such as a multiple-choice vocabulary game or a Jeopardy-type game. By using features in PowerPoint® such as hyperlinks, teachers can enable students to click on a response and receive immediate feedback and reinforcement.

3. PowerPoint® allows teachers to incorporate sounds, pictures, and video clips to provide a variety of sensory strategies. Microsoft.com provides instructions and tutorials on the many different components of the program.

For templates and instructions on interactive games or inserting sounds, visit http://www.microsoft.com/education/vocabblast.mspx. For Microsoft PowerPoint® Jeopardy templates, visit http://www.jmu.edu/madison/teacher/jeopardy/jeopardy.htm.

Word Games

When selecting a game, think carefully about the knowledge students will gain from the activity. For example, finding a list of words in a word search puzzle does little to promote vocabulary acquisition since definitions are not part of the activity. Instead, activities designed to enhance vocabulary acquisition provide students with opportunities to extend their knowledge of the word and use the word in their writing or speech. Providing opportunities for children to connect new vocabulary words with prior knowledge and experiences enhances their understanding of the words.

Blachowicz and Fisher (2009) suggested a variety of word games to assist in vocabulary instruction. Matching games can encourage children to pair words to written definitions, picture definitions, a synonym, an antonym, or a cloze sentence in which the word is used appropriately. Using a scoring method for correct matches may provide additional motivation for students. Students can keep track of points earned and redeem them for rewards that are meaningful them, such as a specified amount of time with a preferred activity or interest.

Other games include Applause, Applause and Thumbs-Up, Thumbs-Down (Beck & McKeown, 2002, 2008). In these games, students use either applause or thumb signals to answer questions such as Would you be eager to take a test? Would you be eager to win $25.00? Providing students with ASD a choice of which game to play may result in increased engagement.

Online Resources

www.randomhouse.com/features/rhwebsters/game.html – This web site features a "hangman" type of game in which students try to beat the dictionary.

www.readwritethink.org – This web site features lesson ideas and materials for a range of reading and writing skills and strategies. Several excellent vocabulary lessons can easily be adapted to fit the needs of students with ASD.

www.vocabulary.com – This resource provides many types of word lists and games for use by both students and teachers in middle school or above.

http://wordinfo.info/words/index/info/search_box/index – This site provides teachers with a search engine to access a multitude of information about a specific word, including the word's origins, family units, and occasionally poems that include the word.

http://www.wordinfo.info/words/index/info/ – This site provides information on thematic units of English words based upon Latin-Greek prefixes, suffixes, and roots.

Teaching Strategies for Independent Word Learning

It would be impossible to individually teach all of the words needed to have a strong vocabulary. Therefore, it is important to teach students strategies they can use to learn word meanings on their own. Three important strategies that can be used for this purpose are **contextual analysis** (using context clues), **morphological analysis** (using word parts), and the use of outside resources such as dictionaries and a thesaurus.

Teaching Students to Use Context Clues

Most words are learned from context. However, not all students are equally skilled at using context to fuel their word learning. Graves (2006) proposed a four-step method for teaching students how to use context clues to infer the meaning of an unknown word. With its consistent structure and link to the terminology and function of a DVD player, this model holds promise for students with ASD.

1. **Play and Question.** Students read the selection carefully while frequently asking themselves if what they are reading makes sense. When students come to a word they do not know, they proceed to the second step.

2. **Slow Advance.** In this step, students read the sentence again and look for clues that may tell them what the word means. If they figure out the meaning, they continue to read. If not, they proceed to the third step.

3. **Stop and Rewind.** In this step, students go back to the previous sentence or two and look for additional cues that may help them figure out the meaning. When students think they have it figured out, they move on to the fourth step.

4. **Play and Question.** This step is slightly different than the first step by the same name because students are now substituting their educated guess about the meaning of the word for the original word to see if the sentence makes sense. If it does, they keep reading. If not, they begin the process again or turn to another strategy such as using word parts to determine the meaning.

Graves (2006) recommended that teachers begin by first explaining the process and use guided practice to walk students through an example of the process in action. Students then have an opportunity to practice independently using the skills they have just learned. Each session should end with a brief review of the strategy and answers to any questions the students may have.

1. **Explain the process.** The opening explanation serves the function of priming, shown to be an effective strategy for students with ASD (Aspy & Grossman, 2008).
2. **Guided practice.** To increase the effectiveness of this instructional step, we suggest preparing a visual aid to help students remember the parts of the process. This can take the form of a picture schedule, a cartoon, or a written list of the steps posted in the classroom.
3. **Practice independently.** Finally, as a general guideline for teaching students with ASD, remember to stick with a pre-established timeline and use rewards or reinforcements as necessary.

The combination of priming, explaining the procedure, using visual aids, sticking to a schedule, and using rewards (Aspy & Grossman, 2008) can be an effective method of improving participation in classroom learning routines (Koegel, Koegel, Frea, & Green-Hopkins, 2003).

In the case of this learning routine, repeated opportunities to practice the sequence will result in students becoming increasingly more confident in their ability to use context clues to infer the meanings of words. Typically, teachers begin by doing more guided practice and less independent practice. Over time, students do more of the talking and practicing without teacher assistance so that they become more independent in using the strategy. As students become familiar with the strategy, it is important to provide guided practice with examples for which the relevant clues come after, instead of before, the unknown word. Eventually, students will learn that *context clues* is a broad term that can include the genre being read, the main events in the story, or the main arguments in informational texts.

Recent research on students' use of contextual analysis suggests that prior knowledge and general reasoning skills play an important role in the process (Wieland, 2008). For students with ASD, it makes sense to scaffold the way they bring these two skills to bear. Although some studies have shown that children with ASD are able to access background knowledge (Saldana & Frith, 2007), they may have problems integrating this background knowledge in meaningful ways (Wahlberg & Magliano, 2004).

Additionally, it is important to recognize that students with ASD may need extra support in the first step: stopping and thinking about what they are reading to determine whether they do, in fact, understand it. Students with ASD (and others who struggle with reading or comprehension more generally) are often unaware that they have to read a word that is unknown to them. For these students, therefore, a significant first step is to realize that they have read (or heard) an unknown word.

One method that may be useful here is think-aloud. In this procedure, the teacher encourages students to stop at the end of every sentence or paragraph to process the meaning. Students can do this by talking about what they have just read, writing or typing about it, or drawing a picture about it. This helps to slow down the reading process so that students are engaged with the words and their meanings rather than merely decoding the words on the page. Drawing and writing about stories has also been shown to increase the ability of students with ASD to answer comprehension questions as well as improve the length and quality of writing samples (Colasent & Griffith, 1998).

Teaching Students to Use Word Parts

Many of the words that students encounter can be broken down into smaller units of meaning. In fact, it is estimated that more than 60% of the new words that students come into contact with while reading "have relatively transparent morphological structure" (Nagy, Anderson, Schommer, Scott, & Stallman 1989, p. 279). When students understand how word parts – base words and affixes – function, they can use this knowledge to independently determine the meanings of new words. There are three specific word parts upon which to focus instruction: prefixes and suffixes (together, known as affixes) and base words.

Prefixes. The 20 most common prefixes in third- through ninth-grade school texts are presented in Table 11.3. Since 58% of all words with prefixes are accounted for by the "big four" – *un-*, *re-*, *in-* *(not)*, and *dis-* (White, Sowell, & Yanagihara, 1989) – it makes sense to begin with these.

The first step is to teach students how to recognize prefixes as separate units that carry meaning. A true prefix can be removed from the remainder of the word, leaving a recognizable word that carries meaning of its own. Thus, *un-* is a prefix in the words *unlock* and *untie,* but not in the word *uncle.* Any lesson on prefixes should begin with the definition of a prefix, including instances and non-instances of prefixes. White et al. (1989) suggested planned instruction for the nine most popular prefixes since these account for the vast majority that students will encounter in their reading materials. Instruction on other prefixes may occur on an as-needed basis.

Table 11.3

20 Most Common Prefixes in Printed School English for Students in Grades 3-9

Rank	Prefix	Percentage
1	un-	26
2	re-	14
3	in-, im-, il-, ir – meaning "not"	11
4	dis-	7
5	en-, em-	4
6	non-	4
7	in-, im- meaning "in" or "into"	4
8	over- "too much"	3
9	mis-	3
10	sub-	3
11	pre-	3
12	inter-	3
13	fore-	3
14	de-	2
15	trans-	2
16	super-	1
17	semi-	1
18	anti-	1
19	mid-	1
20	under- meaning "too little"	1
	All others	3

Adapted from "Teaching elementary students to use word-part clues," by White, T. G., Sowell, J., & Yanagihara, A. (1989). *The Reading Teacher, 42*(4), 302-308. Copyright 1989 by the International Reading Association. Used with permission

Suffixes. As with prefixes, a relatively small number of suffixes account for the vast majority found in textbooks. In fact, 10 suffixes (*-s/-es, -ed, -ing, -ly, -er, -ion, -able, -al, -y*, and *-ness*) account for 85% of all suffixed words. Two types of suffixes exist in our language: inflectional suffixes and derivational suffixes. *Inflectional suffixes* change the grammatical function of the base word, most often by indicating tense or plurality (e.g., *play, playing, played; house, houses*), while the meaning remains the same. When *derivational suffixes* are added to a base word, on the other hand, the new word has a new meaning (e.g., *hope, hopeless; afford, affordable*).

Since inflectional suffixes do not impact meaning, instructional time with suffixes is usually focused on derivational suffixes. Whitehurst et al. (1994) suggested directly teaching derivational suffixes only when they are displayed in the material that students are currently reading, as they can be abstract for students when they are not tied to meaningful segments of text or conversation. Since most native English speakers understand the grammatical functions of inflectional suffixes, Whitehurst and colleagues advocated teaching students to dismantle words to separate the suffix from the root word to enhance understanding. This instruction is often tied to work in spelling, with particular attention paid to changes that occur when a suffix is added, including just adding the suffix, doubling the last consonant, changing *y* to *i*, and deleting the silent *e*.

Many teachers choose to begin discussing affixes by looking at suffixes. Since they appear at the end of the word rather than at the beginning, the base word is apparent. At the beginning of their work with affixes, students usually find it easier to "spot" a suffix than to spot a prefix.

Base words. Academic texts often feature a significant proportion of words with Greek or Latin origins. Terms for new technologies and content-specific vocabulary, in particular, rely heavily on Greek and Latin influences (Padak, Newton, Rasinksi, & Newton, 2008). While most researchers agree that teaching children to dismantle words into their separate parts is a worthwhile strategy, there is disagreement on whether teaching the non-English roots of base words is worthwhile. Traditionally, teaching word roots has been reserved for students in upper grades or for content-area classes. Reasons include the large number of roots that exist, the fact that it can be difficult to identify roots due to spelling differences, and the fact that the relationship between the current English word meaning and the original meaning of the root word is not always clear. However, recent research suggests that students in elementary grades can benefit from breaking down words and using word roots as a strategy to identify meaning units within words (Biemiller, 2005). Table 11.4 provides a suggested list of roots to teach according to grade level.

Table 11.4
Suggested Roots to Teach According to Grade Level

Root Words for Primary/Elementary Students	
Base	**Meaning**
audi-, audit-	hear, listen
graph-, gram-	write, draw
mov-, mot-, mobil-	move
port-	carry
vid-, vis-	see
Root Words for Elementary Students	
cred-, credit-	believe
cur-, curs-, cours-	run, go
dict-	say, tell, speak
duc-, duct-	lead
mis-, mit-	to send
pon-, pos-, posit-	put, place
scrib-, sript-	write
terr-	earth
fac-, fic-, fact-, fect-	do, make
Root Words for Middle School Students	
am(a)-, amat-, phil(o)-	love
fort-, forc-, dynamo-	power, strong
lumen-, luc-, luc photo-	light
nat-, natur-, gen-, gener-	be born, give birth, produce
nov-, neo-	new
omni-, pant-	all, every
spec-, spectscop-	look at, watch
viv-, vit bi(o)	live, life
voc-, vok-, voice phon-	voice, call

Adapted from: "Getting to the Root of Word Study: Teaching Latin and Greek Word Roots in Elementary and Middle Grades," by Padak, N., Newton, E., Rasinski, T., & Newton, R. (2008). In A. E. Farstrup & S. J. Samuels (Eds.), *What research has to say about vocabulary instruction* (pp. 6-31). Newark, DE: International Reading Association. Copyright 1989 by the International Reading Association. Used with permission.

Teaching Students to Use Outside Resources to Learn Word Meanings

For general education students, using references such as the dictionary and thesaurus can be overwhelming without proper planning and instruction. Without support, students are not only frustrated, they are unsuccessful (Miller & Gildea, 1987), as reflected in the following statement by a middle school student whose mother gave her a dictionary to look up the meanings of unknown words in her reading assignment: "I did what you said. I looked up the word to figure out what it meant, but then I didn't understand half the words in the definition, so I had to look those up, too. By the time I finished looking up all those words, I forgot what I was trying to figure out."

Instruction on how to use the dictionary, thesaurus, or any other reference book should begin with an appropriate reference book for the students' grade level and should then follow a model of instruction that is appropriate for teaching any strategy, including contextual analysis and structural analysis. This model, described by Duke and Pearson (2002), consists of five steps:

1. Explicitly describe the strategy, including when and how it should be used.
2. Model the strategy in action.
3. Facilitate students' collaborative use of the strategy.
4. Facilitate guided practice with a gradual release of responsibility.
5. Facilitate independent use of the strategy.

It is critical to remember that in all of these tasks, the student must be an active participant who is constructing her own knowledge about the task at hand. The teacher's role is to facilitate the learning of the strategies through modeling, scaffolding, and discussion (Graves, 2006). Movement toward independence is gradual. Research on the use of collaborative methods such as reciprocal questioning and cooperative learning with students with ASD (see Koppenhaver, this text, Chapter 12) suggests that carefully structured collaborative strategy use may be a particularly important step on the way to independence.

A Student's Guide for Using Strategies

Duke and Pearson's (2002) five-step model is a useful set of steps for teachers to follow as they teach word learning strategies. Similarly, it is helpful for students to have a guide or checklist to follow as they use their newly acquired strategies. In Table 11.5, we provide five parallel steps for students to follow as they use context clues, words parts, and outside resources to learn word meanings on their own. The fourth step is the most important, as it is easy for students to focus so heavily on strategy implementation that they forget to check for meaning.

Table 11.5
Student Guide to Learning Word Meanings

Using Context Clues	Using Word Parts	Using Outside Resources
1. Identify the unknown word.	Identify the unknown word.	Identify the unknown word.
2. Check for clues around the word.	Check for a prefix, suffix, or root.	Check resources (reading all definitions, not just the first one, in a dictionary).
3. Determine a possible meaning.	Determine a possible meaning.	Use information from resource and from the context of the text or conversation to determine word meaning.
4. Check to see if possible meaning makes sense.	Check to see if possible meaning makes sense.	Check to see if meaning makes sense.
5. If not, use another strategy.	If not, use another strategy.	If not, use another strategy.

Adapted from *Vocabulary teaching and learning* by S. Watts-Taffe, 2008, June. Workshop conducted at the Summer Literacy Institute, Topics in Literacy: Bridging the Achievement Gap, Boston.

One of the most important lessons for students to learn about all of these strategies – especially using context clues and word parts – is that they do not always lead to success. By checking to see whether their possible meaning makes sense in context, they can determine whether the strategy was successful or not. This final step may be the most challenging for students with ASD, since it requires shifting attention from the individual word to comprehension of the word in a larger context. Weaknesses in central coherence, as discussed by Baron-Cohen (1995) and others, may make such a shift difficult. Contextual analysis as a word learning strategy may be the hardest, overall, of the three strategies for students with ASD to master. However, focused attention on this strategy holds promise for increasing language comprehension among individuals with ASD.

In order to enhance the usability of the guide in Table 11.5, it may be helpful to add picture or symbol cues for each step (Mesibov, Browder, & Kirkland, 2002). Another suggestion is to use video modeling, in which a student watches a video of a peer engaged in each of the steps. This type of visual support has been shown to be effective in teaching other academic skills to students with ASD (Kinney, Vedora, & Stromer, 2003).

Vocabulary Visits

Many teachers have attested to the benefits of taking children on field trips; however, the restricted resources of both schools and parents often limit the number and range of field trips that can be taken. As an alternative, Blachowicz and Obrochta (2005) described a vocabulary-building technique called Vocabulary Visits. In a Vocabulary Visit, teachers take students on a virtual field trip that engages the senses and increases the development of new concepts and words.

Vocabulary Visits focus on interactive read-alouds that actively engage children in learning new concepts and words. Similar to a typical field trip, the Vocabulary Visit begins with planning the trip. First, teachers must identify a topic of interest for the Vocabulary Visit such as a current science or social studies topic. Next, teachers identify a set of approximately five books that are related to the topic and provide a range of difficulty. After reviewing the books, teachers select target vocabulary words and develop a poster with interesting pictures to stimulate discussion of the topic. The teachers and children are now ready for the Vocabulary Visit. Blachowicz and Obrochta (2005) suggested the following steps to a successful vocabulary visit:

1. **Jump-Start and First Write:** In this step, teachers introduce the topic to stimulate a brief discussion among the students. Then, each student creates a list of personally known words that are related to the topic. For students who have difficulty with handwriting, the list may be typed or dictated to a peer or teacher.
2. **Group Talk**: Next, teachers introduce the topic in a group setting using the poster to stimulate conversation about what the children see, as if children were on a field trip describing the sights. As children name words, teachers write the words on sticky notes and attach to the poster. Teachers carefully facilitate the discussion to help focus children's attention on targeted concepts. Teachers may use other senses besides sight to engage children in discussion.
3. **Reading and Thumbs-Up**: Next, teachers read one of the books that was selected for the unit. This reading should be interactive to encourage discussion about new words. Each time students hear a new word, they give the teachers a "thumbs-up." After the reading, the new words are placed on the poster followed by a short writing activity in which students write about something that they found interesting.
4. **Follow-Up**: The Vocabulary Visit poster remains in the classroom, and the sequence of activities is repeated for the remaining books that were chosen. Students add new words to the poster and may even regroup the way in which the words are posted.
5. **Final Write**: After all five books have been read, students complete two writing activities. The first is a written piece on what they have learned. This may take the form of a home-made book or a book report. The second writing activity consists of making a list of all of the words that they currently know about the topic. Again, this writing process may be done via typing or dictation.

Results from research on Vocabulary Visits (Blachowicz & Obrochta, 2005) indicate that this technique increases students' content knowledge vocabulary and provides an exciting and active way to incorporate both new content and new word knowledge into the everyday curriculum.

Assessing Word Learning

Assessing word knowledge is an arduous task (Pearson et al., 2007). The complexities of assessing word knowledge necessitate a variety of tools to garner information about the various aspects of word knowledge. Any single assessment is likely to be limited. For example, most tests assess receptive but not expressive vocabulary. Tests of receptive vocabulary often require students to match a spoken or written word to a picture, definition, or single sentence context. It is quite possible to know the meaning of a word, or at least an aspect of meaning, that does not match the given choices. Efforts are underway to conduct a large-scale assessment that takes into account gradations in word knowledge (Scott, Flinspach, & Samway, 2007).

For typical children, Blachowicz and Fisher (2009) advocated classroom-based assessments as a way to monitor progress and involve students in self-assessment. They recommend using the Before-Reading Knowledge Rating to ascertain student prior knowledge. Table 11.6 shows a sample chart.

Table 11.6
Knowledge Rating Chart

Word	Never Heard It (Don't Know)	Heard It Before	Know It (Can Define/Use)
eager			
hostile			
rambunctious			
cavern			

For children with ASD, this activity holds great promise, because it includes priming, consistent structure, and visual support, and provides important information for the teacher concerning task demand. In addition to giving the teacher a sense of students' prior knowledge of specific words, it serves to actively engage the students in their own word learning by focusing their attention on the task and supporting them as they attempt to bring background knowledge to the foreground.

Further, vocabulary usage can be assessed using a work sampling system. By collecting pieces of writing and using anecdotal notes to record instances of oral word use, teachers can get a sense of the ways in which students' vocabularies are growing and changing. Finally, think-alouds can be used to ascertain students' ability to use strategies for independent word learning.

Focus on Diversity

English-language learning (ELL) students are the fastest growing population of students in the United States (Hoffman & Sable, 2006) and are at increased risk for reading difficulty (Snow, Burns, & Griffin, 1998). Understanding vocabulary is a vital component of communicating with others in both oral and written formats.

Helman (2008) presented the following key elements of successful vocabulary interventions for ELL students:

- Words are presented to students in meaningful contexts, including texts that are interesting to allow for application of concepts both inside and outside of the classroom setting.
- Lessons motivate students and encourage active participation.
- Interventions are in depth, include repetition and review, take place over time, and go beyond surface-level definitions.
- Lessons involve discussion around text.
- Vocabulary study builds upon what students already know in their home language and may include activities such as introducing the lesson in the home language first or presenting related words or cognates from the home language.
- Students learn to apply useful strategies for word learning, such as morphemic analysis.
- Lessons involve scaffolding, using techniques such as simplified syntax, visual materials, or oral language practice activities.
- Instruction is individualized for each student to meet varying needs and abilities.

Above all, instruction for ELL students should be built upon all of the concepts presented throughout this chapter. The goals for ELL students should be challenging but not impossible to attain.

Assessing Task Demand

As with all students, instruction for students with ASD should begin with an accurate assessment of what students already know along with an inventory of skills that they already possess. This allows for an accurate assessment of the task demands of the lesson in order to ensure that they do not exceed the student's zone of proximal development (Aspy & Grossman, 2008). The Ziggurat Model (Aspy & Grossman) lists three questions to guide the assessment of task demand:

1. **Is this a skill that the student has the ability to perform?** The task demand will be too high if the skill is too difficult for the student, likely resulting in behavior difficulties or avoidance of the task.
2. **Does the student already know how to perform the skill, or is this a skill that will need to be taught first?** The task demands would be too great if the student is expected to perform a skill that he has not yet been taught.
3. **Have you put the necessary supports in place?** It may be necessary to provide priming, visual supports or schedules, or reinforcement in order for the student to be successful at the proposed task.

Conclusion

Little research has focused on vocabulary teaching and learning for students with ASD. In this chapter, we have shared information about the nature of word learning and the characteristics of effective instruction, as evidenced with typically developing students. By considering this information alongside what is known about the nature of ASD, language characteristics of students with ASD, and characteristics of effective instruction for students with ASD, we have suggested a direction for enhancing the vocabulary development of students with ASD.

Research has found that students with ASD are more often successful at decoding words (Nation, Clarke, Wright, & Williams, 2006) than at determining the appropriate meanings of words in context (Joliffe & Baron-Cohen, 1999). In both written and oral contexts, students with ASD often struggle with identifying and applying appropriate word meanings to the larger unit of a conversation or passage as a whole. Thus, building vocabulary, through attention to individual words as well as instruction in word learning strategies, is critical to meeting the larger goal of providing quality literacy instruction to students with ASD.

Chapter Highlights

- Vocabulary knowledge impacts social interactions, academic performance, and classroom engagement.

- There are four types of vocabulary:
  - ✔ Listening
  - ✔ Speaking
  - ✔ Reading
  - ✔ Writing

- Vocabulary is defined as words whose meanings are understood by students, whether or not they can decode the words or recognize them in print.

- There are five levels of word knowledge:
  - ✔ No knowledge
  - ✔ Incorrect knowledge
  - ✔ General knowledge
  - ✔ Narrow knowledge
  - ✔ Rich knowledge

- Word learning is an incremental process that develops over time.

- There are two characteristics researchers utilize to describe words:
  - ✔ Multiple meanings
  - ✔ Interrelatedness

- In order to develop vocabulary, word type and level of word knowledge are important considerations.

- Students with ASD may display a variety of communication disorders that impact their ability to productively use language.

- Three factors interfere with language knowledge and application for students with ASD:
  - ✔ The repetition of words or phrases
  - ✔ The expression of nonsense words
  - ✔ The concept language understanding is not represented by performance

- Effective vocabulary instruction involves teaching the meaning of words, teaching strategies that promote independent word learning, and maintaining a concept-rich learning environment.

- Teaching the meanings of specific words is important for students with ASD, because they may not learn words from contexts.

- Instruction should focus on comprehension words, useful words, academic words, and generative words.

- The factors that increase the likelihood of students learning vocabulary words include:
  - ✔ If words are connected semantically
  - ✔ If there is student interest and prior knowledge
  - ✔ If the words are concrete instead of abstract
  - ✔ If the words are identified as new labels for known words, instead of being viewed as isolated new concepts

- When teaching new words, teachers need to rely on user-friendly definitions and meaningful contexts and build upon prior knowledge. It is essential that teachers use visual representations, engage the students, and provide opportunities for practice.

- It is vital for teachers to provide strategies that consider independent word learning such as
  - ✔ Contextual analysis
  - ✔ Morphological analysis
  - ✔ Outside resources

- When students understand how word parts function, they can use this knowledge to independently determine the meaning of new words.

- Teachers need to focus instruction on word parts (prefix, suffix, base word), because research indicates that students benefit from breaking words down and understanding word roots.

- Teachers are encouraged to use outside resources such as dictionaries and thesauruses through strategy modeling, guided practice, and student collaboration.

- Assessing word learning is complex, and any single measurement is likely to be limited.

- Other assessment methods include work samples and think-alouds.

- It is suggested that teachers refer to the following three guiding questions for assessing task demand:
  - ✔ Is this a skill the student has the ability to perform?
  - ✔ Does the student already know how to perform this skill?
  - ✔ Are necessary supports in place for the student to be successful at this task?

Chapter Review Questions

1. What are three characteristics of word learning that are important for teachers to know? Give an example of each.

2. What is meant by the notion that there are varying levels of word knowledge (or that word knowledge exists on a continuum)? What are the implications for instruction?

3. There are many words that it is important for students to know. How might you develop a plan for selecting which words to teach? What factors should be considered?

4. What are the five elements that characterize effective instruction on the meanings of individual words? Describe one way that each element can be enacted in the classroom.

5. What are three word learning strategies that are worthy of instruction? Why is it important to teach these word learning strategies?

6. Describe Duke and Pearson's (2002) five-step model for strategy instruction. What additional supports can assist students with ASD in learning word learning strategies?

7. Overall, how do the unique characteristics of students with ASD impact the vocabulary learning task? Think specifically about the communication challenges students may face, task demands, and support systems that can be put into place to ensure successful learning.

References

Aspy, R., & Grossman, B. (2008). *Designing comprehensive interventions for individuals with high-functioning autism and Asperger Syndrome: The Ziggurat model.* Shawnee Mission, KS: Autism Asperger Publishing Company.

Baron-Cohen, S. (1995). *Mind blindness: An essay on autism and theory of mind.* Cambridge, MA: MIT Press.

Beck, I. L., Perfetti, C. A., & McKeown M. G. (1982). The effects of long-term vocabulary instruction on lexical access and reading comprehension. *Journal of Educational Psychology, 74,* 506-521.

Beck, I. L., & McKeown, M. G. (2001). Text talk: Capturing the benefits of read-aloud experiences for young children. *The Reading Teacher, 55,* 10-20.

Beck, I. L., & McKeown, M. G. (2002). Questioning the author: Making sense of social studies. *Educational Leadership, 60*(3), 44.

Beck, I., McKeown, M., & Kucan, L. (2002). *Bringing words to life: Robust vocabulary instruction.* New York: Guilford Publications.

Beck, I., McKeown, M., & Kucan, L. (2008). *Creating robust vocabulary: Frequently asked questions and extended examples.* New York: Guilford Publications.

Biemiller, A. (2001). Teaching vocabulary: Early, direct, and sequential. *American Educator, 25*(1), 24-28.

Biemiller, A. (2005). Size and sequence in vocabulary development: Implications of choosing words for primary grade vocabulary. In E. H. Hiebert & M. L. Kamil (Eds.), *Teaching and learning vocabulary: Bringing research to practice* (pp. 223-242). Mahwah, NJ: Erlbaum.

Biemiller, A., & Boote, C. (2006). An effective method for building meaning vocabulary in primary grades. *Journal of Educational Psychology, 98*(1), 44-62.

Blachowicz, C.L.Z., & Fisher, P. J. (2009). *Teaching vocabulary in all classrooms* (4th ed.). Upper Saddle River, NJ: Pearson.

Blachowicz, C., Fisher, P., Ogle, D., & Watts-Taffe, S. (2006). Vocabulary: Questions from the classroom. *Reading Research Quarterly, 41*(4), 524-539.

Blachowicz, C., & Obrochta, C. (2005, November). Vocabulary visits: Virtual field trips for content vocabulary development. *Reading Teacher, 59*(3), 262-268.

Colasent, R., & Griffith, P. L. (1998). Autism and literacy: Looking into the classroom with rabbit stories. *The Reading Teacher, 51,* 414-420.

Chomsky, N. (1957). *Syntactic structures.* Berlin, Germany: Walter de Gruyter GmbH & Co.

Collins, M. F. (2005). IRA outstanding dissertation award for 2005: ESL preschoolers' English vocabulary acquisition form storybook reading. *Reading Research Quarterly, 40,* 406-408.

Dale, E. (1965). Vocabulary measurement: Techniques and major findings. *Elementary English, 42,* 895-901.

Davis, F. (1944). Fundamental factors of comprehension in reading. *Psychometrika, 9,* 185-197.

Dickinson, D., & Smith, M. (1994). Long-term effects of preschool teachers' book readings on low-income children's vocabulary and story comprehension. *Reading Research Quarterly, 29*(2), 104-22.

Duke, N. K., & Pearson, P. D. (2002). Effective practices for developing reading comprehension. In A. E. Farstrup & S. J. Samuels (Eds.), *What research has to say about reading instruction* (3rd ed., pp. 205-242). Newark, DE: International Reading Association.

Eigsti, I., Bennetto, L., & Dadlani, M. (2007). Beyond pragmatics: Morphosyntactic development in autism. *Journal of Autism & Developmental Disorders, 37,* 1007-1023.

Gerber, S. (2003). A developmental perspective on language assessment and intervention for children on the autistic spectrum. *Topics in Language Disorders, 23*(2), 74-94.

Graves, M. F. (2006). *The vocabulary book: Learning and instruction*. New York: Teachers College Press.

Hoffman, L., & Sable, J. (2006). *Public elementary and secondary students, staff, schools, and school districts: School year 2003-2004.* Washington, DC: National Center for Educational Statistics.

Joliffe, T., & Baron-Cohen, S. (1999). A test of central coherence theory: Linguistic processing in high-functioning adults with autism or Asperger syndrome: Is local coherence impaired? *Cognition, 71,* 149-185.

Juel, C., & Deffes, R. (2004). Making words stick. *Educational Leadership, 61*(6), 30-34.

Kinney, E., Vedora, J., & Stromer, R. (2003). Computer-presented video models to teach generative spelling to a child with an autism spectrum disorder. *Journal of Positive Behavior Interventions, 5*(1), 22-29.

Koegel, L., Koegel, R., Frea, W., & Green-Hopkins, I. (2003) Priming as a method of coordinating educational services for students with autism. *Language, Speech, and Hearing Services in the Schools, 34,* 228-235.

Mesibov, G., Browder, D., & Kirkland, C. (2002). Using individualized schedules as a component of positive behavioral support for students with developmental disabilities. *Journal of Positive Behavioral Interventions, 4,* 73-79.

Mezynski, K. (1983). Issues concerning the acquisition of knowledge: Effects of vocabulary training on reading comprehension. *Review of Educational Research, 53*(2), 253-279.

Miller, G. A., & Gildea, P. M. (1987). How children learn words. *Scientific American, 257*(3), 97-99.

Myles, B. S., & Simpson, R. L. (2003). *Asperger Syndrome: A guide for educators and parents* (2nd ed.). Austin, TX: Pro-Ed.

Nagy, W., Anderson, R., Schommer, M., Scott, J., & Stallman, A. (1989, Summer). Morphological families in the internal lexicon. *Reading Research Quarterly, 24*(3), 262-282.

Nagy, W. E., & Scott, J. A. (2000). Vocabulary processes. In M. L. Kamil, P. B. Mosenthal, P. D. Pearson, & R. Barr (Eds.), *Handbook of reading research: Volume III* (pp. 269-284). New York: Longman.

Nation, K., Clarke, P., Wright, B., & Williams, C. (2006). Patterns of reading ability in children with autism spectrum disorder. *Journal of Autism and Developmental Disorders, 36,* 911-919.

National Reading Panel. (2000). *Report of the national reading panel: Reports of the subgroups.* Washington, DC: National Institute of Child Health and Human Development Clearinghouse.

Neuman, S. B., & Dickinson, D. K. (Eds.). (2001). *Handbook of early literacy research.* New York: Guilford Press.

Norbury, C. (2004). Factors supporting idiom comprehension in children with communication disorders. *Journal of Speech, Language and Hearing Research, 47,* 1179-1193.

Padak, N., Newton, E., Rasinski, T., & Newton, R. (2008). Getting to the root of word study: Teaching Latin and Greek word roots in elementary and middle grades. In A. E. Farstrup & S. J. Samuels (Eds.), *What research has to say about vocabulary instruction* (pp. 6-31). Newark, DE: International Reading Association.

Paterson, K. (1977). *Bridge to Terabithia.* New York: HarperCollins.

Pearson, P., Hiebert, E., & Kamil, M. (2007, April). Vocabulary assessment: What we know and what we need to learn. *Reading Research Quarterly, 42*(2), 282-296.

Prizant, B. (1983). Language acquisition and communicative behavior in autism: Toward an understanding of the whole of it. *Journal of Speech and Hearing Disorders, 48,* 296-307.

Prizant, B., & Duchan, J. (1981). The functions of immediate echolalia in autistic children. *Journal of Speech and Hearing Disorder, 46,* 241-249.

Robbins, C., & Ehri, L. C. (1994). Reading storybooks to kindergartners helps them learn new vocabulary words. *Journal of Educational Psychology, 86*(1), 54-64.

Rutter, M., Mawhood, L., & Howlin, P. (1992). Language delay and social development. In P. Fletcher & D. Hall (Eds.), *Specific speech and language disorders in children: Correlates, characteristics, and outcomes* (pp. 63-78). London: Whurr.

Saldana, D., & Frith, U. (2007). Do readers with autism make bridging inferences from world knowledge? *Journal of Experimental Child Psychology, 96*, 310-319.

Scott, J. A., Flinspach, S., & Samway, K. D. (2007, April). *Linking word knowledge to the world: The VINE project.* Paper presented at the annual meeting of the American Educational Research Association, Chicago

Senechal, M., Thomas, E., & Monker, J. (1995). Individual differences in 4-year-old children's acquisition of vocabulary during storybook reading. *Journal of Educational Psychology, 87*(2), 218-229.

Snow, C. E., Burns, M. S., & Griffin, P. (Eds.). (1988). *Preventing reading difficulties in young children.* Washington, DC: National Academy Press.

Stahl, S. A., & Fairbanks, M. (1986). The effects of vocabulary instruction: A model-based meta-analysis. *Review of Educational Research, 42*(4), 24-32.

Stahl, S., & Nagy, W. (2006). *Teaching word meanings.* Mahwah, NJ: Lawrence Erlbaum Associates.

Stahl, S., & Vancil, S. (1986, October). Discussion is what makes semantic maps work in vocabulary instruction. *Reading Teacher, 40*(1), 62-67.

Swensen, L., Kelley, E., Fein, D., & Naigles, L. (2007). Processes of language acquisition in children with autism: Evidence from preferential looking. *Child Development, 78*(2), 542-557.

Tager-Flusberg, H., Paul, R., & Lord, C. (2005). Language and communication in autism. In F. Volkmar, R. Paul, A. Klin & D. Cohen (Eds.), *Handbook of autism and pervasive developmental disorders* (3rd ed., pp. 335-364). Hoboken, NJ: Wiley.

Terman, L. M. (1916). *The measurement of intelligence.* Boston: Houghton Mifflin.

Wahlberg, T., & Magliano, J. (2004). The ability of high functioning individuals with autism to understand written discourse. *Discourse Processes, 38*(1), 119-144.

Watts-Taffe, S. (2008, June). *Vocabulary teaching and learning.* Workshop conducted at the Summer Literacy Institute, Topics in Literacy: Bridging the Achievement Gap, Boston.

Watts-Taffe, S., Blachowicz, C.L.Z., & Fisher, P. J. (2009). Vocabulary instruction for diverse students. In L. M. Morrow, R. Rueda, & D. Lapp (Eds.), *Handbook of research on literacy instruction: Issues of diversity, policy, and equity* (pp. 320-336). New York: Guilford Press.

White, T. G., Sowell, J., & Yanagihara, A. (1989). Teaching elementary students to use word-part clues. *The Reading Teacher, 42*(4), 302-308.

Whitehurst, G. J., Arnold, D. S., Epstein, J. N., Angell, A. L., Smith, M., & Fischel, J. E. (1994). A picture book reading intervention in day care and home for children from low-income families. *Developmental Psychology, 30*, 697-689.

Wieland, K. M. (2008, December). *Contextual vocabulary acquisition in action: Analyzing the reading and reasoning moves made by excellent adolescent readers while deriving unknown word meanings from multiple texts.* Paper presented at the annual meeting of the National Reading Conference, Orlando, FL.

Zevenbergen, A. A., & Whitehurst, G. J. (2003). Dialogic reading: A shared picture book reading intervention for preschoolers. In A. van Kleeck, S. A. Stahl, & E. B. Bauer (Eds.), *On reading books to children: Parents and teachers* (pp. 177-200). Mahwah, NJ: Lawrence Erlbaum Associates, Inc.

Chapter 12
Reading Comprehension

David A. Koppenhaver, Ph.D., Appalachian State University

Learner Objectives

After reading this chapter, the learner should be able to:

- Define and describe reading comprehension

- Explain critical elements of reading comprehension instruction

- Describe typical reading comprehension difficulties in students with ASD

- List and describe research-based best practices in reading comprehension instruction for (a) typically developing students and (b) students with ASD

- Design **guided reading** lessons that support improved reading comprehension in students with ASD

■ ■ ■

Years ago, when I was a first-year language arts teacher, a veteran special educator suggested that my job was much easier than hers. My trivial responsibility, she argued, was teaching children to read, something all children could do. As her clinching argument, she invited me to observe a 12-year-old boy in her classroom who was diagnosed with ASD and moderate intellectual disabilities. She handed him a high school-level science text, which he proceeded to read without a single error. In amazement, particularly given the reading difficulties of many of the students in my mainstream language arts class, I questioned the boy about his reading. He did not respond to many of my questions, and to those he did, his responses were incorrect.

■ ■ ■

That young adolescent's performance was remarkably similar to that of the majority of children with autism spectrum disorders (ASD) with whom I have worked since then in classrooms and clinical environments, and it's the reason why a chapter on reading comprehension instruction is particularly important in a text such as this. Plain and simple, most students across the autism spectrum struggle with comprehending the texts they encounter in school, at home, and in the community. Their learning difficulties are amenable to focused, high-quality instruction based on an understanding of (a) the nature of reading comprehension and reading comprehension instruction, (b) the nature and sources of comprehension difficulties in students with ASD, and (c) the juncture of high-quality reading comprehension instruction and the specific learning needs of students with ASD. Each of these areas will be discussed in this chapter.

Reading Comprehension

Reading comprehension has been defined as an individual's "understanding, recall, and integration of information stated in or inferable from specific text passages" (Tierney & Cunningham, 1984, p. 610). Silent reading with comprehension is "the essence of reading" (Durkin, 1993, p. 12) and, consequently, the ultimate goal of reading instruction (Cunningham, 1993). All other reading skills and abilities (e.g., decoding, sight word knowledge, reading fluency, text structure awareness, or world knowledge) are components of the larger ability to read texts and understand them. Each of these skills is important only to the extent that it contributes to the larger goal of reading silently with comprehension (Erickson, Koppenhaver, & Cunningham, 2006).

Cunningham (1993) reviewed the research on reading comprehension to determine which components were instructionally relevant (i.e., which aspects of reading comprehension could be assessed and taught). His resulting whole-to-part model identified three components: word identification, language comprehension, and print processing. Word identification can be either automatic (i.e., sight words) or mediated (i.e., decoding), language comprehension involves both vocabulary and text structure knowledge, and print processing can be thought of as a synonym for reading fluency.

Reading with comprehension, then, depends on students' knowledge of print, language, and the world, and their ability to actively apply that knowledge in understanding, interpreting, or applying information presented in written texts (Fielding & Pearson, 1994). In actively applying these types of knowledge, readers construct dynamic representations of the meaning of the text that are informed both by their personal sources of knowledge and by the portion of text they have completed at any given point (Kintsch & van Dijk, 1978). These representations support memory, facilitate processing of the text at hand, and enhance subsequent use of what has been read and understood (National Reading Panel, 2000).

Reading Comprehension Instruction

Walt Whitman (1949) provided a clear description of skilled reading comprehension in an essay, *Democratic Vistas*:

> … the process of reading is not a half-sleep, but, in highest sense, an exercise, a gymnast's struggle; that the reader is to do something for himself, must be on the alert, must himself or herself construct indeed the poem, argument, history, metaphysical essay – the text furnishing the hints, the clue, the start or frame-work. (p. 81)

Recognizing, as did Whitman, the complex interplay between reader skill and text, researchers have studied skilled readers as a way to understand what might be taught to improve all students' comprehension of text. Pressley and Afflerbach (1995), in a review of this research, concluded that five characteristics seemed particularly important. Skilled readers apparently:

1. anticipate what they will learn from a text based on their personal background knowledge relevant to the text;
2. monitor their evolving understanding as they read and are aware of which ideas are important and which ideas or words they find difficult or confusing;

3. seek answers to their personal questions or those posed by teachers (i.e., they are goal directed);

4. reflect on what they read (e.g., consider how text events relate to their own life experiences); and

5. read systematically through entire texts, occasionally skipping ahead in antici-pation of key information or rereading previous sections in order to clarify their understanding.

Armed with this understanding, researchers have studied a variety of strategies for teaching all students to engage in one or more of the behaviors of skilled readers. The findings of this research are briefly summarized below with regard to what to teach and how to teach it.

What to Teach

There is strong agreement from multiple perspectives on what should be taught in order to promote reading comprehension as a repertoire of authentic strategies, including (a) prediction and activation of prior knowledge, (b) recognition and use of text structure, (c) development and use of visual representations such as story maps and graphic orga-nizers, (d) summarization skills, (e) comprehension monitoring, and (f) question answering and generation (Duke & Pearson, 2002; National Reading Panel, 2000). Each of these strategies taught individually and in combination has substantial support in the research literature and requires active student involvement in both lessons and application in wider reading beyond the classroom.

How to Teach

Several organizing principles are critical to successful comprehension instruction, regardless of what specifically is taught.

First, teachers should spend substantial time directly teaching, and then monitor-ing guided practice in, strategies while minimizing and carefully directing the time stu-dents spend working independently. In a review of independent work, Rosenshine (1983) concluded that students are generally less engaged during independent work than when they are in instructional groups and that independent work is effective only under specific conditions (see Table 12.1).

Table 12.1
Effective Independent Work Conditions

- Students are prepared specifically for independent work through teacher instruction.

- Teachers guide students through initial independent work task.

- Guided practice immediately precedes independent work.

- Teachers circulate among students during independent work, providing feedback, directing attention, and assisting with understanding.

Second, teachers should be wary of grouping students by ability, since this has been observed to lead to a variety of consequences that do not promote growth in reading comprehension. These include, among other findings, that struggling students in lower ability groups (a) tend to receive lower-quality instruction (Good & Marshall, 1984); (b) have lower self-esteem and develop negative attitudes toward reading (Paratore & Indrisano, 2003); (c) read fewer materials because they read orally more and silently less than higher-ability groups (Allington, 1984); (d) are asked more literal than inferencing or main-idea questions (Allington, 1983); and (e) receive less instructional time in general (Chorzempa & Graham, 2006). Rather than ability grouping, exemplary first-grade teachers have been found to use a variety of large-group, small-group, and partner reading plans (Pressley, Allington, Wharton-McDonald, Block, & Morrow, 2001).

One research-supported alternative to ability grouping is the use of cooperative learning (National Reading Panel, 2000). This heterogeneous instructional grouping seems to work best with reading comprehension instruction when there are group goals, monitoring of each individual's learning success, and an emphasis on students providing explanations rather than correct answers (Pearson & Fielding, 1991). This grouping also increases opportunities for social negotiation of text meaning and peer tutoring, while decreasing the overabundance of teacher talk in the typical classroom (Fielding & Pearson, 1994).

The question of how to organize instructional lessons has been addressed by Cunningham, Moore, Cunningham, and Moore (1983). After analyzing reading comprehension lesson frameworks, the authors concluded that four steps were essential: establishing purposes for readers' comprehension; having students read for the established purpose; having students perform a task that reflects and measures accomplishment of the purpose set; and providing informative feedback concerning student comprehension based on task performance. The authors also noted that many, but not all, effective comprehension lesson frameworks included an additional, and initial, step of cuing access to or developing background knowledge assumed by the text.

Researchers have also reached agreement on how strategies may best be taught (Duffy, 2003; Pressley, 2002). Strategies should be selected for instruction because they are authentic. Teachers should first demonstrate or model application of the strategy, defining what it is and explaining how, when, and why to use it. Next, teachers should consistently emphasize that the focal strategies should be applied flexibly rather than as a sequence of rigid steps. Following this demonstration and explanation, teachers should provide guided practice for students in authentic texts.

Perhaps the easiest practice to implement, and yet the most often neglected when students struggle in learning to read, is providing significant amounts of time for reading (Allington, 1983; Morrow, Gambrell, & Pressley, 2003). Fielding and Pearson (1994) recommended that of the total time allocated for reading instruction, students should spend more time reading than the combined total time allotted to learning about reading and either discussing or writing about what they have read.

Adequate time for reading enables students to (a) practice skills being taught and (b) acquire new knowledge and vocabulary (Nagy, Anderson, & Herman, 1987). Benefits accrue regardless of ability level when (a) there is plenty of choice of what to read on a wide variety of difficulty levels, (b) students are encouraged to engage in multiple readings of favorite texts as well as to read with peers periodically, and (c) regular and frequent opportunities are provided to discuss readings with peers and teachers (Fielding & Pearson, 1994).

The Nature and Sources of Comprehension Difficulties in Students With ASD

In the largest study to date, Nation, Clarke, Wright, and Williams (2006) reported that in a sample of 32 children with ASD, ages 6-15 years, scores on word identification (i.e., isolated word reading and nonsense word reading) and print processing (i.e., error analysis of short passages read aloud) tasks were within normal limits, but reading comprehension scores were approximately one standard deviation below population norms. More than one third of the sample scored two standard deviations below the norm, indicating substantial difficulties in this area. An additional nine children were reported to be unable to read because they lacked the language skills to participate in the unadapted assessments.

While children across the autism spectrum were included in the sample, their scores were not reported separately. The researchers noted that performance was highly variable on each subtest, ranging from floor to ceiling levels. However, children who struggled with reading comprehension in general performed more poorly on the language comprehension measures than the children with average and above-average reading comprehension scores.

IRI Assessment

Many educators use individual reading inventories (IRIs) to informally assess reading performance. Consisting of leveled word lists and passages, IRIs enable educators to examine not only overall reading comprehension ability, but also relative student capability in the three areas of Cunningham's (1993) whole-to-part model: word identification, print processing, and language comprehension.

Nilsson (2008) conducted a critical comparative analysis of eight IRIs that may guide teachers in choosing an instrument best suited to the individual differences of their student(s) with ASD. While noting that the Cooter, Flynt, and Cooter (2006) IRI may be best suited for use with special populations, she reviewed differences in text genre, passage length, illustrations, and question types and formats.

Further, Koppenhaver, Foley, and Williams (2009) provided a rationale and description of how to adapt IRIs for administration to children who rely on augmentative and alternative communication (AAC) for their face-to-face needs (i.e., children who cannot or do not speak). By employing a multiple-choice format, they showed how any individual, who either could reliably point or indicate yes or no, could engage in the assessment. By referencing the assessment process to Cunningham's (1993) diagnostic model of reading, they further demonstrated that assessment results could be used to design effective reading interventions targeting needs in language comprehension, reading fluency, or word identification for students with disabilities, including ASD.

Myles et al. (2002) assessed the reading skills of 16 students with Asperger Syndrome, ages 6-16 years, using an informal reading inventory. Results suggested that students' word identification, print processing, language comprehension, and overall reading performance each was approximately at grade level. O'Connor and Hermelin (1994) reported similar age-appropriate comprehension accompanied by exceptional word reading and print processing in two children with Asperger Syndrome, ages 5 and 8 years, at the beginning of a two-year study.

Given the foundational role of language in reading (Catts & Kamhi, 2005), the pro-files reported in these studies suggest that language comprehension was the greatest area of need for the students because the ability to listen with comprehension typically exceeds the ability to read with comprehension in developing readers (Sticht & James, 1984). This interpretation is further supported by the fact that participants in the Myles et al. (2002) study demonstrated significantly greater difficulties responding accurately to inferential questions than to literal questions.

The results of several studies designed to explore what are thought to be differ-ences in the cognitive or linguistic processes of individuals with ASD help explain some of the difficulties observed in these students when responding to inferential questions. Rumsey and Hamburger (1988) administered intelligence test items to adults with high-functioning autism and found that while participants could comprehend information, their inferences tended to be incorrect. For example, in one item a character heard a loud noise and ran outside where she saw a car by the side of the street and nails all over the road. Participants were asked, "What was the bang?" Besides the correct answer that the tire had popped, incorrect responses included an explosion, sticks of dynamite, or the crash of a truck loaded with nails. Participants demonstrated difficulties in integrating information across multiple sentences to obtain the best response, relying instead more on single-sentence information and their own knowledge of the world.

Minshew, Goldstein, and Siegel (1995) reported a similar finding in their study of 62 individuals with high-functioning autism. Administering a battery of standardized tests, these researchers found inferential comprehension and ability to respond to complex language significantly lower than for typically developing controls matched for age, IQ, gender, race, education, and family socioeconomic status.

Happé (1994) studied general listening comprehension and the ability to infer the motivations of characters' actions and speech among individuals with ASD. Children and adults, ages 8-23 years, who were verbal and possessed varying intellectual capabilities, listened to what the author referred to as "strange stories." They were then allowed to re-read portions or all of the text as desired in order to answer two types of questions: "Is it true, what ___ said?" and "Why did ___ say that?"

The strange stories involved pretending, white lies, figures of speech, irony, and other instances where characters in the story say things they do not really mean (i.e., "What a lovely hairdo!" experiences). The strange stories were intentionally written to be unambiguous to invite a single interpretation of character motivation. Physical story control texts involved descriptions of activities followed by "Is it true that (something oc-

Autism Asperger Publishing Company
PO BOX 23173
Overland Park, KS 66223-0173
Phone: 913-897-1004
Fax: 913-681-9473
www.asperger.net

Packing Slip

DATE	INVOICE #
9/16/2010	79122

PAID

BILL TO	SHIP TO
Yeager, Christina 3415 Oak View Place Cincinnati, OH 45209	Yeager, Christina 3415 Oak View Place Cincinnati, OH 45209

Customer E-mail	P.O. NUMBER	SHIP	VIA	VIA ACCT#
Christina.Yeager@cchmc.org	marketing	9/16/2010	UPS- ground	

QUANTITY	ITEM CODE	DESCRIPTION	CLASS
1	9506	Quality Literacy Instruction for Students with Autism Spectrum Disorders... #9781934575666 (9506)	marketing
1	8801	Shipping and Handling	marketing

Thank you for your contribution!

Please check the accuracy of your e-mail address in the Customer E-mail box and contact billing@asperger.net with any corrections. This will ensure you are updated with our new releases.

Autism Asperger Publishing Company

PO BOX 23173
Overland Park, KS 66223-0173
Phone: 913-897-1004
Fax: 913-681-9473
www.asperger.net

INVOICE

DATE	INVOICE #
9/16/2010	79122

PAID

BILL TO	SHIP TO
Yeager, Christina 3415 Oak View Place Cincinnati, OH 45209	Yeager, Christina 3415 Oak View Place Cincinnati, OH 45209

Customer E-mail	P.O. No.	SHIP DATE	SHIP VIA	VIA ACCT#
Christina.Yeager@cchmc.org	marketing	9/16/2010	UPS- ground	

QTY	ITEM	DESCRIPTION	PRICE EACH	CLASS	AMOUNT
1	9506	Quality Literacy Instruction for Students with Autism Spectrum Disorders... #9781934575666 (9506)	0.00	marketing	0.00T
1	8801	Shipping and Handling	0.00	marketing	0.00

Thank you for your contribution!

Subtotal	$0.00
Sales Tax (0.0%)	$0.00
Balance Due	$0.00

**Please check the accuracy of your e-mail address in the Customer
E-mail box and contact billing@asperger.net with any corrections.
This will ensure you are updated with our new releases.**

curred)?" and "Why will (something else happen)?" No participants with ASD or from the control groups correctly answered fewer than five of six questions about the physical stories, suggesting that the texts were written at an acceptable level of difficulty. Further, participants with ASD were just as likely to provide justifications inferring character motivation in the strange stories as the other participants. However, their justifications were much less likely to be correct or to connect to the specific story content. Thus, unlike studies of preschool-aged children with ASD (Tager-Flusberg, 1992), participants with ASD in this study were able to discuss character motivation but had great difficulties in identifying appropriate character motivation in the strange stories.

In a replication and extension of the Happé (1994) strange stories study, Jolliffe and Baron-Cohen (1999a) employed more difficult strange story and physical control texts to eliminate ceiling effects. Questions following strange stories were similar to those in the original study, including "Was it true what X said?" and "Why did X say that?" Questions accompanying physical control texts did not require interpreting character motivation but did require inferencing beyond text (e.g., "Why did X happen?"). Participants again were allowed and encouraged to read and reread the texts in order to facilitate their explanations in response to "why" questions. Participants were adults with high-functioning autism, Asperger Syndrome, and nondisabled controls. All had average and above scores on full-scale, verbal, and performance IQ measures.

Participants with ASD experienced significantly more difficulty than nondisabled controls in giving context-appropriate explanations for character motivation in the strange stories. Both experimental groups freely used terms to describe motivation but failed to attribute appropriate terms given the specific texts. All participants with high-functioning autism gave at least one context-inappropriate response, and averaged two to three; 12 of 17 participants with Asperger Syndrome did likewise, also averaging one to two. While the group of participants with high-functioning autism did not differ significantly in the accuracy of their responses, they consistently performed at lower levels than the group with Asperger Syndrome.

General comprehension difficulties did not seem to explain performance differences in the two experimental groups, since groups did not differ on the number of errors made on comprehension questions, physical control text responses, or on number of character motivation responses provided. Further, both ASD groups performed comparably to nondisabled controls in the physical control text condition. These data suggest that the central issue for these groups lay in providing context-specific interpretations of character motivation and that the major distinction between the two groups was simply a matter of degree.

In a series of three related experiments, Jolliffe and Baron-Cohen (1999b) examined performance relevant to reading comprehension in students with ASD. All three studies were conducted with two experimental groups, adults with high-functioning autism and adults with Asperger Syndrome, and a control group of nondisabled adults. In experiment 1, participants were asked to read aloud sentences containing homographs (e.g., *tear* in her eye, *tear* in her dress). Both experimental groups were less likely to use the context-appropriate pronunciation, opting instead for the most common pronunciation of the word. That is, they demonstrated difficulties processing information at the sentence level.

In experiment 2, participants were asked to read two- to three-sentence vignettes in which a premise was set (e.g., George left his bath water running.) and the final sentence required a bridging inference to make sense (e.g., George cleaned up the mess in the bathroom.). Participants were asked to select the correct inference (e.g., the bath overflowed) from three alternatives. Participants with high-functioning autism were significantly slower in responding than either the group with Asperger Syndrome or the control group. Both experimental groups demonstrated significantly greater difficulty selecting appropriate bridging inferences than the control group.

In the final experiment, participants were asked to interpret spoken sentences with lexical ambiguity (e.g., "He drew a gun.") or syntactic ambiguity (e.g., "The man was ready to lift.") presented in pairs with other contextual information that invited either a relatively unusual interpretation (e.g., "he drew a picture of a gun" or "the man was ready to be lifted") or a relatively common interpretation (e.g., "he pulled his gun out" or "the man was ready to lift something"). While there were no differences in common lexical or syntactic interpretations, both experimental groups had significantly greater difficulty than controls on less common lexical and syntactic interpretations.

Together, results of the three experiments suggest comprehension difficulties at the sentence and text levels, whether information was read or heard. In each case, individuals with ASD had difficulty applying surrounding text to successfully interpret individual word or inferential text meaning. And in all three experiments, individuals with high-functioning autism tended to have greater difficulty than individuals with Asperger Syndrome.

Prior Knowledge

Three studies have looked within the language component of silent reading comprehension to determine whether or not adults with ASD could draw on prior knowledge to understand what they read. Wahlberg and Magliano (2004) explored the impact of titles and primer texts on story recall. Primer texts consisted of general information providing background to more ambiguous target passages. Participants were able to use the titles and primer text information to activate and employ information at general but not at specific levels. Text recall was greatest when participants had access to both informative titles and primer texts. Participants were unable to use relevant background information to interpret ambiguous statements in the texts.

Saldaña and Frith (2007) explored the question of whether adolescents with ASD could access relevant prior knowledge by measuring the time it took them to read questions related and unrelated to two-sentence vignettes. For example, one relevant item was worded: *The Indians pushed the rocks off the cliff onto the cowboys. The cowboys were badly injured. Can rocks be large?* A parallel irrelevant item was worded: *The Indians pushed the cowboys off the cliff onto the rocks. The cowboys were badly injured. Can rocks be large?* Participants read questions that were relevant to the inference implicit in the vignette more quickly than questions that were irrelevant, suggesting that they were activating appropriate prior knowledge primed by the vignettes. No differences were found in participants' performance whether vignettes addressed physical or social knowledge.

Finally, Norbury and Bishop (2002) investigated the ability of students with high-functioning autism, ages 6-10 years, to engage in two kinds of inferencing in a reading comprehension task. One inference, which the authors described as text-connecting, required participants to integrate information explicitly mentioned in two sentences (e.g., "Michael got the drink out of his bag." and "The orange juice was very refreshing." = "Michael got the orange juice out of his bag."). The other type of inference, described as gap-filling inferences, was what the studies above called "bridging inferences;" that is, requiring participants to integrate their own general knowledge with information in the texts (e.g., inferring that a character was at the beach after reading "The girl put on her swimsuit, but the water was too cold, so she built sandcastles instead."). Texts were written on topics of common knowledge to avoid confounding the results with lack of general knowledge. In addition, participants answered questions about the literal content of the stories.

Unlike the Jolliffe and Baron-Cohen (1999b) study, participants responded to open-ended questions rather than forced-choice items. Students with high-functioning autism were able to make as many inferences as the control group and students with other language impairments, but, as in previous studies, they had greater difficulty in using story information to make inferences appropriate to the specific story contexts.

High-Quality Reading Comprehension Instruction
for Students With ASD

Few intervention studies have specifically addressed reading comprehension in students with ASD (see, e.g., Chiang & Lin, 2007), but existing studies share two important characteristics with the wider reading comprehension instruction research: (a) the studies are theoretically sound and based on best practice principles in mainstream literacy education; and (b) the studies have demonstrated positive learning outcomes attributable to these sound teaching practices.

What Has Been Tried and How It Has Worked

Generating and responding to questions. Teaching typically developing students to generate and respond to questions supports their reading comprehension and comprehension monitoring (National Reading Panel, 2000). Scaffolding strategies found to be particularly effective have included procedural checklists, visual cues, prompts, and question stems (Rosenshine, Meister, & Chapman, 1996).

Recognizing that all of these strategies also have been employed successfully in assisting students with ASD to achieve a variety of social, communicative, and behavioral goals, Whalon and Hanline (2008) incorporated them into a reciprocal questioning intervention. Participants were three 7- to 8-year-old students with ASD and nine general education peers. All students were taught story elements (i.e., setting, characters, event, problem, and solution) in groups consisting of one student with ASD and three general education peers. Then, using a variety of group and individual supports, they were taught to answer and generate questions about the story and to refer to the text as needed in these activities. The three participants increased the range of unprompted questions they generated from 0 to 1 per story at baseline to 1 to 6, 1 to 4, and 0 to 4 during intervention. Further, they increased their unprompted response to questions from zero at baseline to 2 to 6, 1 to 6, and 1 to 5 during intervention.

Different types of questions yielded differing responses. Specifically, questions about characters and settings required the least amount of prompting, whereas problem questions at times required more prompting. Questions that required interpretation or summarization required prompting more often than literal responses found directly in the texts. The study included no formal measures of reading comprehension growth, but in post-intervention interviews, participants with ASD all reported that the intervention helped them better understand what they were reading. Two of the three participants continued to ask questions as they read after completion of the study. Finally, the three participants' parents, after observing videos of the initial and final intervention sessions, agreed that the intervention was valuable and noted various improvements in their child's reading, questioning, and communication skills.

Cooperative learning. This strategy has proven effective with typically developing students in increasing reading comprehension, student discussion, and acquisition of reading strategies (National Reading Panel, 2000). Drawing on this research, Kamps, Leonard, Potucek, and Garrison-Harrell (1995) explored the effects of inclusive cooperative learning groups involving one child with high-functioning autism and two children diagnosed with autism and moderate intellectual disabilities. Direct instruction of vocabulary, story concepts, main idea, sequencing, and story mapping was provided in the classroom along with three cooperative learning activities: peer tutoring in vocabulary, responding to text-based wh- comprehension questions, and a text-based comprehension game. Cooperative learning groups consisted of three general education students and one student with ASD.

Both groups of students demonstrated increased levels of academic engagement and social interaction following the intervention. The participant with high-functioning autism achieved greater reading gains than the two with autism and moderate intellectual disabilities.

Peer tutoring. Another collaborative teaching strategy with a history of success in many different populations and classroom settings is peer tutoring (McMaster, Fuchs, & Fuchs, 2007). Kamps, Barbetta, Leonard, and Delquadri (1994) trained three students with high-functioning autism, ages 8 to 9, and their nondisabled peers to engage in peer tutoring. Three to four times a week following teacher-directed instruction, student pairs spent 25-30 minutes reading aloud a short passage to one another, providing corrective feedback and asking one another wh- questions about the passage.

Thirteen of 14 nondisabled students and all students with ASD demonstrated gains: (a) in reading fluency of 20 or more words per minute, and (b) in reading comprehension as measured by successful response to text-based wh-questions. Participants and their teachers nearly universally reported liking the strategy and believing that it improved their reading.

Procedural facilitation. O'Connor and Klein (2004) explored the efficacy of what they described as procedural facilitation in supporting the reading comprehension of 20 adolescents with high-functioning autism. Participants read modified texts intended to support better comprehension by requiring different responses associated with their reading: answering prereading questions, completing cloze sentences embedded in texts, responding to anaphoric cuing (i.e., identifying which of three possible referents matched each pronoun encountered in the passage), and control passages.

Across conditions, three aspects of participants' reading comprehension were notable. First, when asked to identify the main idea of texts, participants tended to identify the main character or an object in the story regardless of condition. Second, participant retellings of the passages consisted largely of lists of events rather than coherent retellings. Finally, on average, participants answered just half of the literal-level questions correctly. Only the anaphoric cuing procedure significantly increased student passage comprehension. Prequestions contributed to comprehension for students with the highest comprehension ability. This is consistent with previous research with typically developing students, which found that prequestions benefit comprehension under three conditions: (a) when the material to be read is difficult; (b) when the goal is for students to learn only the information from reading that is necessary to answer the questions; and (c) when the information on the pretest is among the most important in the text (Tierney & Cunningham, 1984). The authors proposed that anaphoric cuing benefited comprehension because it caused the students to study the texts more carefully, rereading portions of the texts in order to find the correct answers.

Colasent and Griffith (1998) conducted the sole reading comprehension intervention involving more significantly impaired students with ASD. Participants were three students, 12-15 years old, with ASD and developmental disabilities in a self-contained classroom for students with multiple disabilities. The students had full-scale, verbal, and performance IQ scores ranging from 49-74. Prior to the classroom-based intervention, reading instruction consisted of a functional sight word curriculum (Browder & Lalli, 1991) and story read-alouds from unrelated texts. The students had never received literacy instruction and their individualized education programs (IEPs) included no reading goals.

For the intervention study, teachers read aloud thematically related children's books with rabbits as characters. A scenario was set up in which the students owned a radio station and were interviewed about the stories following each reading. At a prereading background-knowledge step, students were taught about rabbits, and during each reading students engaged in prediction activities.

Participants demonstrated gains in story retelling quality, quantity, and accuracy. Story-related followup drawing and writing activities contributed to further story retelling gains. In addition, student writing samples increased in sentence length and total number of words written across the three stories from pre-intervention performance levels. Finally, an observer noted a variety of behavioral change during the readings and activities, including reduced behavioral outbursts and stereotypic behaviors, increased topic-related comments, and reduced echolalia.

Toward a Clearer Understanding of What Constitutes Best Practice

What emerges from the research is a picture of students with ASD who demonstrate significant, though varying, degrees of reading comprehension difficulties. Students with Asperger Syndrome have scored comparably to typically developing students on global measures of comprehension, but demonstrate difficulties in inferential comprehension tasks. Students with high-functioning autism demonstrate more significant reading comprehension difficulties. That is, it seems that degree, rather than qualitative differences, separates reading comprehension difficulties in students with high-functioning autism from those with Asperger Syndrome. The reading comprehension of more significantly involved students with autism has been investigated in a single study (Colasent & Griffith, 1998). Comprehension difficulties across ASD have included application of text-specific information to derive specific word meanings, making inferences, and relating texts to personal experience.

Three interventions drawn from the best practice literature in general reading comprehension instruction (i.e., cooperative learning, peer tutoring, and reciprocal questioning; see Table 12.2) have demonstrated success in improving the reading comprehension of students with ASD in a few studies. How educators and researchers might begin to more systematically address these identified difficulties is addressed below.

Table 12.2
Interventions Based in ASD Research

Strategy	Research Basis
Cooperative learning	Kamps, Leonard, Potucek, and Garrison-Harrell (1995)
Peer tutoring	Kamps, Barbetta, Leonard, and Delquadri (1994)
Reciprocal questioning	Whalon & Hanline (2008)

Educators

The profile that has emerged from research involving readers with ASD and the success of preliminary studies of reading comprehension interventions suggest several promising practices for educators (see Table 12.3). First, given the prevalent comprehension difficulties reported in the literature, it is sensible for educators to organize reading comprehension around what appears to work best in supporting comprehension learning in typically developing students (Cunningham et al., 1983):

1. Teachers establish purposes for comprehension.
2. Students read or listen for the established purpose.
3. Students perform a task to measure accomplishment of purpose.
4. Teachers provide specific feedback concerning performance.

Table 12.3

Interventions Based on Research in Other Populations

Strategy	Goals
Guided reading lessons	Improved learning from text
Vocabulary and background knowledge tied to specific texts	Improved learning from text, increased understanding of multi-meaning words, and enhanced awareness of importance of context
Repeated reading of text for new comprehension purposes	Increased engagement, text comprehension, and readability of text
Optimal interest	Increased vocabulary learning and comprehension
Selecting texts of optimal interest rather than optimal difficulty	Increased engagement, ability to apply relevant background knowledge, and text comprehension
Summarization	Increased ability to integrate information across sentences
Prediction	Increased ability to apply personal background knowledge in understanding text-specific information
ReQuest and Question-Answer Relationships procedures	Increased ability to ask and answer questions

Guided reading. Given the additional, specific difficulties in connecting world knowledge to text-based inferences (e.g., Wahlberg & Magliano, 2004) that characterize students with ASD, it is also important that what has been an optional, additional step of cuing access to or developing background knowledge for typically developing students (Cunningham et al., 1983) be more consistently and rigorously employed in comprehension lessons for students with ASD.

Supporting Background Knowledge and Comprehension With Webspiration

Barbara Wollak, a speech-language pathologist and assistive technology specialist, uses a variety of technology and instructional strategies in supporting written and oral language development in adolescents. She shared the following story about supporting the comprehension and independence of Deondre (pseudonym), an African-American seventh grader with ASD.

Deondre's IEP listed no reading goals, but his mother told Ms. Wollak that he required assistance in organizing and understanding whatever he read. Deondre told Ms. Wollak that his mind was like a video that kept playing and was difficult to stop. After trying out several graphic organizers to see if they would help Deondre organize his thoughts, Ms. Wollak settled on Webspiration (http://www.mywebspiration.com/), a free, online version of the popular Inspiration graphic organizer software.

As she taught him to use this new tool, Wollak gathered a set of easy texts about African-American leaders to take advantage of Deondre's intense interest in this topic. While reading, Deondre used the rapid-fire feature to take notes quickly as the software organized them for him. Seeing these relationships visually represented in the semantic web view assisted his comprehension, while using the tool across texts increased his understanding of relationships between these famous people. Finally, he switched to the outline view and sent the outline to a word processor in order to extend his newfound understanding to his own writing. Recently Deondre used Webspiration to independently create a family tree for a science project requiring him to show recessive and dominant genes for hair color.

Vocabulary and background knowledge. Students with ASD seem to understand common meanings and pronunciations of individual words, but struggle with contextual use of vocabulary and less frequent meanings and pronunciations (e.g., the difference between *tear* in my eye and a *tear* in her dress). Consequently, within the framework recommended above, it makes sense to preteach key vocabulary from a text to be read during the background-knowledge step. Such instruction should include definitional information and examples, and students should engage in performance that demonstrates relative understanding (e.g., matching word meaning to pictures, acting out or demonstrating the meaning, using writing and speaking to provide additional examples). In this way, students with ASD will be alerted to the specific meaning used in the text; have opportunities to read, write, and discuss them in particular contexts; and improve their ability to use background knowledge to support inferential comprehension.

Technology-Supported Vocabulary Instruction for Diverse Students With ASD

St. Paul (MN) Public Schools serve a diverse population. Specifically, 75% are students of color, and 40% are students from homes where English is a second language and who speak more than 70 languages and dialects. The inclusion program at Highland Park Junior High, with Barbara Wollak's guidance, has designed a systematic way to support vocabulary and comprehension for these students. Each week the instructional team meets to discuss the books to be read that week and the key concepts represented. The team focuses their discussions and planning on so-called Tier 2 vocabulary (Beck, McKeown, & Kucan, 2002). Because of their utility across domains, Tier 2 words (e.g., *fortunate, coincidence, perform, introduce*) have a positive and powerful effect on communication capabilities but are more frequently learned and used in written language experiences. Tier 1 consists of basic words (e.g., *happy, sad, walk, run*) that are common in spoken language, and Tier 3 contains words of low frequency often specific to a particular domain (e.g., *isotope, photosynthesis, philatelist*).

For an American history class, this planning process led to consideration of texts about the Underground Railroad. Wollak searched United Streaming (http://streaming.discoveryeducation.com/index.cfm), YouTube (http://www.youtube.com/) and TeacherTube (http://www.teachertube.com/) for relevant video content. She downloaded a video, edited it to about a 2-minute clip, and added explanatory captions with the free program Capscribe (http://www.capscribe.com/). On this occasion, she typed in the word *escape*, so the students could see it as the video showed and discussed how slaves used the Underground Railroad. After showing the video, Wollak helped the students make personal connections with the target vocabulary by asking them to discuss what they already knew about escape. One student told about how her parents escaped Cambodia by swimming across the Mekong River. Another talked about how the science teacher's snake escaped from its cage. All of this instruction was aimed at supporting students' improved comprehension in their mainstream social studies reading.

Repeated readings and thematically related text. Two additional instructional practices would broaden and deepen understanding of vocabulary and selected themes or topics, as well as comprehension in general: repeated readings of the same text for multiple purposes (Dowhower, 1987) and the use of thematically related texts and units (Colasent & Griffith, 1998; Pressley et al., 2001). Repeated readings, when combined with new purposes for reading, sustain student engagement with a particular text from different perspectives, increasing comprehension and vocabulary learning. Thematically related units and texts increase student use of target vocabulary across instructional experiences and days, contributing to both breadth and depth of vocabulary learning as well as comprehension of central concepts.

Case Example

Tatum was a 5-year-old student with ASD in a classroom serving seven preschoolers with ASD. Tatum demonstrated the benefits of repeated text experiences and the beginnings of text-based comprehension on two occasions. On the first occasion, Tatum and his classmates had heard *Harold and the Purple Crayon* (Johnson, 1983) read aloud several times by their teacher and the school librarian, and the book had been made available to look at during other activities and free play. Toward the end of the week, Tatum was observed engaging in emergent writing with chalk on a portable chalkboard. When asked what he was writing, he began reciting portions of the story intermixed with his own comments and questions, like, "Whatcha doin?"

On another occasion, Tatum's emergent literacy was being assessed at the end of an intervention study (Koppenhaver & Erickson, 2003). In between assessments as I recorded his performance and selected the next task, he was allowed to play with an old, exploratory software program called *The Playroom*. Within the program, he went to a keyboard, where he repeatedly typed the V key, which activated a computer animation of a vulture vacuuming, said, "Vultures vacuum," showed the upper- and lower-case letter V, and made a vacuuming sound. Tatum explored this key, watched, and listened to the animation several dozen times. One of his assessments involved a free-writing sample using the computer keyboard. For much of this assessment, he held the V key down as it typed line after line of V's. When asked to read what he wrote, he pointed to his writing sample and said, "It says, 'Pictures vacuum.' Wanna do that?"

What he demonstrated, among other skills and understandings, in this early, nonconventional performance was an awareness that pictures and text carry meaning. His writing sample indicated his acquisition of *vacuum* as a vocabulary item. His use of *pictures* instead of *vultures* suggested either that he misunderstood what he was hearing, or that he was adapting his reading and listening experience to a new application.

Repeated readings have the added benefit of increasing the readability of a text. That is, a text that is a little too difficult becomes easier each day as it becomes more familiar, as the teacher preteaches vocabulary before reading, as the text is discussed in new ways, and as additional instructional activities accompany the text. This is particularly important since the difference between text that is at an instructional level vs. frustration level may be quite small for students with ASD (Myles et al., 2002). While it is common instructional practice to select texts of optimal difficulty (Fielding & Pearson, 1994), teachers might reduce the risk of selecting texts that are too difficult by instead choosing texts that are easy and hold personal interest for students. Interest correlates with experience and increases the odds of students bringing relevant background knowledge and experiences to the text. In addition, most comprehension strategies do not depend upon difficult text for their application and are more likely to be understood if they are taught in connection with understandable texts.

Using Thematically Related Texts to Support Comprehension in Diverse Students

When a general education American history class was studying the Revolutionary War, the special education literacy class read books not just about the Revolutionary War but also a picture book, *Dia's Story Cloth: The Hmong People's Journey to Freedom* (Cha, 1998). The students were guided in making personal connections and in comparing and contrasting the two texts. The discussion was recorded as a Venn diagram in Inspiration (http://www.inspiration.com) and projected for all the students to see. Among students with ASD were supported in accessing their relevant background knowledge and then applying it systematically in order to better understand their mainstream class's readings and discussions about the Revolutionary War.

Optimal interest. Finding sufficiently easy but optimally interesting text for comprehension lessons can be a challenge for teachers of students who are significantly involved and read at beginning levels despite being in middle or high school. One commercial resource for interesting, easy-to-read texts for students with ASD in upper-elementary, middle, and high school is Don Johnston's *Start-to-Finish Literacy Starters* (http://www.donjohnston.com/products/start_to_finish/literacy/index.html). These stories are written for older students who are emergent or beginning readers. There are currently more than 50 titles in the series with accompanying teaching materials.

Another resource with more than 8,700 titles but fewer quality controls is the Tar Heel Reader web site (http://tarheelreader.org/), a collaborative project between the Department of Computer Science and the Center for Literacy and Disability Studies at the University of North Carolina at Chapel Hill. First introduced in May 2008, the web site enables fast and easy creation of easy-to-read texts of personal interest by teachers and parents of older, beginning readers. Each book that is created becomes available to the Tar Heel Reader community and can be read silently or with computer speech online or downloaded in multiple formats.

Prediction and summarization. While it is important to teach a wide array of reading comprehension strategies, two strategies, prediction and summarization, seem particularly relevant in addressing identified difficulties of students with ASD. Instruction in summarization would teach students how to integrate information across multiple sentences rather than drawing solely on their related background knowledge or simply focusing on individual sentences as they often do in the absence of intervention (Rumsey & Hamburger, 1988).

One very simple and research-tested strategy for teaching students how to identify main ideas by responding to question cues is described by Jitendra, Hoppes, and Xin (2000). Instruction in prediction, particularly if predictions were revisited and revised at multiple points in the text, would systematically engage students in using their background knowledge and connecting it to text-specific information. They could also be guided to read and reread the text in order to check the validity of their predictions. Stauffer's (1969) directed reading thinking strategy is a research-tested and easily implemented strategy for teaching the use of thoughtful and text-based prediction.

Generating and responding to questions. Finally, mainstream reading comprehension research suggests that it is important to teach students how to generate and respond to questions to improve reading comprehension. This is even more critical for students who have ASD. While able to answer literal information questions, these students have been observed to have difficulty answering a variety of other question types, including main ideas, inference, and character perspective or motivation (e.g., Myles et al., 2002). Two research-based strategies seem most applicable for teaching children how to ask and answer questions successfully: reciprocal questioning (Manzo, 1969; Whalon & Hanline, 2008) and question-answer relationships (Raphael, 1986).

Manzo's (1969) ReQuest strategy consists of three steps: teacher and student reading of a targeted short text; student questioning with teacher response, reinforcement, and clarification of intended questions; and exchange of roles in which the teacher asks the student questions to which the student responds or seeks clarification.

Raphael's (1986) QAR strategy helps students learn two categories of question-and-answer relationships: those with answers found in the text and those with answers requiring students' own knowledge and background. The first category, called "In the Book," consists of "Right There" (i.e., questions where the answer is found in a single sentence) and "Think and Search" (i.e., questions where the answer is found across multiple sentences). The second category, called "In My Head," consists of "Author and You" (i.e., questions about what students already know about what the author is telling them and how these two information sources fit together) and "On My Own" (i.e., questions that rely solely on students' knowledge or experience). "Think and Search" questions and "Author and You" are the two types of questions students with ASD have found most difficult to answer. "Think and Search" questions are challenging because of the tendency of individuals with ASD to rely on single-sentence information ("Right There") or their own knowledge of the world ("On My Own") (Rumsey & Hamburger, 1988). "Author and You" questions are difficult for students with ASD because they require readers to interpret the author's intent, a task that has proven difficult in research studies examining theory of mind (Happé, 1994).

Rosenshine et al. (1996) identified a variety of additional teaching techniques that help typically developing children learn to ask and answer questions more successfully, including procedural checklists, visual cues, signal words (i.e., *who, what, where, when, why, how*), and generic question stems (e.g., What is the main idea of…?). Each of these techniques already has a history of success in the ASD literature for teaching a variety of desired behaviors, communication forms, and independent skills (Whalon & Hanline 2008).

Blogging to Learn Questioning and Answering

Observing that many of the students with ASD whom she served experienced difficulties in answering and asking questions, Barbara Wollak initiated two technology-supported writing opportunities.

The first is her e-pals program. Each semester she pairs her students with undergraduate or graduate education students at Appalachian State University. Wollak's students learn how to ask and respond to questions, receive good models of questions and responses, and engage in motivated writing for a real audience. The college students, in turn, learn about the interests, experiences, and literacy skills of diverse students with disabilities.

Wollak's second initiative was her creation of the Virtual Authors blog (http://hpjh.blogspot.com/). Each week she posts a question to which students respond. For example, she posted a short video clip about Martin Luther King at the blog with the question, "What is your dream for America?" For this prompt, responses varied from one student with high-functioning autism, who wrote, "My dream is for real equal rights which means no hidden discrimination," to a student with autism who wrote, "My dream is for real right is love a America." While clearly demonstrating different levels of understanding and expression, both responses, as well as those of other students, were used for instructing students how to formulate and respond to question-answer relationships. The advantage of a blog for this type of instruction is that many students, e-pals, parents, and teachers have the possibility of contributing models and content for instruction that makes sense to students. (For more information, see http://donjohnston.com/wollak-epal/index.html.)

Researchers

Reading comprehension intervention research in ASD currently lags 30 years behind mainstream reading comprehension instruction. That is, the birth of reading comprehension intervention research can be traced fairly specifically to Durkin's (1978-1979) landmark classroom study, which contended that there was little comprehension instruction occurring in public school classrooms, and the publication of Pearson and Johnson's (1978) *Teaching Reading Comprehension*, the first methods text focused on what was known at that time.

What we know about reading comprehension in students with ASD today has been learned largely outside of classrooms, and what we know with certainty about teaching reading comprehension to this population is next to nothing. Researchers such as Kamps et al. (1995) and Whalon and Hanline (2008) have achieved successful learning outcomes by applying best practices from the general education literature. It is important to test the limits of their thinking (i.e., do all best practices in general education apply in ASD, and, if not, what are needed additional strategies, modifications, or considerations?). If all strategies apply, then the real challenge is implementing and studying them on a grander scale than has been attempted in classrooms serving children with ASD.

In a related manner, it is critical to draw more extensively on the wealth of existing reading research in order to design better interventions and to understand intervention outcomes more thoroughly. For example, Social Stories™ are widely employed as a form of behavioral or social intervention for students with ASD (Reynhout & Carter, 2008). Because Social Stories are a text form, ultimately, they depend on student comprehension of the text content for their success in addressing the targeted student behavior.

While there are specific guidelines for the style and format of Social Story sentence types (Gray & Garand, 1993), text difficulty relative to reader or listener skill has seldom been considered. If the Social Stories are to be read, this might be done by examining text readability and the reading levels of the students; or by administering cloze or maze assessments. If the passage is to be read to students, it should be written within their listening comprehension capability. Additionally, because Social Stories represent a comprehension task, it would make sense that they be implemented as guided reading tasks. As presently described in the literature, comprehension questions and checklists seem to be components of implementation (Reynhout & Carter, 2008), but that does not appear to be the case for background knowledge activation/instruction, purpose setting, or followup and feedback described by Cunningham et al. (1983).

Maze Assessment

Developed initially as an alternative reading comprehension assessment (Guthrie, Siefert, Burnham, & Caplan, 1974), the maze procedure has experienced renewed interest in recent years as a curriculum-based measure of reading achievement (Shin, Deno, & Espin, 2000). Maze passages typically are constructed by deleting every fifth to seventh word in a passage and replacing the blank with three alternatives (i.e., the correct word and two alternatives). Administered either to individuals or entire classes, the maze requires a reader to replace each blank in the passage with the correct choice. Repeated administration of maze passages of known reading difficulty can be used as an efficient measure of reader growth and/or reading program effectiveness.

The maze is a particularly appealing assessment for students with ASD, because it requires only a minimal behavioral response, and unlike passage read-aloud measures, which are often used as curriculum-based measures, results are not confounded with skilled word reading in the absence of comprehension. *Cloze Pro*, a software made by Crick Software (http://www.cricksoft.com/us/products/clozepro/default.aspx), greatly eases the process of creating maze passages for teachers, enables computer-based administration, and tabulates results automatically. In a summer literacy camp for adolescents with disabilities (http://www.couragecamps.org), we have observed that some students with ASD respond more readily to maze completion than to wh-questions.

It is representative of what Kliewer and Landis (1999) have identified as "institutional understanding" (p. 89) that only a single study of reading comprehension can be identified with more significantly involved individuals with ASD (Colasent & Griffith, 1998). Thus, no study of reading comprehension instruction has been identified involving students with ASD who require augmentative and alternative communication (Koppenhaver & Erickson, 2009). Yet, 35-40% of individuals with ASD fail to develop functional and communicative language (Mesibov, Adams, & Klinger, 1997).

If, as a society, we do not view persons with ASD as candidates for literacy, why would we teach them to read with comprehension or study how to teach them to read with understanding? Researchers with not only the knowledge and experience to address the complex behaviors and communication of ASD but also the curricular and instructional understanding to plan theoretically sound reading comprehension interventions are few in number. Consequently, if we wish to make significant progress in enhancing reading comprehension instruction for the more significantly involved population of individuals with ASD, it is essential to develop interdisciplinary collaborations.

Two additional issues stem from the complexity of the population – descriptions of participants and synthesizing and reporting of results. Performance means in a population as individually diverse as individuals with ASD (Nation et al., 2006) carry little meaning for individual teachers or families and have little impact on students struggling to learn to read with comprehension. While larger-scale studies are vital to progress in the field, it is critical that researchers report not just whole-group data but also both detailed participant descriptions and outcomes data on subgroups and individuals. The Internet is a valid and valuable way to share such data, which may be too extensive to fit journal page or book chapter limits but might assist in changing outcomes of individual students, teachers, classrooms, or schools. Such data could also become a valuable source of additional intervention studies.

Conclusion

For too long, it has been assumed that the typical profile of students with ASD (i.e., relative strengths with word identification and significant difficulties with comprehension) is the only profile, and that it is immutable. Recent work by Nation et al. (2006) demonstrates that there is greater variability within the ASD population than has been reported previously, although clearly reading comprehension remains a substantial need. Recent intervention studies have demonstrated that reading comprehension is teachable to students with ASD.

As educators, we have an ethical responsibility to believe in the learning capabilities of our students and a professional responsibility to continue problem solving if students are unsuccessful. We have evidence that beyond our specific knowledge of reading comprehension in individuals with ASD, the more general body of reading comprehension research may apply if implemented thoughtfully. Whalon and Hanline (2008) provided a model of one such classroom application with higher-functioning individuals, and Colasent and Griffith (1998) introduced a model for working with more significantly involved individuals with ASD.

As researchers, we have a gap in our ASD portfolio where substantial understanding of a little understood phenomenon, reading comprehension, is needed. We have an enormous body of reading comprehension research involving typically developing students with which to better inform our questions, our research designs, and our data interpretation. One study, focused on writing instruction of a complex student with ASD (i.e., Bedrosian, Lasker, Speidel, & Politsch, 2003), provides a particularly promising blueprint for how we might take on the messy world of classrooms in more systematically studying reading comprehension in ASD. In so doing, we will not only increase understanding of reading comprehension and improve instructional practice, we will also increase learning expectations for the entire spectrum of students with ASD.

Chapter Highlights

- Most students with ASD struggle with comprehending texts.

- Reading comprehension is defined as understanding, remembering, and applying information from text passages.

- Word identification, language comprehension, and print processing are three components that are instructionally relevant in reading comprehension.

- Researchers have examined skilled readers as a way to understand what might be taught to improve all students' reading comprehension.

- Five characteristics are associated with skilled readers:
  - ✔ Anticipation of learning
  - ✔ Monitoring for understanding
  - ✔ Seeking answers to questions
  - ✔ Reflecting
  - ✔ Reading systematically

- Other comprehension strategies include predicting background knowledge, using text structure, developing and using visual representations, and summarization.

- Reading comprehension instruction should include guided practice, monitoring, students working in a variety of peer groups, teacher-demonstrated application, and time for reading.

- Research indicates that language comprehension is the greatest area of need for students with ASD because their ability to listen generally exceeds their ability to comprehend.

- Studies show that students on the autism spectrum have difficulty in integrating information across sentences, identifying appropriate character motivation in stories, and processing information at the sentence level.

- With regard to utilizing prior knowledge, research demonstrates that students with ASD are unable to use relevant information to interpret statements in text.

- Research shows that the following strategies improve reading comprehension for students with ASD:
  - ✔ Cooperative learning
  - ✔ Peer tutoring
  - ✔ Prequestioning techniques

- Students with ASD demonstrate different reading comprehension difficulties.

- Educators are encouraged to organize reading comprehension around what supports comprehension in typically developing children.

- Establishing a purpose for comprehension involves:
  - ✔ Listening for a purpose
  - ✔ Measuring accomplishment of the purpose
  - ✔ Providing performance feedback

- Best practices for educators include preteaching key vocabulary, repeated reading, thematic related units, and teaching students how to respond to reading questions.

- The reading comprehension research reveals:
  - ✔ Future studies need to draw on existing reading research
  - ✔ Future studies need to focus on subgroups and individuals as opposed to large-scale studies

Chapter Review Questions

1. What is Tierney and Cunningham's definition of reading comprehension?

2. What general education strategy has been studied and shown successful for improving the ability of students with ASD to ask questions about text?

3. Do individuals with high-functioning autism or individuals with Asperger Syndrome tend to experience greater difficulties with reading comprehension?

4. What are the two particular advantages of using maze assessment for examining reading comprehension in students with ASD?

References

Allington, R. (1983). The reading instruction provided readers of differing reading abilities. *Elementary School Journal, 83*, 548-559.

Allington, R. (1984). Content coverage and contextual reading in reading groups. *Journal of Reading Behavior, 16*, 85-96.

Beck, I. L., McKeown, M. G., & Kucan, L. (2002). *Bring words to life: Robust vocabulary instruction*. New York: Guilford Press.

Bedrosian, J. L., Lasker, J., Speidel, K., & Politsch, A. (2003). Enhancing the written narrative skills of an AAC student with autism: Evidence-based research issues. *Topics in Language Disorders, 23*, 305-324.

Browder, D. M., & Lalli, J. S. (1991). Review of research on sight word instruction. *Research in Developmental Disabilities, 12*, 203-228.

Catts, H. W., & Kamhi, A. G. (Eds.). (2005). *The connections between language and reading disabilities*. Mahwah, NJ: Lawrence Erlbaum Associates.

Cha, D. (1998). *Dia's story cloth: The Hmong people's journey of freedom*. New York: Lee and Low Books.

Chiang, H., & Lin, Y. (2007). Reading comprehension instruction for students with autism spectrum disorders: A review of the literature. *Focus on Autism and Other Developmental Disabilities, 22*, 259-267.

Chorzempa, B. F., & Graham, S. (2006). Primary-grade teachers' use of within-class ability grouping in reading. *Journal of Educational Psychology, 98*, 529-541.

Colasent, R., & Griffith, P. L. (1998). Autism and literacy: Looking into the classroom with rabbit stories. *Reading Teacher, 51*, 414-420.

Cooter, R., Flynt, E., & Cooter, K. (2006). *Comprehensive reading inventory: Measuring reading development in regular and special education classrooms.* London: Pearson.

Cunningham, J. W. (1993). Whole-to-part reading diagnosis. *Reading and Writing Quarterly: Overcoming Learning Difficulties, 9,* 31-49.

Cunningham, P. M., & Allington, R. L. (2007). *Classrooms that work: They can all read and write* (4th ed.). Boston: Pearson Education.

Cunningham, P. M., Moore, S. A., Cunningham, J. W., & Moore, D. W. (1983). *Reading in elementary classrooms: Strategies and observations.* New York: Longman.

Dowhower, S. L. (1987). Effects of repeated reading on second-grade transitional readers' fluency and comprehension. *Reading Research Quarterly, 22,* 389-406.

Duffy, G. G. (2003). *Explaining reading: A teacher's resource for teaching concepts, skills and strategies.* New York: Guilford

Duke, N. K., & Pearson, P. D. (2002). Effective practices for developing reading comprehension. In A. E. Farstrup & S. J. Samuels (Eds.), *What research has to say about reading instruction* (3rd ed., pp. 205-242). Newark, DE: International Reading Association.

Durkin, D. (1978-1979). What classroom observations reveal about reading comprehension instruction. *Reading Research Quarterly, 15,* 481-533.

Durkin, D. (1993). *Teaching them to read* (6th ed.). Boston: Allyn and Bacon.

Erickson, K. A., Koppenhaver, D. A., & Cunningham, J. W. (2006). Balanced reading intervention and assessment in augmentative communication. In M. E. Fey & R. J. McCauley (Eds.), *Treatment of language disorders in children* (pp. 309-345). Baltimore: Paul H. Brookes.

Fielding, L. G., & Pearson, P. D. (1994). Reading comprehension: What works. *Educational Leadership, 51*(5), 62-68.

Good, T. L., & Marshall, S. (1984). Do students learn more in heterogeneous or homogeneous groups? In P. L. Peterson, L. C. Wilkinson, & M. Hallinan (Eds.), *The social context of instruction: Group organization and group processes* (pp. 15-38). New York: Academic Press.

Gray, C., & Garand, J. D. (1993). Social stories: Improving responses of students with autism with accurate social information. *Focus on Autism and Other Developmental Disabilities, 8,* 1-10.

Guthrie, J. T., Siefert, M., Burnham, N. A., & Caplan, R. I. (1974). The maze technique to assess, monitor reading comprehension. *Reading Teacher, 28,* 161-168.

Happé, F.G.E. (1994). An advanced test of theory of mind: Understanding of story characters' thoughts and feelings by able autistic, mentally handicapped and normal children and adults. *Journal of Autism and Developmental Disorders, 24,* 129-154.

Jitendra, A. K., Hoppes, M. K., & Xin, Y. P. (2000). Enhancing main idea comprehension for students with learning problems: The role of a summarization strategy and self-monitoring instruction. *The Journal of Special Education, 34,* 127-139.

Johnson, C. (1983). *Harold and the purple crayon.* New York: HarperCollins.

Jolliffe, T., & Baron-Cohen, S. (1999a). The strange stories test: A replication with high-functioning adults with autism or Asperger Syndrome. *Journal of Autism and Developmental Disorders, 29,* 395-406.

Joliffe, T., & Baron-Cohen, S. (1999b). A test of central coherence theory: Linguistic processing in high-functioning adults with autism or Asperger syndrome: Is local coherence impaired? *Cognition, 71,* 149-185.

Kamps, D. M., Barbetta, P. M., Leonard, B. R., & Delquadri, J. (1994). Classwide peer tutoring: An integration strategy to improve reading skills and promote peer interactions among students with autism and general education peers. *Journal of Applied Behavior Analysis, 27,* 49-61.

Kamps, D. M., Leonard, B., Potucek, J., & Garrison-Harrell, L. G. (1995). Cooperative learning groups in reading: An integration strategy for students with autism and general classroom peers. *Behavioral Disorders, 21*, 89-109.

Kintsch, W., & van Dijk, T. A. (1978). Toward a model of discourse comprehension and production. *Psychological Review, 83*, 363-394.

Kliewer, C., & Landis, D. (1999). Individualizing literacy instruction for young children with moderate to severe disabilities. *Exceptional Children, 66*, 85-100.

Koppenhaver, D. A., & Erickson, K. A. (2003). Natural emergent literacy supports for preschoolers with autism and severe communication impairments. *Topics in Language Disorders, 23*, 283-292.

Koppenhaver, D. A., & Erickson, K. A. (2009). Individuals with autism spectrum disorders who use AAC. In P. Mirenda & T. Iacono (Eds.), *Autism spectrum disorders and AAC* (pp. 385-412). Baltimore: Paul H. Brookes.

Koppenhaver, D. A. Foley, B. E., & Williams, A. R. (2009). Diagnostic reading assessment for students with AAC needs. In G. Soto and C. Zangari (Eds.), *Practically speaking: Language, literacy, and academic development for students with AAC needs* (pp. 71-91). Baltimore: Paul H. Brookes.

Manzo, A. V. (1969). The ReQuest procedure. *Journal of Reading, 12*, 123-126.

McMaster, K. L., Fuchs, D., & Fuchs, L. S. (2007). Promises and limitations of peer-assisted learning strategies in reading. *Learning Disabilities: A Contemporary Journal, 5*(2), 97-112.

Mesibov, G. B., Adams, L. W., & Klinger, L. G. (1997). *Autism: Understanding the disorder*. New York: Plenum Press.

Minshew, N. J., Goldstein, G., & Siegel, D. J. (1995). Speech and language in high-functioning autistic individuals. *Neuropsychology, 9*, 255-261.

Morrow, L. M., Gambrell, L. B., & Pressley, M. (Eds.). (2003). *Best practices in literacy instruction* (2nd ed.). New York: Guilford Press.

Myles, B. S., Hilgenfeld, T. D., Barnhill, G. P., Griswold, D. E., Hagiwara, T., & Simpson, R. (2002). Analysis of reading skills in individuals with Asperger syndrome. *Focus on Autism and Other Developmental Disabilities, 17*(1), 44-47.

Nagy, W., Anderson, R., & Herman, P. (1987). Learning word meanings from context during normal reading. *American Educational Research Journal, 24*, 237-270.

Nation, K., Clarke, P., Wright, B., & Williams, C. (2006). Patterns of reading ability in children with autism spectrum disorder. *Journal of Autism and Developmental Disorders, 36*, 911-919.

National Reading Panel. (2000). *Teaching children to read: An evidence-based assessment of the scientific research literature on reading and its implications for reading instruction: Reports of the subgroups* (National Institute of Health Pub. No. 00-4754). Washington, DC: National Institute of Child Health and Human Development.

Nilsson, N. L. (2008). A critical analysis of eight informal reading inventories. *Reading Teacher, 61*, 526-536.

Norbury, C. F., & Bishop, D.V.M. (2002). Inferential processing and story recall of children with communication problems: A comparison of specific language impairment, pragmatic language impairment and high-functioning autism. *International Journal of Language and Communication Disorders, 37*, 227-251.

O'Connor, I. M., & Klein, P. D. (2004). Exploration of strategies for facilitating the reading comprehension of high-functioning students with autism spectrum disorders. *Journal of Autism and Developmental Disorders, 14*, 115-127.

O'Connor, N., & Hermelin, B. (1994). Two autistic savant readers. *Journal of Autism and Developmental Disorders, 24*, 501-515.

Paratore, J. R., & Indrisano, R. (2003). Grouping for instruction in literacy. In J. Flood, D. Lapp, J. R. Squire, & J. M. Jensen (Eds.), *Handbook of research on teaching the English language arts* (2nd ed., pp. 566-572). Mahwah, NJ: Erlbaum.

Pearson, P. D., & Fielding, L. (1991). Comprehension instruction. In R. Barr, M. L. Kamil, P. B. Mosenthal, & P. D. Pearson (Eds.), *Handbook of reading research* (Vol. 2, pp. 815-860). New York: Longman.

Pearson, P. D., & Johnson, D. (1978). *Teaching reading comprehension*. New York: Holt, Rinehart, & Winston.

Pressley, M. (2002). *Reading instruction that works: The case for balanced teaching* (2nd ed.). New York: Guilford Press.

Pressley, M., & Afflerbach, P. (1995). *Verbal protocols of reading: The nature of constructively responsive reading*. Hillsdale, NJ: Erlbaum.

Pressley, M., Allington, R. L., Wharton-McDonald, R., Block, C. C., & Morrow, L. M. (2001). *Learning to read: Lessons from exemplary first-grade classrooms*. New York: Guilford.

Raphael, T. (1986). Teaching question answer relationships, revisited. *Reading Teacher, 39*, 516-522.

Reynhout, G., & Carter, M. (2008). A pilot study to determine the efficacy of a social story intervention for a child with autistic disorder, intellectual disability and limited language skill. *Australian Journal of Special Education, 32*, 161-175.

Rosenshine, B. (1983). Teaching functions in instructional programs. *Elementary School Journal, 83*, 335-351.

Rosenshine, B., Meister, C., & Chapman, S. (1996). Teaching students to generate questions: A review of the intervention studies. *Review of Educational Research, 66*, 181-221.

Rumsey, J., & Hamburger, S. (1988). Neuropsychological findings in high-functioning men with infantile autism, residual state. *Journal of Clinical and Experimental Neuropsychology, 10,* 201-221

Saldaña, D., & Frith, U. (2007). Do readers with autism make bridging inferences from world knowledge? *Journal of Experimental Child Psychology, 96*, 310-319.

Shin, J., Deno, S. L., & Espin, C. (2000). Technical adequacy of the maze task for curriculum-based measurement of reading growth. *Journal of Special Education, 34*, 164-172.

Stauffer, R. G. (1969). *Directing reading maturity as a cognitive process*. New York: Harper and Row.

Sticht, T. G., & James, J. H. (1984). Listening and reading. In P. D. Pearson, R. Barr, M. L. Kamil, & P. Mosenthal (Eds.), *Handbook of reading research* (pp. 293-317). New York: Longman.

Tager-Flusberg, H. (1992). Autistic children's talk about psychological states: deficits in the early acquisition of a theory of mind. *Child Development, 63,* 161-172.

Tierney, R. J., & Cunningham, J. W. (1984). Research on teaching reading comprehension. In P. D. Pearson, R. Barr, M. L. Kamil, & P. Mosenthal (Eds.), *Handbook of reading research* (pp. 610-655). New York: Longman.

Wahlberg, T., & Magliano, J. P. (2004). The ability of high function individuals with autism to comprehend written discourse. *Discourse Processes, 38*, 119-144.

Whalon, K., & Hanline, M. F. (2008). Effects of a reciprocal questioning intervention on the question generation and responding of children with autism spectrum disorder. *Education and Training in Developmental Disabilities, 43*, 367-387.

Whitman, W. (1949). *Democratic vistas*. New York: The Liberal Arts Press.

Chapter 13
Writing Instruction

Jennifer C. Wolfe, M.S., Linden Grove School, Ohio

Pamela Williamson, Ph.D., University of Cincinnati

Christina Carnahan, Ed.D., University of Cincinnati

Learner Objectives

After reading this chapter, the learner should be able to:

- List the components of a process approach to writing instruction

- Describe characteristics of students on the autism spectrum that might impede their writing ability

- Describe strategies for adapting writing instruction to address these characteristics

■ ■ ■

Alyssa is a 10-year-old student on the autism spectrum with significant needs. An emergent learner, Alyssa's communication system consisted of rudimentary signs that only those close to her understood. In addition to communication barriers, Alyssa faced challenges with fine-motor skills. Although Alyssa could make marks with a paint brush on paper, her educational team believed that with proper technology, Alyssa could develop writing skills.

After an assistive technology needs assessment, Alyssa received an IntelliKeys©, an oversized keyboard. With this support, Alyssa's teacher, Angela, began developing lessons and activities to promote emergent writing skills. Using Photovoice (see, e.g., Carnahan, 2006), an educational action research technique that pairs students with cameras as a means of sharing visual information about their lives, the paraprofessional in the classroom, Carol, helped Alyssa photograph important things related to her school experiences. Alyssa photographed various areas of the classroom: the cooking area, the sensory area, and the music room. From this array of pictures, Alyssa selected one to begin the task of writing.

The picture Alyssa selected was imported into a Word document, and Alyssa was asked to write about her picture. Alyssa's first "story" was a caption for her picture. As with all emergent writers, her caption was a string of unrelated letters. Angela hopes that through repetition of this activity, Alyssa will begin to understand that letters actually have meaning, and that when people write letters, they have a purpose. Long term, Angela hopes that Alyssa's "writing" will eventually include word boundaries, as well as conventionally written words.

■ ■ ■

Jake is a 15-year-old with high-functioning autism. He attends his neighborhood middle school and is included for all subjects except English. He receives intensive academic instruction for reading comprehension and writing with other students who have special needs. Jake's teacher, Caitlin, read an article by Bedrosian, Lasker, Speidel, and Politsch (2003) reporting on a student with learning disabilities and a student with ASD being paired to work on writing narrative stories together. Although the student with ASD in that study used augmentative and alternative communication and appeared to have more significant needs than Jake, Caitlin wanted to try having Jake write with a boy named Peter who had learning disabilities. The two seemed to have complementary skills. Jake was excellent at spelling, whereas Peter had difficulty spelling and reading.

Caitlin decided to have the boys collaborate on expository writing, as that was the kind of writing expected in their other classes. For example, in their science class, students were required to write a research report about sharks by the end of the first semester.

Luckily, this was a topic of interest to both boys. Jake knew a great deal about sharks, as he was fascinated by the ocean. Caitlin took both boys to the school library where they selected a nonfiction book on sharks written at the third-grade reading level – the boys' instructional reading level. Once back in the classroom, Caitlin reviewed the text features, including the table of contents, the glossary, and the index of the book. She reminded the boys that for report writing, it is not necessary to read the entire book, cover to cover. Instead, she explained, they would develop a list of key words related to the information they wanted in their report and then use the book's features to locate that information. Over the course of the semester, she delivered explicit instruction on key words, searching and scanning, and taking notes from source materials. The boys also received explicit instruction on how to complete a graphic organizer for an expository paragraph. Finally, with the foundation set, the boys crafted a complete paragraph.

■ ■ ■

The importance of teaching all children to write cannot be overstated. Adults with disabilities need to pay bills and write grocery lists; they may wish to write emails to their families and friends. Some may wish to use their talents to become accomplished writers. Thus, writing is especially relevant to self-determination (Wehmeyer & Shogren, 2008).

Children enter school with varied literacy experiences, and students on the spectrum are no exception. Some children have lots of exposure to print. Parents may spend hours interacting with them over a book or reading the cereal box over morning breakfast. Other children have less exposure, perhaps due to early aversive reactions to books and print. As with typically developing children, those on the autism spectrum bring these early experiences to the classroom.

As with reading, students with autism spectrum disorders (ASD) face particular challenges with written expression. Mayes and Calhoun (2006) studied the prevalence of learning disabilities, as defined by using the discrepancy model, among children with different diagnoses, including ASD. Among students with ASD, the discrepancy between IQ and achievement in written expression was significant. Furthermore, these students were able to spell far better than would be predicted by the full written expression scale. In other words, learners on the spectrum have relative strengths in spelling compared to their abilities to create a piece of writing, akin to their relative strengths in word recognition compared to their ability to comprehend text (Koppenhaver & Erickson, 2009).

Writing can be broadly thought of in both physical (i.e., handwriting, typing, alternative augmentative communication [AAC]) and generative terms (i.e., the product, such as report or email). Alyssa's example clearly demonstrates the need to address physical needs first, as being able to "write" is a prerequisite for the generative aspect of writing. Although keyboards are the answer for some of our students, many students with significant needs are unable to use keyboards. Researchers at the Center for Literacy and Disability Studies and the University of North Carolina at Chapel Hill suggest that students with significant disabilities can profit from daily writing instruction when they have "alternative pencils" (Hanser, 2006). Hanser argued that just as typically developing students need not possess conventional writing skills when they first become acquainted with writing implements, children with more significant disabilities need opportunities for emergent writing, as Alyssa's case demonstrates. Whatever developing abilities a student possesses should be used to facilitate emergent writing (e.g., eye gaze, print flip chart, Braille flip chart).

When selecting a writing implement, it is important to consider how much pressure various implements require to make marks on a page. For example, pens require more pressure than pencils, pencils require more pressure than markers, and markers require more pressure than paint brushes.

Hanser (2006) suggested the following guidelines for selecting and using "alternative pencils":

1. Select a tool that has the greatest potential relative to ease of use.
2. Provide access to the entire alphabet, not just letters or letters of the day.
3. Pair the child with the appropriate tool as soon as possible. All children learn by doing. Children do not need to know their letters to begin.

The last point is particularly important. Recently, when we were consulting in a classroom filled with learners with significant needs, we inquired about writing for a particular student. The teacher reported that since the student was "messy with markers," he was no longer allowed to use markers. Yet, for this student, who had fine-motor concerns, markers met Hanser's first recommendation – they were the easiest tool with the greatest potential for generative writing. Writing is similar to a contact sport – students must participate by practicing skills and developing fundamentals. In the process, and in some cases, they make messes. After our inquiry and some discussions about the benefits of allowing the student to use markers, the teacher again made markers available to him.

Writing Development and Theoretical Underpinnings

Development of Writing Ability

As with reading, writing for typically developing children is conceptualized as progressing through stages (Morrow, 2005; Sulzby, 1990). While these stages generally move toward greater sophistication, students do not pass through each stage in a linear fashion. Rather, student writing at any given time may include characteristics from more than one stage. The stages are as follows: (a) drawing as writing, (b) scribbling as writing, (c) letter-like units, (d) nonphonetic letter strings, (e) copying environmental print, (f) invented spelling, and (g) conventional spelling. (See, e.g., http//www.sedubois.k12.in.us/~jblackgrove/stages_of_writing.htm.) As the case of Alyssa demonstrates, while some stages may be skipped (e.g., drawing pictures), students who use AAC to write follow roughly the same paths toward conventional writing.

Initially, typically developing children use pictures to symbolize writing (Morrow, 2005; Sulzby, 1990). If invited, children will "read" their drawings to others, as if the pictures were accompanied by words. This suggests that they understand that one purpose for writing is to convey a message to others. As children become more attuned to the function of print, their writing takes the form of scribbles across the page. At this point, they may begin to hold their writing implement in much the same way as adults. Next, children begin creating letter-like forms. They seem to notice that instead of connected lines, letters are formed individually. However, at this stage, conventional letter forms are not present. During the next stage, letter forms emerge, but there are generally no word boundaries (i.e., spaces between words), and the letters are unrelated (i.e., do not spell words). Often children use letters that are part of their names in these unrelated letter strings. Next, children begin copying down words they find in the environment. They may copy words from their cereal box, or they may write words they see on signs. Word boundaries begin to emerge. During the next phase called invented spelling, students write the letters they know and hear in a word. Although writing begins to look more like conventional writing, word boundaries may still be confused, and vowels are frequently omitted. Finally, conventional spelling emerges. For typically developing children, invented spelling emerges between the end of kindergarten and the end of first grade. Once conventional spelling gives way to conventional writing, different models are needed to explain how writers engage in generating a piece of writing, be it a simple sentence or a narrative paragraph (see Table 13.1).

Table 13.1

Stages of Writing Ability

Drawing	Children draw pictures to represent writing and may verbalize their drawings as if reading aloud. This demonstrates their understanding that writing is used to relay information.
Scribbling	Children begin to scribble as if writing and to hold their pencil or crayon in a manner similar to an adult.
Letter-like units	As children's writing matures, connected scribbles transition into separate, broken lines resembling letters.
Nonphonetic letter strings	Children begin to combine unrelated letters, in an effort to resemble words. They frequently use letters from their own names.
Copying environment print	Children copy words from their surroundings.
Invented spelling	Children's writing begins to resemble conventional style as they incorporate familiar words. However, word boundaries may still be confused and vowels may be omitted.
Conventional spelling	Children achieve correct or standard spelling.

Writing Process Models

Koppenhaver and Erickson (2009) proposed that the whole-to-part (WTP) model of writing is a useful framework for thinking about writing for students on the autism spectrum. The WTP model conceptualizes the cognitive construct of writing as constituent parts that collectively make up a whole (Flower & Hayes, 1981), and is based on the assumption that individual success is a factor of both skill and learning opportunities. Instead of conceptualizing writing as distinct phases that writers move through, from prewriting to publishing, the WTP model is a cognitive process theory of writing that focuses on the decision-making process that a writer engages in during the act of writing.

As this writing process takes shape, the steps of planning, translating, and reviewing occur within the context of the task environment. Work on a piece of writing is inherently discursive, characterized by revisions within each step or sequence of each process. These processes are influenced to a great extent by the writer's long-term memory and his ability to recall knowledge from memory. The parts function together as a whole, and weaknesses in particular parts may be mitigated by strength in other parts. For children with ASD, this suggests that relative strengths in spelling (Mayes & Calhoun, 2006) should be exploited in the process. Table 13.2 compares the typical writing process to the WTP model.

Table 13.2

Typical Writing Process Versus Whole-to-Part Model

Typcial Writing Process	Whole-to-Part Process
Prewriting/brainstorming	Planning
Rough draft	Translating
Editing/revising	Reviewing
Publishing	Publishing

What Does the Research Say?

Based on a review of the literature on effective instructional practices for teaching students with disabilities to write, Vaughn, Gersten, and Chard (2000) suggested that teachers should (a) model the writing process, (b) provide explicit instruction of writing conventions, and (c) provide frequent supportive feedback. Further, Englert (1992) emphasized the "social enterprise of writing" (p. 153), along with the cognitive aspects.

As is true for many disability areas (see, e.g., learning disabilities writing research by Hooper, Swartz, Wakely, deKruif, & Montgomery, 2002), research examining writing in students with ASD is scant. Four studies were found to have investigated writing for students with more significant needs.

Colasent and Griffith (1998) investigated the use of thematic teaching on the reading and writing products of adolescent students in a self-contained classroom in a large urban public school district that included three students with ASD. After building background knowledge around the topic of rabbits, they read several books to students about rabbits and used explicit prompts to facilitate story retellings. They also examined the influence of thematic teaching on student writing samples, comparing samples of writing before and after thematic teaching. After the thematic unit, all three students wrote longer passages and sentences; after the third story, the researchers noted improvements in vocabulary usage.

Bedrosian and her colleagues (2003) investigated a narrative writing intervention for a student with ASD who was using AAC. The researchers paired this student with a peer with a cognitive disability. Baseline data indicated that the boy with ASD was an accurate speller, whereas the boy with cognitive disabilities made far more surface errors due to underdeveloped skills at writing complete stories, but demonstrated more story elements. Thus, the boys' skills were complementary. After a yearlong intervention that emphasized process writing in partners, the use of writing conventions and written expression markedly improved for both boys.

Koppenhaver and Erickson (2003) studied the effects of natural emergent literacy supports for preschoolers with ASD and communication impairments. Essentially, these researchers provided emergent writing supports, including computers and preschool writing toys (e.g., Etch-a-Sketch [The Ohio Art Company], Magna-Doodle [Fisher-Price]), as well as various writing surfaces (e.g., sticky notes, paper, whiteboards, chalkboards) and writing implements (e.g., markers, chalk, crayons, pencils). Reading supports, as well as interaction supports for both reading and writing, were also made available to students. The researchers found that as a result of using these supports, in addition to interest in the materials, the literacy skills of the children became more sophisticated. For example, one child began to write his name conventionally.

Finally, Rousseau, Krantz, Poulson, Kitson, and McClannahan (1994) explicitly taught students with ASD to combine shorter sentences into one longer sentence (e.g., the sentences "the boy is tall, and the boy is blond" is combined to read, "The boy is tall and blond."). The researchers noted that student writing included more adjectives after the intervention, but they suggested that the effects might be due to the fact that the "autistic students (sic) became overly dependent on the visual prompts as discriminative stimuli" (p. 32).

Writing Instruction

All aspects of literacy link tightly to one another (Stewart & Clarke, 2003). Listening and speaking form the basis of communication skills, and while reading is a decoding process whereby words are identified and comprehended, writing is an encoding process whereby ideas are generated and formulated into words on the written page (Buss & Karnowski, 2000). Alyssa, in our opening vignette, learned to communicate using more and more words, and those new words in her budding lexicon can be tapped during meaningful reading and writing activities. Although we do not yet know whether students on the spectrum follow a similar developmental trajectory, understanding typical writing development may provide insight into where to begin instruction.

Sink (1975) distinguished between two approaches to writing instruction: teach-to-write and write-to-teach. Teach-to-write emphasizes formal grammar instruction and, while common in classrooms, it has not proven effective for learners either with or without disabilities. A major concern is that students may learn the mechanics for writing, but have minimal opportunities to actually write. The write-to-teach approach, on the other hand, places emphasis on the primary role of the author. Ideas are shared in written form while structure is taught in the context of the students' writing, not in isolation, or in lieu of students' writing. Both are crucial and should be taught together.

A Process Approach

A process approach to writing instruction, such as write-to-teach, challenges traditional writing instruction by emphasizing the process rather than the finished work product. Assumptions and guidelines include (a) an emphasis on the process of writing leads to the work product, (b) children learn to write by writing, (c) mini-lessons are the means of direct instruction, (d) instruction is based on what the students need to learn at the time, (e) collaboration among students is encouraged, and (f) writing is shared with a wide audience (Calkins,1985; Gillet & Beverly, 2001).

A process approach for students with ASD should provide well-organized materials to support active engagement. This is achieved through careful consideration of student language skills, interests, and needs. This means providing visual supports and explicit instruction (Aspy & Grossman, 2007).

Instructional Strategies

McCarrier, Pinnell, and Fountas (2000) described four instructional strategies to help children of any age who are developmentally emerging writers. These include (a) language experience, (b) shared writing, (c) interactive writing, and (d) independent writing.

Language experience approach (LEA). This approach can be used with a group of children at varied levels of writing experience. This kind of lesson usually begins with a group experience, a field trip or a daily cooking lesson, followed by a group writing experience. For students with memory challenges, experiences may be recorded on video (Ayres & Langone, 2005). Students or support adults might take notes or complete graphic organizers during the experiences (Williams, 1995). Further, photos may be taken during the activity and downloaded in computer programs to prompt writing and illustration.

Generally, a small group of students is seated around a large writing surface (e.g., chart paper, whiteboard, overhead projector), and the teacher leads a conversation about the experience. As the group discusses the experience, the teacher models writing what students say using a think-aloud style. In other words, she utters each word as she writes it on the writing surface. Generally, it is important to record what students say exactly as they say it, as it helps students make connections between utterances and print. It is important to preserve class stories for future reading (Gregory & Kuzmich 2005; McCarrier et al., 2000; Polloway Patton, & Serna, 2005). For example, LEA stories can be transcribed onto pages of a book and placed in the independent reading corner. A photo commemorating the experience may also be added.

Shared writing. Similar to LEA, the shared writing approach involves two or more writers contributing to the creation of text while the teacher transcribes their thoughts. Unlike language experience, the purpose for shared writing is to create text about a unit of study or the retelling of a piece of literature. Emphasis is placed on accuracy of content and sequencing of events while the teacher guides the children in text development. Through group discussion, the teacher encourages students to expand their ideas. This process helps children understand that the purpose of writing can be to inform others (Gregory & Kuzmich, 2005; McCarrier et al., 2000).

Interactive writing. Interactive writing is a process during which students and teachers jointly construct letters, notes, or daily messages (Rycik & Rycik, 2007). Teachers begin lessons by helping students focus on specific topics. For example, when writing a thank-you note to a recent class visitor, the teacher may ask students what they want to say and then model how to format the note. At this point, the teacher also provides opportunities to "share the pen" (p. 97), allowing individual students to write specific letters, words, or punctuation.

Independent writing. Independent writing provides opportunities for students to create their own text. Journal writing is an easy place to start independent writing. It is an authentic activity that students may continue into adulthood. Each student should be provided with a notebook that is only used for journaling. Journals may also be kept on computers. If students have voice output devices, paraprofessionals might act as scribes. If students can point or use eye gaze to indicate choices from an array of pictures, they can select their entry. Entries might be generated from a writing prompt (e.g., What is your favorite computer game?) or student choice. Journals are flexible – students choose an entry at their own level. Generally, students are taught to record the date at the top of each entry.

Dialogue journals are a special kind of journal where students and another person write back and forth. For example, if Jake wrote an entry about sharks, his teacher might write a question next to his entry. Jake then answers the teacher's question as part of his next journal entry. He might also write questions for his teacher. Instead of a teacher, dialogue journals can be written between peers. For example, Jake and Peter might keep a dialogue journal together. Another possibility is to have different responders (e.g., parents, peers, other teachers) each time.

Learning logs are a bit like journals in that they have dates entered at the top of each page, and students write about something they learned during the day. An alternative is to ask students to respond to particular prompts (e.g., Write one thing you learned in math today). Learning logs are an easy way to integrate writing across content areas.

Writer's Workshop

Writer's workshop (WW) is another example of a process approach to writing. It is an instructional method that is individualized and personalized (Calkins, 1994; Graves, 1983). Through WW, teachers dedicate blocks of time to writing. As with independent reading, the amount of time afforded to WW should be based upon student ability. During this time, teachers may provide mini-lessons to either whole-group, small-group, or individual students. Mini-lessons are brief lessons that focus on one aspect of writing. They may be related to a particular skill (e.g., use of punctuation), a revision technique (e.g., reducing the number of overused words, combining short sentences into longer ones), or topic generation. Students also receive instruction through writing conferences, in one-on-one, or small-group discussions with adults or peers.

The general format of WW includes a check-in procedure that informs teachers and other supporting adults of where students are in the writing process. Figure 13.1 shows a sample check-in chart appropriate for an inclusive fifth-grade classroom. Instead of the typical procedure whereby students report orally, the chart is circulated for students to mark where they are in the writing process. If students are working on multiple aspects of writing, they may check more than one blank. No matter what strategy is used, the teacher is able to quickly scan the sheet to see who needs assistance. For example, if Ethan has not requested a conference within a reasonable timeframe, the teacher might approach him to see how he is doing. The chart also affords a long-term picture of student work.

After students check in, they immediately begin working. Depending on the kind of technology students use to write, their writing may be kept in manila folders or in computer files. Every student should have a file of writing pieces in various stages. For example, Sandra's folder contains notes from a story-starting activity that her teachers presented as part of a whole-class mini-lesson, as well as a story based upon a journal entry that she had written about cooking at school. She also included a completed story grammar map that she cowrote with her buddy-reader from the local middle school. In addition, she has an expository piece started on *The Titanic*, one of her special interests, as well as a couple of sentences about her family's vacation. An underlying part of WW is that not all stories have to be completed, just as published authors do not finish every story they begin. In addition, students choose which piece they feel like working on during particular sessions.

Date:							
Name	Brainstorming	Drafting	Revising	Editing	Publishing	Conference needed with peer	Conference needed with teacher
Alyssa							
Sandra							
Ethan							
John							

Figure 13.1. Writer's workshop check-in chart.

Brainstorming and topic selection. There are three purposes for this phase of writing: planning, idea stimulation, and motivation. Teachers stimulate students and motivate them to write. Students are given a chance to brainstorm ideas with peers, developing ideas and listing new and future topics. As students discuss and comment on each other's ideas, they begin to develop a purpose, audience, and genre. At this planning phase, the teacher encourages students to think about ideas for their stories, waiting to address the mechanics and conventions of writing until later in the writing process. Attention to detail at this early stage might increase anxiety regarding feelings of perfectionism and/or fears of failing (Alley & Deshler, 1979).

Developing a topic for students on the spectrum can be challenging. To help their students, Sandra and Julie allowed students to rewrite familiar stories. For example, Justin, a boy with high-functioning autism, loved reading SpongeBob books. During this phase, the paraprofessional worked one-on-one with Justin to brainstorm ideas for his own SpongeBob stories. At first, Justin simply recreated existing stories, but eventually he began writing stories with some variation. For another student, Anna, who was functioning at a lower level, the teachers provided photographs as part of this phase. Finally, teachers afforded students access to Kidspiration®, a software program that helps students link ideas by concept.

Students with ASD have a narrow focus when it comes to their favorite topics. That is, they tend to accumulate vast knowledge about specific subjects and have a strong ability to recall factual information about topics of interest (Abisgold, 2007). Teachers should not be concerned if students continue to choose the same topics for their writings (Stevens & Englert, 1993). Students can be encouraged to expand their knowledge about their favorite topics of interest and focus their writing on different aspects in each paper. Eventually, they can be encouraged to expand their writing repertoire by exploring new subjects that are similar to their topic of interest.

Drafting. During the drafting stage, students are encouraged to write without regard for surface features (e.g., spelling, punctuation), as those aspects of writing are attended to during editing. For students like Jake, who naturally attend to surface features, this may be distressing. Out of respect for Jake, Caitlin did not force the drafting/editing separation, as she did with other students in the class. Instead, she provided Jake with resources to spell words conventionally (e.g., word processor, individualized dictionary, dictionary) to mitigate his stress.

Revision. During revision, writers evaluate the content and cohesiveness of their writing. Revision and drafting may occur simultaneously. For students on the spectrum, even editing may occur simultaneously with writing. Conferencing with a peer or the teacher may be especially helpful in reducing student anxiety during revision (Vaughn et al., 2000). Many students with ASD have difficulty asking for help (Thomas et al., 1998); using the check-in procedure described above may be helpful here by making each step, including conferencing, a requirement.

Many students on the spectrum have difficulty giving or receiving feedback during teacher and peer conferencing (Nash, 2003) due to a lack of understanding that others may think differently than they do (Kaufman & Gentile, 2002). To mitigate this, prewritten questions may be part of the process. Peer conferencing begins with the writer reading his or her piece aloud to a select peer. Next, the writer asks a sequence of questions designed to get feedback about her or his story. For example, writers might ask these questions:

1. What did you find interesting about my piece?
2. What do you want to hear more about?
3. What did you find confusing?

Editing. To facilitate editing, teacher-developed checklists are useful. Checklists should contain mechanical writing elements that students have been taught. Figure 13.2 shows a checklist for beginning writers. It is designed for students to first check their own writing and then ask a peer to check it.

Element	Self-check	Peer check
Ending punctuation (**. ? !**)		
Spelling		
Sentences begin with capital letters (**T**he dog went to school.)		
Names begin with capital letters (**A**nn, **J**ohn)		

Figure 13.2. Editing checklist for beginning writers.

Publishing. In the WW sense of the term, publishing means creating a final, error-free product. Published products may be displayed in the classroom, or they may be celebrated with a performance (e.g., a poetry reading). Students with ASD may not be responsive to social praise during the writing process, especially during the presentation phase when their classmates want to celebrate one another's accomplishments (Mesibov, Sheal, & Schopler, 2005). Some students may prefer a reward or reinforcement more specific to their special interest such as time alone to draw (Attwood, 2003). This should be agreed upon during the preplanning stage.

Sentence Frames and Other Supports for Emerging Writers

Writing frames provide structure and visual support, two important elements for students on the spectrum. Writing frames are flexible tools that can be used for different genres of writing (e.g., poetry, narrative writing, expository writing). They can also be tailored to meet the needs of individual students. For example, after reading the story *Brown Bear, Brown Bear* by Bill Martin, Jr. and Eric Carle (1992), writers might independently generate one idea by completing the following sentence: "Brown bear, brown bear, what do you see? I see a _____ looking at me." Some students might use printed words, others select a picture to complete the sentence frame, while still others select from preprinted index cards. Frames increase in sophistication with student abilities. Figures 13.3 and 13.4 show examples of paragraph frames.

Valentine's Day – A Natural Writing Occasion

To take advantage of an authentic purpose for writing, Dabney and Karen, two teachers in an inclusive classroom, planned a weeklong integrated unit around Valentine's Day. To build anticipation for the holiday, they selected a variety of books to read aloud to their class. They also planned several writing activities.

After reading aloud *Mouse's First Valentine* (Thompson, 2002), a story about a mouse who makes a Valentine for her sister, the class dictates a list of reasons why people like to make Valentines for those they love. In this exercise, Dabney writes what they say on a piece of chart paper, and in anticipation of the class discussion, Karen programmed some appropriate reasons into Lisa's voice output device (e.g., because they are your friend, to tell someone that you love them) so that she could contribute to the conversation. Next, Karen modeled how to complete the paragraph frame shown in Figure 13.3. She selected two reasons from the class-generated list and filled in a copy of the sentence from the overhead projector. She was careful to utter each word as she wrote, and then asked the students to independently fill in their own paragraph frame. The teachers and paraprofessionals circulated during this work. (It should be noted that all of their students were in different writing stages.) When they found students using scribble writing, they asked them to "read" what they wrote and then carefully printed what the student "read" under the student's scribble writing. Once again, Lisa "dictated" her choices to Karen.

The teachers also set up a writing center where students could make Valentines for their friends. They made available red, pink, and white paper, paper doilies, lots of stickers, and different-colored markers and crayons for decorating. A local grocery store had donated a batch of envelopes left over from its greeting card rack. There were also rubber stamps of each letter of the alphabet and a variety of Valentine shapes. To provide visual models, the teachers put out Valentine cards they had collected over the years. Students could copy messages from the old cards onto new ones for their friends.

The variety of materials would support all of the emerging writers in their classroom except for Lisa. For her, the teachers programmed several common Valentine greetings into her device (e.g., Happy Valentine's Day, Be Mine). In the writing center when shown pictures of classmates, Lisa was able to "dictate" to a paraprofessional what she wanted her cards to say.

Valentine Cards

Name _____

I like to give my friends Valentines because:

_____.

_____.

Figure 13.3. Paragraph frame with topic sentence.

When students are ready to begin writing a topic sentence with two details, the paragraph frame in Figure 13.4 might be useful. This example was created for students engaged in a thematic unit about space. After reading several books about Earth, students were asked to use the writing frame to write about what they learned. Notice that, visually, the topic sentence is in larger font to represent the "bigger" nature of that idea.

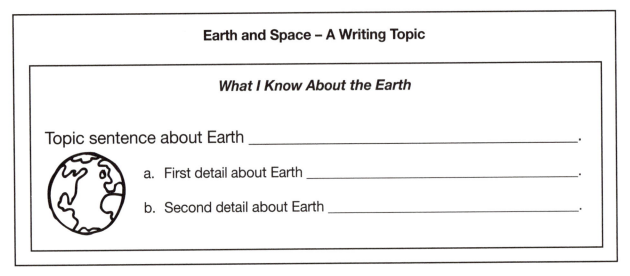

Earth and Space – A Writing Topic

What I Know About the Earth

Topic sentence about Earth _____.

    a. First detail about Earth _____.

    b. Second detail about Earth _____.

Figure 13.4. Paragraph frame without topic sentence.

Other visual supports for emergent writers include word walls and individualized writing dictionaries. Word walls refer to classroom walls used to display words after they have been introduced to students. Individualized dictionaries are little paper books where the student or an adult can record a word of interest to the student. Word walls and individualized dictionaries are both organized alphabetically and can facilitate writing words conventionally with some independence. To facilitate connection to the meanings of words, small pictures representing the meaning of individual words may be added. Students can be taught to search word walls and dictionaries for the words they wish to use in their writing. Deciding which support to use depends upon each student. For students on the spectrum, who need visual stimulation to be at a minimum, individualized dictionaries are best.

Since reading and writing are linked, visual supports used as part of reading instruction may also be used for writing instruction. For example, the story grammar map used to list story elements as part of reading comprehension may be used to help students identify the same elements for a story they are writing. For expository writing, a Venn diagram completed when comparing and contrasting information on a particular topic may also be used to compose an essay comparing the topics.

Technology

Sturm and Koppenhaver (2000) described the benefits of the cognitive approach model to teach writing to students with disabilities when combined with technology. They found a variety of software programs to support students with composition.

Crick Software Ltd. (1997). *Clicker plus* [computer program]. Northhampton, UK: Author. (Available from Don Johnston Inc., 26799 West Commerce Drive, Volo, IL 60073)

Don Johnston Inc. (1998). *Co:writer* [computer program]. Volo, IL: Author. (Available from Don Johnston Inc., 26799 West Commerce Drive, Volo, IL 60073)

Don Johnston Inc. (1990). *WriteOutloud* [computer program]. Volo, IL: Author. (Available from Don Johnston Inc., 26799 West Commerce Drive, Volo, IL 60073)

Information Service, Inc. (1989). *Write away 2000* [computer program]. St. Johns, NF, Canada: Author. (Available from Information Resources Incorporated, P.O. Box 7056, Water Street, St. Johns, NF, Canada A1E3Y3)

Inspiration Software. (1997). *Inspiration* [computer program]. Portland, OR: Author. (Available from Don Johnston Inc., 26799 West Commerce Drive, Volo, IL 60073)

Intellitools, Inc. (1996). *Intellitalk* [computer program]. Novasto, CA: Author. (Available from IntelliTools, Inc., 55 Leveroni Court, Suite 9, Novato, CA 94949)

Web Support for Writing
http://www.autisminspiration.com/public/main.cfm
http://www.autism-society.org
http://www.med.unc.edu/ahs/clds/
http://www.nwp.org/
http://www.route66literacy.org/
http//www.sedubois.k12.in.us/~jblackgrove/stages_of_writing.htm.
http://shop.augcominc.com/
http://tarheelreader.org/write-a-book/
http://www.321learn.net/

Conclusion

Self-determination is a person's desire to manage her own life (Wehmeyer & Shogren, 2008). Writing instruction is especially relevant to a student's self-determination because many life skills (e.g., money management, correspondence) require written expression in one form or another (Bakken & Parette, 2008). As is true for typically developing students, students on the spectrum should have an "alternative pencil" in place as soon as possible to facilitate emergent literacy skills (Hanser, 2006). Students should be exposed to daily balanced literacy lessons that integrate reading and writing. Because of language differences, it is particularly important that these activities be situated in the context of meaning. Teachers and support professionals must consistently help students make the critical connections between spoken and written language.

Chapter Highlights

- All children enter school with varied literacy experiences, but children with ASD face particular challenges with written expression.

- Writing is composed of physical (handwriting, typing, and AAC) and generative aspects.

- Children with more significant disabilities need opportunities for emergent writing; student abilities (e.g., eye gaze) should be used to facilitate this stage.

- Writing for typically developing children is conceptualized in stages that include:
  - ✔ Drawing
  - ✔ Scribbling
  - ✔ Letter-like units
  - ✔ Nonphonic letter strings
  - ✔ Copying environment print
  - ✔ Invented spelling
  - ✔ Conventional spelling

- The whole-to-part (WTP) model of writing is a useful framework that focuses on the writer's decision-making process.

- The writing process involves planning, translating, and reviewing. These three elements are influenced by the writer's long-term memory.

- For effective instruction, research suggests that teachers:
  - ✔ Model the writing process
  - ✔ Provide explicit instructions of writing conventions
  - ✔ Provide frequent supportive feedback

- Research examining writing in students with ASD is scant, but suggests that thematic teaching, pairing students with complementary skills, providing supports, and manipulating sentences are effective practices in developing writing skills.

- All aspects of literacy link tightly to one another.

- The "Teach to Write" approach focuses on grammar, whereas the "Write to Teach" approach focuses on the role of the author.

- There are four major strategies to promote writing:
  - ✔ Language experience
  - ✔ Shared writing
  - ✔ Interactive writing
  - ✔ Independent writing

- Journal writing is an example of an independent writing tool that can be used in a variety of ways; journals can be kept on computers, entries can be generated from pictures, and paraprofessionals can act as scribes.

- Other tools that promote independent writing include sentence frames, learning logs, word walls, and individualized writing dictionaries.

- Writer's workshop (WW) is another instructional method that enhances students' writing. During this time the teachers may provide whole-group mini-lessons or pull individual students to present a mini-lesson. The workshop involves:
  - ✔ Brainstorming
  - ✔ Drafting
  - ✔ Revising
  - ✔ Editing
  - ✔ Publishing
  - ✔ Peer conference
  - ✔ Teacher conference

Chapter Review Questions

1. How did Alyssa benefit from the use of an oversized keyboard?

2. What types of strengths and weaknesses did Jake and Peter bring to their collaboration?

3. What are four instructional strategies to help engage emergent writers in the writing process?

4. Describe several visual supports that can be implemented to help students write and edit their work more independently.

References

Abisgold, C. (2007). *Professional advice, school zone educational intelligence.* Retrieved June 8, 2009, from http:www.schoolzone.co.uk/resources/articles/GoodPractice/classroom/Special_needs/Advice.asp

Alley, G., & Deshler, D. (1979). *Teaching the learning disabled adolescent: Strategies and methods.* Denver, CO: Love.

Aspy, R., & Grossman, B. G. (2007). *The Ziggurat model.* Shawnee Mission, KS: Autism Asperger Publishing Company.

Attwood, A. (2003). Understanding and managing circumscribed interests. In M. Prior (Ed.), *Learning and behavior problems in Aspergers Syndrome* (pp. 126-147). New York: Guilford Press.

Ayres, K. M., & Langone, J. (2005). Intervention and instruction with video for students with autism: A review of the literature. *Education and Training in Developmental Disabilities, 40(2),* 183-196.

Bakken, J. P., & Parette, H. P. (2008). Self-determination and persons with developmental disabilities. In A. F. Rotatori, F. E. Obiakor, & S. Burkhardt (Eds.), *Autism and developmental disabilities: Current practices and issues. Advances in special education, Volume 18* (pp. 221-234). London: Emerald Group Publishing Group Limited.

Bedrosian, J. L., Lasker, J., Speidel, K., & Politsch, A. (2003). Enhancing the written narrative skills of an AAC student with autism: Evidence-based research issues. *Topics in Language Disorders, 23(4),* 305-324.

Buss, K., & Karnowski, L. (2000). *Reading and writing literary genres.* Newark, NJ: International Reading Association.

Calkins, L. M. (1985). "I am the one who writes." *American Educator: The Professional Journal of the American Federation of Teachers, 9*(3), 26-29.

Calkins, L. M. (1994). *The art of teaching writing* (2nd ed.). Portsmouth, NH: Heinemann.

Carnahan, C. (2006). Engaging children with autism and their teachers. *Teaching Exceptional Children, 39*(2), 44-50.

Colasent, R., & Griffith, P. L. (1998). Autism and literacy: Looking into the classroom with rabbit stories. *The Reading Teacher, 51,* 414-420.

Englert, C. S. (1992). Writing instruction from a sociocultural perspective: The holistic, dialogic, and social enterprise of writing. *Journal of Learning Disabilities, 25,* 153-172.

Flower, L., & Hayes, J. R. (1981). A cognitive process theory of writing. *College Composition and Communication, 32,* 365-387.

Gillet, J. W., & Beverly, L. (2001). *Directing the writing workshop: An elementary teacher's handbook.* New York: The Guilford Press.

Graves, D. H. (1983). *Writing: Teachers and children at work.* Portsmouth, NH: Heinemann.

Gregory, G. H., & Kuzmich, L. (2005). *Differentiated literacy strategies for student growth and achievement in grades K-6.* Thousand Oaks, CA: Corwin Press.

Hanser, G. (2006). Fostering emergent writing for children with significant disabilities: Writing with alternative pencils. *Technology Special Interest Section Quarterly, American Occupational Therapy Association, 16*(1). Retrieved January 14, 2009, from http://www.med.unc.edu/ahs/clds/files/Alt%20 Pencil%20Order%20UPD.pdf

Hooper, S. R., Swartz, S. W., Wakely, M. B., deKruif, R.E.L., & Montgomery, J. W. (2002). Executive functions in elementary school children with and without problems in written expression. *Journal of Learning Disabilities, 35,* 610-621.

Kaufman, J. C., & Gentile, C. A. (2002). The will, the wit, the judgment: The importance of an early start in productive and successful creative writing. *High Ability Students, 13*(2), 115-123.

Koppenhaver, D. A., & Erickson, K. A. (2009). Individuals with autism spectrum disorders who use AAC. In P. Mirenda and T. Iacono (Eds.), *Autism spectrum disorders and AAC* (pp. 385-412). Baltimore: Paul H. Brookes.

Koppenhaver, D. A., & Erickson, K. A. (2003). Natural emergent literacy supports for preschoolers with autism and severe communication impairments. *Topics in Language Disorders, 23,* 283-292.

Martin, B. Jr., & Carle, E. (1992). *Brown Bear, Brown Bear*. New York: Henry Holt & Company.

Mayes, S. D., & Calhoun, S. L. (2006). Frequency of reading, math, and writing disabilities in children with clinical disorders. *Learning and Individual Differences, 16,* 145-157.

McCarrier, A., Pinnell, G. S., & Fountas, I. C. (2000). *Interactive writing: How language and literacy come together, K-2*. Portsmouth, NH: Heinemann.

Mesibov, G. G., Shea, V., & Schopler, E. (2005). *The TEACCH approach to autism spectrum disorders.* New York: Kluwer Academic/Plenum Publishers.

Morrow, L. M. (2005). *Literacy developing in the early years: Helping children read and write* (5th ed.). Boston: Pearson.

Nash, M. (2003). The secrets of autism: The number of children with autism and Asperger's in the United States is exploding. Why? In K. Freiberg (Ed.), *Educating exceptional children* (pp. 85-93). Guilford, CT: McGraw Hill/Dushkin.

Polloway, E. A., Patton, J. R., & Serna, L. (2005). *Strategies for teaching learners with special needs.* Upper Saddle, NJ: Prentice Hall.

Rycik, M. T., & Rycik, M. T. (2007). *Phonics and word identification: Instruction and intervention, K-8.* Upper Saddle, NJ: Prentice Hall.

Rousseau, M. K., Krantz, P. J., Poulson, C. L., Kitson, M. E., & McClannahan, L. E. (1994). Sentence combing as a technique for increasing adjective use in writing by students with autism. *Research in Developmental Disabilities, 15,* 19-37.

Sink, D. M. (1975). Teach-write/write-teach. *Elementary English, 52,* 175-177.

Stevens, D. D., & Englert, C. S. (1993). Making writing strategies work. *Teaching Exceptional Children, 26*(1), 34-39.

Stewart, D. A., & Clarke, B. R. (2003). *Literacy and your deaf child: What every parent should know.* Washington, DC: Gallaudet University Press.

Sturm, J., & Koppenhaver, D. A. (2000). Supporting writing development in adolescents with developmental disabilities. *Topics in Language Disorders, 20*(2), 73-92.

Sulzby, E. (1989). Assessment of writing and children's language while writing. In L. Morrow & J. Smith (Eds.), *The role of assessment and measurement in early literacy instruction* (pp. 83-109). Englewood Cliffs, NJ: Prentice Hall.

Thomas, G., Barratt, P., Clewly, H., Joy, H., Potter, M., & Whitaker, P. (1998). *Asperger syndrome-practical strategies for the classroom: A teacher's guide.* London: The National Autistic Society.

Thompson, L. (2002). *Mouse's First Valentine.* New York: Simon & Schuster Books.

Vaughn, S., Gersten, R., & Chard, D. J. (2000). The underlying message in LD intervention research: Findings from research syntheses. *Exceptional Children, 67,* 99-114.

Wehmeyer, M. L., & Shogren, K. A. (2008). The self-determination of adolescents with intellectual disability. In S. Lopez (Ed.), *Positive psychology perspective series volume III: Growing in the face of diversity* (pp. 89-108). Westport, CT: Greenwood Publishing Group.

Williams, K. (1995). Understanding the student with Asperger's Syndrome: Guidelines for teachers. *Focus on Autistic Behavior, 10,* 1-8.

Paraprofessionals Providing Quality Literacy Support for Students With Autism Spectrum Disorders

Betty Y. Ashbaker, Ph.D., Brigham Young University

Kate Snyder, M.Ed., Middletown City Schools, Ohio

Christina Carnahan, Ed.D., University of Cincinnati

Pamela Williamson, Ph.D., University of Cincinnati

Learner Objectives

After reading this chapter, the learner should be able to:

- Describe the role of the paraprofessional in supporting literacy development in individuals with ASD

- Identify the elements of paraprofessional supervision that can improve overall quality of services to students

- Describe a shared philosophy and how one is created

- Describe the components of reading

- Identify strategies paraprofessionals can use to support literacy development in individuals with ASD

■ ■ ■

A Picture of Support – Paraprofessionals in Action

Nancy and Ellen are paraprofessionals in John's self-contained classroom. All three have been in the field long enough to have witnessed students with ASD growing so reliant on one-on-one support that instead of support, a codependent relationship evolved. This team agreed in their joint mission statement that in order to preserve student independence, no one person would be assigned to a particular student. Rather, John provided training to Nancy and Ellen, so that as paraeducators, they could deliver high-quality literacy support to students.

This year, they have six students who function in the moderate to intense range. All students have established communication systems – two students are using PECS (Picture Exchange Communication System; Frost & Bondy, 2002), two students are using voice output devices, and two students use oral language to communicate.

The team has embedded all language arts instruction into thematic units. In addition to typical life-skills units, units have been developed around student interests. For example, Sam is into things that move in the water, whereas Anna is interested in cars. So the team developed a transportation unit to incorporate these interests. The team decided up-front what should be programmed into student output devices and how visual materials (e.g., Boardmaker® pictures, photographs printed from Google Images) would support student learning. The team has made adjustments as needed.

The daily schedule is posted for all to see, and includes station teaching, as well as some limited whole-group lessons. Each station provides a written protocol of exactly how to teach the station, affording all students access to standardized procedures.

During the opening day of the transportation unit, John engaged the students in whole-group instruction. He created an interactive chart version (Hieronymus & Moomaw, 2001) of the "Wheels on the Bus," which was set to music. Each part of the bus was represented with a picture that had Velcro on the back. Students, with assistance from Nancy and Ellen, took turns adding their picture to the interactive poster. Next, students were grouped in pairs and sent to stations.

John facilitated reading instruction. He worked on students' language and reading skills. For this unit, Nancy supported students in the writing center while Ellen supported students in the independent reading center. In the writing center, Nancy took student "dictation" around topics of interest. In the reading center, Ellen read to one student as the other student looked through a self-selected book. A scan of the room suggested that all teachers and students were engaged in literacy activities.

■ ■ ■

Nancy, John, and Ellen understand that literacy is the cornerstone of self-advocacy, independence, and self-determination. They recognize that although designing quality literacy instruction for students with significant communication needs using a balanced approach is complex, it is crucial to helping students attain the lifelong goal of self-determination.

> "In a world constructed around the assumption that everyone has the basic skills of literacy and where literacy and freedom are indissolubly linked, to be illiterate is to be unfree."
>
> Koichiro Matsuura, Director-General of UNESCO, on International Literacy Day (September 8, 2002)

In order to develop balanced instruction for his students with autism spectrum disorders (ASD), John relies on his paraprofessionals for support. The paraprofessionals make substantial contributions to instructional effectiveness. This is especially true given appropriate planning and infrastructures, as well as proper training and supervision (Giangreco & Doyle, 2002; Hofmeister, Ashbaker, & Morgan, 1996; Pickett, 1986; Salzberg & Morgan, 1995).

To maximize the benefits of paraprofessional support for students with ASD, participation in classrooms must be carefully planned and implemented at all levels. This chapter discusses how paraprofessionals can support literacy development for students with ASD. Specifically, we will explore resources for supervision and training, what paraprofessionals need to know about quality literacy instruction, and strategies they can use to support literacy development for students with ASD.

Training and Supervision

As described in the opening vignette, paraprofessionals provide both academic and social-behavioral support to students with ASD across the school day. However, it is important to ensure appropriate use of paraprofessionals' time so as not to compromise their effectiveness. Giangreco and Broer (2005) urged schools to deliberately match assignments to personnel's skills, training, and certification, as well as to students' needs. Moreover, they cautioned that inadequate orientation, role clarification, training, and supervision can limit paraprofessionals' effectiveness.

Paraprofessionals typically undertake a variety of roles and responsibilities in educational settings. A 2008 study by the National Center for Education Statistics (NCES) indicated that the average special education paraprofessional worked in five different classes per week and served 21 students, 15 of whom have disabilities. French (1998) studied the activities most paraprofessionals performed on a weekly basis and summarized them as shown in Table 14.1.

Table 14.1
Roles and Responsibilities of Paraprofessionals

- One-on-one instruction
- Small-group instruction
- Large-group instruction
- Data collection/observation
- Preparation/planning
- Reproducing/typing instructional materials
- Playground/hall/bus supervision
- Attending meetings/inservices
- Behavior management
- Storytelling/reading aloud

Since much of their responsibility involves instruction, paraprofessionals need guidance in content-specific instructional strategies (Giangreco, Edelman, & Broer, 2001). That is, they must know and be able to implement evidence-based academic and social behavioral interventions (Causton-Theoharis, Giangreco, Doyle, & Vadasy, 2007). Further, paraprofessionals need guidance in understanding the individual needs of each student with ASD, and strategies to meet these needs.

Paraprofessionals should receive training and direct supervision to effectively support students with ASD in the classroom. However, regulations do not specify what constitutes "direct supervision" and whose responsibility it is to supervise paraprofessionals under either the No Child Left Behind Act of 2001 or the Individuals with Disabilities Education Improvement Act (2004). These laws do provide nonregulatory guidance.

While many districts designate an administrator (e.g., building principal) to manage and evaluate paraprofessionals, ultimately classroom teachers are responsible for supervising paraprofessionals in classrooms. Therefore, it is important that general education and special education teachers play an active role in providing ongoing guidance and professional development (Pickett, 2008).

Many teachers report that collaborating with and supervising paraprofessionals in their classrooms is a challenge (Causton-Theoharis et al., 2007). This may, in part, be due to lack of explicit, written plans or explicit instruction for paraprofessionals (French, 2001). In order to mitigate some supervision challenges, the IDEA Partnership Paraprofessional Initiative Report to the U.S. Department of Education, Office of Special Education Programs (2001), included the following recommendations for administrators:

1. Differences in staff roles and responsibilities must be adequately understood in order to organize and schedule staff to meet individual learners' needs.

2. One individual (i.e., teachers, administrators, related services personnel) should be responsible for scheduling and supervising paraprofessionals. This individual should receive training on how to supervise individuals.

3. Administrative support is needed to ensure common planning time, acquisition of appropriate equipment and resources, and development of professional environments for instruction.

4. Families must understand who is directing and monitoring the performance of paraprofessionals/assistants.

Initial Support of the Paraprofessional's Role

Interviews. A paraprofessional is generally hired under a broad and generic job description. It is in the best interest of the teacher/teachers who will work alongside the paraprofessional to be included in the interview process and the hiring decisions, especially when hiring someone who will be expected to support literacy instruction. During the interview, the paraprofessional could be provided the school/district procedures, handbooks, and basic school information (school map, evacuation or lock-down plans, student behavior policies, use of photocopier and other equipment, etc.), as well as an outline of the evaluation process.

Teachers. Additionally, information must be provided about the classroom related to specific roles (Ashbaker & Minney, 2007; French, 2003; Giangreco et al., 2001; Morgan & Ashbaker, 2001; Pickett, Likins, & Wallace, 2003; Riggs & Mueller, 2001). The teacher might supply information regarding specific duties and responsibilities in the classroom and school settings. Examples of literacy-related responsibilities include reading with individual students or small groups and playing games that reinforce literacy skills (Causton-Theoharis et al., 2007). Paraprofessionals might also provide support as students work independently on projects during reader's or writer's workshop, organize learning materials, or deliver instruction with teacher guidance (e.g., the teacher plans and delivers the lesson initially; the paraprofessional observes and reteaches the lesson).

Administrators. Administrators can help the paraprofessional understand the organizational structure of the school, emphasize the importance of the supervisor's role, and communicate their personal interest in the paraprofessional through a brief interview conducted upon hiring. Although a teacher is likely to be the direct manager or supervisor of a paraprofessional, as mentioned, the school building administrator is often the designated supervisor and generally has the final say in continued employment.

It is beyond the scope of this chapter to provide an in-depth discussion of strategies for training and supervising paraprofessionals. A list of resources is provided at the end of the chapter for further reading. The remainder of this chapter discusses ways in which paraprofessionals can support literacy instruction for students with ASD.

Paraprofessionals and Quality Literacy Instruction

Shared Philosophy

Critical to the development of quality literacy instruction for students with ASD is the creation of a shared philosophy among instructional staff (Carnahan, Williamson, Clarke, & Sorenson, 2009). Giangreco and his colleagues (1999) defined a *shared philosophy* as "a statement of what is aspired to, rather than necessarily what currently is" (p. 2). Such a statement should include a summary of the team's values, goals, and desires for the school year. Establishing such a commitment can create consistency and predictability in both instruction and classroom management.

Developing a shared commitment begins with agreement upon a set of values or beliefs, in this instance, specifically related to literacy instruction. Next, creation of a set of observable, measurable statements identifying how the values and beliefs translate to action provides a behavioral framework for the team. Sprick, Garrison, and Howard (1998) recommended posting the shared philosophy and guidelines in the classroom in a location that is visible to everyone in the room. For example, a team might enlarge the statement of its shared philosophy to poster size and hang it in a prominent location in the classroom (Carnahan et al., 2009).

John, Nancy, and Ellen created a shared philosophy specifically about literacy instruction. Their shared philosophy contains both the ideas to which they are committed and an outline for implementation.

A Shared Philosophy for Literacy Instruction

We believe in and are committed to:

- The understanding that reading requires meaningful comprehension
- An integrated, balanced approach to reading instruction that addresses students' strengths and needs
- Instruction that includes meaningful literacy experiences for all students

To represent our beliefs in the classroom, we will:

- Be consistent in our instruction and interaction with students.
- Know each student's strengths and needs in reading through ongoing assessment and collaboration with other team members.
- Be responsive to the needs of every student in the classroom by providing differentiated literacy experiences.
- Provide explicit praise and feedback to students that identify their achievements (e.g., "You looked at the picture to help you with the word. Great job!").

What Paraprofessionals Need to Know About the Components of Literacy and Learning for Individuals with ASD

The majority of this textbook has discussed specific strategies for quality literacy instruction for individuals with ASD. Two of the most important points paraprofessionals need to understand are that (a) all individuals deserve access to and can develop some literacy skills; and (b) providing integrated, balanced literacy instruction every day is critical for promoting independence and quality of life. Other important information presented in the following will help paraprofessionals structure their instruction.

The National Reading Panel (2000) identified phonological awareness, word identification, fluency, vocabulary, and comprehension as the factors primarily involved in reading. Paraprofessionals supporting reading instruction should know these components and how they are integrated to build quality literacy instruction. Further, it is critical that paraprofessionals understand how learning characteristics of many individuals with ASD influence reading development, particularly because paraprofessionals often work closely with individuals with ASD. Paraprofessionals can improve their practice by providing instruction that reflects an understanding of both the components of reading and the learning characteristics of individuals with ASD (see Table 14.2).

Table 14.2

Important Points for Paraprofessionals Regarding Literacy for Students With ASD

Big Ideas

- Communication is a part of literacy. Literacy instruction incorporates instruction around communication.

- Comprehension is more than the sum of all of its parts.

- Instruction related to the various components of reading should not occur in isolation.

ASD and the Components of Reading

- ***Phonological awareness.*** A reader with good phonological awareness is able to distinguish words, syllables, and phonemes as distinct units. This skill is critical to good reading because it supports a reader's ability to sound out words (Gillet, Temple, & Crawford, 2004).

- ***Word recognition.*** Word identification is a skill that can be accomplished four ways: recognizing the word by sight; guessing the word using cues (initial letters, preceding words, pictures, and topic knowledge); decoding; and analogy (Caldwell, this text, Chapter 4). Paraprofessionals should know that research suggests that individuals with ASD demonstrate strengths in decoding and word calling (Chiang & Lin, 2007; Myles et al., 2002; Nation, Clarke, Wright, & Williams, 2006), but should always consider the specific strengths and skills of the individual(s) with whom they are working.

- ***Fluency.*** Accuracy, automaticity, and prosody are the three components of fluency. An accurate and automatic reader is able to identify words correctly and without hesitation. Reading with correct prosody requires reading with expression to convey meaning and with attention to punctuation. Gillet et al. (2004) emphasize that the development of greater fluency allows readers to focus more on comprehension and having meaningful experiences with texts. Paraprofessionals should recognize that while accuracy and automaticity may be relative strengths, prosody may be challenging for individuals with ASD due to their social and cognitive differences.

- ***Vocabulary.*** Paraprofessionals need to support the use and acquisition of basic words, comprehension and content-area words, useful words, academic words, generative words, and idiomatic and figurative words/expressions (Jacobs & Watts-Taffe, this text, Chapter 11). Whenever possible, paraprofessionals need to emphasize using words in meaningful ways.

- ***Comprehension.*** It is important that paraprofessionals understand that individuals with ASD have differences in cognitive processing that may have a significant impact on comprehension. To support comprehension for students on the spectrum, paraprofessionals should be acquainted with various strategies to facilitate student prediction and activation of background knowledge, recognition and use of text structure, use of visual representations such as story maps and graphic organizers, summarization skills, comprehension monitoring, and question answering and generation (Duke & Pearson, 2002; Koppenhaver, this text, Chapter 12; National Reading Panel, 2000). In addition, paraprofessionals should be well versed in methods to promote active engagement in literacy experiences, such as integrating students' interests into the activity.

Strategies to Support Literacy Development for Students With ASD

In addition to information about literacy development, paraprofessionals need to understand the importance of well-structured learning environments and learning materials for students with ASD. They also need to understand and be able to support quality instruction. Table 14.3 highlights big ideas related to instruction and strategies paraprofessionals must understand when working with students with ASD.

Table 14.3
Instructional Considerations for Paraprofessionals

Big Ideas About Instruction

- Students with ASD benefit from external organization to learn.

Strategies Paraprofessionals Might Use to Support Literacy Development

- *Set visual boundaries.* Clearly defined boundaries help students with ASD understand the expectations in each area of the classroom (Mesibov, Shea, & Schopler, 2005). These boundaries minimize distractions and help students attend to learning materials. Simple strategies such as using bookshelves or colored tape to create boundaries can increase understanding and academic engagement for students with ASD.

- *Use visual supports.* Visual supports include materials such as visual schedules, timers, to-do lists, structured work systems, graphic organizers, etc. These interventions promote increased engagement and learning for students with ASD. By clearly indicating what will come first, next, and last, visual supports decrease anxiety and focus attention. Paraprofessionals can prepare picture or written schedules for daily or weekly activities. They might provide specific, concrete beginning and endings for activities using tokens, timers, or checklists, even for activities that may continue over several days or class periods.

- *Capitalize on student interests.* In the opening vignette, the teaching team recognized the unique interests of students in their classroom. They used student interests to develop integrated language arts themes to develop literacy skills.

- *Understand and implement specific teaching strategies.* Paraprofessionals need to be trained to deliver instruction using evidence-based strategies. Examples include:

  ✔ *Systematic instruction.* Systematic teaching strategies often incorporate discrete trial instruction (DTI) (Iovanne, Dunlap, Huber, & Kincaid, 2003). During DTI, students respond to a direction or cue presented by a teacher or paraprofessional. The instructional team then uses systematic prompting (i.e., least-to-most prompting, error correction) and reinforcement to increase accuracy and independence (Kates-McElrath & Axelrod, 2006; Leblanc, Ricciardi, & Luiselli, 2005).

  Note: Though systematic, explicit instruction is important for teaching specific skills, integrated instruction that connects individual skills to larger concepts and promotes generalization is crucial.

Table 14.3 (cont.)

✔ ***Prompting.*** West and Billingsley (2005) described systematic prompting as "supplementary stimuli that increase the probability that desired behaviors will be emitted by students and be reinforced, in the presence of natural cues for those behaviors" (p. 131). Prompting serves as an instructional tool that increases students' ability to engage in a variety of literacy activities and tasks (Heckaman, Alber, Hooper, & Heward, 1998). Prompting strategies include time delay, least-to-most and most-to-least prompting strategies, simultaneous prompting, and graduated guidance (Heflin & Alberto, 2001; Snell & Brown, 2007; Worely & Schuster, 1997). Prompts are a necessary and valuable tool for teaching students with ASD. However, overuse of prompts or failure to use prompts in a systematic way may keep students from mastering a skill. Thus, prompts should be systematically planned; that is, when educational teams plan to use prompts, they should also plan to systematically fade these prompts as soon as possible.

✔ ***Reinforcement.*** Reinforcement refers to the use of consequences that increase the likelihood a behavior will occur (Skinner, 1953). Reinforcement is crucial for teaching students new skills and ensuring that they maintain these skills over time (Heflin & Alberto, 2001; Maurice, Green, & Luce, 1996). Heflin and Alberto described several guidelines for using reinforcement. First, increasing positive interactions often increases student responses. Second, linking reinforcers to desired behaviors is important when designing reinforcement schedules. Finally, varying reinforcement so students do not become satiated or bored with one particular item or object is critical. To do this, instructors conduct preference assessments and identify several items of interest to the child.

✔ ***Priming.*** Students with ASD find it easier to participate in classroom routines and activities when they have had an opportunity to prepare. This concept, known as priming, is an antecedent intervention, in which students preview learning materials before actual instruction occurs (Koegel, Koegel, Frea, & Green-Hopkins, 2003). Priming has been effectively used to increase both appropriate social behaviors and academic responding. When priming, the paraprofessional (or other adults, peers) and the student review learning material in advance of the lesson. Examples of literacy materials that may be primed include reading materials, vocabulary, and reading strategies. Paraprofessionals can use priming techniques by working with the teacher to obtain in advance an outline of curriculum subjects or books that will be presented to the class. Paraprofessionals can identify materials, like a video or other related support materials, that will provide background knowledge related to the upcoming topic. The paraprofessional may show these materials to the student or discuss key concepts to prepare him or her for unfamiliar content or future classroom activities. This preliminary exposure may help the student get ready for a lesson when it is presented to the class (Koegel et al.). Further, Marks and colleagues (2003) suggested involving parents by having them read with their children at home, so they have a basic understanding of what will be presented in a lesson the next day. School personnel can provide the student with an extra set of texts for home to prevent forgetting needed academic materials. Priming strategies can be used to prepare students for new activities or concepts. Whereas homework can be beneficial as an *extension* activity for many students, for students with ASD, it might be better as a *preteaching* activity (Marks et al.).

Conclusion

Increasing numbers of paraprofessionals provide services to students with ASD, and many are assigned to focus on literacy support. Through careful planning, training, and appropriate delegation of tasks, administrators and teachers can support the success of paraprofessionals; and paraprofessionals, in turn, can facilitate the growth of literacy skills in students with ASD. As students increase literacy skills, they develop a means of improving self-expression and social interaction – vital to their success.

Chapter Highlights

- Paraprofessionals make substantial contributions to instruction.

- To maximize the benefits of paraprofessional support for students with ASD, participation must be carefully planned and implemented at all levels.

- It is encouraged that instructional assignments be matched to personnel's skills, training, and certification, as well as student needs.

- Paraprofessionals must know and be able to implement evidence-based interventions.

- Even though paraprofessionals will benefit from guidance, regulations do not specify this issue; thus, classroom teachers are responsible for supervising paraprofessionals.

- The IDEA Partnership Paraprofessional Initiative Report identified four recommendations for administrators:
  - ✔ Understand staff roles and responsibilities
  - ✔ Make a trained individual responsible for scheduling and supervising paraprofessionals
  - ✔ Provide administrative support
  - ✔ Make families aware of the paraprofessional's role

- Teachers should be involved in the paraprofessional interviewing process to supply details about classroom duties and responsibilities.

- Administrators can help paraprofessionals understand the organizational structure of the school.

- It is crucial to literacy instruction for individuals with ASD to develop shared philosophy among instructional staff. The philosophy should include a summary of team values, goals, and desires for the school year.

- The literacy components that paraprofessionals need to know include:
  - ✔ All individuals deserve access to literacy skills
  - ✔ Providing integrated balanced literacy instruction daily is important

- Major factors involved in reading include phonological awareness, word identification, fluency, vocabulary, and comprehension.

- Instructional considerations for paraprofessionals include visual boundaries to help students learn without distractions, provision of visual supports, and capitalizing on student interests. Other instructional considerations involve systematic prompting to increase the likelihood of appropriate student behavior, providing reinforcement, and priming in order to allow the students to preview learning.

Chapter Review Questions

1. Why is it important to include paraprofessionals in supporting literacy development in individuals with ASD?

2. Under the existing nonregulatory guidance, who is responsible for supervising paraprofessionals in the classroom?

3. What is the importance of an instructional team having a shared philosophy?

4. State at least three strategies a paraprofessional can use to support literacy development in individuals with ASD.

5. List the components of reading. Describe how the learning differences of individuals with ASD impact at least one of those components.

References

Ashbaker, B. Y., & Minney, R. B. (2007). *Planning your paraprofessionals' path: An administrator's legal compliance and training guide.* Horsham, PA: LRP.

Carnahan, C. R., Williamson, P., Clarke, L., & Sorenson, R. (2009). A systematic approach for supporting paraeducators in educational settings: A guide for teachers. *TEACHING Exceptional Children, 41*(5), 34-43.

Causton-Theoharis, J., Giangreco, M., Doyle, M., & Vadasy, P. (2007). Paraprofessionals: The "sous chefs" of literacy instruction. *TEACHING Exceptional Children, 34(2),* 60-64.

Chiang, H. M., & Lin, Y. H. (2007). Reading comprehension instruction for students with autism spectrum disorders. *Focus on Autism and Other Developmental Disabilities, 22*(4), 259-267.

Duke, N., & Pearson, P. D. (2002). Effective practices for developing reading comprehension. In A. E. Farstrup & S. J. Samuels (Eds.), *What research has to say about reading instruction* (3rd ed., pp. 205-242). Newark, DE: International Reading Association.

French, N. K. (1998). Working together: Resource teachers and paraeducators. *Remedial and Special Education, 19*(6), 357-368.

French, N. K. (2001). Supervising paraprofessionals: A survey of teacher practices. *The Journal of Special Education, 35,* 41-53.

French, N. K. (2003). *Managing paraeducators in your school: How to hire, train, and supervise non-certified staff.* Thousand Oaks, CA: Corwin Press.

Frost, L., & Bondy, A. (2002). *PECS: The picture exchange communication system training manual* (2nd ed.). Cherry Hill, NJ: Pyramid Educational Consultants.

Giangreco, M. F., & Broer, S. M. (2005). Questionable utilization of paraprofessionals in inclusive schools. *Focus on Autism and Other Developmental Disabilities, 22*(3), 149-158.

Giangreco, M. F., CichoskiKelly, E., Backus, L., Edelmen, S. W., Broer, S. M., CichoskiKelly, C., & Spinney, P. (1999, March). Developing a shared understanding: Paraeducator support for students with disabilities in general education. *TASH Newsletter, 25*(1), 21-23.

Giangreco, M. F., & Doyle, M. B. (2002). Students with disabilities and paraprofessional supports: Benefits, balance, and band-aids. *Focus on Exceptional Children, 34*(7), 1-12.

Giangreco, M. F., Edelman, S. W., & Broer, S. M. (2001). Respect, appreciation, and acknowledgement of paraprofessionals who support students with disabilities. *Exceptional Children, 68*(1), 485-498.

Gillet, J. W., Temple, C., & Crawford, A. N. (2004). *Understanding reading problems: Assessment and instruction.* New York: Pearson.

Heckaman, K., Alber, S., Hooper, S., & Heward, W. (1998). A comparison of least-to-most prompts and progressive time delay on the disruptive behavior of students with autism. *Journal of Behavioral Education, 8*(2), 171-201.

Heflin, L. J., & Alberto, P. (2001). Establishing a behavioral context for learning for students with autism. *Focus on Autism and Other Developmental Disabilities, 6*(2), 93-101.

Hofmeister, A. M., Ashbaker, B. Y., & Morgan, J. (1996). Paraeducators: Critical members of the rural education team. In rural goals 2000: Building programs that work. *16th Annual National Conference Proceedings of the American Council on Rural Special Education* (ACRES), Baltimore. (ERIC Document Reproduction Service No. ED 394 757)

IDEA Partnerships. (2001). *IDEA partnership paraprofessional initiative: Report to the U.S. Department of Education, Office of Special Education Programs.* Arlington, VA: Council for Exceptional Children.

Individuals With Disabilities Education Improvement Act of 2004, Amendments to IDEA Section 612.14B iii (2004).

Iovanne, R., Dunlap, G., Huber, H., & Kincaid, D. (2003). Effective educational practices for students with autism spectrum disorders. *Focus on Autism and Other Developmental Disabilities, 18*, 150-165.

Kates-McElrath, K., & Axelrod, S. (2006). Behavioral interventions for autism: A distinction between two behavior analytic approaches. *The Behavior Analyst Today, 7*(2), 242-252.

Koegel, L., Koegel, R., Frea, W., & Green-Hopkins, I. (2003). Priming as a method of coordinating educational services for students with autism. *Language, Speech, and Hearing Services in Schools, 34*, 228-235.

Leblanc, M., Ricciardi, J., & Luiselli, J. (2005). Improving discrete trial instruction by paraprofessional staff through an abbreviated performance feedback intervention. *Education and Treatment of Children, 28*(1), 76-82.

Marks, S. U., Shaw-Hegwer, J., Schrader, C., Longaker, T., Peters, I, Powers, F., & Levine, M. (2003). Instructional management tips for teachers of students with autism spectrum disorder (ASD). *TEACHING Exceptional Children, 51*(1), 50-54.

Maurice, C., Green, G., & Luce, S. (1996). *Behavioral interventions for young children with autism: A manual for parents and professionals.* Austin, TX: Pro-Ed.

Mesibov, G., Shea, V., & Schopler, E. (2005). *The TEACCH approach to autism spectrum disorders.* New York: Kluwer Academic/Plenum Publishers.

Moomaw, S., & Hieronymus, B. (2001). *More than letters: Literacy activities for preschool, kindergarten, and first grade.* St. Paul, MN: Red Leaf Press.

Morgan, J., & Ashbaker, B. Y. (2001). *A teacher's guide to working with paraeducators and other classroom aides.* Alexandria, VA: Association for Supervision and Curriculum Development.

Myles, B. S., Hilgenfeld, T., Barnhill, G., Griswold, D., Hagiwara, T., & Simpson, R. (2002). Analysis of reading skills in individuals with Asperger Syndrome. *Focus on Autism and Other Developmental Disabilities, 17*(1), 44-47.

Nation, K., Clarke, P., Wright, B., & Williams, C. (2006). Patterns of reading ability in children with autism spectrum disorder. *Journal of Autism and Developmental Disorders, 36*, 911-919.

National Center for Educational Statistics. (2008). *The condition of education 2008.* Retrieved January 15, 2009, from nces.ed.gov/pubsearch/pubinfo.asp?pubid=2008031

National Reading Panel. (2000). *Report of the National Reading Panel teaching children to read: An evidence-based assessment of scientific-based literature on reading and its implications for reading instruction.* Washington, DC: National Institute of Child Health and Human Development.

No Child Left Behind Act (NCLB) of 2001, 20 U.S.C. § 6301 *et. seq.* (2002).

Pickett, A. L. (1986). *Paraprofessionals in special education: The state of the art – 1986.* New York: National Resource Center for Paraprofessionals in Special Education, New Careers Training Laboratory, Center for Advanced Study in Education, City University of New York. (ERIC No. ED 276 209)

Pickett, A. L. (2008). Roles and responsibilities of paraeducators working with learners with developmental disabilities: Translating research into practice. In H. Parette & G. R. Peterson-Kalran (Eds.), *Research-based practices in developmental disabilities* (2nd ed., pp. 501-520). Austin, TX: Pro-Ed.

Pickett, A. L., Likins, M., & Wallace, T. (2003). *The employment and preparation of paraeducators.* New York: National Resource Center for Paraprofessionals in Education and Related Services. Retrieved December 6, 2007, from http://www.nrcpara.org/resources/stateofart/

Riggs, C. G., & Mueller, P. H. (2001) Employment and utilization of paraeducators in inclusive settings. *The Journal of Special Education, 35*, 54-62.

Salzberg, C. L., & Morgan, J. (1995). Preparing teachers to work with paraeducators. *Teacher Education and Special Education, 18,* 49-55.

Skinner, B. F. (1953). *Science and human behavior.* New York: Macmillan.

Snell, M., & Brown, F. (2007). *Instruction of students with severe disabilities.* Columbus, OH: Pearson Education.

Sprick, R., Garrison, M., & Howard, L. (1998). *CHAMPS: A proactive and positive approach to classroom management.* Eugene, OR: Pacific Northwest.

West, E., & Billingsley, F. (2005). Improving the system of least prompts: A comparison of procedural variations. *Education and Training in Developmental Disabilities, 40*, 131-144.

Worely, M., & Schuster, J. (1997). Instructional methods with students who have significant disabilities. *The Journal of Special Education, 31*, 82-83.

Training Resources for Paraprofessionals

A variety of resources for teachers working with paraprofessionals in classroom settings are compiled on the web site http://www.nrcpara.org/training. The following resources describe strategies for supporting paraprofessionals in schools.

- Ashbaker, B. Y., Morgan, J., Enriquez, J. (2004). *Preparing for teamwork. A training program for teachers and Latino paraprofessionals.* Provo, UT: Brigham Young University.

- Ashbaker, B.Y., & Morgan, J. (n.d.). *Teamwork and evaluation for teachers and para-educators. A staff development training program for teachers and paraeducators as members of the instructional team, with supplemental video vignettes and participant manual.* Provo, UT: Brigham Young University.

- French, N. K. (2003). *Managing Paraprofessionals in your school: How to hire, train, and supervise paraeducators.* Thousand Oaks, CA: Corwin.

- Morgan, R. L., Gee, T., Merrill, Z., Gerity, B. P., & Brenchley, R. (1998). *Colleagues in the classroom: A video-assisted program for teaching supervision skills.* Logan, UT: TRIPSED.

- Pickett, A. L. (n.d.). *A training program: To prepare teachers to supervise and work effectively with paraeducator personnel.* National Resource Center for Paraprofessionalsavailable through the NRCP. Available at http://www.nrcpara.org/training/children

- Pickett, A. L. (1997). *A training program to prepare teachers to supervise and work more effectively with paraprofessional personnel.* Available from National Resource Center for Paraprofessionals. www.nrcpara.org

- Pickett, A. L., Faison, K., & Formanek, J. (2006). *A core curriculum and training program to prepare paraeducators to work in inclusive classrooms serving school-age students with disabilities.* Available from National Resource Center for Paraprofessionals. www.nrcpara.org

- Pickett, A. L., & Gerlach, K. (Eds.). (2003). *Supervising paraeducators: A team approach.* Austin, TX: Pro-Ed.

Index

E

F

G

H

definition, 9–10
experiences of individuals with ASD, 10–13
generalizing skills, 72–74
impact of communication skills, 138–143
importance, 22
situation models, 22–23, 103
visual, 10, 169
See also Emergent literacy; Reading; Writing
Literacy instruction
authentic, 13, 401
balanced, 190–192
guiding principles, 13–14
integrated approaches, 90, 112, 208
models, 9–10
roles of paraprofessionals, 413, 414–418
for students with ASD, 13–14
See also Balanced instruction; Instructional strategies
Literacy-rich environments, 166
See also Print-rich environments
Literal level, 102, 106
Literal thinking, 12, 25, 26, 146, 326
Logographic stage, 96
Logos, 167–168, 169, 223–224

M

Magliano, J. P., 364–365
Manzo, A. V., 375
Marten, C., 272–273
Masonheimer, P. E., 167
Matthew Effect, 93
Mayer-Johnson Company, 195
Mayes, S. D., 389
Maze assessments, 377, 378
McClannahan, L. E., 394
McIntosh, L., 10
McKeown, M., 324
Mean fluency rates, 297
Mean length of utterance (MLU), 133
Memory
impairments, 258
for rote facts, 32, 47, 73
Mesibov, G., 8
Metalinguistic skills, 131–132, 141–142
Microsoft PowerPoint. *See* PowerPoint
Minority students, reading achievement gaps, 110–111
See also Diversity
Minshew, N. J., 256, 362
Mirenda, P., 10, 35, 262, 275
Miscues
analysis, 97, 295–296, 316
recording, 293
MLU. *See* Mean length of utterance

Moore, D. W., 359
Moore, S. A., 359
Morphemes
bound, 34
definition, 132
development, 132–133
study of, 139
Morphological analysis, 336, 338–340
Morphology, 139
Motivations
for reading, 104, 292
special interests and, 14
of students with ASD, 192–194, 327
Motor difficulties, 35, 71, 224, 390
Movement, 240
Music, 240
Myles, B. S., 361

N

NAEP. *See* National Assessment of Educational Progress
Nagy, W. E., 103, 325
Names, writing, 241
Narratives, oral, 226
Narrative text, 104, 106
Nation, K., 256, 379
National Assessment of Educational Progress (NAEP), 110, 298
National Center for Education Statistics, 411–412
National Professional Development Center on Autism Spectrum Disorders (PDA), 48
National Reading Panel (NRP), 196, 301, 333, 415
National Research Council (NRC), 23, 109
Neologisms, 326
Neuman, S. B., 166
Nilsson, N. L., 292, 361
No Child Left Behind Act, 90, 111, 412
Nonsense words, 95–96, 97, 326
Nonwords, decoding, 257
Norbury, C. F., 365
NRC. *See* National Research Council
NRP. *See* National Reading Panel

O

Obrochta, C., 344
O'Connor, I. M., 367
O'Connor, N., 361
Online resources
assessment instruments, 93
on augmentative communication, 159
blogging, 376

on environmental print, 187
games, 244, 335
images, 52
for instructional design, 195
on language, 159
on literacy, 159
for literacy instruction, 36
texts, 374
visual supports, 52
vocabulary instruction, 260, 335
word games, 335
for writing, 403
Onsets, 92, 98, 267
Oral language development, 88–89, 220–221, 258–259
See also Prosody; Speech
Orthography. *See* Spelling
Osterling, J., 143
Overselective attention, 11

P

PA. *See* Phonological awareness
Paired reading, 305
PALS. *See* Phonological Awareness Literacy Screening
Paragraph frames, 400–402
Paraprofessionals
hiring, 413
knowledge needed, 415–416
literacy instruction, 413, 414–418
roles and responsibilities, 411–412, 413
shared philosophies, 414–415
supervision, 412–413, 414
training, 412–413, 424
Paris, A. H., 100
Paris, S. G., 100
Parsing, questioning, and rephrasing (PQR) strategy, 307
PDA. *See* National Professional Development Center on Autism Spectrum Disorders
Peabody Picture Vocabulary Test-IV (PPVT-IV), 230
Pearson, P. D., 342, 377
Peers
conferencing with, 399
paired reading, 305
tutoring, 367, 369
Performance reading, 238–239, 305–306
Perspective taking. *See* Theory of mind
Phonemes
blending, 93, 94, 272
definition, 222
deletion, 93, 94
perceiving, 91
producing, 134–135

Appendix A:
Chapter Review Answers

Chapter 1

1. There are many definitions of literacy. Generally speaking, literacy skills incorporate reading, writing, listening, speaking, viewing, and any other communication skill necessary for an individual to have increased, meaningful engagement with his or her environment (e.g., home and school communities) and those in it.

2. Students with ASD demonstrate differences in the way they perceive their worlds. These differences influence the ability to integrate new experiences or knowledge with existing knowledge and to act based on what one knows. Cognitive processing differences may cause students with ASD to have difficulty with literacy skills. For example, because students with ASD are prone to literal interpretations of language, they may need specific instruction in how to understand or use figurative language when reading or writing.

3. All students should have access to quality literacy instruction, and literacy experiences should be authentic, functional, and student centered. This means that quality literacy experiences are based on what is known about the cognitive processing style of ASD while incorporating the special interests of each student.

Chapter 2

1. Contributions from the reader (e.g., student characteristics, background knowledge), the text (e.g., length, genre, text difficulty), and the context (e.g., teaching strategies) influence reading comprehension, or the development of a situation model consistent with the text.

2. ToM is the capacity to (a) recognize the thoughts, beliefs, and intentions of others and understand that these mental states are different from our own; and (b) use this understanding to predict the behavior of others. Recently, Baron-Cohen has begun to also discuss the ability to empathize and systematize in the context of ToM.

EF involves organizing the cognitive processes; EF skills are important for maintaining goal-directed behavior such as organizing, planning, implementing, and self-monitoring.

CC refers to the brain's ability to process multiple chunks of information in a global way, connecting them and viewing them in context, in order to determine a higher level of meaning.

3. Differences in ToM, EF, and CC may influence reading comprehension as manifested by:

   - Difficulty understanding the thoughts and predicting behaviors of characters in a passage.

   - Difficulty making inferences or answering inference questions.

   - Significant focus on small details, which may influence the ability to understand the main ideas of a passage and integrate information for meaningful purposes.

   - Difficulty accessing relevant background knowledge and integrating new knowledge with existing knowledge.

   - Limited self-monitoring globally for comprehension and for specific errors.

4. Examples may include, but are not limited to, situations in which an individual:

   - Reads a passage without understanding the main idea and/or becomes absorbed by very small details.

   - Has difficulty linking text to relevant background information; the individual begins talking about a situation (s)he experienced that is related, but not relevant to the story.

   - Reads a passage containing a great deal of figurative speech, but only interprets it literally.

   - Lacks an understanding of character motive, or is not empathetic to the emotions of the characters in a story.

- Has difficulty organizing the actual task of reading a passage; the reader may struggle to begin the reading process, become confused or easily lose his place while reading, or not understand the purpose for reading.

- Has difficulty monitoring/self-monitoring comprehension.

- Struggles to integrate new knowledge with existing.

Chapter 3

1. Using strategies designed around student strengths increases the likelihood of students being actively engaged in instruction. Strategies that help students with ASD to better organize themselves, attend to relevant information, and gain meaning from literacy activities are recommended.

2. Educators can segment the classroom space to help students better understand what literacy activities will be taking place in specific locations. Examples include using labels, signs, rugs, color cues, shelves, and desks to clarify locations. In addition, educators can remove or reduce auditory and visual distractions. This will help students to focus on salient information.

3. Visual schedules can help a student with ASD better understand when activities will be occurring throughout the day. This increases predictability and can help reduce a student's anxiety about when events will take place.

4. Using task analysis to help break down complex literacy tasks into smaller steps can be beneficial, along with using positive reinforcement when steps are mastered. Effective prompting can help ensure student success as well.

5. Educators can use novels, magazines, newspapers, instruction booklets, menus, advertisements, maps, comic books, videos, and/or audio books. These may increase engagement, as students may be more interested in these materials and, therefore, be more likely to participate.

6. Educators should reduce adult prompting as soon as skills are mastered so students do not become reliant on adult presence or support to demonstrate skills. In addition, embedding reinforcement into activities will reduce the need for adults to provide additional reinforcement. Finally, encouraging self-management strategies during literacy instructions is helpful.

7. Educators can use technology in a number of ways. Technology may be used to create supports such as visual schedules and work systems. In addition, technology can be used to deliver instruction. Video and PowerPoint® have proven to be effective forms of instruction and can be applied easily to literacy activities.

Chapter 4

1. Phonological awareness; phonics, fluency, vocabulary, and comprehension.

2. Awareness of words in sentences; awareness of syllables in words; awareness of sounds within syllables.

3. Through tasks that ask children to segment words, say words without a certain sound, blend sounds, and substitute sounds.

4. Sight recognition, prediction, decoding, and analogy.

5. Logographic, alphabetic, and automatic word identification.

6. Oral reading of words and text, miscue analysis, running records.

7. Fluency consists of three components: accuracy, automaticity, and prosody.

8. By measuring reading rate as words per minute or correct words per minute.

9. Receptive vocabulary includes listening comprehension and reading vocabulary. Productive vocabulary includes speaking vocabulary and writing vocabulary.

10. Formation of a text base (microstructure and macrostructure) and a situation model.

11. Reader word-level skills, reader prior knowledge, reader motivation, text structure, text difficulty, and readability level.

12. By asking questions, student retelling, and thinking aloud.

Chapter 5

1. Language and literacy development are complex processes that consist of many essential components, including syntax, semantics, morphology, pragmatics, metalinguistics, phonological awareness and phonics, transaction, and stance. Because language and literacy are interconnected, all of these components are described in this chapter.

2. a. Communication is often a core deficit associated with ASD; it includes the following: (a) delay in or lack of development of spoken language or gestures; (b) impairment in the ability to initiate or maintain conversation; (c) repetitive and idiosyncratic use of language; and (d) lack of pretend play (DSM-IV-TR; American Psychiatric Association, 2000). In addition, frequently there is a failure to acquire and use joint attentional skills, symbols (Woods & Wetherby, 2003), and theory of mind (Walenski, Tager-Flusberg, & Ullman, 2006).

    b. Additionally, children with ASD typically use object words and nouns more commonly than other types of vocabulary words, such as actions or emotions (Walenski et al., 2006). They rely on a relatively narrow range of grammatical constructions and reduced use of forms that initiate social interaction, such as questions. Because many children with ASD have echolalia, they often demonstrate reversal of personal pronouns (e.g., using *you* rather than *I*) (Tager-Flusberg, Paul, & Lord, 2005). Frequently, individuals with ASD interpret text literally and have difficulty understanding that other people have different thoughts, ideas, and opinions about the meaning of the words on the page. All of these components affect their ability to gain meaning from the text.

3. Because of the deficits exhibited by children with ASD, many benefit from augmentative communication, whether low-tech communication boards, computer software, or high-tech speech-generating devices. Specific therapeutic techniques may include the following: semantic webbing, aided language stimulation, and access to a keyboard.

Chapter 6

1. Teachers who are designing literacy-rich environments for students with ASD may need to take into the account the following:

   - Potential sensory sensitivity

   - Need for structure and organization

   - Need for visual supports and schedules

   - Low, medium, and high assistive technology to provide access

   - Designation of certain areas of the classroom for certain activities or routines

2. All students benefit from literacy-rich environments. Examples include:

   - Word walls

   - Use of environmental print

   - Availability of a variety of print and genres of writing

   - Opportunities for communication, reading, and writing throughout the environment

   - Inclusion of culturally and linguistically diverse literacy materials.

3. The letter should include reference to some of the following factors: brain-friendly instruction; the importance of the connection between home, community, and school; the importance of visual literacy; the importance of choice of literacy activities; building on prior learning and student strengths; and taking into account sensory preferences.

4. Many examples are provided throughout the chapter.

5. This must include the objective, procedure, and method for evaluation.

Chapter 7

1. Balanced literacy instruction incorporates both holistic and explicit instruction. The instruction is theme based and occurs in blocks of time whenever possible; themes incorporate students' interests and strengths. Additionally, balanced literacy instruction incorporates reading, writing, and word work every day.

2. A well-organized physical environment and learning materials are crucial to meeting the learning style of students with ASD by increasing student engagement and learning. The physical space should be structured to provide students with an understanding of what activities will take place in each area of the classroom. Such organization promotes student understanding of classroom rules and expectations, attention (limits distraction), and engagement in learning activities.

3. Exemplary teachers:

    *   *Motivate learners and build excitement about learning:* Link to topics of interest to grab student attention and gradually expand these interests to a wide range of topics.

    *   *Build strong relationships:* Explicitly teach students to engage in social activities and relationships.

    *   *Link instruction to individual needs:* Assess the individual needs of each learner, identify the strengths and interests of each student and use these as a basis for instruction, recognize the needs of individuals with ASD for external organization (well-organized physical space and learning materials), and use visual instruction whenever possible.

    *   *Use holistic and explicit instruction:* Develop the instructional context before teaching. Help students make connections between prior knowledge and experience and new learning material. Link skills taught during one-on-one instruction to the natural environment and the theme or concept being addressed. Plan opportunities to practice and generalize new skills in many different settings. Reinforce key social, behavioral, and academic concepts in every facet of the student's day.

- *Organize literacy-rich environments:* Recognizing the needs of many individuals with ASD for external organization, exemplary teachers organize their classrooms to highlight necessary materials that are well organized.

- *Have strong organizational and management skills:* Use rules and routines to build predictable learning environments, teach clearly defined rules, and promote understanding of routines.

- *Integrate instruction across the school day:* Recognizing that many individuals with ASD need support to generalize skills and knowledge across environments, exemplary teachers embed instruction throughout the day by incorporating literacy-based skills in all content areas.

- *Develop strong home-school connections:* Build relationships and communication with families and community organizations to increase teaching efficiency and effectiveness, increase generalization, and promote problem solving. Strategies include the creation of email groups, monthly or quarterly team meetings, communication notebooks, home visits (or visits to therapy centers, etc.), and planned phone conferences.

4. Teachers use assessment data to select strategies from different learning theories to provide appropriate instruction to meet the needs of each individual learner.

5. Answers will vary, but should include attention to/descriptions of both holistic and explicit experiences and teacher- and student-directed experiences.

6. Answers will vary, but should address issues of motivation and excitement for learning, building relationships with students, aligning instruction to individual learning needs, creating print-rich environments, and maintaining a well-organized environment. Additionally, answers should incorporate a balance between student- and teacher-directed activities and holistic and explicit instruction.

Chapter 8

1. Emergent literacy theory suggests that children develop literacy knowledge long before they can read and write in the conventional sense and before formal schooling through participation in early exploratory reading and writing behaviors.

2. The two processes involved in reading include (a) information obtained from the code-related aspects of the printed word (e.g., what is gleaned from alphabet knowledge and phonological awareness); and (b) information obtained from understanding the meaning associated with the printed word (e.g., what is gleaned from vocabulary, background knowledge, context).

3. Despite many emergent literacy interventions that have been shown to be effective with children from vulnerable populations (e.g., children with developmental disabilities, severe language impairments, children from backgrounds of economic disadvantage, and children learning English as a second language), it is unclear whether these interventions are applicable to children with ASD.

4. Many meaning-based and code-related skills may be embedded in an interactive shared book reading session. Shared book reading is highly adaptable to different kinds of texts (e.g., electronic storybooks), different reading levels, and different contexts (e.g., whole-group, small-group, and individual).

Chapter 9

1. The purpose of phonics and word study instruction is to facilitate word recognition in order to promote fluency, as it leads to greater comprehension of texts. As part of a balanced literacy curriculum that takes an integrated approach to teaching both reading and writing to foster meaning making, phonics and word study should incorporate words and word components that are in active use through a variety of classroom literacy activities. Students on the spectrum are often able to recognize and decode words, but they are not necessarily able to derive meaning from those words once decoded. As a result, students with ASD would particularly benefit from word study instruction as presented in this chapter, as it shows teachers how to:

a. Determine the developmental spelling phase that most aptly fits where the student currently is;

b. Work with students to increase their knowledge of how letters and sounds combine to make meaningful words; and

c. Provide a variety of research-based activities and strategies to increase word knowledge and awareness, building these activities into other literacy events in the classroom.

2. Phases and three characteristics of each phase of spelling development: (As the review question asks for only three characteristics for each phase, readers are encouraged to review Table 9.2 (on pp. 263-265) for additional characteristics.)

a. Emergent
   - Scribbles or lines on paper representing what the student describes as words or stories
   - Graphic representation of words using the letters for the initial or most recognizable sounds in those words
   - Beginning awareness of concepts of print (i.e., left to right; return sweep; spacing)

b. Letter-name alphabetic
   - Students begin to spell words based on the correspondence between the letter name and the sound it represents
   - Beginning and ending consonants, and strong vowels, often correctly reproduced in written representations of words
   - By the end of the phase, ability to spell many common and single-syllable words

c. Within-word
   - Students understand basic spelling patterns
   - Overuse of common patterns when reproducing long vowel sounds
   - High-frequency words and short-vowel words are consistently spelled correctly

d. Syllables and affixes
   - Students correctly spell long and short vowel patterns
   - Ambiguous vowel and consonant patterns, and high-frequency words are correctly rendered
   - Confusion in spelling now rests in syllable junctures and use of affixes

e. Derivational relations
- General mastery of the previous developmental phases
- Students now spell correctly most words derived from common English ortho-graphic patterns
- Confusion in spelling now rests in words that rely on common spelling patterns from foreign language derivations

3. Descriptions of implementation of strategies will vary depending on the individual classroom context. Key ingredients for instruction include:

- Ascertaining and incorporating student spelling developmental phase

- Integrating a variety of reading and writing activities that key into student interests and developmental phase, using a balanced approach to literacy instruction

- Making meaning from the text at the word, sentence, and passage level

- Providing opportunities for students to personally connect with the texts read

- Examples of strategies include:
  - Concept sorts
  - Word sorts
  - Word hunts
  - Word journals
  - Interactive writing
  - Writing journals
  - Other student opportunities to write

4. Traditional spelling models offer students an often disconnected set of words for rote memorization, with assessment conducted on a weekly basis. Because many students with ASD are proficient at decoding, but not at making meaning, such traditional spelling instructional designs do not support the processes necessary for them to develop an understanding of the words themselves when encountered in print. The developmental model offered here incorporates spelling instruction with the perspective that students' understandings of spelling follow recognizable phases and that these phases share characteristics that can be observed through their writing. Mastery of the phases leads to greater fluency and, if part of a balanced approach to literacy instruction, greater comprehension of written texts.

5. Spelling inventories list words representing each phase of spelling development. The groups of words are arranged chronologically to follow the order of acquisition for the concepts included at each phase. The inventories are used to determine specific features that are being applied correctly and incorrectly by students, in order to aid in subsequent instruction.

Chapter 10

1. Factors include the student's (a) cognitive profile, (b) attention, (c) prosodic differences, (d) background knowledge, (e) purpose for reading, and (f) reading levels.

2. Text readability influences fluency (e.g., variety of words used, variety of spelling patterns of words included, number of high-frequency words, length/complexity of sentences).

3. Fluency should be assessed by determining the correct number of words per minute (CWPM) as well as prosody.

4. Progress monitoring is an appropriate use of a short piece of text.

5. Fluency is only one facet of reading. Multiple measures should be used that address comprehension, word recognition, use of background knowledge, and so on.

Chapter 11

1. • Word learning is incremental; it develops gradually over time with repeated and varied experiences.

   • Words may have multiple meanings that may be unrelated (e.g., *nail* can mean something that you hammer or the hard piece at the end of your finger or thumb).

   • Knowledge of one word is directly linked to knowledge of other words; understanding the word *deciduous,* for example, is linked to understanding other words, such as *trees, leaves,* and *seasons.*

2. Students understand words at varying levels based upon their experiences with those words. Students may have no knowledge, incorrect knowledge, general knowledge, context-bound knowledge, or rich decontextualized knowledge. This means that a one-size-fits-all instructional strategy is not effective. Teachers must effectively assess students' depth of knowledge and incorporate instructional strategies to meet students at their current level of knowledge.

3. Words to teach should include basic words, words that are essential to understanding a selection or unit of study, useful words, academic words, generative words, and idiomatic and figurative words. Teachers should aim for fewer words with depth of understanding rather than for a large number of words with less understanding. Teachers should consider students' prior knowledge, interest, and whether and how those words relate to other words the student already knows.

4. • *Provide a user-friendly definition* – Give students a definition using everyday language.

   • *Provide a meaningful context* – Use the words in a context that is meaningful and interesting to the student.

   • *Activate students' prior knowledge and help them build semantically related categories of words and concepts* – Connect the new word to students' experiences.

   • *Actively engage students* – Ask the students to use the new word.

   • *Provide a lot of practice* – Provide opportunities throughout the week for students to use the new word.

5. • *Contextual analysis* – using context clues

   • *Morphological analysis* – using word parts

   • *Using outside resources* – dictionary and thesaurus

   • Not all students learn words from context alone; therefore, it is important that students have strategies to determine the meanings of unknown words.

6. • Explicitly describe the strategy, including when and how it should be used.

   • Model the strategy in action.

   • Facilitate students' collaborative use of the strategy.

   • Facilitate guided practice with a gradual release of responsibility.

   • Facilitate independent use of the strategy.

   • Make students active participants. Teachers may provide a checklist or guide for students to follow, including picture or symbol cues for each step; video modeling or peer modeling may be helpful.

7. Students with ASD display inconsistencies in their language abilities and may have a variety of communication disorders that interfere with their ability to use language. They may display echolalia, use neologisms, use overly specific or proper words, use odd phrasings of words, use words without truly comprehending the meaning, and they may interpret language quite literally. Performance on language tasks also may not provide an accurate picture of a student's true understanding of a given word. Tasks should relate to student interests and take place in meaningful contexts. Tasks and goals should be challenging but attainable. Visual support systems, including video modeling and picture/symbol schedules, may assist students in word learning.

Chapter 12

1. An individual's understanding, recall, and integration of information stated in or inferable from specific text passages.

2. Reciprocal questioning.

3. Individuals with high-functioning autism.

4. It requires only minimal behavioral response (i.e., multiple-choice selection), and the results are not confounded with skilled word reading in the absence of comprehension.

Chapter 13

1. Alyssa's example clearly demonstrates the need to address physical needs first, as being able to "write" is a prerequisite for the generative aspect of writing. As Alyssa's case demonstrates, children with significant disabilities need opportunities to engage in emergent writing. Whatever developing abilities a student possesses should be used to facilitate emergent writing.

2. Jake is a student with high-functioning autism, whereas Peter has learning abilities. Jake was excellent at spelling but Peter had difficulty with both spelling and reading. The two boys seem to have complementary skills. The two boys have common interest in a topic, which makes the collaboration possible.

3. McCarrier, Pinnell, and Fountas (2000) described four instructional strategies to help children of any age who are developmentally emerging writers. These include (a) language experience, (b) shared writing, (c) interactive writing, and (d) independent writing.

   Language experience approach – used with a group of children at varied levels of writing experience

   Shared writing – involves two or more writers contributing to the creation of text while the teacher transcribes their thoughts

   Interactive writing – students and teachers jointly construct letters, notes, or daily messages

   Independent writing – students create their own text

4. Visual supports for emergent writers include word walls and individualized writing dictionaries. Word walls refer to classroom walls used to display words after they have been introduced to students. Individualized dictionaries are little paper books where the student or an adult can record a word of interest to the student. Story grammar maps used to list story elements can help students identify elements for a story they are writing. For expository writing, a Venn diagram completed when comparing and contrasting information on a topic would be used to compose an essay comparing the topics.

Chapter 14

1. Increasing numbers of paraprofessionals provide support services to individuals with ASD. Paraprofessionals can make substantial contributions to instructional effectiveness by providing direct, evidence-based literacy instruction under the direction of the classroom teacher.

2. Although many districts assign management and evaluation of paraprofessionals to an administrator, classroom teachers are ultimately responsible for supervising paraprofessionals in the classroom.

3. A shared philosophy can create consistency and predictability in both instruction and classroom management.

4. Visual boundaries, visual supports, student interests, or specific teaching strategies (systematic instruction, prompting, positive reinforcement, and priming).

5. • Phonological awareness
     – Word recognition
     – Fluency
     – Vocabulary
     – Comprehension

   • Research suggests that individuals with ASD demonstrate differences in cognitive processing that may have a significant impact on comprehension.

   • Research suggests that individuals with ASD demonstrate strengths in decoding and word calling.

   • Accuracy and automaticity may be relative strengths for individuals on the spectrum; prosody may be challenging.

Appendix B:
Glossary

A

Academic words. Words critical to understanding and participating in school routines and learning processes.

Aesthetic stance. Emphasis by the reader on the feelings and ideas while reading that may include past psychological events.

Alternative pencils. Any functional substitute for a pencil that a student prefers to use as an implement for written expression such as a marker, paint brush, technology, or even a physical indicator such as an eye gaze.

Assistive technology. Any item, piece of equipment, or product system that is used to increase, maintain, or improve functional capabilities of individuals with disabilities.

Attention. The cognitive energy expended in the effort to process a task.

Augmentative communication. An alternative form of communication that is used when an individual cannot use speech to communicate; includes a range of systems from low-tech communication boards to computer software or high-tech speech generating devices.

Automaticity. The ability to gain meaning from a text without the conscious attention required by decoding.

B

Balanced literacy. Model of literacy instruction that includes both holistic and explicit instruction, as well as daily attention to reading, writing, and word work.

Base word. Word that stands alone and carries meaning, although its meaning may be altered by the addition of a prefix or suffix.

Basic words. Words essential to daily life activities and routine social interactions as well as words that occur frequently in text.

Brain-friendly learning. Using teaching methods consistent with what we know about how the brain processes, stores, and retrieves information.

C

Central coherence. The brain's ability to process multiple chunks of information in a global way, connecting them and viewing them in context, in order to determine a higher level of meaning.

Chaining. Reinforcing individual responses occurring in sequence to form a complex behavior.

Closed sort. An instructional strategy where groups of words with particular sounds or features are supplied on cards for students to sort into categories to learn common word patterns.

Code-related processes. The ability to understand the structural aspects of print related to phonological awareness, alphabet knowledge, print concepts, and emergent writing.

Cognitive-constructivist. The theory that the construction of meaning from a text includes contributions from the reader, the text, and the context.

Cognitive processing style. The patterns of thinking that characterize the way individuals with ASD process or take in, integrate, and apply information.

Communication. The sending and receiving of messages.

Comprehension. The "process of simultaneously extracting and constructing meaning through interaction and involvement with written language" (RAND Reading Study Group, 2002, p. 11).

Comprehension words. Words essential to understanding a given reading selection or unit of study.

Concept sort. A strategy that provides students with easily identifiable picture cards that can be sorted into relational categories.

Contextual analysis. Method of determining the meaning of a word or passage based on clues from the surrounding text.

Contextual information. Description of situations in which a word might be used and/or examples of the word's meaning in various settings, situations, or contexts.

Culture of autism. The notion of "predictable patterns of thinking and behavior" specific to autism spectrum disorders.

D

Definitional information. Facts pertaining to the meaning of a word.

Differentiated instruction. Planning and implementing instruction (i.e., ways for students to acquire and demonstrate knowledge) that incorporates each learner's unique learning styles.

Dramatic storytelling and retelling. An activity in which children invent and act out stories or retell stories heard or read.

Ɛ

Echolalia. The immediate or delayed repetition of the speech of others.

Efferent stance. Focus by the reader on facts from the text that affect the overall meaning of the text.

Emergent literacy perspective. The view that children participate in exploratory reading and writing behaviors long before they can read and write in the conventional sense and before formal schooling.

Environmental print. Words and text encountered daily in routine activity (e.g., street and store signs, package labels, and logos).

Etymology. The study of words, often with an emphasis on their origins and derivations.

Executive function. The set of skills or abilities involved in organizing cognitive processes; EF skills are important for maintaining goal-directed behavior (organizing, planning, implementing, self-monitoring).

Exemplary teachers. Motivate learners, building strong affective relationships with students, creating excitement about content, adjusting instruction to meet individual needs, creating literacy-rich physical environments, and having strong organizational and management skills.

Explicit instruction. Systematic teaching designed to target specific skills or strategies.

Expressive language. The ability to produce language; includes how we share our thoughts, ideas, and feelings.

F

Fluency. The combination of accuracy, automaticity, and prosody when reading.

G

Games. One type of play for targeting emergent literacy skills.

Grapheme. Written representations of the sounds made by phonemes (e.g., the letters *ph* or *f* to represent the sound /f/).

Guided reading. Refers to any instructional activity in which a teacher directs one or more students in ways intended to increase their ability to apply word identification or comprehension strategies in text (Cunningham & Allington, 2007). Teachers guide student reading by providing them with *reading purposes* in order to increase their success in reading with comprehension (Tierney & Cunningham, 1984). *Background knowledge:* Sometimes called prior knowledge or world knowledge, refers to the existing knowledge that readers have before reading a text. Background knowledge is acquired through experiences and facilitates comprehension. For example, more readers in Australia would have well-developed background knowledge about the game of cricket, while readers in the United States would be more apt to have greater understanding of the game of baseball than of cricket. Consequently, Australian readers would typically have greater understanding of a text about cricket, while American readers would typically read a baseball passage with greater understanding.

H

Hyperlexia. The ability to fluently decode and/or recognize words without the ability to describe the meaning of the words, sentences, or paragraphs.

I

Idiomatic and figurative words. Commonly used expressions that cannot be interpreted literally.

Information processing. A model of learning that describes how learning occurs through the perception of environmental stimuli, how the sensory input is processed, and how information is stored in memory.

Intentional communication. Also referred to as goal-directed communication; includes making eye contact, using gestures and vocalizations that are consistent and ritualized, waiting for a response, and remaining persistent until the communication goal is met.

Interactive reading. Style of reading that allows the adult reader to actively involve the student in the kinds of cognitively challenging tasks that enhance both vocabulary acquisition and retention.

Interactive routines. Predictable, repeated actions written down as a schedule or chart.

Interactive writing. A process in which a teacher leads a class of students in jointly constructing a letter, story, list, or another type of writing in order to demonstrate concepts of print. Often this is done on a large, poster-sized piece of paper, with individual students and the teacher taking turns physically writing or adding punctuation.

Intonation/prosody. The melody of speech; includes pitch changes (rising or falling) to signal the mood of an utterance.

Invented spelling. Usually seen most during the early phases of spelling and writing acquisition, this is the process used by students to create spellings of words based on the individual letters heard or articulated during pronunciation.

J

Joint attention. Coordinated attention to the same object, activity, or topic; includes at least two people.

Juncture. Pausing after meaningful phrasing during reading.

L

Language experience activities. An activity in which the teacher guides a discussion and written record of some shared experience.

Language experience approach. An instructional strategy that engages a group of emergent learners in the activity of writing by first sharing a group experience such as a field trip and then recalling the experience later as a group and using agreed-upon written language to describe what they shared.

Listening comprehension. Defined similarly to reading comprehension, but instead of reading a text, students listen as the text is read aloud to them.

Literacy. Generally speaking, the ability to read, write, view, listen, and otherwise communicate with others.

M

Meaning-based processes. Global understanding of printed words and sentences related to vocabulary, grammatic understanding, and narrative production.

Metalinguistic skills. The use of language to analyze, study, and understand language.

Morpheme. The smallest unit of letters in a word that holds meaning (e.g., *thank-* and *-ful* in the word *thankful*).

Morphological analysis. Method of determining the meaning of a word based on the structure of a word (i.e., base word, prefix, and suffix).

Morphology. The study of morphemes; includes prefixes and suffixes.

Music and movement. Enlarged-print versions of lyrics written as interactive charts.

N

Neologism. Nonsense words, created by the speaker, that have been assigned specific, consistent meanings.

O

Orthography. The writing system of a language, referring specifically to the arrangement of letters and patterns of letters resulting in meaning.

Overselective attention. Attention to a limited number of environmental cues at one time.

P

Paraprofessional: An individual in a teaching-related position who is trained and responsible for specialized assistance to students in elementary and secondary schools. Paraprofessional is often interchanged with terms such as *paraeducator, instructional assistant*, and/or *classroom assistant*.

Phoneme. The smallest unit of sound in a language. Phonemes can be represented by a single letter or by a single combination of letters.

Phonemic awareness. The ability to identify and recognize the individual phonemes in spoken language.

Phonics. The system by which letters and sounds are connected to make words and meaning in written form.

Phonological awareness. The ability to perceive words, syllables, and phonemes as discrete units.

Phonology/phonological awareness. The ability to manipulate sounds; this general term includes skills such as initial phonemic awareness, sound isolation, rhyming, blending, segmentation, and syllable deletion.

Pitch. The rise and fall of voice during reading.

Positive reinforcement. Contingent presentation of a reinforcer following a response that increases the likelihood of the response occurring again.

Pragmatics. The use of language to express intentions and get things done in the world.

Prefix. Meaningful unit attached to a base word, at the beginning (e.g., *dis* as in *disregard*), that is not a word by itself.

Priming. A strategy used to prepare students for learning in which the student is given support in reviewing instructional materials, routines, or activities before they occur.

Prior learning. The knowledge base that students bring to the educational setting.

Prompting. Providing cues to students to increase the probability of desired responses.

Prosody. The ability to read with expression through the application of oral language features, including stress, pitch, and word juncture.

R

Reading. A highly complex act of cognition that involves both print processing skill and comprehension.

Reading comprehension. Describes an individual's "understanding, recall, and integration of information stated in or inferable from specific text passages" (Tierney & Cunningham, 1984, p. 610).

Reading the room. A sight word strategy that involves labeling objects and people in the student's immediate environment.

Receptive language. The understanding of language; includes the comprehension of words, sentences, and stories.

Reinforcement. The use of consequences that increase the likelihood a behavior will occur, as defined by Skinner (1953).

S

Scaffolding. Providing students with support that allows them to complete activities they would not otherwise be able to accomplish.

Scaffolds. Temporary strategies provided by educators that support student learning of new skills and concepts.

Schema. An association or group of knowledge or experiences.

Segmented space. Using physical and/or visual boundaries in a classroom environment to differentiate areas.

Semantic networks. Ways in which word meanings are connected and stored in one's memory.

Semantics. The meanings of words; often used synonymously with the word *vocabulary*.

Sensory sensitivity. Aversion to a particular sensory stimulus.

Shared book reading. A style of book reading in which the adult and child have rich conversations about the content and pictures in a text.

Shared philosophy. A statement created by an instructional team that describes the team's values, goals, and desires for the school year and outlines a framework for translating those beliefs to action.

Signing-in and signing-up. An activity in which children write their name on a piece of paper when they come to school in the morning or for turn-taking purposes.

Situation model. A mental representation a reader creates based on information presented in the text, which is integrated with background knowledge.

Speech. The production of sound; includes articulation, phonology, voice, and fluency.

Spelling inventory. A spelling test formulated and used for diagnostic or formative assessment; includes words that illustrate particular features in written words found in the English language.

Stress. Word emphasis during reading.

Structural analysis of words. The process of breaking down a word into its component parts for meaning.

Student interests. Activities, objects, people, and ideas most important to an individual student.

Sufficient exemplars. Use of many examples and a variety of materials when teaching skills/concepts.

Suffix. Meaningful unit attached to a base word, at the end (e.g., *less* as in *helpless*), that is not a word by itself.

Supervision. The process of giving critical direction, support, and guidance to ensure quality performance.

Suprasegmentals. Aspects of communication, such as inflection, stress, rhythm, tone of voice, loudness and speaking rate, that change the meanings of words and phrase

Symbolic play. One object represents another object in play.

Syntax. The structure of a sentence, including word order; also referred to as grammar.

Systematic instruction. A planned sequence for instruction that builds from basic to more complex concepts or skills and is based on information from individual student assessments.

T

Task analysis. Breaking complex behavior into its component parts.

Theory of mind. The ability to recognize the thoughts, beliefs, and intentions of others, understand that these are different from our own, and use this understanding to predict behavior.

Transaction. The idea that both the text and the reader are changed through the reading process; meaning (i.e., comprehension) occurs through the transaction that occurs between the reader and the text.

V

Variability. The range in emergent literacy skill knowledge and skills between and within young children.

Video modeling. Teaching desired behaviors through video demonstration.

Visual boundaries. Physical structures and supports integrated into a classroom environment that distinguish one area from another and help to clarify classroom expectations.

Visual literacy. The ability to interpret and make meaning from information presented in the form of an image.

Visual modifications. Changes to the environment or learning stimuli that enhance the use of visual inputs and processing.

Visual schedules. Use of a visual means to communicate sequence of upcoming activities or events.

Visual supports. Materials that enhance instruction and direction in the classroom by presenting expectations and procedures in a visual format. Examples include timers, to-do lists, visual schedules, token boards, and structured work systems.

Vocabulary. The words used and understood while reading. Vocabulary includes basic words, comprehension and content-area words, useful words, academic words, generative words, and idiomatic and figurative words/expressions.

W

Whole-to-part model. A cognitive theory of writing whereby the writer filters the thoughts or ideas to be written first through an outline or planning process, second through a word description or translating process, and then through a review or rewriting process, out of which the story is finally shaped and told.

Word families. Groups of words that are related, either by spelling patterns or etymology (e.g., the -at family includes words like *sat*, *fat*, *cat*, and *hat*).

Word hunt. A lesson strategy that allows students to search for specific types of words or word patterns in texts or environmental print.

Word identification. The process of matching letters and letter units to sounds and attaching meaning to the resulting pronunciation.

Word journal. A student notebook where students collect and record novel or interesting words and spellings.

Word recognition. The ability to recognize words by sight, to guess words using cues, to decode, and to use analogy.

Word work/word study. Systematic and explicit investigation of words and word parts that facilitates understanding of spelling patterns and meanings.

Word walls. A systematically organized collection of words displayed in large letters on a wall or other surface (they are designed to promote group learning and provide visual support for targeted vocabulary).

Work systems. An organizational system that provides students with visual information about what to do.

AAPC Textbooks

Meeting the Mandate for Highly Qualified Educators

AAPC Textbooks Are Classroom-Ready

If you're teaching a college course or preparing for an in-house training, AAPC Textbooks can help. We make the process easy and convenient while adhering to the gold standard in the field by offering with each textbook ...

- Chapter PowerPoint™ Presentations
- Chapter Tests
- Comprehensive Exams
- Case Study Ideas
- Recommendations for In-Class Activities
- Project Ideas
- Paper Topic Ideas
- Supplemental PowerPoint™ Presentations

All support materials are easily tailored to a specific instructor's needs
www.aapctextbooks.net

Advance praise for *Quality Literacy Instruction for Students with Autism Spectrum Disorders*

"The authors promote a balanced perspective to provide differentiated literacy instruction and discuss effective incorporation of technology. This is a must-have text for anyone who is interested in understanding why individuals with ASD struggle to comprehend and apply what they have read in order to help emergent readers become proficient readers."

– L. Juane Heflin, Ph.D., Associate Professor, Georgia State University

Intervention

New!
Quality Literacy Instruction for Students with Autism Spectrum Disorders

Having effective literacy skills enhances the quality of life of all individuals, including those with autism spectrum disorders. Bringing together experts from both the autism and reading fields, this textbook provides a detailed discussion of literacy instruction, thus supporting professionals and families alike in building lifelong literacy instruction geared to the needs of students on the autism spectrum. Using case examples, the textbook brings theory and research to practice, thus meeting the mandate for evidence-based practice.

Teachers and families alike will have access to theoretical, practical, and pedagogical implications associated with providing students on the spectrum access to quality, balanced literacy instruction. ISBN 9781934575666

Edited by Christina Carnahan, Ed.D., and Pam Williamson, Ph.D.; foreword by Kathleen Quill, Ed.D.

Code 9506 (Textbook) **Price: $59.00**

Foundations/Characteristics

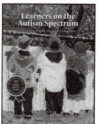

2009 ASA Literary Work of the Year Award!
Learners on the Autism Spectrum: Preparing Highly Qualified Educators

This text responds to the escalating need to prepare highly qualified educators with essential knowledge and practical skills to support diverse learners on the autism spectrum. Covering a range of critical topics and themes, this edited volume brings together leading experts representing diverse disciplines and perspectives (i.e., researchers, therapists, educators, parents, and adults on the autism spectrum) for a comprehensive look at the core issues related to individuals with autism spectrum disorders. ISBN 9781934575079

Edited by Kari Dunn Buron, M.S., and Pamela Wolfberg, Ph.D.; foreword by Carol Gray

Code 9504 (Textbook) **Price: $59.00**

Intervention Strategies and Comprehensive Planning

Based on the ASA Award-Winning Book
Designing Comprehensive Intervention for Individuals with High-Functioning Autism and Asperger Syndrome: The Ziggurat Model

While it is relatively easy to find information describing specific interventions, it is difficult to find information on how to develop a comprehensive intervention plan. This textbook presents a process and framework for designing interventions for individuals of all ages with ASD while staying consistent with recent special education trends, including response to intervention (RTI), evidence-based practices, and positive behavioral supports. ISBN 9781934575093

Ruth Aspy, Ph.D., and Barry Grossman, Ph.D.; foreword by Gary Mesibov, Ph.D.

Code 9502 (Textbook) **Price: $59.00**

Social Skills Programming

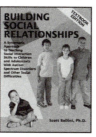

Based on the ASA Award-Winning Book
Building Social Relationships: A Systematic Approach to Teaching Social Interaction Skills to Children and Adolescents With Autism Spectrum Disorders and Other Social Difficulties

This textbook addresses the critical need for social skills programming for children and adolescents with autism spectrum disorders and other social difficulties. Unlike other resources, this book presents a comprehensive model that incorporates five fundamental steps: assess social functioning, distinguish between skill acquisition and performance deficits, select intervention strategies, implement intervention, and evaluate and monitor progress. Rather than promoting a single strategy, the model details how to organize and make sense of the myriad social skills programs and resources available. ISBN 9781934575055

Scott Bellini, Ph.D.

Code 9500 (Textbook) **Price: $59.00**

AAPC Textbooks

A Division of AAPC

P.O. Box 23173

Shawnee Mission, Kansas 66283-0173

www.asperger.net